Dynamics of Knowledge-Intensive Entrepreneurship

Knowledge-intensive entrepreneurship lies at the core of the structural shift necessary for the growth and development of a knowledge-based economy, yet research reveals that the EU has fewer young leading innovators, and Europe's new firms do not adequately contribute to industrial growth. This is especially true in the high R&D intensive, high-tech sectors. This structural malaise, undermining Europe's growth potential, is well diagnosed, but poorly understood.

This volume fills this important gap by exploring new firms that have significant knowledge intensity in their activity and develop and exploit innovative opportunities in diverse sectors. Through an evolutionary and systemic approach to entrepreneurship, focusing on knowledge-intensive entrepreneurship as both a micro and a macro phenomenon and analysing firms in the context of various socio-economic models, the authors explore firms' creation and origins around the world, their organization, strategies and business models as well as the role of innovation systems and institutions in their formation and growth.

This comprehensive research text is vital reading for academics, researchers and students of high-tech and knowledge intensive entrepreneurship as well as those with an interest in industrial dynamics, innovation management and public policy.

Franco Malerba Professor of Industrial Economics, University of Bocconi, Italy.

Yannis Caloghirou Professor of Economics of Technology and Industrial Strategy at the National Technical University of Athens, Greece.

Maureen McKelvey Professor of Industrial Management, Institute of Innovation and Entrepreneurship, University of Gothenberg, Sweden.

Slavo Radosevic Professor of Industry and Innovation Studies, University College London, UK.

RIOT! Routledge Studies in Innovation, Organization and Technology

Dynamics of Knowledge-Intensive Entrepreneurship

Business strategy and public policy

**Edited by Franco Malerba,
Yannis Caloghirou,
Maureen McKelvey and
Slavo Radosevic**

LONDON AND NEW YORK

First published 2016
by Routledge

2 Park Square, Milton Park, Abingdon, Oxfordshire OX14 4RN
52 Vanderbilt Avenue, New York, NY 10017

Routledge is an imprint of the Taylor & Francis Group, an informa business

First issued in paperback 2019

British Library Cataloguing in Publication Data
A catalogue record for this book is available from the British Library

Library of Congress Cataloging in Publication Data
Dynamics of knowledge-intensive entrepreneurship : business
strategy and public policy / edited by Franco Malerba, Yannis
Caloghirou, Maureen McKelvey and Slavo Radosevic.
    pages cm. – (Routledge studies in innovation, organizations and
    technology)
    Includes bibliographical references and index.
    1. Entrepreneurship–Europe. 2. Knowledge management–Europe.
    3. Information technology–Economic aspects–Europe. 4. Technological
    innovations–Economic aspects–Europe. I. Malerba, Franco, 1950-
    HB615.D984 2015
    658.4'038–dc23   2015005696

ISBN: 978-1-138-02528-8 (hbk)
ISBN: 978-0-367-86898-7 (pbk)

Typeset in Sabon
by Wearset Ltd, Boldon, Tyne and Wear

Contents

Figures

Tables

Contributors

Yannis Caloghirou is Professor of Economics of Technology and Industrial Strategy and Head of the Innovation and Entrepreneurship Unit at the National Technical University of Athens (NTUA). He is leading two research groups – at the Laboratory of Industrial & Energy Economics – the first on 'Innovation and Entrepreneurship Studies' and the second on the study of the 'Information Society and the Knowledge-based Economy'. In this capacity he has acted as a scientific coordinator in a number of European research projects in the broader area of socio-economic research. He has served in top policy-making positions in Greece among them as Secretary General for Industry and as Secretary for the Information Society. He has also sat in a number of EU high-level expert and policy groups, among them as co-Rapporteur of the EU High-Level Policy group on the Socio-Economic Benefits of the European Research Area. He has also extensive work experience in industry as well as in policy advisory and policy design and evaluation positions. Prof. Caloghirou has written extensively on topics related to his research in scholarly journals, edited books and the popular and business press.

Roberto Camerani is Research Fellow at the Science Policy Research Unit (SPRU), University of Sussex. He holds a PhD in Science and Technology Policy Studies at SPRU. He also has an MSc in Innovation and Industry Analysis in the same institution and a degree in Economics at Bocconi University, Milan. Before joining the University of Sussex he worked in a number of research projects at CRIOS (Center for Research on Innovation, Organization and Strategy), Bocconi University, and INGENIO (CSIC-UPV, Valencia). His main research interests include the economics of innovation, the adoption and diffusion of innovations, entrepreneurship and innovation in the creative and cultural industries, self-employment and freelance work, job satisfaction and well-being.

Nicoletta Corrocher is a lecturer in Applied Economics at Bocconi University and Research Fellow at CRIOS (Center for Research on Innovation, Organization and Strategy), Bocconi University. She obtained a PhD in Economics and Management of Innovation at the Sant'Anna School of

Advanced Studies and an MSc in Science and Technology Policy at the Science Policy Research Unit (SPRU), University of Sussex. Her main research interests concern the diffusion of innovations and industrial dynamics – particularly in ICT industries and service sectors – and the emergence of eco-innovations in the framework of sustainable development. She has published in international journals such as the *Journal of Evolutionary Economics, Regional Studies, Research Policy, Journal of Information Technology, Telecommunications Policy, Technological Forecasting and Social Change* and *Industry and Innovation.*

Víctor Ferreira has taught at the Polytechnic Institute of Leiria, Portugal. He is a Fellow of the Research Centre for Rapid and Sustainable Product Development (CDRSP). He is currently the Executive Director of the D. Dinis Business School in Leiria. He is also a founder and partner of Look and Go, an innovative start-up in Portugal.

Roberto Fontana is currently an Associate Professor in Applied Economics at the University of Pavia and Research Fellow at CRIOS (Center for Research on Innovation, Organization and Strategy), Bocconi University, Milan. He received his PhD in Science and Technology Policy Studies at SPRU, University of Sussex. He is the advisory editor of the *Journal of Evolutionary Economics.* He has published research on innovation diffusion and standardization, product innovation, demand and its implications for the dynamics and structural evolution of industries with particular reference to high technology sectors.

Astrid Heidemann Lassen is Associate Professor of Innovation Management. She works at the Center for Industrial Production, Department of Business and Management, Aalborg University, Denmark. She is an expert in knowledge-intensive entrepreneurship, corporate entrepreneurship and user centred innovation, and her research includes detailed empirical work to understand the complex processes of developing organizational innovation capabilities based on a balanced approach to exploration and exploitation in both established companies and entrepreneurial ventures. Her publications are published in international academic journals and academic books.

Hartmut Hirsch-Kreinsen, Dr. rer.pol., Dipl.Wirtsch.Ing. (Business Administration and Engineering) is Professor at the TU Dortmund University, and has been Chair of Economic and Industrial Sociology since 1997. From 1980 to 1997 he was a research associate at the TH Darmstadt University and the Institute for Social Research Munich (ISF München). His working fields are economic and structural change, development of production work, new technologies and industrial innovation. He is a visiting professor at several foreign universities and a member of national and international advisory councils in the field of innovation policy.

YoungJun Kim is currently a professor at the Graduate School of Management of Technology, Korea University, in Seoul, Korea. Before joining Korea University, he taught at Seoul National University and Texas A&M International University, USA. His areas of research interests include technology management, technology strategy, technology transfer and commercialization, R&D and innovation policy, and technology economics. He has published more than 20 papers in Social Science Citation Index (SSCI) journals and several book chapters (OECD, Taylor & Francis). He is currently a member of the Presidential Advisory Council on Science and Technology in Korea.

Jens Laage-Hellman is Associate Professor of Industrial Marketing. He works in the Division of Industrial Marketing, Department of Technology Management and Economics, Chalmers University of Technology, Sweden and at the Institute for Management of Innovation and Technology (IMIT). His research focuses mainly on technological innovation, especially networking and collaboration. Over the years, he has been involved in numerous studies dealing with the development and commercialization of new technologies and products in a variety of industries, including e.g. steelmaking, mechanical engineering and biotechnology/life sciences. His current research interest is primarily focused on the life sciences, and in particular commercialization of academic research.

Daniel Ljungberg is Assistant Professor of Innovation and Entrepreneurship. He works at the Institute of Innovation and Entrepreneurship, Department of Economy and Society, School of Business, Economics and Law, University of Gothenburg, Sweden. His research has predominantly been focused on analysing the role and activities of universities and academics in the knowledge economy, specifically focusing on their relation with industry and their role in industrial innovation processes. His main research interests include academic patenting and entrepreneurship, university-industry interaction and the economics of universities.

Patrick Llerena has been Professor in Economics since 1988 at the Faculty of Economics and Management, University of Strasbourg; and is CEO of the Foundation University of Strasbourg, researcher and former director of the Bureau d'Economie Théorique et Appliquée (CNRS UMR n°7522), University of Strasbourg, France. He has published numerous articles in academic journals and edited books in the following fields: innovation economics; economics of science; theories of the firm and of organization; scientific and innovation policies; and decision theory under uncertainty. He was, from 2005 to 2011, co-cocoordinator of a Network of Excellence funded by the EU: DIME 'Dynamics of Institutions and Markets in Europe'. He was, from 2009 to 2013, a member of the 'Expertkommission für Forschung und Innovationen' (EFI), Berlin, Germany. He has been, since 2011, the first member of the Higher Level Economic Policy Expert Group 'Innovation for Growth' (I4G).

Franco Malerba is Professor of Applied Economics at Bocconi University, Milan. He is President of CRIOS (Center for Research on Innovation, Organization and Strategy), Bocconi University, Editor of *Industrial and Corporate Change*, Advisory Editor of *Research Policy* and Associate Editor of the *Journal of Evolutionary Economics*. He received his PhD in Economics from Yale University and has previously been Director of CESPRI and KITeS Research Centers; President of the International Schumpeter Society and of EARIE (European Association of Research in Industrial Economics). In 2012 he won the Schumpeter Prize. He has conducted economic research for the EU and has been a member of the several EU High-Level Panels on innovation and innovation policy. He has been the author of a large number of books and articles on innovation, industrial organization, industrial dynamics, economic development and public policy.

Sunil Mani is Professor at the Centre for Development Studies, Trivandrum, Kerala, India. His most recent publication is, with Richard Nelson (eds, 2013), *TRIPS Compliance, National Patent Regimes and Innovation, Evidence and Experience from Developing Countries*, Cheltenham, UK and Northampton, MA, USA.

Astrid Marinoni is a PhD student in Strategic Management at Rotman School of Management, Toronto. She holds a BS in Business Administration and an MS in Economics and Management of Innovation and Technology from Bocconi University, Milan. Her main area of interests is the economics of innovation and entrepreneurship. During her working experience at CRIOS (Center for Research on Innovation, Organization and Strategy) research centre at Bocconi University, she focused on projects involving spin-offs, pre-entry experience, employee mobility and knowledge flow.

Maureen McKelvey is Professor of Industrial Management. She works at the Institute of Innovation and Entrepreneurship, Department of Economy and Society, School of Business, Economics and Law, University of Gothenburg, Sweden. She is a research fellow at the Institute for Management of Innovation and Technology (IMIT). Her research addresses innovation and entrepreneurship. An underlying theoretical proposition from an evolutionary and Schumpeterian paradigm is that innovation and entrepreneurship are closely related to processes of creating, accessing and diffusing knowledge and opportunities. Her research focuses upon economics and management of innovation, with many publications in academic journals and also academic books.

Manuel Mira Godinho is a Full Professor of Economics at ISEG, the Economics and Business School of the University of Lisbon, Portugal, and a member of the Research Unit on Complexity and Economics (UECE). His main research focuses and publications are in intellectual property rights, innovation and knowledge-based entrepreneurship. He has also worked as a consultant for public and private organizations in the areas of innovation and science and technology policy.

Aimilia Protogerou holds a PhD in Business Strategy and Industrial Policy and is Research Fellow at the Laboratory of Industrial and Energy Economics- National Technical University of Athens (LIEE-NTUA). Her research interests revolve around strategic management of technology and innovation, technology policy and cooperative research and development, innovation networks and knowledge-intensive entrepreneurship. She has contributed as a researcher and principal researcher to a large number of related research projects, mainly financed by the EU and the Greek National Secretariat of Research and Technology. She has published her work in international journals such as *Industrial and Corporate Change, Economics of Innovation and New Technology, Science and Public Policy, Journal of Technology Transfer* and *European Management Journal*.

Slavo Radosevic is Professor of Industry and Innovation Studies at (UCL) University College London. His main research interests are in science, technology, industrial change, foreign direct investments and innovation policy in central and eastern Europe (CEE). He has published extensively in international journals in these areas. He favours empirically oriented and policy-relevant research projects, based in neo-Schumpeterian economics. He acts as an expert for the European Commission, OECD, UNESCO, UNIDO, World Bank, UNECE and Asian Development Bank and for several governments in CEE. He also has significant policy-making experience in Croatia and ex-Yugoslavia at the highest policy level.

Isabel Schwinge, MA, was a research associate, lecturer and PhD candidate at the Chair of Economic and Industrial Sociology of TU Dortmund University, Germany (2009–2014). The title of her dissertation is 'The paradox of knowledge-intensive entrepreneurship in low-tech industries – using the example of cases from the German textile industry' (forthcoming). She studied Sociology, Political Sciences and Ergonomics at Technische Universität Braunschweig. Her main research interests are institutional entrepreneurship in low-tech industries, inter-organizational processes of innovation along supply chains and sustainable economies.

Valerio Sterzi was educated at Bocconi University, Pompeu Fabra University and University of Bergamo, where he received his PhD in 2009. He is currently a researcher at Gretha, CNRS, and Assistant Professor of

Economics at the University of Bordeaux, where he is also programme director of Master 1 'Ingénierie des Risques Économiques et Financiers' (IREF). He teaches Econometrics at undergraduate and graduate levels, as well as an undergraduate course in Macroeconomics. His research interests are mainly in Economics of Innovation and Technological Change. He has published in several international journals, such as *Research Policy, World Development, Journal of Evolutionary Economics, Journal of Socio-Economics, Science and Public Policy* and *Tijdschrift voor economische en sociale geografie*.

Aggelos Tsakanikas is Assistant Professor in the field of economic evaluation of technological systems, at the Laboratory of Industrial and Energy Economics (LIEE), National Technical University of Athens. He has also worked in the Foundation for Economic and Industrial Research (FEIR/IOBE) as Head of Research and as Research Director. He has participated in various European projects in the area of socioeconomics research and entrepreneurship. His main research interests and most of his published work are in the area of technology strategy of the firm, business strategy, economics of innovation, entrepreneurship and relevant public policies. He has also been involved in numerous sectoral studies, quarterly reports on the Greek Economy, studies on entrepreneurship and competitiveness, and information society. He is also a member of the Greek research team that participates in the Global Entrepreneurship Monitor Programme.

Nicholas S. Vonortas is Professor of Economics and International Affairs at The George Washington University. He is a faculty member of the Department of Economics and of the Center for International Science and Technology Policy (CISTP). He has served as the Director of both the CISTP and of the adjustment graduate programme. He is now the director of PhD Candidacy at the Department of Economics. He is currently an editor of the journal *Science and Public Policy*. Professor Vonortas also holds the São Paulo Excellence Chair in Innovation Policy at the Universidade Estadual de Campinas (UNICAMP), Brazil during the period 2014–2019. Professor Vonortas' teaching and research interests are in industrial organization, in the economics of technological change, and in technology and innovation policy. He holds a PhD and an MPhil in Economics (New York University), an MA in Economic Development (Leicester University) and a BA in Economics (University of Athens).

Xiaobo Wu is Qiushi Chair Professor of Strategy and Innovation Management, Dean of School of Management, Director of National Institute for Innovation Management and Director of Global Zhejiang Entrepreneur Research Center, at Zhejiang University. He is also the director of the Zhejiang University–Cambridge University Joint Research Center for Global Manufacturing and Innovation Management. He used to serve as the Senior Vice President of International Council for Small Business.

Esin Yoruk is Research Fellow at SSEES (School of Slavonic and East European Studies), UCL (University College London) in the UK. She obtained her DPhil from SPRU (Science and Technology Policy Research), University of Sussex, UK. She holds a BSc in Materials Science and Metallurgical Engineering and an MSc in Economics. Her research interests are about technological change and innovation, technological capability, technology acquisition, innovation systems, knowledge networks, knowledge-intensive entrepreneurship, clean technologies and emerging technologies particularly with regard to medium and high technology manufacturing sectors.

Andrei Yudanov is Professor of Economics, Department of Economics, at the Financial University under the Government of the Russian Federation, Moscow. He is a Doctor of Economic Science (DSc) and a member of the editorial boards of the *Russian Management Journal* and *'The Modern Competition' Journal*, Moscow. He obtained the Award of the Government of the Russian Federation. He has participated in numerous international research projects – among them 'Big Business and the Wealth of Nations' and 'Business History Around the World', organized by Alfred D. Chandler; and AEGIS, a project of the European Commission's FP 7. Current fields of scientific interest are: high-growth firms ('gazelles'), low-tech innovations, knowledge intensive enterprises, entrepreneurship, theory of competition.

Preface

There are several reasons why a reader concerned with innovation and entrepreneurship will find this book interesting and worth reading. First, this book examines an important type of entrepreneurship – namely, knowledge-intensive entrepreneurship – which is very much associated with innovation and with knowledge generation and diffusion and which is present both in high-tech and low-tech sectors as well as in R&D and non-R&D-based activities. Second, this volume is a research-intensive intellectual product combining a conceptual framework with extensive empirical research based on a detailed field survey of more than 4,000 new firms in Europe and on 86 in-depth case studies examining high-tech and low-tech manufacturing sectors as well as Knowledge Intensive Business Services (KIBS). Third, the book has a strong comparative dimension as the research studies knowledge-intensive entrepreneurship in different contexts, within both sectors and countries. More precisely, this book examines knowledge-intensive entrepreneurship in these manufacturing and service industries and in different countries in Europe (Nordic, Continental, Anglo-Saxon, Southern European, Eastern European ex-planning economies) and in the BRICS economies (Russia, China and India). Fourth, this book develops an approach for designing a system of policies for the promotion of the knowledge-intensive entrepreneurship.

This book is the result of almost ten years of EU-funded research effort conducted by a network of prominent research units active in the field of innovation and entrepreneurship studies, across and beyond Europe. This research venture was initiated with the KEINS project[1] and was advanced and further deepened with the AEGIS[2] project. More specifically, ideas, concepts and data used in this book emerged from extensive research and dense intellectual communication in the context of AEGIS (Advancing Knowledge-Intensive Entrepreneurship and Innovation for Economic Growth and Social Well-being in Europe), a four-year large-scale EU-funded research project.

As such, this book and the underlying research project, represent so far the largest and the most comprehensive empirical research effort in understanding the important phenomenon of knowledge-intensive entrepreneurship.

Research that forms the basis for this volume has been the collective effort of a number of European and non-European organizations: Cespri/KITES/ CRIOS of Università Commerciale 'Luigi Bocconi' Milan, National Technical University of Athens, Institute for Management of Innovation and Technology Gothenburg, Max Planck Gesellschaft zur Förderung der Wissenschaften e.v., Lunds universitet, Universiteit Utrecht, Technische Universität Dortmund, Université Louis Pasteur, University College London, Unidade de Estudos sobre Complexidade e Economia, Aalborg Universitet, University of Sussex, Institute of Economics, Hungarian Academy of Sciences, Centre for Economic Studies, University of Economics and Management Prague, The Finance Academy under the Government of the Russian Federation, Zhejiang University China, Centre for Development Studies India, Center for Social and Economic Research Warsaw, Universiteit Maastricht and Croatian Employer's Association. We are grateful to all colleagues from these organizations for excellent cooperation and team effort.

We would like to thank all the participants and discussants at the multiple conferences and workshops held during the AEGIS project, which were hosted at Bocconi University, the National Technical University of Athens, University College London, the Technical University Lisbon, and at the EC DG Research in Brussels. In particular, George Licht, Bo Carlsson, Tasssos Gianitisis and Johan Van den Bossche have participated in workshops and commented on work in progress. We appreciate their contribution. Rapahel Koumeri and Soumi Papadopulou from PLANET S.A. have been the project coordinators of AEGIS and have skilfully managed the project while Marianne Paasi and Pia Laurila from the European Commission (DG Research and Innovation) have followed the project and have provided continuous support and suggestions. Global Data Collection Company and its CEO Kees-Jan Mars contributed decisively to the successful implementation of the AEGIS survey by collecting data across ten countries. Dario Lamacchia skilfully helped in the final editing of the book. Finally, Sinead Waldron of Routledge has been a great editor from the publisher side. We thank them all.

Franco Malerba, Yannis Caloghirou. Maureen McKelvey
and Slavo Radosevic
Milan, Athens, Gothenburg and London, January 2015

Notes

1 European DG Research, *Knowledge Base Entrepreneurship: Institutions, Networks and Systems*, EU project n.CT2-CT-2004–506022.
2 AEGIS, *Advancing Knowledge-Intensive Entrepreneurship and Innovation for Economic Growth and Social Well-being in Europe*, Grant Agreement number 225134.

1 Introduction

Franco Malerba, Yannis Caloghirou,
Maureen McKelvey and Slavo Radosevic

1 Introduction

Entrepreneurship has become increasingly recognized as an important topic in society, as demonstrated through

i The increasing interest on the entrepreneurial practice as a choice for professional career.
ii The widespread conviction that entrepreneurship can play a vital role in promoting innovation, economic growth and well-being.

In particular, research on entrepreneurship (Carlsson *et al.*, 2013: 913) has 'flourished in recent years and is evolving rapidly'. Today, the domain of entrepreneurship research 'can be seen as a subfield within several disciplines, each with its own perspective on the subject matter ... representing a variety of research traditions, perspectives, and methods'. There is a growing number and an increasing variety of relevant publications.

Over the last 10–15 years, the literature on entrepreneurship includes a variety of genres, such as academic research based, professional-practical and popular. Indeed, many books of all kinds are published, from theoretical and conceptual, to applied research based and handbooks, to biographies of entrepreneurs, compendiums of practical information for start-ups, guides and manuals and even 'cookbooks' with oversimplified recipes. Moreover, they deal with all sorts of entrepreneurship, such as female, youth, academic, engineering, high tech, corporate, social, etc. So, on the one hand, we can see a relatively recent explosion of interest. On the other hand, we can see a long tradition. This is an evolving and very dynamic academic field, which can be attributed to the heterogeneous, multi-dimensional and complex character of the entrepreneurial phenomenon. That is why entrepreneurship as a field of research can be found in relation to different, distinct intellectual traditions, in relation to the different perspectives and methods used, and in relation to several disciplines (economics, management, sociology, business and business history, etc.) literature.

So, why do we believe that there is room for yet another book on this matter? What is the value-added of this book compared to others of a similar vintage?

This book addresses one specific type, namely Knowledge Intensive Entrepreneurship (KIE), which we consider quite important in the modern economy. Knowledge intensive entrepreneurial ventures are new firms that have significant knowledge intensity in their activity and develop and exploit innovative opportunities in diverse sectors. These firms do not operate only in high tech sectors but also in services and in particular knowledge intensive business services (KIBS), and low tech industries; their activities focus not only on science and R&D based knowledge but also on new knowledge stemming from professional and business practice. In terms of innovation, they include design and other formal and informal types of innovative activities. A detailed discussion on KIE definition can be found in Chapter 2, which deals with the conceptual foundation of this volume. This book explores KIE ventures in terms of creation and origins, organization, strategies and business models as well as the role of innovation systems and institutions in its formation and growth.

The challenges of developing KIE lie at the core of the EU growth malaise and its structural shift towards knowledge based economy. The EU has fewer young leading innovators, particularly in new high R&D intensive sectors. Europe's new firms do not play a significant role in the dynamics of industries, especially in the high tech industries. In addition, Knowledge Intensive Entrepreneurial ventures can play a significant role in fostering the competitiveness of low- and medium-low technology (LMT) industries, which have a considerable weight in Europe. In this respect, KIE ventures can upgrade and improve the position of European business firms active in LMT sectors in the new emerging international division of labour. These kinds of structural deficiency problems of the European industry are well diagnosed but very little is known about the micro dimension of this major EU challenge. In order to understand why the creative destruction process as well as the industrial restructuring process in the EU encounters significant obstacles, while undermining Europe's growth, a potential much better understanding of the micro dimension of this process is required.

Furthermore, KIE can be considered as a mechanism to grow out of the crisis in the framework of a much needed European growth policy, however properly adapted to the different contexts and capacities across different countries in Europe. The formulation and implementation of a new growth agenda for Europe – based on a strategy for activating knowledge – is an 'absolute must' in order to upgrade EU position in the emerging division of labour in the globalization era. In this context, KIE as a transformative mechanism converting useful knowledge into economic activities and innovative new ventures is the key driving force of an innovation-led and high-growth potential path.

The AEGIS research and this book

This book explores KIE conceptually and empirically by generating new evidence based on large-scale surveys, case studies, and analyses on various sectors and countries. It is the selection of results from the large-scale collaborative project AEGIS (Advancing Knowledge-Intensive Entrepreneurship and Innovation for Economic Growth and Social Well-being in Europe, Grant Agreement number 225134) which was part of the 7th Framework Program in the Social Science and Humanities (SSH) and was managed by the consultancy firm PLANET.

Participants included:

- Cespri/KITeS/CRIOS, Università Commerciale 'Luigi Bocconi', Milano
- Laboratory of Industrial and Energy Economics at the National Technical University of Athens, Athens
- Institute for Management of Innovation and Technology, working with University of Gothenburg
- Max Planck Gesellschaft zur Förderung der Wissenschaften Jena
- Lundsuniversitet Lund
- Universiteit Utrecht
- Technische Universität Dortmund
- Université Louis Pasteur Strasbourg
- University College London
- Unidade de Estudos sobre Complexidade e Economia
- Aalborg Universitet Denmark
- University of Sussex Brighton
- Magyar tudomanyos akademia kozgazdasagtudomanyi intezet (Institute of Economics, Hungarian Academy of Sciences) Hungary
- Centrum ekonomickych studii Vysoke skoly ekonomie a managementu, o.p.s. (Centre for Economic Studies, University of Economics and Management)
- Finansovaya akademiya pri pravitelstve rossiyskoy federacii (The Finance Academy under the Government of the Russian Federation) Russia
- Zhejiang University China
- Centre for Development Studies Trivandrum India
- Centrum analiz spoleczno- ekonomicznych- fundacja naukowa (Center for Social and Economic Research) Poland
- Universiteit Maastricht, The Netherlands
- Croatian Employer Association.

This volume goes beyond the traditional, exclusively person-centred view of entrepreneurship by adopting an evolutionary and systemic or network approach to entrepreneurship. In particular, this volume introduces the following series of research topics to advance the state-of-the-art:

- organization-centred and network-centred view of entrepreneurship;
- focus on entrepreneurship as both micro and macro phenomena;
- attention to cultural and organizational issues;
- concentration on both high and low technology sectors, including manufacturing, and services;
- focus on activities exploiting non-scientific or non-R&D practice based innovations;
- extension of the analysis beyond supply, to the demand side of the entrepreneurial phenomenon;
- analysis in the context of various socio-economic models and systems of innovation in Europe;
- comparison of European patterns with those of other leading emerging economies such as China, India and Russia;
- systemic view of the entrepreneurship and, consequently, of the associated policy implications;
- focus on factors that affect dynamic organizational capabilities which are instrumental to knowledge intensive entrepreneurship.

Section 2 provides a brief discussion on a previous study on KIE (Malerba, 2010). In Malerba (2010) the major findings of the previous EU project called *KEINS (Knowledge base entrepreneurship: institutions, networks and systems)* are presented: it represents the base, both empirical and theoretical, upon which the AEGIS project was later developed. Section 3 explains how the AEGIS project has advanced the state-of-the-art, defined around five contributions. Section 4 discusses the contributions of each chapter, in relation to these themes

2 The KEINS legacy about knowledge intensive entrepreneurship

This book greatly refines and expands the approach and the findings of an earlier EU-funded project called KEINS on knowledge intensive entrepreneurship and innovation systems. KEINS has been a research project on knowledge based entrepreneurship *KEINS (Knowledge base entrepreneurship: institutions, networks and systems,* EU project n.CT2-CT-2004–506022) supported by European DG Research and carried out by seven European research centres. They are: CESPRI – now CRIOS, Bocconi University, Italy; Max Plank Institute Jena, Germany; IMIT working with Chalmers University of Technology, Sweden; Beta – University Louis Pasteur, France; University College London, United Kingdom; Cisep University of Lisbon, Portugal; and Case Research Center Warsaw, Poland. A selection of papers from the KEINS project have been published in the book *Knowledge Intensive Entrepreneurship and Innovation Systems: Evidence from Europe* (Malerba, 2010).

In the following pages we briefly discuss the main results from KEINS and from Malerba (2010) in order to introduce the advancements presented in this book. KEINS and Malerba (2010) developed a view of KIE quite close to the one used in this book. KEINS examined entrepreneurship as dealing with innovation and change and as knowledge operators, dedicated to the utilization of existing knowledge, the integration and coordination of different knowledge assets, and the creation of new knowledge, and engaged in the development of new products and technologies. In particular, KEINS has examined KIEs in Europe along four different perspectives: the quantitative relationship between KIE, industrial dynamics, economic growth and regional development; the creation of new firms in knowledge intensive sectors in Western Europe and in Central and Eastern Europe as inserted in various types of innovation systems; the analyses of KIE across technologies and specific industries; KIE in terms of academic entrepreneurship and patenting. Let's briefly highlight the main results.

2.1 The relationship between KIE, economic growth and regional development

KEINS found that KIE affects economic growth and regional development. For example, for 440 counties in Germany in 2000, Audretsch and Keilbach (in Malerba, 2010) show that KIE entrepreneurship in general, and also high tech entrepreneurship (entry in sectors that have an R&D intensity greater than 2.5 per cent) and ICT entrepreneurship (entry in ICT sectors), have a positive role in German regional economic performance. High knowledge intensity (i.e. high technology sectors or ICT) affects entrepreneurship by providing more entrepreneurial opportunities and entrepreneurship affects economic performance through increase in competition and increase in diversity.

What are the main features of KIE in industrial dynamics? Mamede, Mota and Godinho (in Malerba, 2010) examine the dynamics of KIE in Portugal between 1995 and 2000, using two classifications, the OECD one that considers high and medium technology industries plus knowledge based services, and the other one that considers industries that are in the 10 per cent of industries with the highest average proportion of employees holding a university degree. Entrepreneurship in industries that are knowledge based has higher survival rates and higher growth rates than entrepreneurship in other industries. In these industries entry is less responsive to incentives (in terms of price cost margins or industry growth), and more to other factors such as the behaviour of incumbents and competition (low concentration) and limited economies of scale.

2.2 Small scale surveys in Western Europe and in Central and Eastern Europe

What are the characteristics of KIE in Western Europe and Central and Eastern Europe when we consider a system perspective? Two specific firm small scale surveys have been administered by KEINS. For Western Europe Lenzi *et al.* (in Malerba, 2010) in KEINS explore the characteristics of KIE in Germany, France, UK, Italy, Sweden and Portugal. Knowledge intensive entrepreneurs have been selected as a group of new firms that innovate within a very short time after their establishment and are both knowledge based (i.e. active in science based and science driven sectors) and technology based (i.e. patenting in sophisticated and dynamic technological contexts). Ninety-nine companies have been examined. They have been divided according to three broad regions: Germany, Northern Europe and Latin Countries (France and Italy) and three sectors: biotechnology, electronics and medical devices. The major findings are that venture capital is very important, in Germany and Northern countries and in biotechnology. Banks on the contrary are more relevant for medical devices and local and regional authorities for biotechnology. In general, IPR (licensing and patent) is important for founding a new firm. All types of firms reported specialized labour as key for their survival and success. Networks are considered always important for a large part of firms, while more than 40 per cent of firms do not consider important the links with universities. Collaborations with previous employers are more frequent in Nordic Countries and in biotechnology, and R&D is the main area of collaboration. The success of knowledge based entrepreneurs is based on the uniqueness of their products. In addition, marketing skills and customer services are important in electronics and medical devices. Most of the firms offer a product for a specialized market which is unrelated to the founder's previous employer. And the level of human capital is confirmed high: most founders have a PhD or a Master's. Differences across countries (Germany, Nordic Countries and France/Italy) are related to degrees of development of, and the ease of access to, financial markets, and the different functions and effectiveness of the university system. The first one affects the probability of entry into entrepreneurship. The second affects the educational profile of founders, the frequency of collaborations with the private sector and the rate of university spin-offs. On the other hand, major differences across sectoral systems refer to the competences, the knowledge endowment, the inheritance from, and the relationship with the previous employer, and the types of customers. Ultimately, the combination and interplay of both country and technology specific elements strongly affect and shape the initial decision of entry into entrepreneurship as well as the early evolution of new innovative firms.

For Central and Eastern Europe, Radosevic, Savic and Woodward (in Malerba, 2010) examine KIE in Hungary, Lithuania, the Czech Republic, Croatia, Poland and Romania from a survey of 304 firms in six countries. The results of the survey show that knowledge based entrepreneurs usually start their careers in the business sector rather than in the scientific sector, and start knowledge intensive firms in order to take advantage of market (i.e. commercial and financial) opportunities. These entrepreneurs bring knowledge about products and technology from their previous employment and then develop new markets with their new firms. In that respect, KIE in CEECs can be considered as a market repositioning activity. Technological opportunities are frequently mentioned as a key rationale for establishing companies only in the Hungarian sample, where more entrepreneurs come from the science sector. KIEs in CEEC are not 'gazelles'. The key factor in KIE firms' growth is most often firm specific capabilities which do not always involve R&D. Based on what the firms have identified as their success factors, Radosevic *et al.* (2010) have grouped firms in three types: new technology based firms, 'networkers' and companies whose success is based on 'customer-oriented organisational capabilities'. The most common developmental barrier in domestic markets is the low level of demand on those markets. This is followed by high labour costs, increased competition and lack of public support. Firms fall into two groups with respect to the kinds of barriers that were most important for them. For the first group the main barriers concern skills shortages and high labour costs. For the second group, the major barriers are related to finance (lack of access to finance and of public support). Compared to standard companies in CEE, which tend to limit their strategic interactions for innovation to value chain partners such as buyers and suppliers, the networks of KIEs are broader and more frequently involve innovation system actors (research institutes, universities), including professional networks (fairs and exhibitions). Finally for different types of KIEs different networks are important. In general, these are either vertical (foreign and domestic value chains) or horizontal (links with the domestic public research system).

Based on this survey and on case studies of several Central and eastern Europe Countries, Radosevic (KEINS, 2007) identifies some general features of KIE in new member countries (NMS) of the European Union. In NMS there is a limited domestic demand for knowledge based products and activities, including public sector demand. This is even more so for knowledge intensive services. Local networks do not play a major role. However, customers have an increasing relevance, particularly in software, because customization is important for the success and growth of firms. Knowledge is usually developed in-house, except in internet based business.

2.3 A first exploration of KIE across technologies and sectors

How relevant is KIE in terms of new innovators in a technology? Camerani and Malerba (in Malerba, 2010) have examined new innovators in terms of companies and other organizations that patent for the first time in 12 technologies with a high rate of change, ranging from ICT, to semiconductors, to pharmaceuticals and biotechnology, to machine tools. The authors have used patents applications at the EPO in the period 1990–2003 in Europe, the United States and Japan. They find that innovative entry is a very frequent phenomenon: on average more than 40 per cent of the patenting firms in a technological class in every period did not patent before in that class. And more than 25 per cent of new innovators in a technology never patented before in any other technological class – in a sense they are de novo technological entrants. The importance of new innovators differs across technologies: de novo innovators are particularly high in ICT, medical engineering and measurement instruments, and low in semiconductors and chemicals. However, the relevance of new innovators in terms of total number of patents is much less relevant. This means that innovative entrants start innovating with very few patents and are smaller than incumbent innovators: this is similar across technologies and across countries. If technological entry is quite common, persistence in innovative activity is more difficult: around half of the firms continue to have only one patent. Those firms that enter and become persistent innovators keep patenting in the same technological field in which they entered. Again, no major differences in this respect across countries and sectors seem relevant.

2.4 Academic entrepreneurship

Academic entrepreneurship can be examined ether through academic start-ups, or through the contributions that academics provide to innovative activity. Using these perspectives, Lissoni, Llerena, McKelvey and Sanditov (KEINS, 2007) have examined academic patenting in France, Italy and Sweden. They show that in those countries academic scientists have signed more patents than previously estimated in other studies. This re-evaluation of academic patenting in Europe comes by considering all patents signed by academic scientists active in 2004, both those assigned to universities and the many more held by business companies, governmental organizations and public laboratories. From these KEINS data, universities' contribution to total domestic EPO patent applications in France, Sweden and Italy appears not to be much less intense than that of their US counterparts: 4 per cent in the EU and 6 per cent in the USA. Specific institutional features of the university and research systems in the three countries (IPR arrangements, the institutional profile of national academic systems and the research contracts) contribute to explain these different ownership patterns between the USA and Europe. In Europe between 60 and 80 per cent of academic patents were owned by business companies, 14 per cent by individuals and only 10 per cent by universities in France and Italy. In the USA, 69 per cent of academic patents are owned by universities. In Europe businesses own 57 per cent of academic patents in pharmaceuticals and 85 per cent in electronics. This difference depends on the funding of research and on the exploitation strategies of patents. However, university ownership of patents, albeit small, has increased in all the three European countries considered.

Lissoni (in Malerba, 2010) combines a relational analysis on inventors' data with the results of a short questionnaire submitted to a subset of Italian academic inventors, and with data on their scientific publication record and CVs. Lissoni finds that that brokerage and gatekeeping positions are very few, and are held by scientists with both a large number of patents and a strong publication record. These scientists are better than colleagues when it comes to keeping in contact with industrial researchers. Network ties between academic and industrial researchers may be short-lived as far as knowledge exchanges are concerned, but may serve well other purposes. Some of them, especially those who have signed patents only for one or two different assignees, are likely to keep in touch mainly for research or research funding purposes. Others, such as those academic inventors with many different assignees and/or assignees such as public consortia, may nurture their personal links outside universities for more strategic purposes.

3 Contributions of this book

As compared to KEINS and Malerba (2010), the current book greatly advances our knowledge of KIE for the following reasons:

- a more fine grained conceptual, and systemic analysis of KIE, considered as an organization-centred and network-centred entrepreneurship, exploiting also non-R&D and practice based innovations;
- a very large scale European Survey regarding more than 4,000 firms;
- a very detailed set of 86 case studies;
- an expansion on the sectors examined;
- a discussion of KIE in the context of various countries and systems of innovation in Europe;
- a comparison of European patterns with those of other emerging economies, by examining KIE in three BRICS countries – namely China, India and Russia;
- a system of policies view for promoting KIE, which can be seen as a gradual merger between Entrepreneurship Policy and Knowledge and Innovation Policies.

This book delves into the analysis of a particular type of entrepreneurship – KIE – which combines knowledge intensive content and innovative performance. In this regard, the main research questions we address are: What kind of animal is KIE? Why does KIE differ from other forms of entrepreneurship? In order to answer these questions, a variety of empirical instruments are used (survey, case studies, social network analysis, patent analysis, etc.) in order to better measure and understand a multifaceted phenomenon.

A central part of this book (and of the AEGIS project) is the AEGIS survey. The AEGIS survey was conducted in 4004 firms, with detailed questionnaires completed and filled by the interviewer during a telephone interview with one of the firms' founders. It was carried across ten European countries: UK, Germany, France, Italy, Sweden, Denmark, Greece, Portugal, Croatia and Czech Republic. The sample firms are independent young entities founded between 2001 and 2007, with an average age of 7.1 years. All firms have been in operation for at least four years, and therefore it can be assumed that they have managed to exceed the critical three-year survival threshold. The majority of them (63.6 per cent) are micro firms, i.e. they employ up to nine full-time persons. Almost 90 per cent are small firms, as they employ less than 50 persons, while at the same time only a very small share of them (0.28 per cent) can be regarded as large or very large firms (>250 persons). The surveyed firms belong to different sectors: high and medium to high technology manufacturing, low and medium to low technology manufacturing, and KIBS. A broad range of questions in the survey regarded the origin, the organizational structure, the strategy and the performance of KIE. The AEGIS survey has supplied a unique opportunity to understand better the characteristics and features of KIE in Europe. Several of the chapters in this book are based on the AEGIS survey and explore several aspects of KIE. Thus, the AEGIS survey allows for analysis to be carried out at various levels (the founding team, the firm and the contextual characteristics) and numerous dimensions (different levels of knowledge intensity in their activity, different innovative performance, etc.). In particular, knowledge intensity level is measured on the basis of firms' knowledge seeking activities, innovation performance, initial knowledge capital and human capital. Moreover, this book places the AEGIS survey in the context of the most known surveys on entrepreneurship like the Entrepreneurship Indicators Programme (EIP) of OECD and EU, the research based on Global Entrepreneurship Monitor (GEM) and the KfW/ZEW Start-up Panel and others.

Taken together, the chapters in this book make the following five major contributions. They:

- develop theoretically and conceptually the notion of knowledge intensive entrepreneurship;
- offer rich evidence on the behaviour and organization of 4,000 knowledge intensive enterprises in ten European countries;
- present extensive case studies and meta-studies of KIE providing detailed and articulate understanding of the opportunities, challenges and behaviour of KIE ventures;
- provide a comprehensive understanding of sectoral differences in characteristics of KIEs and support the view that KIE cannot be narrowly associated with high tech sectors (both in manufacturing and services), but is equally present in low tech activities;
- present comparative evidence and analysis on KIE in countries of Western Europe, Central and Eastern Europe as well as China, India and Russia.

This book is intended for the research community in the field of innovation studies and entrepreneurship research as well as the policy-shaping and policy-making circles in the public policy field that relate to entrepreneurship. Furthermore, its readership includes managers, business analysts, engineers and business persons with an interest in knowledge intensive innovative entrepreneurial activity. In this respect, a particular segment of potential readers includes young would-be entrepreneurs originating from interested students, academics and researchers as well as coaches, mentors and funding professionals. Last but not least, opinion makers, media people and business and technology analysts will find this volume an important reference.

4 Overview of the book

This book has four parts that reflects the main themes and areas of contribution. There is a *conceptual analysis* which defines what KIE is and then an operalization of the concepts through an empirical analysis of KIE in Europe through the AEGIS *survey*, conducted in ten European countries, and through more in-depth analysis of KIE with a very large number of detailed *case studies* and meta-analyses. Then KIE is studied in different *sectors* and in different *countries:* Western European, Eastern European and some new emerging countries, i.e. three of the BRICS. The final theme presents the *policy* implications and suggestions of this book.

In the following pages a brief presentations of the book and chapters is provided. The four parts are the following:

I   Analysing and measuring KIE: the conceptual framework, the survey and the case studies
II KIE in different sectors
III KIE in different countries
IV Designing and implementing a system of policies for promoting KIE

The brief presentation of the content and the contributions of the 16 chapters included in these parts are summarized below:

Part I Conceptualizing and empirically studying KIE – survey and case studies

Using the notion of KIE theoretically and conceptually developed in Chapter 2, the remaining chapters in the first part of the book provide rich empirical evidence based either on the large scale AEGIS survey or on a series of detailed case studies and meta-studies.

More specifically, in Chapter 2, Franco Malerba and Maureen McKelvey provide a conceptualization of knowledge intensive entrepreneurship – including a specific definition and process model – which can be used in relation to theories, constructs and indicators and draw implications for public policy makers and managers. They first examine specific aspects of knowledge intensive entrepreneurship in the literature, and then move on to propose a broad conceptual framework that takes into account the system and the process dimension of KIE. Knowledge intensive entrepreneurship is considered a key socio-economic phenomenon that drives innovation and is at the base of the economic growth of countries.

In Chapter 3 Yannis Caloghirou, Aimilia Protogerou and Aggelos Tsakanikas present selected findings from the AEGIS survey which aimed at identifying motives, characteristics and patterns in the creation and growth of young firms across ten European countries. The AEGIS survey could be considered as a pilot exercise for the design of a new instrument aiming at the monitoring and study of KIE in Europe on a regular basis. The chapter provides evidence on the founding team's characteristics, the firms' formation phase, the market environment and the opportunities it provides for growth, the firms' strategies, innovation and business model as well as the firm performance and the effect of economic crisis.

In Chapter 4, Yannis Caloghirou, Aimilia Protogerou and Aggelos Tsakanikas develop a taxonomy of firms' entrepreneurial behaviour, based on the AEGIS survey. The empirical taxonomy identifies three types of entrepreneurial ventures which exhibit distinct KIE characteristics. In particular, the 'all-around KIE' group shows a balanced emphasis on knowledge seeking activities (both in-house and from external sources), on new-to-market product innovation, and on process and organizational innovation. On the other hand 'world-class KIE' emphasizes new-to-world product innovation drawing from in-house knowledge which in turn draws from high quality human capital (both in terms of founders and workforce). The 'modest KIE' group focuses on new-to-firm product innovation drawing on external industry knowledge sources and, in general, it appears less knowledge intensive and innovative compared to the other two groups.

In Chapter 5, Nicholas Vonortas and YoungJun Kim analyse empirically aspects of managing risk in young small enterprises on the basis of the AEGIS survey data. Young companies treat technology risk as unsystematic or diversifiable and, thus, try to manage it actively and to decrease it through strategic networking. On the other hand, competition risk, market risk and financial risk seemed to be considered systematic – largely depending on external factors – and, consequently, do not lend themselves easily to management.

In Chapter 6 Maureen McKelvey, Daniel Ljungberg and Astrid Heidemann Lassen present 86 in-depth case studies of knowledge intensive entrepreneurship from different industries and countries. They focus upon the venture creation process, involving close interactions between the entrepreneur, the firm, and the surrounding eco-system and environment. The cases mostly offer a managerial perspective on the process, from the sources of ideas, through opportunities and strategies, to outcomes and interactions with external networks.

In Chapter 7, Maureen McKelvey, Daniel Ljungberg and Astrid Heidemann Lassen discuss the different types of opportunities and knowledge which are identified during the start-up phase and realized through the management and development phase of knowledge intensive ventures. The meta-analysis of 86 case studies across different countries and sectors suggests that the creation of opportunities and importance of knowledge networks is as much present in 'high tech' as in 'low tech' sectors. Nevertheless, the propensity and direction of KIE appears to be influenced by the specific sectoral and national institutional contexts.

Part II KIE in different sectoral systems

In the second part of the book, which goes from Chapters 8 to 12, different types of sectors are discussed, providing evidence that KIE can be found across the economy.

In Chapter 8 Roberto Fontana, Franco Malerba and Astrid Marinoni use the AEGIS survey data to reveal the different types of sectoral systems in which KIE takes place. Starting from the framework of sectoral system, several relevant dimensions have been isolated: knowledge and its sources, the benefits coming from relationships and networks, the type of participation in formal agreements and the instruments of intellectual property protection. Five different sectoral profiles have been identified suggesting that the environment in which young knowledge intensive enterprises are active is very diverse and, therefore, strategies for knowledge access, networking and innovation protection should also take into account the specific characteristics of the sectoral system a firm operates in.

In Chapter 9, Hartmut Hirsch-Kreinsen and Isabel Schwinge move the analysis to low and medium technology industries and examine whether KIE activities can be identified in these sectors. Their analysis is based on case study research in 27 firms, either established or young ones, in four European countries. Four types of firms are distinguished: a demand driven type, a science and technology driven type, a capability driven type and a competitive pressure driven type. The conceptual value of this typology is that it advances the theoretical understanding of opportunities for KIE activities in low tech industries. The findings show that KIE stretches well beyond high tech and knowledge intensive sectors and start-up firms.

In Chapter 10, Aimilia Protogerou and Yannis Caloghirou examine the role and impact of dynamic capabilities (DCs) in the context of new ventures using the large data set of the AEGIS survey. Their analysis support the assertion that dynamic capabilities – such as market and technology sensing, new product development, networking and collaborative technology agreements – are present in newly established firms that in their majority are micro and small firms. Dynamic capabilities are based on the firm's knowledge base, which consists of knowledge assets and human capital. Dynamic capabilities also exist in low tech firms, although capabilities such as technical adaptation and technology collaborative agreements are present to a smaller degree compared to high tech firms.

In Chapter 11 Jens Laage-Hellman and Maureen McKelvey focus on the dynamics of developing and managing a KIE venture relative to the wider innovation system. Their empirical approach is based upon a case study of a company which is active in the Swedish medical technology industry. The case study provides an understanding of how one specific firm relies upon the innovation system to access and further develops knowledge and resources. More specifically, it reveals the role of a network in providing resources as well as of the different types of networks that the KIE venture develops over time. The medical technology sector is heavily regulated, and therefore companies must meet particular sectoral conditions related to clinical studies, if they are to be able to identify and exploit innovative opportunities.

In Chapter 12 Roberto Camerani, Nicoletta Corrocher and Roberto Fontana examine product innovation in a very dynamic knowledge intensive industry characterized by rapid technical change. Relying upon a comprehensive database of 585 innovative products in the Digital Audio Player (DAP) industry marketed between 2011 and 2009, they analyse the product differentiation strategy of firms distinguishing between de-novo entrants and diversifiers. Their findings highlight a substantial variety of supply in the industry as convergence towards a similar design is rather low. In addition to this, convergence is also low across types of entrants as de-novo firms look for ways of fending off competition from more 'resource-rich' diversifiers. These findings suggest that, despite the presence of an undisputable leader (Apple), there is much more variety of strategy and innovative products in the industry than one could expect. Their analysis shows the need to nurture and sustain variety in order to promote innovation in knowledge intensive industries.

Part III KIE in different countries

In the third part of the book KIE is studied at the country level: Chapters 13–15 give a comparative evidence and analysis on KIE in countries of Western Europe, Central and Eastern Europe as well as China, India and Russia.

In Chapter 13 Slavo Radosevic and Esin Yoruk examine the factors influencing the entrepreneurial strategies of firms based on an in-depth survey of 60 knowledge intensive companies in four Central and East European (CEE) countries. The analysis is framed within the entrepreneurial orientation framework exploring the extent of autonomy, innovativeness, risk-taking, pro-activeness, competitive aggressiveness as well as sheds light on their networking strategies. The picture that emerges from the analysis is sharply different from the dominant 'individual – opportunity nexus' as depicted in the GEM style of research on entrepreneurship. Firms in CEE countries, either organizational spin-offs or new start-ups, are geared towards exploiting existing knowledge based on previous experience and recognizing new market opportunities. They are repositioning themselves in terms of markets or products, but not in terms of technology. In that respect, CEE entrepreneurship is of a cumulative and evolutionary rather than disruptive nature.

In Chapter 14, Victor Ferreira and Manuel Mira Godinho analyse the relationship between innovation and KIE through an innovation production function approach that uses a set of explanatory variables that reflect various factors linked to innovation systems. In order to measure regional innovation in the EU's NUTS 2 regions they built a composite variable, using patent applications together with trademarks. Analysis suggests that this measure may be appropriate to identify innovation that is not as technologically intensive as the one typically captured by patent counts. Furthermore, it demonstrates that traditional factors (such as the level of business R&D, schooling and wealth) have a statistically significant effect on the production of knowledge (the composite of patents and trademarks); while at the same time entrepreneurship in KIBS seems to play a significant role.

In Chapter 15 Franco Malerba, Sunil Mani, Valerio Sterzi, Andrei Yudanov and Xiaobo Wu examine KIE in three new emerging economies: China, India and Russia. They provide a quantitative analysis of the growth of KIE in terms of new innovators and new patenting activities in the three countries using patents granted by the European Patent Office. Then they go in depth to discuss the main features of KIE in China, India and Russia highlighting their main differences. They also discuss in detail the common factors behind the emergence of KIE, particularly in China and India: among them the most relevant ones include the growth in income and domestic market opportunities; the increase in skills and education and in the supply of engineers, technicians and managers; the growth of R&D; the increase of policy support; the rise in venture capital; the spread of information and communication technologies and the flow of returnees from advanced countries.

Part IV Designing and implementing a system of policies for promoting KIE

A final chapter regards the public policy implications of this book. In Chapter 16 Yannis Caloghirou, Patrick Llerena, Franco Malerba, Maureen McKelvey and Slavo Radosevic draw public policy and business strategies issues resulting from the analyses and chapters presented in this volume. The conclusions go well beyond the current focus on entry of new small KIE ventures and focus on a systemic perspective and on the differentiated ecologies – i.e. sectors, countries, markets, etc. – for the growth of KIE ventures. They provide specific policy recommendations for the promotion of KIE and strongly argue the need for a system of policies approach linking knowledge, innovation and entrepreneurship in a national and European context. In this respect innovation policy – more broadly know-ledge policy – and entrepreneurship policy should be integrated. Moreover, entrepreneurship policy should be differentiated from traditional SME policy as it addresses issues related to a different stage of the life cycle of the firm. In addition, the need for evidence based entrepreneurship policy should be covered by adopting a regular European Entrepreneurship Survey (EES) conducted with a unified methodology in all EU countries.

References

Carlsson, B., P. Braunerhjem, M. McKelvey, C. Olofsson, L. Persson and H. Ylinenpää (2013), 'The evolving domain of entrepreneurship research', *Small Business Economics*, Volume 41, Issue 4, pp. 913–930.

KEINS (2007), 'Knowledge base entrepreneurship: institutions, networks and systems' Project no. CT2-CT-2004-506022 DG Research, European Union, Brussels.

Malerba, F. (ed.) (2010), *Knowledge-Intensive Entrepreneurship and Innovation Systems: Evidence from Europe*, London: Routledge.

Part I
Survey and case studies

2 Conceptualizing knowledge intensive entrepreneurship
Definition and model

Franco Malerba and Maureen McKelvey

1 Introduction

This chapter proposes a conceptualization of knowledge intensive entrepreneurship (KIE), including a definition and a process model of the dynamics over time which take into account the interactions between KIE ventures and innovation systems. This chapter provides a broad foundation for understanding and analysing KIE at two levels, namely as a particular type of entrepreneurial venture and as a dynamic phenomenon.

Much research has been conducted on a huge variety of issues related to entrepreneurship in general as well as different types of entrepreneurship. Some approaches categorize entrepreneurship as the event of starting a firm, while other approaches focus on specific aspects, such as entrepreneurs' traits or the role of cognition in identifying opportunities. Distinguishing elements of knowledge intensive entrepreneurship – as compared to entrepreneurship in general – are the roles of innovation, knowledge and innovation systems. This system view contrasts KIE from much existing research on entrepreneurship which has focused upon more specific types of entrepreneurship such as the one dependent upon science and universities – namely academic entrepreneurship – or new technology based firms. Because this chapter emphasizes concepts, models and indicators, only a few selected references are made: We suggest that the interested reader examine the selected bibliography in this chapter, references in other chapters in this book as well as the literature review in McKelvey and Lassen (2013a).

Thus the concept of KIE is narrower than entrepreneurship in general, but it is broader than specific types of entrepreneurship, such as academic entrepreneurship. This implies that KIE may rely upon a range of types and sources of relevant knowledge, and that they can be found also in low and medium tech sectors as well as in services. The definition of KIE also has impacts upon research strategies in that we move beyond more simple measures (such as for example statistics about entrepreneurs in high tech sectors) and search for a variegated set of indicators in order to more precisely define the characteristics and dimensions of KIE across the economy.

In sum, the concept of KIE provides a broad definition of entrepreneurship which is dependent upon knowledge and innovation systems and which can be applied across all types of sectors.

This chapter also goes on to propose a process model of the dynamics of knowledge intensive entrepreneurship over time. This model is based upon an analysis of entrepreneurship, which draws from the insights of evolutionary economics, a Schumpeterian view and the innovation system approach. By doing so, our conceptualization of KIE moves away from a person-centric view of entrepreneurship and instead includes a broader view of individuals and companies seen in relation to the linkages, networks and other actors in the society. This process model considers entrepreneurs as agents involved in using, generating and transforming knowledge. It emphasizes that the dynamics of resources and capabilities of entrepreneurs are conditioned by linkages and networks related to innovation systems, which include institutions and which influence the development and diffusion of relevant knowledge.

In particular, the specific structure and characteristics of innovation systems are important because they help condition the type and range of network linkages available to the entrepreneur and to the evolution of the KIE venture. These external network linkages within an innovation system refer to the relationships among agents, including firms as well as many other organizations. In our conceptualization, linkages within innovation systems matter because they influence the entrepreneur's access to resources and also their perceptions about which innovative opportunities can be developed through science, technology and markets. Hence, networks are essential because they are links to potential sources of knowledge, new capital, new employees, strategic alliance partners, and service providers (such as lawyers, accountants and consultants). Moreover, these networks in innovation systems also allow entrepreneurs to share others' information and assessments about market and technological opportunities as well as lessons learnt from their own entrepreneurial activities. Thriving regions and nations generally boast a wide array of both formal and informal network structures within national, regional and sectoral innovation systems.

The conceptualization of KIE as proposed in this chapter forms the foundation upon which the AEGIS project and this book have been developed. By using advanced design, market and technological knowledge, KIE ventures are crucial agents that can stimulate innovation, foster industrial renewal, introduce new business models and drive economic growth and societal well-being across the economy. While the purpose of this book is to provide overall evidence about KIE, the purpose of this chapter is to provide a conceptualization of KIE – including a specific definition and process model – which can be used in relation to theories, constructs and indicators and derive implications for public policy and managers.

Section 2 presents the definition of a KIE venture, consisting of four characteristics. Section 3 continues the discussion of definitions, by placing the KIE definition in relation to definitions of other types of new ventures, which are influential and can be found in the literature. Section 4 provides the process model of the dynamics of knowledge intensive entrepreneurship over time, including a brief positioning in the literature. Then Section 5 elaborates how this conceptualization can provide a platform that can let researchers define their empirical contributions – as well as to specify where and why they have chosen different variables – for analysis based upon official statistics, surveys and case studies. The reason is that a new concept and construct requires a careful consideration of research strategies, data and indicators, with advantages and disadvantages of different research strategies. Finally some concluding remarks can be found in Section 6.

2 Defining knowledge intensive entrepreneurship at the firm level

This section provides a definition of the specific characteristics of knowledge intensive entrepreneurship at the firm level, called KIE venture below. This definition provides a framework within which it is possible to compare and contrast different KIE ventures and to distinguish KIE ventures from other types of entrepreneurial firms, and hence other types of entrepreneurship. This definition of KIE ventures aims to characterize firms that either have not explicitly been the focus of attention in the literature or that have previously been studied in various ways. This definition has inspired in one way or another several empirical chapters that constitute this book.

A definition of KIE takes into account four basic characteristics: *KIE firms are new firms that are innovative, have a significant knowledge intensity in their activity and exploit innovative opportunities in diverse sectors and contexts.*

This definition is more related to the KIE venture as an organization, than to the person, or entrepreneur per se. Naturally, specific individuals are quite important for the dynamics of the development of KIE organization and venture, as is well recognized in entrepreneurship research, but the definition here focuses upon characteristics by which we can identify and analyse KIE ventures. The four main characteristics, which are elaborated below, are: (1) new firms; (2) innovative; (3) with a significant knowledge intensity in their activity; and (4) which exploit innovative opportunities in diverse sectors and context.

2.1 New firms

A first key characteristic of the definition of KIE ventures is that these should represent new firms. This excludes firms that have existed for a long period as well as corporate entrepreneurship, which occurs internally in an existing organization.

One aspect is defining when a new organization exists, independent from a parent organization. As discussed in later chapters, the boundaries between new firms and organizational units that are created but are still dependent from an existing firm are not always easy to define. Existing firms are often the source of new firms, and this research would like to get beyond ideas of entrepreneurial orientation, although this is sometimes difficult to do, and especially in the context of Eastern Europe (see Chapter 13) and of traditional low and medium tech industries (see Chapter 9). Boundaries matter. For example, a spin-off firm can be included in this definition, if the new venture is independent from the parent organization. However, a new organization which is essentially a subsidiary of a large existing firm without independent decision making is not included. Making a clear boundary is crucial, however, and particularly for surveys and quantitative work, while a case study may follow a longer period before the venture was created.

A related topic is how new is 'new' when it comes to operationalize the concept to firms in the economy. In entrepreneurship literature and statistics, new is often defined as eight years. Hence 'new' firms are defined as firms that are less than eight years old and such a definition has been used as appropriate for the AEGIS survey (see Chapter 3). Usually, this operationalization can also be used for quantitative studies and for cross-sectional data based upon official statistics. This can also be used in case studies following the development of KIE ventures in terms of main variables and processes (see Chapters 6 and 7). However, this time limit does not always make sense in qualitative work like case studies that have a longitudinal approach, given that we are also interested in the antecedents of the KIE ventures.

2.2 Innovative

Another characteristic is that the KIE ventures must be innovative, i.e. the novel ideas must be innovative in economic terms. Innovation can be categorized in many ways, with usual dichotomies ranging between product-process, radical-incremental and service-product. In empirical terms, this may be measured in different ways, including traditional measures such as patents and measures developed in the Community Innovation Survey (such as a high percentage of products and services sold that were new to the market). Thus, these characteristics exclude firms that sell standard goods and services or that only focus on traditional and established technologies.

Moreover, a profit motive has to be there in order to characterize KIE (even within the public sector), thus excluding categories like NGOs, lifestyle or hobby firms, and social entrepreneurship. Again, the boundaries are sometimes fuzzy, such that social entrepreneurship is sometimes defined as entrepreneurship, which solves a societal problem, but these may sell goods and services, hence could have a profit motive. Public sector may also generate many new ideas, but which are later commercialized by firms rather than the public sectors. For our purposes, the characteristic of innovative includes both the idea of novelty and of economic impact, or intention of profit.

2.3 Significant knowledge intensity

A third characteristic is that KIE ventures need to have a significant dimension of knowledge intensity in their activity. Knowledge can come from many domains, including advanced science and technology but also including market, design, creative and other types of knowledge.

This can be analysed in many ways. In empirical terms, knowledge intensity can be measured through a variety of ways, where measures may be valid either across sectors or for specific sectors. Knowledge intensity can be measured, for example, as investment in research and development in manufacturing; networking with universities; or advanced human capital for service industries. Case studies have also suggested that entrepreneurial firms in sectors defined as low and medium tech may use a variety of knowledge (see Chapters 6, 7 and 9).

A key aspect is the novelty of knowledge, as related to innovation. Thus, this characteristic excludes a firm, which has a knowledge that is primarily based upon repetitive and routinized knowledge, or based on established technologies that are used without improvements or novel areas of applications.

2.4 Exploit innovative opportunities

Finally, we can expect to find KIE ventures exploiting innovative opportunities. Opportunities may be driven by the rapid development of (potential) markets and of technology or by combinations of creative knowledge and design. Moreover, opportunities tend to emerge over time, during the development of a firm and/or sector, as they are identified and tested in the market place. The literature on business model offers a way to identify key attributes of the firm, which help it exploit the key knowledge and gain revenues from users and stakeholders.

Empirically, no existing statistics can provide a clear measure of opportunities, given that they emerge over time and are often related to the attributes of individual entrepreneurs and of KIE ventures. Therefore, in the context of AEGIS and this book, our aim has been more modest. We are looking to examine whether or not our initial statement is correct, that KIE ventures can exploit innovative opportunities in diverse sectors and different contexts. These sectors can range from manufacturing to services, and from high tech to traditional industries and the countries with their national institutional context can range across Europe, in the context of this book.

Moreover, this characteristic should provide us attributes of the business models that can be studied, which can be analysed both in surveys and case studies. The KIE ventures should have business models, which depend upon relevant knowledge integrated into the exploitation of innovative opportunities in order to create value and growth at the firm level.

2.5 What the definition of KIE excludes and highlights

The above definition and discussion of the four characteristics has provided us aspects of what is excluded and what is included in the definition. Figure 2.1 positions our work by explaining the foci that are excluded.

The key aspects that are excluded from the definition of KIE are: firms that sell standardized goods and services; firms based upon repetitive and routinized activities or established technologies; firms with products with no improvements; NGOs, lifestyle firms and other organizations without profit motives.

Let us summarize now the main characteristics and the definition of KIE highlights, as found in Figure 2.2.

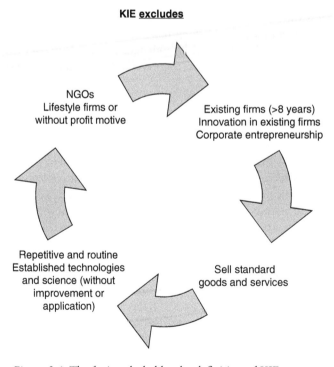

Figure 2.1 The foci excluded by the definition of KIE.

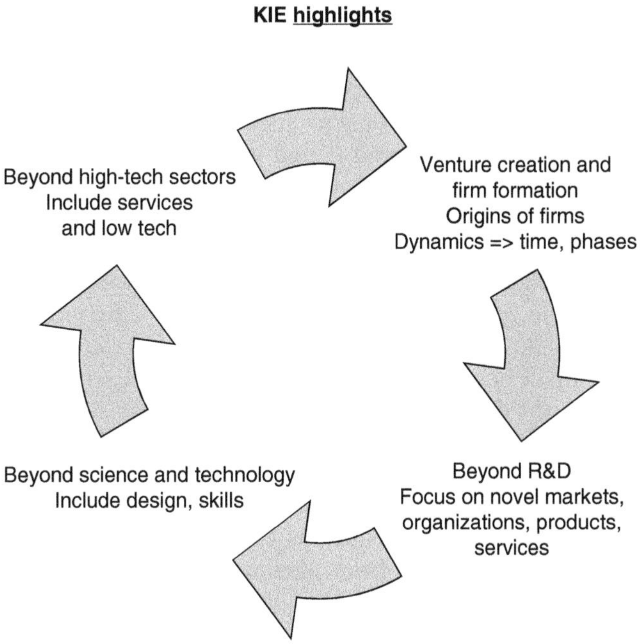

KIE highlights

Beyond high-tech sectors
Include services
and low tech

Venture creation and
firm formation
Origins of firms
Dynamics => time, phases

Beyond science and technology
Include design, skills

Beyond R&D
Focus on novel markets,
organizations, products,
services

Figure 2.2 What KIE highlights.

The first characteristic (that KIEs are new firms) highlights venture creation and firm formation, leading to a focus on aspects such as origins and sources of firms as well as their dynamics over time. The second characteristic (that they are innovative) leads to us to focus upon R&D, novel products and services, new markets and organizations and so on. The third characteristic (that they have a significant knowledge intensity in their activity) means that we have to move beyond traditional indicators of science and technology and also include other dimensions such as design, complementary skills and so on. The fourth (the ability to exploit innovative opportunities in diverse sectors) takes the analysis beyond the traditional studies of R&D intensive sectors, to also consider services and low tech sectors.

3 Knowledge intensive entrepreneurship and other types of entrepreneurship

In this section we provide a discussion of similarities and differences between KIE and other types of entrepreneurship that exist in the literature and in the policy domain. The first aspect relates to the general definition of entrepreneurship. On the one hand, the definition of a KIE venture narrows down the construct from the general concept of entrepreneurship, when measured as starting a company or entrepreneurial intent (or orientation). The other aspect is the relation to other existing concepts. Thus, on the other hand, by addressing the four characteristics, the definition also brings together aspects of entrepreneurship which have previously been addressed in a more fragmented way such as more specific types of entrepreneurship dependent upon science and universities. We would like to acknowledge some of them. Indeed, overlap with some existing definitions is to be expected, even if our definition covers a more defined space than a general definition of entrepreneurship, such as starting a firm.

The first aspect to address is that KIE can be seen as a particular sub-set of entrepreneurship in general. General definitions of entrepreneurship exist, such as in the GEM survey, and these often associate entrepreneurship with the start-up of new firms. The GEM survey[1] has a series of indicators, which have been defined to measure the three main categories of Entrepreneurial Activities, Entrepreneurial Aspirations and Entrepreneurial Attitudes. The indicators measure aspects such as business ownership rates in the population (e.g. percentage of people between 16 and 64 years old in the population) as well as aspects such as expected growth rather than fear of failure (e.g. to prevent them from starting a business). GEM identifies new companies and entrepreneurship in general, but does not provide finer grained indicators that could link start-up firms with the characteristics defined here, such as innovation, knowledge and systems in society. In contrast, to be considered a KIE venture, a firm must meet all four of the characteristics defined above.

The second aspect is that there are a variety of related influential definitions that already exist. The definition of KIE cannot be seen as synonymous with them, for reasons explained below. One thing to point out is that KIE ventures are not necessarily 'gazelles'. 'Gazelles' are defined as fast growing firms (Birch, 1987; Birch et al., 1995) and can be measured in that they maintain consistent expansion of both employment and turnover over a prolonged period. The expansion is often seen as 'exceptional'. There is no single definition of what constitutes an 'exceptional' growth rate, but 20 percent and more per annum is a common definition. This kind of entrepreneurship is also frequently associated with innovation and organizational change. These firms are defined on the basis of empirical data related to growth rates, and tend to be found in high tech sectors. They are not therefore defined based upon their specific internal characteristics but on growth characteristics. Even though 'gazelles' tend to account for a small minority of new ventures, they have attracted much attention from business analysts, economists and policy makers due to their potential for contribution to economic growth and competitiveness. Naturally, some KIE ventures can be gazelles, but many KIE ventures may not meet these criteria, and some gazelles are not KIE ventures.

Another concept is that of new technology based firms (NTBFs) and related concepts like academic entrepreneurship. In the existing literature, these types of concepts are generally associated with the firm being associated with a specific source and type of knowledge, or else their linkages to universities. For example, in one influential article to define the niche orientation of firms, Autio (1997) proposes to classify NTBFs into two groups: (1) Science-based firms. These utilize the results of generic research and transform them into basic technologies or application specific technologies, by developing very sophisticated products or services with a broad scope of application; (2) Engineering-based firms. These apply basic technologies to the development of new products or services addressing specific customer needs. Academic entrepreneurship and NTBFs have often been given a great deal of attention by academics and policy makers during the last decades. The interest has been stimulated by the recognition of NTBFs' contribution to economic development, industrial renewal, and job and wealth creation (see Storey and Tether, 1998 for a review on European NTBFs). These firms are seen as an important channel of technology transfer from R&D institutions to the commercial sector because NTBFs help the diffusion and commercialization of the results of basic and applied R&D carried out by public research and educational institutions (Chamanski and Waago, 2001). However, NTBFs do not necessarily guarantee innovation, enhance economic performance or generate faster rates of economic growth (Wong *et al.*, 2005). Indeed, also here, there are differences in various related types of definitions and classifications. The classification of NTBF primarily focuses upon the technical assets (scientific, engineering), while the literature on academic entrepreneurship focuses upon the role of students and/or academics working at public research organizations like universities and institutes in stimulating entrepreneurship. In contrast, the KIE is not limited to one type of advanced knowledge nor to one source of that knowledge, and also tries to capture the translation of scientific and technological assets into economic value creation and the interactions and impact on innovation system.

Moreover, much work has focused upon firms active in high tech sectors, which has been a major focus of studies in recent decades. The OECD has proposed to divide firms according to the sectors to which they belong into high tech, medium-high tech, medium-low and low technology sectors (Hatzichronoglou 1997). This classification of sectors into these four categories was based upon direct R&D intensity and R&D embodied in intermediate and investment goods. The OCED has continued to work with these categories for the ISIC revisions (and Eurostat for the NAC revisions). Within high technology sectors, key areas for innovation studies include information and communication technology (ICT), biotechnology and nanotechnology.[2] While the majority but not all firms active in high tech sectors would be included in our definition of KIE ventures, many KIE ventures are not within high tech sectors and may be found in low and medium tech sectors as well as service sectors. Hence, starting with statistics on high tech sectors only captures a fragment of the KIE ventures defined here.

Our definition of a KIE venture presents a type of entrepreneurship that is broadly defined, where the venture is new, innovative, uses advanced design, market and technological knowledge, and exploits innovative opportunities in forming business models in many sectors and contexts.

4 A conceptual framework for knowledge intensive entrepreneurship, leading to a process model

4.1 General aspects of conceptualization

This section proposes a general framework for conceptualization and the analysis of knowledge intensive entrepreneurship, which brings together the entrepreneur, venture and innovation system. Our proposed framework of KIE has three pillars united in our analysis, namely: an evolutionary view, a Schumpeterian perspective and an innovation system framework. In an evolutionary approach (Nelson and Winter, 1982) entrepreneurship triggers change and entrepreneurs introduce variety into the economic system through innovation. This entrepreneurship is in contrast with routines and routine behaviour. From our perspective, Schumpeter's key insight was that change is endogenous to economic systems: change is not imposed from outside, but rather is generated within. Schumpeter argued that fundamental changes in existing activities as well as the introduction of entirely novel activities would keep providing the 'fuel' to the capitalist engine (Nelson, 1996; Hanusch, 1999). In an innovation system framework (Edquist, 1997), innovators are part of a system of actors and relationships. We take these three macro arguments as a foundation for our perspective, specifically that entrepreneurship triggers variety, that this change is endogenous to the economic system, and that innovation systems shape firms' actions and performance.

Just for a brief digression of the theoretical basis for our perspective, one should remember that already a long time ago Schumpeter identified some of the aspects discussed in this chapter. Schumpeter considered entrepreneurship as dealing with *new activities and innovation*. As Schumpeter's (1934: 74) statement claims: 'The carrying out of new combination we call "enterprise"; ... the individuals whose function is to carry them out we call "entrepreneurs"'. In this perspective entrepreneurship deals with the setting up and the owning of a new business or new activities but there should also be characteristics of novelty or change. As a consequence, entrepreneurship is an activity that faces uncertainty and has the goals of creating something new: a technology, a product, an organization, a market. In *Capitalism, Socialism and Democracy* (1942), Schumpeter makes a very specific argument about the role of innovations in economic transformation. In the chapter 'The Vanishing of Investment Opportunities', Schumpeter reacts to contemporary arguments about why capitalism would 'stop' working. 'The main reasons for holding that opportunities for private enterprise and investment are vanishing are these: saturation [of wants/demand], [decline of] population, [no more] new lands, [end of] technological possibilities, and ... investment opportunities belong to the sphere of public rather than private investment' (1942: 113). In contrast to these pessimistic views, Schumpeter's argument is that capitalism will indeed keep functioning. 'There is what may be described as the "material" the capitalist engine feeds on, i.e., the opportunities open to new enterprise and investment' (ibid.). From this, we have turned our focus upon innovative opportunities. 'The fundamental impulse that sets and keeps the capitalist engine in motion comes from the new consumers' goods, the new methods of production or transportation, the new markets, the new forms of industrial organization that capitalist enterprise creates' (1942: 82). These quotes capture an intellectual heritage to define our starting position of what is fundamental about the relationships between entrepreneurship and innovation with economic transformation and the creation of new opportunities.

As explained in the introduction, our conceptualization of KIE moves away from a person-centric view of entrepreneurship and instead takes a broader view of the linkages and networks within the society. This conceptualization considers entrepreneurs as agents involved in generating and using knowledge, and emphasizes the fact that their resources and capabilities are conditioned by their linkages and networks with society through innovation systems, institutions and the broader development of knowledge.

To specify and summarize our conceptualization of the phenomena of KIE, the following propositions can be put forth:

- Large investments in knowledge generation (R&D) do not lead automatically to economic growth.
- The existence of a transformative mechanism (such as entrepreneurship) determines the effectiveness of the conversion of knowledge into economic activity. The mechanism varies over time and depends very much on a wide variety of socio-economic factors, including the institutional set-up, cultural factors and the prevailing intellectual climate.
- Much of existing research focuses upon the level of skills of the entrepreneurs as individuals and the types of their activities. According to this view, entrepreneurship can be undertaken by highly skilled individuals or groups of individuals, and the new organizations (i.e. new firms) may also come from existing organizations as in the case of spin-offs and spin-outs.
- In addition, characteristics such as the origin, type, knowledge and sustainability of entrepreneurship also matter, and make a difference for innovation and performance.
- KIE is strongly related to innovation and KIE is often based on innovative technologies and new knowledge. This has a direct impact on the

level of technological knowledge and innovation in the economy, and relevant effects in challenging established firms.

- Opportunities for innovation play a key role in KIE. Entrepreneurs act on these opportunities given their resources, capabilities and strategies.
- KIE adds a perspective on innovation systems including institutions and knowledge base to the notion of entrepreneurship. Entrepreneurs are part of sectoral, regional and national systems that affect their origin, growth and performance.
- Demand – private as well as public – plays a key role in affecting knowledge intensive entrepreneurship, innovation and economic growth.
- The interplay between science, technological advancement and human resources remains key for the emergence and growth of KIE.
- Regional contexts rich in knowledge may generate more entrepreneurial opportunities. A host of other factors, such as institutions, laws, traditions and culture shape the amount of entrepreneurship capital that is specific to a region.
- KIE is highly sector specific. Its features and impact depend on the knowledge base, the main public and private actors and the institutions that are present in a sector.
- KIE is also quite relevant in low tech sectors and traditional industries. A rich knowledge base may exist also in traditional sectors, although the sources and patterns may differ.
- KIE is present in service sectors. Here, the specific features of KIE may differ as compared to manufacturing, in terms of specifically in the key role of human capital, development of creative industries and co-generation of services with the user.
- Entrepreneurial dynamics are generated when systems, market and institutional factors are aligned with firm specific capabilities and when they mutually reinforce each other over time. Hence, entrepreneurship is inextricably linked to the ability of companies to develop dynamic capabilities over time.
- A broad set of public policy instruments affect the link between KIE, economic growth and social well-being. These public policy instruments reflect both the supply side – such as more traditional approaches related to science and technology, education, industry structure, risk finance, and the like – and the demand side – such as lead markets, public procurement, etc.

Thus, these propositions help us understand the context of entrepreneurship, based upon our conceptualization that KIE must be understood as a systemic and dynamic phenomenon, which affects the overall outputs of the economy.

Beyond the traditional economic thinking about the structure of incentive-reward in stimulating activities like entrepreneurship, our model in fact incorporates contextual elements. More specifically, the existence, direction and amount of KIE depends critically also on the other factors like the institutional set-up, the cultural factors and the prevailing intellectual climate. Institutional set-ups generate either a variety of barriers or a variety of opportunities within which KIE as dynamic transformative mechanism influences long-term growth. Hence, understanding the specific variables and processes which stimulate or hinder the processes requires a synthetic and systematic definition of the phenomena of KIE in relation to specific aspects of the context.

From this definition of the phenomena, a key issue to explore further is the relationship between the KIE ventures and the innovation systems. Several consequences can be derived.

One consequence of an innovation system view is that knowledge intensive entrepreneurs are active in quite different contexts or types of innovation systems. Three types of innovation systems stand prominently: national innovation systems (Lundvall, 1993; Nelson, 1993), sectoral systems (Malerba, 2002) and regional and local systems (Cooke, 2001). Each of the three main types of innovation systems may affect KIE in different ways and through different mechanisms.

Another consequence in particular is the linkages with context, which are relevant for the birth, working and dynamics of KIE ventures. Taking this broader perspective on innovation systems into account implies that in addition to business firms, we must also analyse how other actors in the innovation system are in relationship and exchange knowledge with KIE. Two examples can be given to explain the logic. For example, one key actor is constituted by public research organizations like universities and institutes. In fact, universities are involved in generating KIE ventures, and in shaping their impact on society. Academic organizations play a particular role in generating opportunities, in that they create advancements in new knowledge and technologies, which often reach commercial exploitation. This takes place through a person ('the academic entrepreneur') that embodies the necessary scientific and technological knowledge, or through licensing and other transfer mechanisms. Another example refers to users. Many processes of KIE generation in fact are driven by users. Users matter, as they may stimulate or even create entrepreneurship and innovation in various ways and intensity, generally through knowledge related to market opportunities and customer demands.

4.2 A process model of KIE dynamics

We now turn to our proposed process model of KIE dynamics, as visualized in Figure 2.3. The main purpose of this section is to work from the definition of KIE ventures presented in Section 2 and focus upon the dynamics over time. As mentioned above, the elements in our model

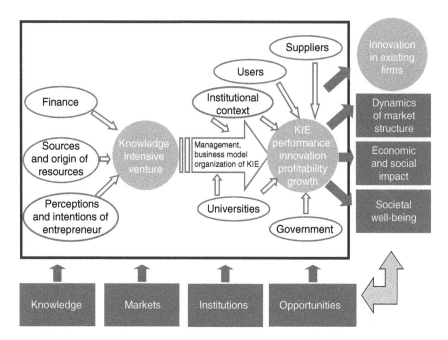

Figure 2.3 The process model of KIE dynamics.

combine evolutionary economics, Schumpeterian perspective and the innovation system view.

In Figure 2.3 one may find the representation of the dynamic development of a KIE venture with a main box and four variables at the bottom, which set the conditions for KIE entrepreneurship. At the far right of the main box broad outcomes related to the dynamic impacts are presented.

4.2.1 Development of the KIE venture: central box

Within the central box, the representation of the KIE entrepreneurial venture over time is given. The central box represents the development of the KIE venture, defined in relation to the context. The variables are based upon an extensive literature review (see McKelvey and Lassen, 2013a, 2013b). On the far left, three key input variables are identified: finance, origin of the entrepreneur and personal traits. The big arrow in the centre of Figure 3.2 identifies the importance of many internal firm attributes (especially management and organization), which affect how a specific firm will develop over time and the actual output at the KIE level in terms of innovation, profitability and growth. At the same time, these outputs are influenced by the sectoral, national and regional innovation system, here represented by suppliers, users, universities and competitors, and by the institutional context. The central box thus represents the development of the KIE venture, and the set of interactions with the surrounding environment.

4.2.2 *Variables setting dynamic conditions: arrows from bottom of model*

The four variables at the bottom affect the on-going process by setting conditions: they are knowledge, markets, institutions and opportunities.

The first dimension relates to *Knowledge*, which we define in relation to scientific, engineering and design knowledge, as well as to application knowledge (such as industrial problem solving and specific areas of products and services). With the term knowledge we refer to systematic problem solving knowledge. KIE are considered knowledge operators, dedicated to the utilization of existing knowledge, the integration and coordination of different knowledge assets, and the creation of new knowledge. KIE firms are engaged in the development of new products and technologies and in the launch of new activities and organizations that intensively use advanced knowledge. As just mentioned, one type may be new and existing scientific and technological knowledge that can be used for commercial purposes or for bringing products to markets. Other types may be market, design, creative and other advanced knowledge used in the innovation process by the firm.

The second dimension is that of *Markets*. The concept of 'markets' implies a focus on the demand side of entrepreneurship as well as an emphasis on the processes of competition and selection among firms. The focus on demand means paying a lot of attention to the knowledge and preferences of customers and consumers as drivers of innovation and entrepreneurial opportunities. The concept stresses the role of interactions between KIE and large firms. In fact many feedback loops and innovative ideas come from large firms as a type of knowledgeable industrial users. This focus on competition and selection means to consider KIE as a part of a more general market dynamics, in which other competitors such as established firms interact or compete with KIE.

The third dimension is that of *Institutions*. The analysis of institutions has been a core building block of the innovation system approach. The KIE conceptual model takes a broad definition of institutions: institutions refer to both formal and informal rules that shape economic outcomes. The institutional setting greatly affects the emergence as well as the performance of KIE ventures in various ways. More specifically, institutions include norms, routines, common habits, established practices, rules, laws, standards and so on, that shape entrepreneurship cognition and action and affect their interactions with other agents. Institutions differ greatly in terms of types of impact upon the behaviour of entrepreneurs. These impacts can range from the ones that impose enforcements on KIE to the ones that are created by the interaction among agents (such as contracts); from more binding to less binding; from formal to informal (such as patent laws or specific regulations vs traditions). Many institutions are national (such as the patent system), while others are specific to sectoral systems, such as sectoral labour markets or sector specific financial institutions.

The fourth dimension is *Innovative Opportunity*. Our focus upon the exploitation of innovative opportunities moves from a focus upon the technological and scientific knowledge per se to its exploitation in business models within an innovation system. This book recognizes that entrepreneurs in KIEs must mobilize their understanding of knowledge and innovation systems, in order to create value. Therefore, we must move beyond the traditional view in entrepreneurship literature that opportunity identification and capture is an attribute of the individual entrepreneur: opportunities arise from a broader range of knowledge, market and institutional changes. In particular, innovative opportunities are 'the possibility to realize an economic value inherent in a new combination of resources and market needs, emerging from changes in the scientific or technological knowledge base, customer preferences, or the inter-relationships between economic actors' (Holmén *et al.*, 2007: 37). 'Innovative opportunities' is a somewhat more complex concept than the ones which exist in the literature, including entrepreneurial, technological and productive opportunities. In our view, an innovative opportunity is more than a new technology or an individual perception or the mobilization of an internal bundle of resources in the firm. Firms in fact must put together all these elements in order to innovate. Consequently, an innovative opportunity must consist of at least the following three conceptual elements in order for actors to have the possibility to observe and act upon the potential inherent in an idea (Holmén *et al.*, 2007): a perceived economic value for someone, a perceived possibility that the resources needed to realize the opportunity can be mobilized, and a perceived possibility that at least some part of the generated economic value can be appropriated by the actor pursuing the opportunity. Taken together, these three elements imply that the KIE venture must identify the value to a customer, mobilize the resources, and capture the economic benefits from innovating, usually through their business model.

4.2.3 Outcomes and broad impacts: arrows to right hand side

On the far right, the broad impact of KIE is represented. KIE has three main impacts at the level of the economy and society: dynamics of market structure, economic and social impact, and society well-being. These dimensions matter a lot in the longer run, and particularly to public policy makers.

In a broader context, the impacts of KIE upon the economy and society are quite different and above all, introduce novelty/variety and stimulate change, which then becomes endogenous to the economy. The phenomena of KIE can have a major impact on market structure if KIE fosters competition, challenges established leaders and introduces new actors in the economic scene, increasing the variety of competences and firms in an industry. Moreover, KIE can also have a major economic and social impact by affecting employment and skills and changing the composition of the labour force and the economy, with major implications for education and training activities and vocational interests. Finally new technologies, products and services can result in new consumption patterns and create opportunities in the form of new goods and services offered for final consumption, thus changing societal well-being.

5 Moving forward in the empirical analysis of knowledge intensive entrepreneurship

This section moves on to issues related to empirical analysis. Capturing empirically KIE ventures as well as the process of KIE dynamics is a stimulating but sometimes tricky task: hence careful attention must be paid to dimensions and details. Moreover, different research strategies and methods have their own advantages and disadvantages and sometimes limit the research questions that can be answered. Our starting-point in this chapter – and reflected in the book as a whole – is that a wide variety of quantitative and qualitative data and research strategies may be used for somewhat different purposes. This section should thus help explain the book, and stimulate readers to new research on knowledge intensive entrepreneurship.

5.1 Research strategies and indicators for KIE ventures

The definition of KIE venture found in Section 2 provided some discussion of how to measure the four characteristics and both Section 2 and Section 3 discussed the important issue of defining the boundaries of the desired population. Given that the construct KIE did not exist before, careful attention needs to be taken for what is considered inside, or outside the population.

Table 2.1 provides an overview and examples of quantitative and qualitative data when investigating each characteristic of the KIE venture. Each research strategy has strengths and weaknesses.

In terms of the characteristic of new firms, a quantitative approach tends to rely on databases concerning a population of relevant firms, while a qualitative approach tends to focus on few firms, selected on the basis of an illustrative or theoretical rationale. The database can focus upon firms that are younger than eight years, and many times, the focus is upon the

Table 2.1 Examples of quantitative and qualitative approaches and data each characteristic of a KIE venture

Characteristic of KIE	Quantitative approach	Qualitative approach
New firm	Databases of populations of firms New firms: younger than eight years old Firm: incorporated	Few firms, selected based on illustrative logic or theoretical rationale New firm: historical trajectory, also before firm formation Individual entrepreneur, team, organization of the venture
Innovative	Distinction among types of innovations, such as product, process and organization Patents, such as EPO or USTPO Use of OECD definitions and CIS indicators, such as percentage of sales in new goods and services	Possibility to go deeper in depth about the types of innovations involved Can ask respondent to define innovative orientation or outputs Quantitative data can also be used
Significant knowledge intensity	R&D intensity (often at sector level) Human capital, such as level of education (often at sector level) Intangible assets (see OECD definition of intangible investments)	Examine in detail the relationship between firm innovation and growth and the knowledge of the firm Can ask the respondent to identify the relationship between development of and markets
Exploit innovative opportunities in diverse sectors and contexts	Include stratified sample of firms in the population (e.g. from high tech, low tech and service sectors or from different countries) Self-reported surveys can relate identification of opportunities (source, idea) to firm strategies	Understand how entrepreneurs/team can identify, act upon and exploit innovative opportunities Link to the innovation system Explain how venture perceives economic value; mobilizes resources; and appropriates economic value

KIE venture rather than the individual entrepreneur, at least in official statistics. When only a few firms are analysed, then usually a longitudinal and thick descriptive approach can be used, often linking the individual entrepreneur to the development of the KIE venture.

In terms of the characteristic of innovative, both research strategies can benefit from existing taxonomies and classifications which define innovation. A quantitative approach built upon existing statistics must use existing measures – such as patents or sales – whereas as a quantitative approach based upon a self-reported survey may use a richer set of indicators, such as those found in the Community Innovation Survey (CIS). Qualitative approaches can also have the respondent explain in which way the KIE venture was innovative, albeit at the risk of losing comparability across firms.

In terms of significant knowledge intensity, the two research strategies may differ more significantly. A quantitative approach may use a series of indicators, such as R&D intensity, human capital or intangible assets while a qualitative approach allows a richer look at the feedback loops and interactions between the development of knowledge, human resources, and the transformation and growth of the firm. In addition, a qualitative approach also allows the respondent to explain how the development of knowledge (such as technological knowledge) was developed in response to potential markets.

In terms of exploiting innovative opportunities in diverse sectors and contexts, from a quantitative approach some of the measurement problems can be addressed by having samples (stratified samples) within the population. Self-reported surveys can also link the identification of different types of opportunities to firm strategies. Obviously, all the characteristics of innovative opportunities can be better addressed by case studies.

Finally, in a more dynamic sense, both quantitative and qualitative research strategies can address a series of questions that follow up the discussion of the process model of KIE dynamics which was visualized in Figure 2.3. Based upon the process model of KIE dynamics, six broad areas of inquiry can be identified. They are: (1) origin of the company, entrepreneurial experience and inputs; (2) evolution and life-cycle of the company; (3) sources and types of new knowledge; (4) business model; (5) firm performance and type of innovation; (6) innovation system context. Each of these main areas of inquiry tends to have extensive literature, as well as a series of possible indicators that can be used in quantitative and qualitative analysis. Table 2.2 includes the dimensions and constructs, the literature and main themes as well as the types of proxies that can be used in the empirical analysis.

Let us now turn to the three main types of research strategies and data, with advantages and disadvantages for each of them.

Table 2.2 Dimensions and constructs of KIE and the related quantitative indicators

Dimension or construct Relevant theories	Proxy or indicator
Origin of the company; entrepreneurial experience; inputs *Literature on spin-outs and spin-offs of different types (corporate, academic and independent)* *Literature on specific role of large companies or of the dynamics of regions*	Spin-off firm or not Founder background, such as experience and skills of founder Origin of the company in terms of main product/service Resources at start of company Financing (private, VC, banks, companies) Role of large companies (corporate VC, customer) Role of public policy Role of demand
Evolution and life-cycle of company *Literature on opportunities, such as identification, recognition, exploitation* *Literature on small company dynamics, such as strategy, survival, management*	Formation (formal incorporation) Historical data about the firm Growth/decline of sales and employment Life-cycle events of the firm Competitive advantages Strategies for growth Gazelles (if applicable) Competition on the market Main collaborators
Sources and types of new knowledge used at firm level *Literature on sources, impact and role of knowledge for companies* *Literature on relationship between knowledge, invention, innovation and entrepreneurship*	Internal resources such as human capital and R&D External resources such as alliances and networks Sectoral categorizations of high tech, low tech and service Type of background; level of education and skills of entrepreneur(s) Level of education and skills of employees Sources of knowledge, such as universities, customers, companies, users Access to external knowledge

Business model
Literature on business models, strategy and organization

- Types of products and services offered; types of innovations introduced
- Analysis of the profitability of products and services
- Customer/stakeholder focus
- Internal organization of resources for knowledge exploration and exploitation

Firm performance, type of innovation
Literature on factors for success and failure
Literature on opportunity realization

- Dynamics of sales and employees
- Number of innovations
- Relevance of inventions for new product and sales (ex number of new products in last five years)
- Patents
- Market share
- Profits

Innovation system context
Literature on innovation systems, such as sectoral, regional and national

- Linkages with customers
- Sources of knowledge such as universities, PRO and suppliers
- Types of collaboration for knowledge flows
- Role of universities
- Dynamics of the specific industry or region

5.2 Quantitative analysis based upon official statistics

Rich sources of data for quantitative analysis are the ones based upon various types of official statistics. While not always perfect for capturing the concept at hand, this type of data does have many advantages, including the fact that these data are gathered through official bodies, present a certain degree of homogeneity, and are often available in time-series. Several of the chapters in this book rely extensively on this type of data, specifically Chapter 12 (Competing for product innovation in knowledge intensive industries: the case of the Digital Audio Players), Chapter 14 (The determinants of innovation: a patent- and trademark-based analysis for the EU regions) and Chapter 15 (Knowledge based entrepreneurship and emerging economies). Moreover, many other chapters include various types of official statistics as input or background data, such as Chapter 13 (Entrepreneurial strategies of knowledge intensive firms in Central and Eastern Europe).

The common types of data used are briefly discussed here. A first way to identify KIE is by looking at all the new firms active in sectors with a *high R&D intensity* – sectors known as high tech sectors. However, this indicator assumes that all new firms that enter a high technology sector have to be innovative or are knowledge intensive. This assumption is quite strong. Moreover R&D can be used as a proxy for scientific and technological knowledge in manufacturing, but it is not appropriate for services. In addition, it confines the analysis only to high technology sectors, while KIE is active also in low and medium tech sectors. Similarly, some research focuses upon the particular role of high tech industries in the dynamics of regions, by using data on entrants in specific regions. The remarks advanced above on the problems related to the use of specific quantitative indicators (new firms in R&D intensive sectors) hold also here.

Instead of focusing upon R&D intensity, another way to use official statistics regards all *new firms that use highly skilled human capital*, irrespective of the sector. Here one could examine and classify individual firms based upon the level and type of human capital. Human capital can be measured in terms of the education of the entrepreneur, the overall education and the skills of the labour force, and so on. In this way, also new firms active in the so called traditional sectors may be considered KIE through indicators of skilled labour. However, this approach works better for education than for the skills of the employees of the new ventures (which are usually not available in the statistics on the population of firms).

A third way is to examine *new firms that are also new innovators, measured by patents*. Patents are sometimes considered a measure of the innovativeness of companies. The basic assumption is that all new firms engaged in patenting activities are innovative enterprises. This measure of 'innovative' through patents provides advantages because it is possible to analyse patenting firms across industries and over time (because patents cover all the sectors and technologies). On the other hand, many new innovative ventures do not patent, patents are not equally relevant to all industries and technologies and from a patent an innovation does not necessarily emerge. So, while having the advantage of examining a whole population of patenting companies, this indicator has the disadvantage of being confined to that fraction of the innovative firms that decide to use IPR in order to protect their technological activities.

A fourth approach is to examine particular types of entrepreneurship, through *specific ad-hoc databases*. For example, a common means of analysing academic entrepreneurship is commercialization by scientists through patents and start-up companies (see review in Perkmann *et al.*, 2013). The existing literature using these measures assume that the university plays a particular role in stimulating KIE, and that this phenomena can be studied through analyses of university scientists or researchers who start new companies. However, there are major underlying assumptions about the particular role of entrepreneurship based upon scientific advances and skills which can in turn generate start-ups and innovation (if coupled with market and application knowledge).

5.3 Surveys that are designed by the researcher, based upon self-reported data

Another way to move forward in empirical analysis is through surveys that are designed by the researcher and based upon self-reported data. As compared to official statistics, they may suffer from lack of homogeneity of the data and low response rates, but have the advantage of better covering the concepts and variables of interest, e.g. a better match between construct and indicator. As compared to case studies, surveys can take into account a much larger number of firms and contexts and in the same time examine several aspects of KIE (seen at one specific time period) that cannot be covered by official statistics.

The AEGIS project is an example of such type of survey. It was a major survey conducted across Europe and based upon the definitions and model found in this chapter. Chapter 3 (The AEGIS survey: a quantitative analysis of new entrepreneurial ventures in Europe) presents the main empirical findings. The AEGIS survey was designed to expressly identify, address and measure the existence, characteristics and performance of KIE, by first using the definition of KIE to identify firms within a database of new firms, and then asking a series of questions related to firm level variables and concerning the origin, characteristics, business model and impact from, and on, the wider innovation system environment.

Table 2.3 explains how the six dimensions presented above were specifically addressed in the AEGIS survey.

In this book, in addition to Chapter 3 the following chapters have been written based upon the AEGIS survey. They are: Chapter 4 (Knowledge-intensive entrepreneurship: exploring a taxonomy based on the AEGIS

Table 2.3 Main variables related to each of the six dimensions of the AEGIS survey

Dimension or construct	Proxy or indicator
Origin of the company	Experience and skills of founder
Entrepreneurial experience	Details on the start-up process like funding and previous work experience
Evolution and life-cycle of the company	Formation (formal incorporation); historical data
Sources and types of new knowledge used at firm level	Internal resources such as human capital and R&D; external resources such as alliances and networks
Business model	Questions related to strategy; how the company senses and seizes business opportunities
Firm performance, type of innovation	Sales; employees; factors defined as relevant for success or as obstacles; relevant capabilities
Innovation system context	Linkages (role of customers, the sources of knowledge such as universities, public research organizations, suppliers) Impact of the institutional and market environment

survey), Chapter 5 (Managing risk in new entrepreneurial ventures), Chapter 8 (Knowledge intensive entrepreneurship in different sectoral systems: a taxonomy) and Chapter 10 (Dynamic capabilities in young knowledge-intensive firms: an empirical approach).

5.4 Case studies

Another way to advance our understanding is to develop case studies. In this project, case studies are usually of some KIE ventures examined over time but they may also concern populations of case studies in certain contexts (like the one regarding low tech industries or specific countries). Case studies may primarily focus upon qualitative data but may also combine them with quantitative data in multiple case study design. Case studies may be chosen upon a sampling strategy, which implies that the companies have first to be identified through surveys or analyses of the total population and then be selected for the relevant case studies. Most case studies are chosen for their rich insights into specific feedback loops and dynamics relative to a specific question. Tables 2.1 and 2.2 have already introduced a series of issues that can be addressed through case studies. The advantage of a case study is that it can follow the history of the individual entrepreneur; the venture creation; the organization, strategy and evolution of the firm; and the specific role of the institutional context of the relevant innovation system. Case studies can also be used to develop deeper theoretical understanding and new models, such as for the internal model of KIE venture development (McKelvey and Lassen, 2013a). Several chapters in this book employ a case study as a research strategy. They include: Chapter 6 (Structuring the process of knowledge intensive entrepreneurship: empirical evidence and descriptive insights from 86 AEGIS case studies), Chapter 7 (Opportunities and knowledge intensive entrepreneurship: a meta-analysis of 86 case studies of ventures), Chapter 9 (Knowledge-intensive entrepreneurship in low-technology industries), Chapter 11 (How networks and sectorial conditions affect commercialization in a KIE venture in the medical technology industry: a case study of Aerocrine) and Chapter 13 (Entrepreneurial orientation of knowledge-based enterprises in Central and East Europe). It must be noted that Chapter 13 is a good example of combination of use of different types of data, ranging from case studies, to official statistics, to data from a survey.

6 Concluding remarks

This chapter offers the conceptual basis upon which this book has been written. Our aim is that this chapter will also stimulate more work on the subject, with implications for conceptualization and theoretical analyses, for empirical work and for public policy.

For theoretical work, the framework advanced in this chapter regarding the definition and conceptualization of KIE and the process model should have some implications for further research and open up developments along different directions. In our purpose the conceptual model should relate to the need to clearly explain the linkages between firm, knowledge and innovation systems, as well as the mechanisms at the base of the dynamics of KIE. Current approaches and theories of entrepreneurship address mainly one variable or level at the time, and often disregard the linkages among the various dimensions of entrepreneurship, the interactions with the innovation system and the evolutionary process that takes place when the new ventures develops and grows. This book offers an example of how a system and process view of entrepreneurship can unravel new dimensions of entrepreneurship, such as the one discussed in Chapters 5 (managing risk), 6 (process and dynamics), 8 (the role of the sectoral context), 9 (dynamic capabilities) and 12 (innovative strategies). In particular, the future direction is to further develop and deepen the analysis of the process and the linkages (as presented in Section 4 and in Figure 2.3 of this chapter). More can be done to analyse more in depth and to explain how and why these linkages affect KIE formation, strategy and organization, its dynamics over time and the outcomes in terms of growth and well-being.

For empirical work, the implications from this chapter are the need, if possible, to combine cases with surveys and quantitative analyses in order to provide a broad, complete and articulated view of KIE and at the same time to go deeper in order to disentangle the emergence, growth and dynamics of KIE. This book taken as a whole provides one good example of this effort and offers an integrated view of KIE. If only one type of empirical work can be conducted – be cases, surveys or quantitative analyses – it is important to define well what specific dimensions can be unravelled by the analysis, as the chapters of this book taken individually do. This is so for cases, as one may find in Chapters 6 and 7 (meta-analysis of KIE ventures), 9 (KIE in low technology industries), 11 (the case of a medical technology firm); for surveys, as done in Chapters 4 (a taxonomy of KIE), 8 (the role of sectoral systems in affecting KIEs) and 13 (KIE in Central and eastern Europe) or for quantitative analyses, as done in Chapter 14 (the use of patents and trademarks for assessing KIE in EU regions). Hence, the book as a whole provides a variety of research methods and data, to address a series of related issues.

Finally, for public policy, the implications are that each policy instrument and policy goal may address a specific aspect of KIE, but it must also be related to the overall processes. And that more than one instrument should be combined for fostering KIE. This discussion will be developed more in detail in Chapter 16. Anticipating some of the points advanced there, the policy implications of this chapter highlight the need of maintaining a process view and a system dimension of KIE. This implies that policies should use several instruments at a time and that systems of policies rather than single, isolated and uncoordinated ones should be used. This requires that policies for KIE have to be coordinated and integrated and that they should take into account both the short run as well as the long run.

Notes

1 See Global Entrepreneurship Monitor (GEM) Key Indicators and Definitions at http://gemconsortium.org/docs/download/414.
2 In OECD 2011, the sectors classified according to ISIC rev 3 are as follows. High-technology industries include: Aircraft and spacecraft; Pharmaceuticals; Office, accounting and computing machinery; Radio, TV and communications equipment; and Medical, precision and optical instruments. Medium-high-technology industries include: Electrical machinery and apparatus; Motor vehicles, trailers and semi-trailers; Chemicals excluding pharmacueticals; Railroad equipment and transport equipment; Machinery and equipment. Medium-low-technology industries include: Building and preparing of ships and boats; Rubber and plastics products; Coke, refined petroleum products and nuclear fuel; Other non-metallic mineral products; and Basic metals and fabricated metal products. Low-technology industries include: Manufacturing; Wood, pulp, paper, paper products, printing and publishing; Food products, beverages and tobacco; and Textiles, textile products, leather and footware.

Selected bibliography on KIE

Audretsch, D.B. and Keilbach, M. (2007) 'The localisation of entrepreneurship capital: evidence from Germany', *Papers in Regional Science*, 86: 351–365.

Audretsch, D.B. and Keilbach, M. (2010) 'Entrepreneurship and growth', in Malerba, F. (ed.) *Knowledge-Intensive Entrepreneurship and Innovation Systems*, Routledge, London, UK and New York, NY.

Audretsch, D.B., Thurik, R., Verheul, I. and Wennekers, S. (eds) (2002) *Entrepreneurship: Determinants and Policy in a European–U.S. Comparison*, Kluwer Academic Publishers, Dordrecht.

Autio, E. (1997) 'New, technology-based firms in innovation networks symplectic and generative impacts', *Research Policy*, 26: 263–281.

Birch, D. (1987) *Job Creation in America: How Our Smallest Companies Put the Most People to Work*, Free Press, New York, NY.

Birch, D., Haggerty, A. and Parsons, W. (1995) *Who's Creating Jobs?* Cognetics Inc., Boston, MA.

Breschi, S., Malerba, F. and Mancusi, M.L. (2010) 'Survival of innovative entrants in knowledge based sectors', in Malerba, F. (ed.) *Knowledge-Intensive Entrepreneurship and Innovation Systems*, Routledge, London, UK and New York, NY.

Brink, J. and McKelvey, M. (2010) 'Diversity of knowledge-intensive entrepreneurial firms: struggling biotech firms despite opportunities', in Malerba, F. (ed.) *Knowledge-Intensive Entrepreneurship and Innovation Systems*, Routledge, London, UK and New York, NY.

Buenstorf, G. (2010) 'Knowledge-based entrepreneurship and international technology transfer in the German laser industry', in Malerba, F. (ed.) *Knowledge-Intensive Entrepreneurship and Innovation Systems*, Routledge, London, UK and New York, NY.

Camerani, R. and Malerba, F. (2010) 'Patterns of technological entry in different fields: an analysis of patent data', in Malerba, F. (ed.) *Knowledge-Intensive Entrepreneurship and Innovation Systems*, Routledge, London, UK and New York, NY.

Chamanski, A. and Waago, S.J. (2001) 'Organizational performance of technology-based firms: the role of technology and business strategies', *Enterprise and Innovation Management Studies*, 2(3): 205–223.

Cooke, P. (2001) 'Regional innovation systems, clusters, and the knowledge economy', *Industrial and Corporate Change*, 10: 945–974.

Edquist, C. (1997) *Systems of Innovation: Technologies, Institutions, and Organizations*, Pinter, London.

Florida, R. (2002) *The Rise of the Creative Class: And How It's Transforming Work, Leisure, Community and Everyday Life*, Basic Books, New York, NY.

Garnsey, E. and Heffernan, P. (2005) 'High-technology clustering through spin-out and attraction: the Cambridge case', *Regional Studies*, 39: 1127–1144.

Garnsey, E., Stam, E. and Heffernan, P. (2006) 'New firm growth: exploring processes and paths', *Industry and Innovation*, 13: 1–20.

Garnsey, E., Lorenzoni, G. and Ferriani, S. (2008) 'Speciation through entrepreneurial spin-off: the acorn-ARM story', *Research Policy*, 37: 210–224.

Hanusch, H. (1999) *The Legacy of Joseph A. Schumpeter*, two vols, Edward Elgar, Cheltenham, UK and Northampton, MA.

Hatzichronoglou, T. (1997) 'Revision of the high-technology sector and product classification', OECD Science, Technology and Industry Working Papers, No. 1997/02, OECD Publishing, Paris.

Holmén, M., Magnusson, M. and McKelvey, M. (2007) 'What are innovative opportunities?', *Industry and Innovation*, 14: 27–45.

Kirzner, I.M. (1973) *Competition and Entrepreneurship*, University of Chicago Press, Chicago, IL.

Klepper, S. (2001) 'Employee startups in high-tech industries', *Industrial and Corporate Change*, 10: 639–674.

Klepper, S. and Sleeper, S.D. (2005) 'Entry by spinoffs', *Management Science*, 51: 1291–1306.

Knight, F. (1921) *Risk, Uncertainty and Profit*, University of Chicago Press, Chicago, IL.

Lenzi, C., Bishop, K., Breschi, S., Buenstorf, G., Llerena, P., Malerba, F., Mancusi, M.L. and McKelvey, M. (2010) 'New innovators and knowledge intensive entrepreneurship in some European sectoral systems: a field', in Malerba, F. (ed.) *Knowledge-Intensive Entrepreneurship and Innovation Systems*, Routledge, London, UK and New York, NY.

Lissoni, F. (2010) 'Academic inventors as brokers: an exploratory analysis of the KEINS database', in Malerba, F. (ed.) *Knowledge-Intensive Entrepreneurship and Innovation Systems*, Routledge, London, UK and New York, NY.

Lundvall, B.Å. (ed.) (1993) *National Innovation Systems: Towards a Theory of Innovation and Interactive Learning*, Pinter Publishers, London.

Malerba, F. (2002) 'Sectoral systems of innovation and production', *Research Policy*, 31: 247–264.

Malerba, F. (ed.) (2010) *Knowledge-Intensive Entrepreneurship and Innovation Systems*, Routledge, London, UK and New York, NY.

Malerba, F. and Orsenigo, L. (1999) 'Technological entry, exit and survival: an empirical analysis of patent data', *Research Policy*, 28: 643–660.

Mamede, R., Mota, D. and Godinho, M.M. (2010) 'Are the dynamics of knowledge intensive industries any different?', in Malerba, F. (ed.) *Knowledge-Intensive Entrepreneurship and Innovation Systems*, Routledge, London, UK and New York, NY.

McKelvey, M. and Lassen, A.H. (2013a) *Managing Knowledge Intensive Entrepreneurship*, Edward Elgar Publishers, Cheltenham, UK.

McKelvey, M. and Lassen A.H. (2013b). *How Entrepreneurs Do What They Do: Case Studies of Knowledge Intensive Entrepreneurship*, Edward Elgar Publishers, Cheltenham, UK.

Nelson, R.R. (1993) *National Innovation Systems: A Comparative Analysis*, Oxford University Press, New York, NY.

Nelson, R.R. (1996) *The Sources of Economic Growth*, Harvard University Press, Cambridge, MA.

Nelson, R.R. and Winter, S.G. (1982) *An Evolutionary Theory of Economic Change*, Belknap Press of Harvard University Press, Cambridge, MA.

Perkmann, M., Tartari, V., McKelvey, M. *et al.* (2013) 'Academic engagement and commercialisation: a review of the literature on university–industry relations', *Research Policy*, 42(2): 423–442.

Radosevic, S., Savic, M. and Woodward, R. (2010) 'Knowledge intensive entrepreneurship in Central and Eastern Europe: results of a firm level survey', in

Malerba, F. (ed.) *Knowledge-Intensive Entrepreneurship and Innovation Systems*, Routledge, London, UK and New York, NY.

Schumpeter, J.A. (1934) *The Theory of Economic Development*, Oxford University Press, New York, NY.

Schumpeter, J.A. (1942) *Capitalism, Socialism and Democracy*, Harper & Row, New York, NY.

Storey, D.J. and Tether, B.S. (1998) 'Public policy measures to support new technology-based firms in the European Union', *Research Policy*, 26(9): 1037–1010.

Wong, P.K., Ho, Y.P. and Autio, E. (2005) 'Entrepreneurship, innovation and economic growth: evidence from GEM data', *Small Business Economics*, 24: 335–350.

3   The AEGIS survey

A quantitative analysis of new entrepreneurial ventures in Europe

Yannis Caloghirou, Aimilia Protogerou and Aggelos Tsakanikas

1 Introduction

The recent economic crisis has turned out to be one of the most severe of the last decades. The costs are already significant across most European countries and are illustrated both in the strong negative impact on economic activity, but also in unemployment. Furthermore, economic recovery at least at the beginning of 2015 seems to be rather weak, indicating that new challenges have emerged at the policy level, especially in terms of entrepreneurship policies. The importance of entrepreneurship in creating new jobs and economic growth seems to be even more crucial today in order to restore growth.

However, policy makers need to further understand the determinants and the obstacles to entrepreneurship in order to analyse the effectiveness of different policy approaches. They need evidence and facts with internationally comparable empirical data when possible. Specifically the creation of new ventures is a discrete process that requires specific attention, when formulating entrepreneurship policies.

AEGIS project aimed at analysing various aspects of the knowledge-intensive entrepreneurial (KIE) ventures. According to the AEGIS conceptual framework,[1] KIE ventures are new firms; that are innovative; that have significant knowledge intensity in their activities; and that exploit innovative opportunities in diverse sectors – including high-tech, traditional low-tech manufacturing industries, and services. These 'special' new ventures build on innovation, use or/and diffuse new knowledge and can be sustainable even under credit crunch conditions. KIE ventures arguably can support growth and employment to a greater extent than the usual new ventures that are created in Europe every day. As survival rates are rather disappointing and the majority of new firms do not grow in terms of employment, further research on the identification and promotion of these 'special' ventures is necessary.[2] These ventures are important because they contribute directly to changing the dynamics and the characteristics of the existing pool of ventures. But they also have an indirect spill-over effect: they challenge existing firms and they push them to innovate as well.

Therefore, they can support at least two of the main pillars of the EU 20–20 strategy: smart (KIE vs 'copy-paste' entrepreneurship) and sustainable (not just plenty of new ventures, but sustainable ones in adverse times) growth.

The main empirical instrument of the AEGIS project was the AEGIS survey, which differs substantially from other instruments that are currently used to measure entrepreneurship in Europe:

- It is not a collection of secondary indicators, (OECD-Eurostat Entrepreneurship Indicator Programme), thus it does not suffer from limited availability of indicators across countries.
- It is not a general population survey, based on individual entrepreneurs (i.e. SMEs Eurobarometer Survey on Entrepreneurship) or even nascent entrepreneurs (Global Entrepreneurship Monitor).
- It is not a cross-sectoral survey for measuring R&D and innovation indicators (Community Innovation Survey).
- It covers ten European countries representing the Nordic model (Sweden and Denmark), the Anglo-Saxon model (UK), the continental model (Germany, France, Italy), the Southern European model (Greece, Portugal), as well as two ex-planned economies (Czech Republic and Croatia).

Various dimensions of KIE are examined in the survey: demand, institutional factors, innovation models and business strategies, their dynamic capabilities, etc. By this way we are able not only to identify motives, characteristics and patterns in the creation and growth of new firms, but also pinpoint those crucial elements that distinguish KIE and less KIE or modest KIE firms. It is, therefore, the first time that in-depth empirical data will be used to identify typologies of firms across sectors and countries that possess specific characteristics, allowing us to classify them by their knowledge-based intensity.

2 Methodology

2.1 Preparation of the survey: sample, sectors and method

A commercially available database, Amadeus,[3] containing harmonized financial data for 12 million European entities that publish their balance sheets, was selected for the sampling.[4] The selection of the sectors follows the rationale that has been developed in the AEGIS conceptual framework (see Chapter 1). The aim was to cover most of the high-technology manufacturing sectors, along with some medium-tech sectors, some low-technology manufacturing sectors (as classified by OECD taxonomy) and Knowledge Intensive Services (KIBS). The full list of the selected sectors is shown in Table 3.1.[5]

Table 3.1 The selected sectors for the AEGIS survey

	NACE *rev. 1.1*
High-technology manufacturing sectors	
Aerospace	35.3
Computers and office machinery	30
Radio-television and communication equipment	32
Manufacture of medical, precision and optical instruments	33
Pharmaceuticals	24.4
Medium to high technology manufacturing sectors	
Manufacture of electrical machinery and apparatus	31
Manufacture of machinery and equipment	29
Chemical industry (excl. pharma)	24 (excl. 24.4)
Low-technology manufacturing sectors	
Paper and printing	21, 22
Textile and clothing	17, 18, 19
Food, beverages and tobacco	15, 16
Wood – furniture	20, 36
Medium to low manufacturing sectors	
Basic metals	27
Fabricated metal products	28
KIBS sectors	
Telecommunications	64.2
Computer and related activities	72
Research and experimental development	73
Other business services activities	74.1, 74.2, 74.3, 74.4, 74.5, 74.8*

Note
* Selection of 4-digits sectors. Only some 74.87 (other activities) excluded.

A crucial dimension of the survey was the criterion used to define 'newly established firms'. After considering advantages/disadvantages of either a very recent year (i.e. 2008–2009) or a much earlier year (i.e. 1999) firms that were established from 2001 to 2007 were selected. This allows the analysis of both some older and already well-established firms and some newer ones. By the time of the survey (late 2010, beginning 2011), firms that were established in 2007 would have been in operation for at least three years, so they would have managed to surpass the period of 3.5 years which according to the literature is crucial for survival (Bygrave and Hunt, 2004). Furthermore, eligible firms for the survey were firms that were actually: (a) new and not just new legal entities; (b) firms that were not subsidiaries of another company, or the legal result of a merger/acquisition; (c) independent firms, meaning not a spin-off from an established company with more than 25% ownership. To investigate this issue, specific screening questions were used in the introductory part in the survey.

Telephone – CATI type – interviews were selected as the most suitable method for the implementation of the survey. The respondent should be a founder or if not available, a partner, a CEO or the Managing Director.

In terms of completed questionnaires the target was set to 4,000 responses. A minimum of 200 responses was decided for the two smallest countries participating in the survey (Croatia and Czech Republic), whereas other countries were grouped based on their size of the economy. For France, Germany and Italy the target was set to 570 responses and for the rest the target was set to 330 responses. This 'country correction' of the sample was necessary to assure that the final sample should be of adequate size in order to perform a solid statistical analysis at the national level.

A 'sectoral correction' was also required when the population universe was examined throughout. As it was expected, firms from KIBS sectors represent the vast population of newly established firms in all countries participating in the survey. Though this reflects the gradual shift from manufacturing to services in most developed economies, it would not be desirable to conduct a survey that would include, i.e. 3,000 firms from the KIBS sectors despite the fact that this is representative of the population. Hence, it was decided to increase the high and low technology sectors' participation in the sample (by 5 and 2.5 percentage points) in each country and decrease the KIBS sample. Furthermore we had also to set a minimum of 40 responses per sector within the country to allow a sectoral analysis at the national level.[6] All these limitations lead to the sample structure presented in Table 3.2.

2.2 Implementation of the survey

Global Data Collection Company[7] was appointed for the execution of the interviews. The survey was launched in September 2010 and was completed in March 2011.[8]

Table 3.2 Sample targets per country and sectoral group

Country	Total	Distribution		
		High	Low	KIBS
Croatia	200	40	108	52
Czech Rep.	200	40	76	84
Denmark	330	40	69	221
France	570	70	195	305
Germany	570	70	170	330
Greece	330	40	171	119
Italy	570	70	293	207
Portugal	330	40	163	127
Sweden	330	40	105	185
UK	570	60	177	333
Total	4,000	510	1,527	1,963

One of the major problems that occurred during the implementation of the survey was the eligibility of the firms to be surveyed. The introductory screening questions led to a substantial number of screen-outs; that is, firms that may be willing to participate but were not eligible. These screen-outs affected significantly the sample sizes, as they didn't follow a specific pattern per country.

The main problem was the year of establishment. All firms that have changed their legal status or generally have been under any legal changes (transformations, name change, etc.), are reported as new entities in most business registries. So by extracting firms established, i.e. in 2005, we actually get a mixed set of companies: those that are indeed new firms created that year, along with other new legal entities, but not actually new firms. The latter had to be screened out. Screen-outs from the other set of screening questions (independent firm, subsidiaries, mergers, acquisitions, etc.) were much more limited (below 10% combined).[9] Limited availability in certain sectors per country were also noticed.

Table 3.3 presents detailed statistics about the survey's outcome. A total of 4,004 usable responses were obtained, while achieving more or less the national and sectoral targets.[10] The total response rate of the survey was 31.2%.

2.3 The questionnaire

The questionnaire used in the survey includes the following sections:

A   General information about the firm: basic firm demographics are retrieved.
B   General information about founder or founding team: characteristics of the founding team (gender, educational background, prior occupation, professional experience, etc.) were provided for up to four founders.
C   Firm's formation process: questions about the factors that have affected the formation process of the firm, such as networks, work experience, etc. and the sources of financing.
D   Market environment: questions about the market environment and the opportunities it provides, the level of competition, the factors that have helped them in creating and sustaining their competitive advantage, the obstacles and the institutional barriers that arose during the firm's expansion were examined. The aim was to identify how the environment and the structure of demand may differentiate, thus leading to different market opportunities.
E   Strategy: questions about the business strategy and the way a firm builds its capabilities, by sensing and seizing opportunities, the sources of knowledge it uses to explore these opportunities and the mechanisms it uses to achieve excellence.

Table 3.3 Survey response per country/sectoral group

	Responses				Screen-outs	Refusals	Response rate[1] (%)	Incidence rates[2] (%)
	High manufacturing	Low	KIBS	Total				
Croatia	35	115	50	200	201	113	63.9	38.9
Czech Republic	25	92	83	200	321	327	38.0	23.6
Denmark	34	69	227	330	787	756	30.4	17.6
France	68	196	306	570	1,906	1130	33.5	15.8
Germany	67	160	330	557	2,883	1774	23.9	10.7
Greece	22	184	125	331	369	521	38.8	27.1
Italy	57	316	207	580	445	560	50.9	36.6
Portugal	31	170	130	331	235	324	50.5	37.2
Sweden	34	108	192	334	501	1376	19.5	15.1
UK	47	192	332	571	2934	1939	22.7	10.5
Total	420	1,602	1,982	4,004	10,581	8,820	31.2	17.1

Notes
1 Response rate is calculated as: completed responses/completed + refusals.
2 Incidence rate is calculated as: completed responses/completed + refusals + screen-outs.

F   Innovative performance and business models: questions about the innovative capacity and performance of firms are included in this section, along with the intellectual property protection methods used and the R&D activity of the firm.

G   Firms' performance and impact of the economic crisis: basic facts about firms' recent market performance in terms of sales, employment, investments, etc., and the effect of the financial crisis on their performance.

3 Main results

3.1 Firms and their founders: some basic trends

3.1.1 The majority of new ventures are micro firms

The majority of the surveyed firms (63.6%) are micro firms at least in terms of full-time employees (employment up to 9 full-time persons) (Figure 3.1). Almost 90% across countries are small firms (<50 persons), while only 0.3% are large or very large firms.[11] This means that new firms all over Europe, even in France or Germany, start as small firms, but they usually remain small.

As it is expected, the share of micro firms active in KIBS is slightly larger (80%) than the relative share of firms in the high-tech and low-tech group of sectors (61.6% and 65.3% respectively). This is probably a result of the fact that generally in manufacturing firms, the average firm size is large due

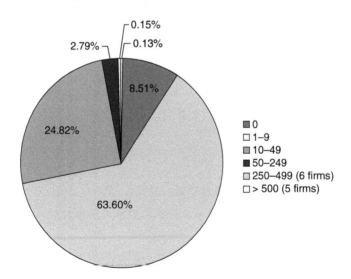

Figure 3.1 Firms' size in terms of (full time) employment (*N* = 3,973) (source: Aegis Survey, data processing by LIEE/NTUA).

to the nature of the activity and the high fixed capital formation that is necessary in most manufacturing activities to achieve high scale economies.

Interviews revealed that founders that create a new firm sometimes do not quit from their old job, but they just devote some part of their time to run the business. They might also follow this pattern in terms of possible employees. So they seem to prefer to hire some part time employees rather than hiring full time employees.

Results show that 41.6% of the firms have at least one part time employee. In fact 7% of these, some 118 firms, have solely part time employees and no full time employees. Furthermore, one out of three firms has more than half of their personnel as part time employees. These results indicate that part time employment in start ups, but also in newly born firms, is quite common, across countries.

The largest share of firms using part timers is observed in Germany (62%) and the smallest in Croatia (26%). Furthermore, the share of firms employing people on a part time basis does not differentiate significantly across the three sector groups.

3.1.2 Educational level of employees

Two out of three firms (64.9%) have at least one employee with a university degree. This on the other hand means that one-third of the firms do not employ anyone with a degree (founders included).

The share of firms employing university graduates is well below sample average for some countries such as Denmark (51.5%) and Italy (52.4%) while for other countries such as Croatia (83.5%), Greece (76.1%), Czech Republic (75.5%), the opposite holds. However, the average number of university degree holders is 5.6 employees per firm and does not differentiate significantly across countries.

Half the firms of the sample employ postgraduates. The majority of these firms have employees with a master's degree while there are 438 firms (11%) that employ PhD degree holders. There are countries with significant differences among the two educational levels (Croatia, Greece, UK, Portugal). For example while 83.5% of the Croatian firms employ university graduates, only 30% of them employ postgraduates. The specific finding may be attributed to factors related to the educational level of employees in these countries' general population or even to the sector distribution of firms within country samples. For example, more than half of the firms in Croatia, Greece and Portugal are active in the low-tech group of sectors. The firm's sector classification determines to a certain extent the educational level of its human capital.

Furthermore, if we compute the ratio of the sum of all employees with a university or master/PhD degree to the sum of all employees, then almost 30% have a university degree and 14% a master/PhD, but with significant variation among countries.

Table 3.4 Employees with a university degree

	% of firms employing university graduates	University graduates employees (mean)	Total employees (mean)	% of total employees with a university degree*	Firms employing post-graduate holders (masters/ PhD) (%)	% of total employees with a master or PhD*
Croatia	83.5	5.7	19.5	25	30.1	3.5
Greece	76.1	7.9	21.7	28	44.4	7.4
Czech Republic	75.5	5.6	15.9	27	77.4	25.0
UK	72.3	6.1	11.7	37	46.8	10.6
Portugal	69.8	5.2	21.4	17	33.8	4.1
Germany	67.1	5.3	12.5	29	72.5	24.1
Sweden	61.7	4.3	6.5	41	40.4	24.7
France	58.1	5.0	6.5	44	62.3	35.0
Italy	52.4	5.4	14.6	20	54.1	12.3
Denmark	51.5	4.5	9.5	24	42.4	14.8
Total	64.9	5.6	13.1	28	52.2	14.3

Source: Aegis Survey, Data processing by LIEE/NTUA.

Note
* Adding all employees in the surveyed firms.

Besides, the share of firms active in KIBS is higher than that of high- and low-tech in terms of university level and postgraduate level employment. More specifically, 74% and 66% of firms in KIBS have university and postgraduate employees while the relative percentage in the low-tech firms is 54% for university-degree holders and 36% for postgraduates. In addition, the average number of university and master's degree holders is higher in KIBS than it is in low-tech firms.

3.1.3 Small sized founding teams

The size of the founding team is well recognized in the literature. Larger teams are more likely to bring in valuable resources (including human capital, social capital and financial resources) and therefore can play a supporting role under changing environmental conditions which are typical of new ventures. Furthermore, teams with a higher number of founders are assumed to be in a better position to recognize opportunities. The larger the founding team, the more heterogeneous it is in terms of competences, knowledge, wisdom and experience, and therefore it can face more effectively everyday problems. In addition, there may be psychological benefits to co-founders (Bird, 1989) and the mutual support structures which sometimes exist within a team can increase the satisfaction and performance of team members (Janz *et al.*, 1997). However, there is also evidence related to the negative aspects of multi-founder ventures which deal with issues of monitoring, shirking and distributing incentives (e.g. Mosakowski, 1998) and group conflict (Amason and Sapienza, 1997).

Survey results reinforce the small sized founding teams across countries. In fact the share of solo ventures in Denmark (56%), Croatia (52%) and Sweden (56%) exceed significantly the total sample share (37%), while the opposite holds for Italy (21%) and Portugal (24%).

Results do not differ significantly in terms of sector: Solo firms represent the 34% of firms in high tech sectors, 39% of low tech and 37% of KIBS, while 93%, 96% and 94% are founded by up to four partners.

AEGIS survey results reinforce the widely observed problem of the limited female participation in entrepreneurship, as only 18% of all the

Table 3.5 The size of the founding team (%)

No. of founders	HR	CZ	DK	FR	DE	EL	IT	PT	SE	UK	Total
1	52	35	56	45	37	27	21	24	56	35	37
2	33	41	26	34	30	36	35	49	26	40	35
3	11	12	10	13	13	19	23	12	12	11	14
4	3	8	5	4	10	11	12	9	3	8	8
5	1	3	2	2	6	3	4	4	2	2	3
6+	1	1	2	3	4	3	5	3	1	4	3

Source: Aegis Survey, Data processing by LIEE/NTUA.

founders examined are women. In many European countries the rates of women creating new business activities (Allen *et al.*, 2008) are still limited, indicating an underexploited pool of possible dynamism. Global Entrepreneurship Monitor's (GEM) annual surveys of early-stage activity entrepreneurship indicate that women account for roughly one in three of the world's entrepreneurs (Allen *et al.*, 2007). Women's intellectual potential and their contribution to Europe's competitiveness are not being maximized. Table 3.6a shows that although slight variations exist, female entrepreneurship is generally limited across countries.

In addition, although males dominate founding teams in all three sectoral groups, a slightly higher percentage of women founders is observed in the low-tech sectors (Table 3.6b).

3.1.4 Almost four out of nine firm founders do not hold a university degree

Education is generally found to be positively related to the likelihood of survival of new firms and firm growth. Figure 3.2 indicates that 43% of the founders are non-university degree holders. However, the larger part of the remaining 57% includes postgraduate and PhD degree holders (35%).

Table 3.6a Gender synthesis of founding teams (number of founders in parentheses)

Country	Male founders (%)	Female founders (%)
Croatia (N = 324)	79	21
Czech Republic (N = 382)	83	17
Denmark (N = 560)	88	12
France (N = 1,049)	80	20
Germany (N = 1,164)	89	11
Greece (N = 735)	84	16
Italy (N = 1,389)	78	22
Portugal (N = 725)	74	26
Sweden (N = 559	82	18
UK (N = 1,166)	81	19
Total (N = 8,053)	82	18

Source: Aegis Survey, Data processing by LIEE/NTUA.

Table 3.6b Gender synthesis of founding teams (sector results)

Sector	Male founders (%)	Female founders (%)
High-tech (908 founders)	88	12
Low-tech (3,091 founders)	77	23
KIBS (4,054 founders)	84	16

Source: Aegis Survey, Data processing by LIEE/NTUA.

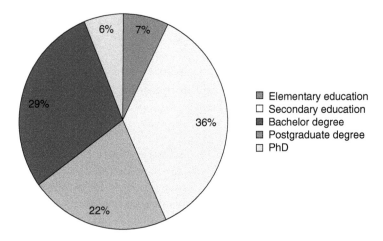

Figure 3.2 Highest educational attainment of founders (*N*=7,589) (source: Aegis Survey, data processing by LIEE/NTUA).

Table 3.7 shows the highest educational attainment of founders. The share of founders that are non-university degree holders differentiate across countries. The highest value is observed in Portugal (52%) and the lowest in Greece and Sweden (29% and 31% respectively).

In terms of sectors, the share of founders who are non-university degree holders is larger for low-tech firms (60%) than in high-tech sectors (50%) and KIBS (28%). Almost half of the founders of KIBS firms hold postgraduate and PhD degrees (48%) compared to only 29% and 18% in high- and low-tech manufacturing sectors respectively.

Table 3.7 Highest educational attainment of founders (number of founders in parentheses) (%)

Country	Up to secondary education	Bachelor degree	Postgraduate degree	PhD	Total
Croatia (319)	32	57	9	2	4
Czech Republic (366)	48	5	42	4	5
Denmark (503)	35	24	37	4	7
France (974)	36	18	39	8	13
Germany (1,068)	38	3	48	11	14
Greece (714)	29	47	19	5	9
Italy (1,332)	65	2	29	4	18
Portugal (704)	52	39	8	2	9
Sweden (531)	31	32	31	6	7
UK (1,078)	40	36	18	6	14
Total (7,589 founders)	43	22	29	6	100

Source: Aegis Survey, Data processing by LIEE/NTUA.

3.1.5 Prior sectoral experience matters for founding a firm: almost 12 years of professional experience is reported

The majority of the founders (41%) were working in a firm at the same industry, before the establishment of their company, while another 19% were working in a different industry (Table 3.8). A 15% had prior founding experience, either with a firm still in operation (10%) or with a firm that has ceased operation (5%). Hence, 75% of the founders have some sort of past industry experience, while for only 6% of the founders, this firm was their first employment.

In an entrepreneurial team, prior industry experience is important because members of the team are likely to share knowledge and information and thus greater knowledge of industry practices and routines will be available to the entire team. Moreover, this pool of knowledge is often distinct from the knowledge that a single team member accumulates directly (Reagans *et al.*, 2005). Especially prior founding experience represents a source of domain specific knowledge that an entrepreneur can use during the start-up stage of a new venture. Shane and Stuart (2002) point out that prior founding experience can help entrepreneurs raise start-up capital, speed a prospective new venture's transition to a liquidity event and avoid outright failure of the future new firm. In the same line of argument, Hsu (2004) points out that entrepreneurs with prior founding experience may have increased likelihood of venture capital funding for their current venture than those founders that do not.

Founding experience does not vary significantly across countries or sectors. However, Italy has quite a large share of founders with some founding experience (28%) while France and Sweden have the smallest relative shares (7% and 8% respectively).

Furthermore the professional experience of founders in the same industry or field that their company is active in is, on average, 12 years, with minor variations across countries (Table 3.9). Founders in the high-tech firms have even more experience (almost 14 years) compared to founders in low-tech and KIBS.

3.1.6 Technical knowledge and managerial skills the most important expertise of the founders

The main areas of expertise of the founders have to do with the tacit knowledge and the skills developed during formal education, but also during their previous employment. More than half of the founders responded that they have technical knowledge and 45% have general management skills. (Figure 3.3).

Technical and engineering knowledge is the most important expertise area of founders across countries with the exceptions of Germany and Portugal where general management skills have equal/slightly more frequent

Table 3.8 Last occupation of founders

Last occupation	Number of founders	HR	CZ	DK	FR	DE	EL	IT	PT	SE	UK
Owner of a firm still in existence	830 / 10%	42 / 13%	45 / 12%	43 / 8%	41 / 4%	136 / 12%	88 / 12%	236 / 17%	96 / 13%	27 / 5%	76 / 7%
Owner of a firm that has ceased operations	436 / 5%	16 / 5%	13 / 3%	21 / 4%	34 / 3%	37 / 3%	50 / 7%	151 / 11%	43 / 6%	15 / 3%	56 / 5%
Employee in the same industry	3,338 / 41%	139 / 43%	147 / 38%	260 / 46%	411 / 39%	491 / 42%	350 / 48%	400 / 29%	266 / 37%	272 / 49%	602 / 52%
Employee in a different industry	1,553 / 19%	67 / 21%	49 / 13%	132 / 24%	314 / 30%	158 / 14%	126 / 17%	187 / 13%	158 / 22%	145 / 26%	217 / 19%
Self-employed	867 / 11%	11 / 3%	86 / 23%	42 / 8%	61 / 6%	202 / 17%	37 / 5%	219 / 16%	53 / 7%	55 / 10%	101 / 9%
University or research institute employee	165 / 2%	3 / 1%	10 / 3%	13 / 2%	23 / 2%	43 / 4%	16 / 2%	11 / 1%	5 / 1%	18 / 3%	23 / 2%
Government employee	155 / 2%	17 / 5%	2 / 1%	28 / 5%	16 / 2%	16 / 1%	4 / 1%	18 / 1%	14 / 2%	8 / 1%	32 / 3%
Unemployed	203 / 3%	11 / 3%	3 / 1%	2 / 0%	57 / 5%	10 / 1%	33 / 4%	25 / 2%	34 / 5%	6 / 1%	22 / 2%
This is his/her first job	506 / 6%	18 / 6%	27 / 7%	19 / 3%	92 / 9%	71 / 6%	31 / 4%	142 / 10%	56 / 8%	13 / 2%	37 / 3%
Total	8,053 / 100%	324 / 100%	382 / 100%	560 / 100%	1,049 / 100%	1,164 / 100%	735 / 100%	1,389 / 100%	725 / 100%	559 / 100%	1,166 / 100%

Source: Aegis Survey, data processing by LIEE/NTUA.

Table 3.9 Average professional experience

Country	Average years of experience
Sweden	13.8
Greece	13.7
UK	13.6
Germany	12.2
France	12.2
Italy	12.0
Denmark	11.1
Czech Republic	10.9
Croatia	10.7
Portugal	9.6
Total	12.2

Source: Aegis Survey, data processing by LIEE/NTUA.

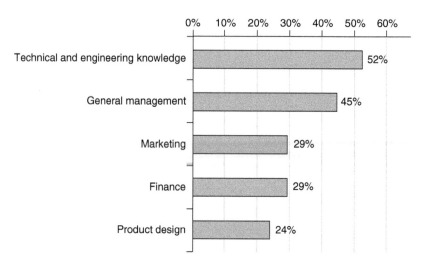

Figure 3.3 Main areas of expertise of the founders (N = 7,792) (source: Aegis Survey, data processing by LIEE/NTUA).

Note
* percentages do not add up to 100 per cent due to multiple responses.

incidence among founders. Technical and engineering knowledge is more prominent among founders in high-tech firms than those in low-tech and KIBs. General management skills appear in a larger share of founders in low-tech sectors and KIBs than in high-tech.

3.1.7 Founders' age

Almost 70% of the founders are over 39 years old (Figure 3.4), so they cannot be considered as young.[12] This trend holds more or less for most of the countries (Table 3.10) and corroborates with founders' experience (over 12 years). Only 5% of the founders belong to the 18–29 age group indicating that despite policies to support young entrepreneurship it seems that survival of new firms is positively related with age and experience: you might be able to influence the birth rates of firms in Europe by supporting young entrepreneurs but this does not necessarily translate to higher survival rates.

In terms of sectors, the share of founders over 39 years of age (73%) is slightly larger in the high-tech sector group than it is in the other two (67–68%).

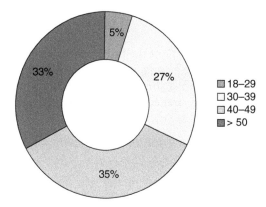

Figure 3.4 Founders' age (*N* = 8,053) (source: Aegis Survey, data processing by LIEE/NTUA).

Table 3.10 Founders' age (number of founders in parentheses) (%)

Country	18–29	30–39	40–49	>50	Total
Croatia (324)	4	28	32	36	100
Czech Republic (382)	6	37	30	28	100
Denmark (560)	3	23	38	35	100
France (1,049)	4	25	38	33	100
Germany (1,164)	5	24	37	33	100
Greece (735)	4	22	38	36	100
Italy (1,389)	8	27	34	31	100
Portugal (725)	7	44	28	21	100
Sweden (559)	3	26	33	38	100
UK (1,166)	4	21	37	38	100
Total (8,053 founders)	5	27	35	33	100

Source: Aegis Survey, data processing by LIEE/NTUA.

3.2 *The formation process*

3.2.1 *Limited spin-off formation*

The formation process of a firm is an important dimension of measuring entrepreneurship and provides useful information for policy design. In this perspective Santarelli and Vivarelli (2007: 455) by providing an extensive survey on the determinants of new business creation note that 'since founders are heterogeneous and may make entry mistakes, policy incentives should be highly selective, favouring nascent entrepreneurs endowed with progressive motivation and promising predictors of better business performance'.

New firms may stem from a pre-existing organization, being a company spin-off or a university spin-off. Company spin-offs can be defined as those firms that used to be a division of an incumbent firm and subsequently were transformed to independent entities. A university spin-off is 'a new company founded to exploit a piece of intellectual property created in an academic institution' (Shane, 2004: 4).

Results (Table 3.11) show that only 14% of the firms that participated in the survey originated from a pre-existing organization, almost exclusively from another firm (97%). Only 14 firms are university spin-offs, six of which are located in UK, indicating very limited academic entrepreneurship.

3.2.2 *Work experience and market knowledge the most important factors for firm formation*

The most important factor for the formation of the new firms was the professional experience in the same industry, followed by market knowledge and skills. Technical and engineering knowledge in the field along with

Table 3.11 Company and university spin-offs

	Number of spin-offs	% of the national sample	University	Company
			No. of firms	
Croatia	13	6.5		13
Czech Republic	8	4.0		8
Denmark	38	11.5		38
France	36	6.3	2	34
Germany	90	16.2	4	86
Greece	10	3.0		10
Italy	192	33.1	1	191
Portugal	65	19.6	1	64
Sweden	24	7.2		24
UK	82	14.4	6	76
Total	558	13.9	14	544

Source: Aegis Survey, data processing by LIEE/NTUA.

founders' personal networks established during their previous career path are also rated as very important formation factors. Although the availability of capital, the existence of a large customer and market changes are assessed as very or extremely important formation factors by almost half of the respondents, they are also considered as factors of low or no importance by a considerable percentage of firms. Design knowledge and technological changes seem to be either very/extremely important formation factors or factors of low importance for an approximately equal share of firms (Table 3.12).

Ranking of these factors does not change significantly at the country level. Some minor variations emerge, i.e. technical and engineering knowledge that seem to be a more important factor for Greek firms than for Swedish ones. The availability of finance is generally considered as a factor of mild impact on company set-up, but it appears to be more important for German and Italian firms than it is for Danish or Swedish firms. Professional experience, market and engineering knowledge seem to be the most prominent creation determinants also across sector groups. However, technical knowledge, design knowledge and opportunity deriving from technological change are perceived as more significant by the high-tech sector group of firms, a fact that can be attributed to the nature of high-tech products/artifacts.

3.2.3 Own resources the main financing source of the new ventures

The role of financing new ventures is of paramount importance, especially during these turbulent times. Despite the fact that the last decade was a period of growth for Europe and many financing instruments were made available, results show that new ventures are primarily funded by founders themselves. More than 92% of these new firms were financed to some extent by their founders' savings (Table 3.13). This is not surprising, as the idea behind entrepreneurship is of course to financially invest in an idea. What can be surprising is the fact that they provided on average, almost 80 per cent of the total funding, while 57% of the firms relied solely on their founders' savings, both considered as very high.

Bank loans are the next most important funding source. However, it has been used only by 28% of firms and accounts, on average, for half of the total funding. Family members finance 10% of the start-ups offering on average 43% of the total funding. Other sources of funding (government, local authorities grants, EU funds or even venture capital), were used by a small number of firms, despite the fact that they represented on average over a third of the investment.

Own financial resources are the most significant funding source in all countries. It is the use of banks that varies across countries and it is used by 41% of Italian firms but only by 14% of the Croatian firms. The use of government funding is generally limited. Although no significant sectoral

Table 3.12 Formation factors

	Mean	Std. dev	Firms that have responded (%)	
			Not important/low importance*	Very/extremely important**
Work experience in the current activity field	4.31	1.07	8	83
Market knowledge	4.05	1.01	7	73
Technical/engineering knowledge in the field	3.83	1.34	17	68
Networks built during previous career	3.74	1.23	16	63
Availability of finance	3.33	1.34	27	47
Existence of a large customer	3.25	1.37	29	47
Opportunity deriving from a new market need	3.27	1.25	25	46
Design knowledge	3.04	1.41	36	41
Opportunity deriving from technological change	2.98	1.35	36	38
Opportunity deriving from new regulations or institutional requirements	2.49	1.32	52	24
Opportunities in a public procurement initiative	2.09	1.29	65	16

Source: Aegis Survey, data processing by LIEE/NTUA.

Notes
* Responses of 1 or 2 in a 1–5 Likert scale.
** Responses of 4 or 5 in a 1–5 Likert scale.

Table 3.13 Funding sources for new firm creation

	% of firms funded	Average funding (%)
Own financial resources	92	79.3
Banks	28	51.6
Family member	10	42.6
National government or local authorities	7	33.9
Venture capital	5	44.7
EU funds	3	33.9
Previous employer	2	44.2

Source: Aegis Survey, data processing by LIEE/NTUA

variations emerge, manufacturing firms either from low- or high-tech sectors have used banks to a greater extent than firms from KIBS, as higher capital requirements cannot easily be afforded by own financial savings.

3.3 The market environment

3.3.1 New ventures but not new markets

The firms that participated in the survey assessed the level of competition that they face by stating if 'many', 'few' or 'no other business competitors', offer the same products and/or services to potential customers.[13] As it is well expected, the majority of the examined firms (almost 60%) responded that they operate in an environment with many competitors (Table 3.14). A significant 7% however respond with no competition at all, representing firms that have created a niche market; that is they have managed to create a new market for their novel products/services in which they have built their competitive advantage.

Since not only new firms, but firms that have been established as early as 2001 participate in the sample, it is not surprising to find that the majority of them operate in a relatively competitive environment. Of the 'newer' firms (i.e. established in 2006–2007), 60% of them operate in a market with many competitors.

One could think that even these new firms are old enough to have no competition at all. The creation of a niche market could be a rather short-term effect of the initial launching of a new firm. Once a new firm (a start-up) creates a market, soon some competition turns up either from established firms or from even newer firms. So it could be possible that when focusing only on start-ups, that a higher percentage of them could enter in a new market with an innovative product/service.

Results from GEM surveys, where the focus is specifically on early stage entrepreneurship (firms less than 42 months old) are similar: two-thirds of

Table 3.14 Level of competition (%)

	Many competitors	Only few competitors	No other competitors
Croatia	55.0	36.0	9.0
Czech Rep.	65.0	32.5	2.5
Denmark	53.6	38.2	8.2
France	52.8	39.8	7.4
Germany	60.0	33.9	6.1
Greece	58.3	36.0	5.7
Italy	59.5	33.8	6.7
Portugal	71.0	22.7	6.3
Sweden	56.6	29.9	13.5
UK	58.7	35.9	5.4
Total	58.7	34.3	7.0
High tech	40.0	49.8	10.2
Low tech	60.1	33.4	6.5
KIBS	61.5	31.8	6.8

Source: Aegis Survey, data processing by LIEE/NTUA.

European firms operate in a highly competitive environment, while only 6% declare that they have no business competitors.[14]

Hence, below 10% of new firms could be considered as a destructive wave of entrepreneurial activity that creates new markets. This on the other hand could be a crucial characteristic of KIE, even as just an output innovation indicator: a knowledge-based venture could be a firm that creates such new markets, where no competition, at least at the mid-term, exists.

Sectoral results reinforce the assumed significant innovative behaviour of high-tech manufacturing firms: more than 10% of these firms are operating in such a unique environment. However, the fact that 104 low-tech firms (6.5%) also classify themselves in this group is interesting. It turns out that they are mostly firms from textile and clothing, food and beverages.

3.3.2 Main market: domestic SMEs

Almost 21% of AEGIS firms reported that they focus exclusively on local/ regional markets. More than one-third of the firms reported that at least 80% of their sales[15] are promoted in the local markets, so they can be also considered as mainly local firms. By using the 51% criterion, it turns out that 37% of the sample is mainly involved with the national markets.

But the most interesting part of the sample is the one that reports significant export activity. A total of 91 firms (2.4% of the sample) reported that they focus exclusively on international markets. Generally 5% of the sample reports that over 85% of their sales were promoted abroad and 11% report that their main market (51% of the sales) is abroad. Alternatively, 43% of the firms responded that they sold during 2007–2009 at least 1% abroad, which on the other hand also means that 57% did not try or were unable to sell anything abroad during that period.

Czech firms seem to be the most extrovert ones, as an average share of 22% of firms' sales is exported. On the other hand French firms with a strong internal and regional market have rather limited exporting activity. If we focus on the most extrovert firms, i.e. those 402 firms that reported over 60% of their sales were promoted abroad, country variations are reinforced. Czech firms represent 5% of the sample, but they represent 9% of these 402 extrovert firms. A total of 18% of the sample from this country (the highest among the participating ones) belongs to this group. Croatia, Denmark, Portugal and the UK are also in the same trend, as 11–13% of their firms are being classified as extrovert. On the other hand, France mainly and then Italy, seem to be significantly underrepresented in this group of firms.

Firms from high-tech sectors are more active in the international markets, as they sell on average 24% of their turnover abroad (13% in low tech and KIBS). Generally almost 20% of high-technology firms sell more than 60% of the turnover abroad.

The majority of the surveyed firms (44%) identified as their most important customer (single answer) other SMEs (Table 3.15). Of the sample, 29% have important large firms as main customers, whereas final consumers are the major client for only 12.5% of the sample. This is not surprising as no retail/wholesale trade or hotels/restaurant sectors are included in the survey.[16] Only 9.1% of the examined firms have the public sector as a major customer.[17]

Table 3.15 Most important customer (%)

	Large firms	SMEs	Final consumers	Public sector	Not specified
Croatia	29.0	44.0	15.0	7.5	4.5
Czech Rep.	27.5	55.0	9.5	5.5	2.5
Denmark	26.7	37.9	12.7	11.5	11.2
France	26.0	39.8	17.0	13.0	4.2
Germany	29.4	46.9	13.5	5.6	4.7
Greece	35.6	43.2	9.7	9.7	1.8
Italy	30.5	45.5	13.8	7.6	2.6
Portugal	24.5	54.4	10.0	4.8	6.3
Sweden	31.1	42.5	11.4	8.1	6.9
UK	31.5	39.8	9.3	13.1	6.3
Total	29.3	44.1	12.5	9.1	5.0
High tech	35.0	41.4	9.8	8.1	5.7
Low tech	26.8	45.9	16.6	6.4	4.2
KIBS	30.1	43.2	9.7	11.4	5.5

Source: Aegis Survey, data processing by LIEE/NTUA.

The share of final consumers as major customers is slightly increased in low-tech sectors (16.6%). This is mainly the result of food and beverages, textile industry and furniture, as firms from these sectors have invested also in developing either distribution channels to end customers or even retail points, at least in some of the countries included in the sample. Furthermore more than 10% of firms from KIBS sectors (mostly consulting) have the public sector as their main customer, which of course jeopardize their position in the market, once public spending decreases.

3.3.3 Quality but also price competition prevails

A competition that is based on quality is the main characteristic of the business environment, as perceived by 61% of the examined firms. Price competition is also an important factor along with a need for innovation since success is based on continuous launching of new products/services.

Firms also evaluated the impact of specific factors in creating and sustaining competitive advantage (Table 3.16). The most important factor is the capability to adapt products/services to the specific needs of different customers/market niches. Four out of five firms responded that the specific factor has a significant impact on competitive advantage. The capabilities

Table 3.16 Business environment

	Mean	Std. dev.	% of firms that	
			Disagree/ strongly disagree	Agree or strongly agree
Quality competition is prevailing	3.67	1.21	17.6	61.0
Price competition is prevalent	3.44	1.32	24.4	51.6
A company only succeeds if it is able to launch new products/ services continuously	3.35	1.31	26.0	48.4
The activities of our major competitors are unpredictable and competition is very intense	3.29	1.27	26.5	44.7
The speed of technological changes is high	3.25	1.37	30.6	45.7
Customers regularly ask for new products and/or services	3.11	1.34	32.2	39.2
The lifecycle of products is typically short	2.62	1.51	48.6	29.2

Source: Aegis Survey, data processing by LIEE/NTUA.

Note
Valid N: 4,004.

of offering high quality product/services at a premium price and novel products/services follow. On the other hand R&D activities or networking with scientific organizations may be important in augmenting the research base of a firm, but do not seem to have helped in creating or sustaining competitive advantage. The same holds for establishment of alliances with other firms. So any form of collaboration either with other firms or scientific agents seems to be correlated negatively with the core advantages of the examined firms. Hence, it seems that firms try to build impediments to imitation in order to hinder existing competitors from duplicating the resources and capabilities that form the basis of their competitive advantage (Besanko *et al.*, 2009). Firms may be open in various other activities but they feel that creating an advantage and sustaining that advantage cannot be a result of collaboration and, surprisingly, of R&D activities.

In eight out of the ten countries firms agree on the most important factor for their competitive advantage. Only in Sweden and Germany the capability of adaptation to different customers is outweighed by the capability to offer quality products at a premium price (Table 3.17). In Italy

Table 3.17 Factors affecting competitive advantage

	Mean	*Std. dev.*	*% of firms that responded*	
			*No impact/ low impact**	*Significant or huge impact***
Capacity to adapt products/ services to the specific needs of different market niches	4.22	0.99	6.5	81.5
Capability to offer high quality product/services at a premium price	3.73	1.18	15.0	62.0
Capability to offer novel products/services	3.68	1.17	14.8	61.2
Capability to offer expected products/services at low cost	3.27	1.18	24.7	42.1
Marketing and promotion activities	3.23	1.28	28.9	44.7
Establishment of alliances/ partnerships with other firms	2.95	1.31	35.8	36.6
R&D activities	2.94	1.36	37.5	37.0
Networking with research organizations	2.25	1.30	61.4	19.3

Source: Aegis Survey, data processing by LIEE/NTUA.

Notes
*   Responses of 1 or 2 in a 1–5 Likert scale.
** Responses of 4 or 5 in a 1–5 Likert scale.
Valid N: 4004.

and Croatia the importance of R&D activities is significantly higher than the overall ranking. These factors are ranked almost the same way in all sectoral groups, with the exception of R&D activities, which are ranked higher in high-tech sectors. Furthermore, alliances are more important in KIBS than in other sectors, as KIBS may act as facilitators, carriers or sources of innovation of other companies and industries (den Hertog, 2000).

3.3.4 Market risks and funding the usual barriers to growth

Firms evaluated also the extent to which specific factors have acted as obstacles to the firm's growth and the expansion of its business activities (Table 3.18). A first look at the results reveals that generally a limited number of firms were too critical on the obstacles they have faced/face. Of the firms, 40% have pinpointed market risk/uncertainty and difficulties in attracting funding for growth investment, but also difficulties in recruiting highly skilled employees as the most important obstacles.

Market risk and difficulties in funding seem to impede firms in Croatia, Greece and Italy to a greater extent than in other countries. Fiscal problems and credit crunch conditions especially in the latter two, have probably affected responses. On the other hand in the Czech Republic, Germany and Portugal the major problem is finding the right people, as difficulties in recruiting highly skilled personnel is ranked at the top of the list. Lack of technological know-how was evaluated higher in Greece and

Table 3.18 Obstacles to growth

	Mean	Std. dev.	% of firms that responded	
			Not at all/low extent*	To significant/ great extent**
Market risk/uncertainty	3.23	1.2	26.3	42.4
Difficulty in finding the necessary funding for growth investments	3.02	1.5	40.5	41.2
Difficulties in recruiting highly skilled employees	2.99	1.4	38.3	40.3
Difficulty in finding business partners	2.56	1.3	49.3	23.3
Technology risk/uncertainty	2.27	1.2	58.9	15.5
Lack of technological know-how	2.26	1.2	60.6	17.0

Notes
* Responses of 1 or 2 in a 1–5 Likert scale.
** Responses of 4 or 5 in a 1–5 Likert scale.
Valid N: 4,004.

Croatia, than in other countries, while in Sweden, Denmark, Germany and the UK it was considered important by a limited number of firms.

Difficulties in funding are the major obstacle in high-technology sectors, but with a narrow lead with respect to market risk. Generally, firms from high-tech sectors have evaluated higher all obstacles, without though differentiating from other sectors in terms of ranking their importance.

In the same context, firms were asked to evaluate institutional barriers that may have affected their growth or expansion of activities (Table 3.19). Again one can notice that the impact of these barriers is considered as rather mild. The two major exceptions are the high tax rates and the time-consuming processes for licensing. Schivardi and Torrini (2008) highlight policies related to taxation and regulation as possible explanations for differences in firm size distributions. Generally, however, the extent to which this is really a serious barrier differs among countries, as in some countries it may be the most important factor, but responses generally are rather mild. The red tape that involves licensing was also considered as important

Table 3.19 Institutional barriers to growth and expansion

	Mean	Std. dev.	% of firms that responded	
			No barriers/ some*	Serious/very serious barriers**
High tax rates	3.52	1.4	26.2	56.6
Time consuming regulatory requirements for issuing permits and licences	3.11	1.5	38.2	44.1
Rigid labour market legislation	2.98	1.5	38.6	39.0
Continuously changing taxation regulations	2.93	1.5	42.2	37.7
Government officials favour well-connected individuals	2.70	1. 6	48.3	33.5
Poorly enforced competition law to curb monopolistic practices	2.64	1.5	51.6	30.4
Bankruptcy legislation makes immense the cost of failure	2.41	1.5	56.5	24.8
Poorly enforced property rights. copyright and patent protection	2.33	1.4	60.4	21.4
Strict property. copyright and patent protection	2.14	1.3	65.3	15.6

Source: Aegis Survey, data processing by LIEE/NTUA.

Notes
* Responses of 1 or 2 in a 1–5 Likert scale.
** Responses of 4 or 5 in a 1–5 Likert scale.
Valid N: 4,004.

barrier by 44% of the firms, while other possible barriers seem to significantly impede less than 40% of the firms.

High tax rates are the most important institutional barrier in all countries, but with significant differences in terms of intensity. Firms from countries that are in a process of fiscal consolidation (Greece, Italy, Portugal), but also Croatia and to some extent Czech Republic, have ranked the specific factor very high. On the other hand, in Sweden and the UK all barriers have been evaluated below the mean of 3, indicating that a limited number of firms feel that their growth was impeded by these factors. Generally if we compose an average indicator of the responses obtained in all items, Croatia, Portugal mainly and then Greece and Italy would be the countries where the effect of these institutional barriers is considered important by large parts of the sample, compared to other countries.

Although results do not differ significantly in terms of sectors, firms from manufacturing seem to face bigger problems than firms from KIBS. The high degree of specialization and up-to-date expertise of KIBS, which derive from abundant client contact, may subsequently contribute to growing demand and this growth can be persistently strengthened as their services link ever more tightly to clients' strategies (Toivonen, 2004).

These results comply also with results from the World Economic Forum's Global Competitiveness report,[18] where tax rates and tax regulation come up as a major obstacle in the examined countries, along with government bureaucracy. Therefore, problems of that nature seem to be the same either for new firms or established firms.

3.4 Firm strategies

3.4.1 Dynamic capabilities and sources of knowledge

A list of 11 statements related to the sensing and seizing of opportunities in the business environment were used as proxies for the dynamic capabilities of the surveyed firms (Table 3.20). Results show that firms have evaluated their performance rather generously: more than 60% of the firms have (strongly) agreed on seven out of the 11 statements. Changing practices based on customer feedback ranked first, along with observing and adopting best practices in the sector. The understanding of new opportunities to better serve customers was ranked equally high. These capabilities are related with identifying market opportunities and relate to the firm's capability to stay in touch with its client base. Almost 65% of the firms responded that their employees share practical experiences, a human capital capability, focusing on internal firm characteristics. On the other hand more than 65% of firms responded that they do not have a formal technical or an R&D department.

Firms were also asked to evaluate the importance of specific sources of knowledge for exploring new business opportunities. The purpose of this

Table 3.20 Sensing and seizing opportunities

	Mean	Std. dev.	% of firms that responded	
			Disagree/ strongly disagree	*Agree or strongly disagree*
We change our practices based on customer feedback	3.97	1.16	12.2	73.7
Our firm actively observes and adopts the best practices in our sector	3.91	1.18	12	69.3
We quickly understand new opportunities to better serve our customers	3.88	1.06	10.6	70.3
Employees share practical experiences frequently	3.72	1.39	19.5	65.4
Our firm regularly considers the consequences of changing market demand in terms of new products/services	3.70	1.17	15.5	62
Our firm is quick to recognize shifts in our market (e.g. competition. regulation. demography)	3.64	1.13	14.9	58.3
Our firm responds rapidly to competitive moves	3.63	1.18	16.5	57.6
We implement systematic internal/external personnel training	3.15	1.37	31	41.5
Design activity is important in introducing new products/ services to the market	3.12	1.53	35.8	45.2
There is a formal engineering and technical studies department in our firm	2.19	1.51	64.5	23.6
There is a formal R&D department in our firm	2.13	1.49	66.2	21.6

Source: Aegis Survey, data processing by LIEE/NTUA.

Note
Valid N: 3,891.

question was to identify and evaluate the significance of specific linkages that can act as sources of knowledge and technology for the firm and therefore support its knowledge-intensive entrepreneurial activity.

Clients or customers are the most important source of knowledge for the majority of firms (Table 3.21). Suppliers were the second most important source, followed closely by in-house know-how and competitors. Participation in funded programmes and generally external R&D

Table 3.21 Sources of knowledge for exploring new opportunities

	Mean	Std. dev.	% of firms that responded	
			Not (that) important*	Important/very important**
Clients or customers	4.41	0.91	4.5	85.8
Suppliers	3.36	1.34	26.4	50.6
In-house (know-how, R&D laboratories)	3.27	1.51	30.3	53
Competitors	3.27	1.18	23.8	43.2
Trade fairs. conferences and exhibitions	2.95	1.28	35.4	35.1
Scientific journals, trade or technical publications	2.87	1.28	37.5	33
Universities	2.12	1.25	65.1	16
Public research institutes	2.10	1.21	65.5	14.3
External commercial labs/R&D firms/technical institutes	2.04	1.20	67.2	14.2
Participation in nationally funded research programmes	1.90	1.22	72.2	13.9
Participation in EU funded research programmes	1.87	1.26	73.4	14.5

Source: Aegis Survey, data processing by LIEE/NTUA

Notes
*   Responses of 1 or 2 in a 1–5 Likert scale.
** Responses of 4 or 5 in a 1–5 Likert scale.
Valid N: 4,004.

were ranked at the bottom of the list, corroborating previous results where collaborative R&D was not considered as important for creating competitive advantage. Firms seem also to prefer participating in trade fairs and conferences and reviewing scientific or technical journals to a greater extent than establishing collaboration with universities or public research institutes.

The results are consistent across countries and sectors at least for the factors at the top and the bottom of the list: clients/customers are by far the major source of knowledge in all countries and sectors. However, firms from high-tech sectors have generally evaluated higher all items, indicating their stronger effort to acquire knowledge.[19] Firms from KIBS seem to pay more attention to in-house sources of knowledge, whereas competitors are slightly used more as sources of knowledge in low tech than in other sectors.

3.4.2 Relationships with customers is the main networking activity

Firms evaluated the extent to which networks that they have gradually created contribute to various operations. The purpose of this question was to determine the importance of interpersonal and inter-organizational relationships to specific operations of the company. It is assumed that these linkages can be viewed as the media through which entrepreneurs gain access to a variety of resources such as information, advice and problem solving held by other actors.

By far the most important outcome of any networking activity is contacting customers (Table 3.22), as the client base of a firm is the essence of any business activity. Selecting proper suppliers is the second most important activity, followed by recruiting skilled labour. These two activities are better undertaken when the information asymmetry that is included in such transactions is reduced. Firms need to acquire precise and reliable information on possible suppliers and their advantages, rather than testing in practice their capability to deliver. Trial and error, fine-tuning or failures in selecting the right suppliers may cause significant delays or even damage a firm's reputation. Any information that entrepreneurs can have from their networks might be crucial in their strategy. The same holds for recruiting skilled personnel. Examining and evaluating CVs or even undertaking interviews with possible candidates for a job might not offer the type of information that a previous employer can provide.

Table 3.22 Contribution of the networks to various activities

To...	Mean	Std. dev.	% of firms that responded	
			Not important*	Important/very important**
...contacting customers/clients	4.10	1.19	11.1	75.6
...selecting suppliers	3.35	1.39	27.2	50.8
...recruiting skilled labour	3.33	1.44	27.9	51.9
...developing new products/ services	3.27	1.30	26.3	46.9
...collecting information about competitors	3.17	1.22	27.7	41.3
...managing production and operations	3.01	1.40	35.6	40.2
...accessing distribution channels	2.89	1.37	38.8	35.4
...advertising and promotion	2.84	1.34	41.0	32.9
...assistance in arranging taxation or other legal issues	2.79	1.33	41.8	31.1
...assistance in attracting funds	2.40	1.39	55.9	24.2
...exploring export opportunities	2.37	1.44	57.8	25.5

Source: Aegis Survey, data processing by LIEE/NTUA.

Notes
* Responses of 1 or 2 in a 1–5 Likert scale.
** Responses of 4 or 5 in a 1–5 Likert scale.
Valid N: 4,004.

On the other hand, networks do not seem very helpful in terms of exploring export opportunities or attracting funding. The first could be explained by the fact that it is usually more difficult to create an international network, while its size might not be crucial. The second factor could be explained by the fact that any networking or generally any soft ties are becoming less important when real money is involved. Lending money to someone is not the same thing as giving references for a job candidate, that is why only one out of four firms considered it as important.

Firms from all countries agreed on the most important networking activity. Selecting suppliers and recruiting skilled labour were also evaluated as important, with small variations in the respective rankings. In Germany, however, accessing distribution channels was considered as the second most important factor, whereas in Italy developing new products/services was ranked second. In terms of sectors, although selecting suppliers is highly affected by networks in manufacturing, this is not the case for KIBS. Two basic structural characteristics of KIBS, recognized by Miles *et al.* (1995), may explain this differential, first they use their knowledge to produce intermediary services for their clients' production processes, and second, they support supplier industries. In the latter, networks seem to better help in recruiting skilled labour and developing new products/services or even in collecting information about competitors.

Furthermore, firms were also asked to indicate the extent to which they have participated in various types of formal agreements to share knowledge and expertise or mitigate risks and share expenses (Table 3.23).

Half of the firms have rarely or never participated in any sort of agreement, not even a subcontracting agreement. Only 17–20% of the firms

Table 3.23 Participation of firms in various types of agreements

Company has participated in	Mean	Std. dev.	% of firms that responded	
			Not at all/ rarely	*Very often/ often*
...subcontracting	2.48	1.42	52.3	27.3
...strategic alliances	2.22	1.39	61.2	20.7
...technical cooperation agreements	2.12	1.27	63.0	17.3
...marketing/export promotion	1.93	1.22	70.6	13.8
...licensing agreements	1.81	1.24	75.6	13.3
...R&D agreements	1.69	1.10	79.2	9.6
...research contract-out	1.49	0.95	85.9	5.9

Source: Aegis Survey, data processing by LIEE/NTUA.

Notes
*   Responses of 1 or 2 in a 1–5 Likert scale.
** Responses of 4 or 5 in a 1–5 Likert scale.
Valid N: 4,004.

participate often in strategic alliances or other technical cooperation agreements and even less (13–14%), in marketing/export promotion or licensing agreements. These results reinforce the non-collaborative trend that has been identified previously in other questions. Only in Germany, Italy and in Croatia is subcontracting not ranked first. In Germany networking was considered most important in creating strategic alliances followed by subcontracting, whereas in Croatia and Italy the technical agreements ranked first. Subcontracting is the major type of agreement also across sectors. However, technical agreements were ranked higher than strategic alliances in manufacturing sectors differing in that aspect from KIBS.

3.5 Innovative performance and business models

3.5.1 Two out of three firms have introduced product innovation

Product innovation involves the introduction into the market of new or significantly improved products.[20] AEGIS results show that only 64% of the sample has introduced some new or significantly improved goods or services during the last three years (Table 3.24). These goods and services represented almost 40% of the firms' sales (on average), while this activity was not linked to any public support initiatives for almost three-quarters of these firms. The share of innovative firms is slightly larger (70%) within the high-tech sector, compared to the other two sectoral groups (62% for KIBS and 64% for low tech). It should be stressed that these results are higher than CIS results in all countries in the sample, which is rather expected as CIS is a survey across all sectors of the economy.[21]

Table 3.24 Product innovation (number of innovative firms in parentheses)

	% of innovative firms	New to the firm*	New to the market*	New to the world*
Croatia	69 (138)	88	72	17
Czech Republic	69 (138)	75	41	7
Denmark	59 (196)	44	59	22
France	54 (309)	56	57	22
Germany	60 (334)	69	64	23
Greece	70 (231)	83	59	14
Italy	74 (430)	59	51	20
Portugal	67 (223)	35	41	37
Sweden	62 (207)	69	55	25
UK	60 (342)	71	51	28
Total	64 (2,548 firms)	64	55	22

Source: Aegis Survey, data processing by LIEE/NTUA.

Note
* Percentages do not add to 100% as multiple responses were reported.

However, most of the innovative goods or services introduced by the examined firms were only 'new to the firm' (64%) i.e. they have already been available from competitors in the market. A large share of firms (55%) stated that their innovative products were 'new to the market', i.e. they were launched in the specific market before competitors, but they may have already been available in other markets as well. Only 22% characterized their innovative products as 'new to the world', i.e. they were the first to introduce them in all markets domestically or internationally.

In Croatia, Greece and Czech Republic the share of firms that introduced products just 'new to the firms' was larger than the sample average. As a consequence, Czech Republic and Greece also report the lowest shares of 'new to the world' innovations, whereas in Portugal, 37% of firms launched 'new to the world products' during 2007–2009. The share of firms that launched 'new to the world' products is larger in the high-tech group (36%) than it is in the other two groups.

3.5.2 Significant organizational innovation

Process and organizational innovation were also explored in the survey.[22] Results reveal that 73.4% of the sample introduced some sort of process or organizational innovation during 2007–2009.[23] Half of the surveyed firms have introduced new or significantly improved knowledge management systems and various supporting process activities (i.e. maintenance systems or purchasing operations, accounting or computing). Changes in methods of manufacturing and in logistics, supply chain and distribution activities have been undertaken by smaller firm shares (43% and 35% respectively). Finally, only three out of ten founders reported a major change to the organization of work within their company, such as changes in the management structure.

In terms of countries (Table 3.25), 60% of the Greek firms and 75% of the Italian firms have introduced major changes in manufacturing methods (well above their relative sample share of 43%), compared to only 24% in Sweden and 21% in UK. Furthermore, 71% of the firms in Croatia and 68% in Portugal have introduced new or significantly improved supporting activities for their production processes.

The share of firms that have introduced process innovations is higher for manufacturing sectors, while major changes in knowledge management systems are more intense in KIBS (52%).

3.5.3 Two out of three firms spend at least 1% of their sales on R&D

Two out of three firms reported some R&D activity, while almost 10% in all countries (except Czech Republic and Greece) report that they spend more than 50% of sales on R&D. However, the average expenses reported by the surveyed firms represent on average, 13% of their sales. The largest

Table 3.25 Process and organizational innovation (% of firms)

	During 2007–2009 has the firm introduced new or significantly improved…				
	Methods of manufacturing	Logistics, supply chain, delivery or distribution methods	Supporting process activities	Knowledge management systems	Changes in managing structure
Croatia	50	56	71	69	32
Czech Republic	51	36	60	64	37
Denmark	31	26	43	40	28
France	38	20	27	42	24
Germany	32	32	42	40	24
Greece	60	49	59	47	36
Italy	75	53	66	65	32
Portugal	53	46	68	57	46
Sweden	24	27	30	36	28
UK	21	23	47	50	37
Total	43	35	49	50	31
High-tech	49	38	53	45	29
Low-tech	55	44	51	48	32
KIBS	32	27	47	52	31

Source: Aegis Survey, data processing by LIEE/NTUA.

R&D share in sales is observed in Italy and Croatia (17%), and the lowest in Greece (9.1%) and Czech Republic (9.5%). R&D expenses are higher in the high-tech sector group (15.7%) and KIBS (14%), while in the low-tech group of sectors it is only on average 10% of sales.

3.5.4 Semi-formal means of intellectual property protection methods: confidentiality agreements and lead time advantages rather than patents or copyrights

Intellectual property has a significant role in firms' innovation processes and competitive strategies. The protection of these rights can take various forms, from formal arrangements to completely informal ways. Formal protection methods include industrial property rights (patents and trademarks) and copyright. Semi-formal protection methods are also based on law but they do not entail any official registration. They are usually contracts (e.g. confidentiality agreements) that can be used similarly with formal protection methods (to protect knowledge and information) but they can also be employed to 'legitimate' the relationships of a firm with its partners and employees. Most of the different types of informal protection methods do not usually entail legal ways of protection. Some of them are closely related to more formal methods such as contracts, and they may even be based on legal rights (e.g. secrecy). In addition, some methods are embedded in standard working practices within the firm (e.g. complexity of design) and they are not valid in a legal sense (Päällysaho and Kuusisto, 2011).

Results show protection of intellectual property in the newly established firms examined is primarily informal or semi-formal, across countries. Confidentiality agreements are used by approximately 55% of the innovating firms, while complexity of design is used by 46% of them. Formal methods such as patents and copyrights are used only by 16.5% and 27.5% respectively. Trademarks, despite being an informal protection method, are used by 41%, possibly representing a marketing tool as customers can recognize the products of a specific trader.

These findings can be attributed to the fact that informal protection methods are often much simpler and faster to introduce than formal protection methods. They also can be maintained with limited resources which are very important especially for newly established firms. On the other hand formal protection methods, mainly IPRs, require major financial and human resources if they are to be exploited thoroughly in business. Finally, 281 out of the 2548 firms that reported some innovative activity, did not use any of the aforementioned intellectual property protection methods (Table 3.26).

In terms of sectors, patents are more important for high-tech firms (29%) while copyright is a more popular formal protection method among KIBS firms (used by 32% of them). Confidentiality agreements are used by the major part of KIBS firms, while secrecy is used by a smaller share of

Table 3.26 Intellectual property protection methods (number of firms in parentheses) (%)

	Patents	Trademarks	Copyrights	Confidentiality agreements	Secrecy	Lead-time advantages on competitors	Complexity of design
Croatia (138)	15	43	33	41	49	68	63
Czech Republic (138)	13	26	20	48	28	42	21
Denmark (196)	15	24	28	62	56	84	44
France (309)	16	39	17	49	24	38	46
Germany (334)	21	44	37	75	71	64	57
Greece (231)	15	67	33	47	35	11	39
Italy (430)	14	39	14	40	20	71	46
Portugal (223)	19	53%	20	38	43	77	48
Sweden (207)	14	45	35	62	52	38	40
UK (342)	19	30	41	74	40	41	44
Total (2,548 firms)	17	41	27	55	40	54	46

Source: Aegis Survey, data processing by LIEE/NTUA.

firms in the low-tech sector compared to the other two groups. Lead-time advantage on competitors and complexity of design are employed quite extensively in all three sector groups but they seem to be more popular in the high-tech sector.

3.6 Firms' performance and the impact of the economic crisis

3.6.1 More than half the sample with up to €0.5 million annual turnover

Almost 80% of the firms that participated in the survey are rather small firms in terms of turnover as they have an average turnover (2007–2009) below €1 million. In fact one out of three had a turnover only up to €250,000, indicating the small size of these new firms. Only 4% of the sample can be considered as relatively large companies, making over €10 million, with variation across countries. At the sectoral level, KIBS firms are significantly smaller than manufacturing. More than 60% of the KIBS sample had a turnover below €500,000 compared to 40% in high-tech manufacturing and 47% in low-technology sectors.

In terms of profits, the performance of the surveyed firms is rather disappointing (Table 3.27). Of the surveyed firms, 12.4% reported on average losses during the examined period, which could be even higher, if we note that almost the same percentage of firms refused to respond to the specific question.[24] Besides almost half the sample reported profits up to €50,000, which could be considered as a non-viable business outcome. Of course, taking into consideration the low turnovers reported for the same period of time, these results are not surprising. On the other hand, these results could be explained to some extent by the fact that maybe some of these companies are still in the depreciation phase of the investments they have made, so they have to report losses in their balance sheets.

In terms of sectors 17% of high-tech firms report profits above €150,000 compared to only 10% in the other two sectoral groups. Losses

Table 3.27 Financial performance during 2007–2009

Turnover	% of surveyed firms	Profits	% of surveyed firms
Up to €500,000	53.4	Losses	12.4
€500,000–1,000,000	25.1	Up to €50,000	46.7
€1–10 million	10.3	€51,000–200,000	21.2
€10–50 million	3.9	>€200,000	7.1
DN/refused	7.3	DN/refused	12.6
Total	100		100

Source: Aegis Survey, data processing by LIEE/NTUA.

are mostly reported by low-tech companies, taking into consideration the non-responses as well.

Apart from the average size characteristics, the trend during this period is also important to evaluate their actual performance. Two out of three firms in the sample reported an average increase in their sales during the period 2007–2009 – in the midst of the financial crisis – almost for all countries participating in the survey (Table 3.28). One out of three has achieved an average growth above 25%, representing the fastest growing part of the sample. Most of them come from Business services (NACE 72), but also from high-tech sectors (NACE 31 and 32) and chemicals (NACE 24).

On the other hand, one out of five firms reported a negative trend, while 10% of the sample faced a significant decrease of sales (over 25%). Some 500 firms reported a rather neutral effect. The average growth of sales for the firms in the sample (excluding 2% outliers on both edges[25]), is +22% (median of +10%).

In terms of employment, the majority of firms reported small changes, leading to a rather neutral effect. More than 42% grew in size during the examined period, while 15.4% increased their employment by at least 50%. Almost 190 firms doubled their size during this period, but this should be treated cautiously.[26] The average growth in employment (trimmed mean as previously), of the whole sample is +15%.

In Sweden and Greece, more than half of the sample created some new jobs in the examined period, while in Croatia and Czech Republic only one-third of the sample reported the same. On the other hand, in Denmark, almost 18% of the firms in the sample reported that they shrank significantly during the examined period, as the number of employees decreased by more than 15%. Firms for the high-technology sectors seem to perform slightly better than others, since half of the sample created some new jobs in the examined period, compared to only 42% that did the same from low-technology and KIBS sectors.

Firms provided also estimation about their exporting activity. The vast population reported a neutral trend, but this again should be treated cautiously. We cannot identify whether firms classified in this group are firms that export and had a neutral trend in their exports or are just non-exporting firms. On the other hand, 20% of firms showed an increasing exporting activity compared to 5.2% with the opposite trend.

Table 3.28 Average trend during 2007–2009 (% of firms)

	Decrease	*Stable*	*Increase*
Sales	20.1	13.7	66.2
Employment	12.7	44.5	42.7
Exports	5.2	74.0	20.9

Source: Aegis Survey, data processing by LIEE/NTUA.

Portuguese firms report some remarkable exporting activity as 34% of the sample report an increasing trend in their exports, along with 27% of Croatian firms. Poor performance on the other hand is shown by French and German firms (only 16% on the positive side). Furthermore, firms from high-tech sectors perform better than other firms; one out of three reports an increasing trend, while 11.3% of them increased their exports by over 50% during 2007–2009.

Firms were asked to provide some additional data for the last available financial year (2010), at least by the time of the survey (Table 3.29). Results during the crisis (2010) are indeed milder than the ones during 2007–2009, but not that worse. A significant 60% of the sample was estimating an increase of sales, while 23% was optimistic enough to expect a growth of over 25%. Some 30% increased the number of jobs that they offer; however, the vast majority (60%) reported no changes in employment. On the other hand, firms did not seem to perform badly in 2010 in their exporting activity, as the same percentage (20%) as in the previous period increased exports.

3.6.2 The impact of the crisis

The survey included also a more straightforward question that aimed at relating the financial effects of the crisis during 2009. Results show a negative effect in sales for the 44% of the sample (Table 3.30). On the other hand a quarter of the firms, despite the crisis, managed to increase their sales by over 5%. Croatian firms suffered the most, as 32% suffered from a very significant decrease (>–20%), followed by French and Italian firms (20%).

As was identified earlier, exports are not seriously affected, to some extent because not all firms of the sample export. On the other hand,

Table 3.29 Financial performance for 2010

Sales (N = 3,657)	(%)
Decrease	21.2
Stable	19.4
Increase	59.5
Employment (N = 3,699)	%
Decrease	10.2
Stable	59.6
Increase	30.1
Exports (N = 3,654)	%
Decrease	4.2
Stable	76.1
Increase	19.8

Source: Aegis Survey, data processing by LIEE/NTUA.

Table 3.30 Impact of the current economic crisis on firms in terms of sales

	Sales	Exports	Employment	Profits	Investments
Significant increase (>5%)	25.4	11.2	17.0	22.5	23.2
No significant changes (+/−5%)	30.5	74.0	63.4	35.7	55.6
Slight decrease (−5% to −10%)	14.2	4.5	6.7	13.7	6.7
Significant decrease (−10% to −20%)	13.1	3.9	5.2	11.8	5.8
Very significant decrease (>−20%)	16.9	6.4	7.7	16.3	8.6
Total	100	100	100	100	100

Source: Aegis Survey, data processing by LIEE/NTUA.

signals from high-tech sectors are rather mixed: while there is 15.8% that managed to increase exports by more than 5%, another 10.7% suffered from a decrease of more than 20%. The vast majority of firms from all sectors though and especially from KIBS, reported no significant changes.

More than 63% of the whole sample reported no significant changes in terms of employment during 2010. Greek firms had to dismiss some of their employees to a greater extent than firms in other countries. More than 22% of them decreased employment by more than 10%, followed by 17% in Croatia. Despite the tight economic activity in Portugal, only 7% of the Portuguese firms had to reduce their personnel, while 27% report that they managed to create new jobs. France is the country with the lowest percentage of firms that increased employment (8.7%). Sectoral differences are rather small, as firms from all sectors seem to have behaved the same.

In terms of profits,[27] despite the crisis, 22.5% of the sample reported a significant increase above 5%, whereas 36% reported no significant changes. This means that almost 60% of the sample was only marginally affected by the crisis. This is not the case however for Croatian and French firms, where more than 55% reported decrease in profits, followed by Czech firms which also had their profitability seriously affected. Danish and German firms on the other hand seem to be the ones which show the lowest impact. High-tech firms seem to be only marginally affected by the crisis in terms of profits as more than 60% report either increase or minor changes.

Investments on the other hand follow more or less the sales trend. Despite reduced liquidity and credit crunch conditions almost in all countries that participate in the survey, the majority of the firms examined (56%) reported no significant changes, while another 23% increased their investments. There is a variation among countries, however. On one hand almost half the sample from Portugal reported a significant increase in investments, whereas in UK only 13.1% reported the same. Of the Croatian firms, 25% had their investment plans seriously reduced while in the Czech Republic only 16% reported the same. It should be stressed however that usually investment plans last longer than a one-year period. So some long-term investments may have started earlier than the examined period, meaning that they may have assured funding before the crisis and therefore are continuing in the hot period of crisis. Furthermore, a part of an investment – depending on the funding scheme – could be fuelled by revenues generated by the investment itself. Possibly new investments could be highly affected by credit crunch conditions, but this cannot be identified in the obtained data.

Despite similar overall trend across the three group sectors, manufacturing shows a rather unaffected performance compared to KIBS, as 27% of the sample increased investments. This could be attributed to the character of those investments. In manufacturing usually higher initial capital requirements than in services but also invested capital, force for the completion of an investment, despite a worsening of the economic environment. On the other hand in KIBS, it could be easier to postpone or delay parts of an investment, which usually refers to buildings or equipment of different scale than manufacturing.

Finally, firms were asked to sketch the business environment that would be created in the post-crisis period, despite the fact that the recovery seems slower than anticipated. Most of the firms agreed on the liquidity problems in their value chain. Customers or suppliers that face liquidity problems were considered by almost 65% of the sample as a new element for the business relationships in the years after the crisis (Table 3.31). A supplier that fails to deliver because of lack of funding for his business; or needing higher cash payments; an important customer that cannot pay on time, may affect the cash flow of even the healthiest firm in a sector. This seems to be the greater fear of the firms that participated in the survey, along with a more general problem of shrinking liquidity (58% of positive answers). The same percentage of firms agreed on the increasing borrowing costs after a long period of rather low interest rates in Europe. On the positive side, five out of nine firms agree also that new opportunities will arise in the post-crisis period, as restructuring could help in healthier economic conditions, leading maybe to a new growth cycle in certain sectors.

As the extent and the consequences of the crisis vary in the countries represented in the survey, the views of the respondents differ significantly across them. In the Czech Republic, Croatia, Greece, Italy, Portugal, but also the UK the major consequence of the crisis is the liquidity problems of the customers/suppliers that affect the cash flow in the value chain. Italian and French firms are the most pessimistic in terms of opportunities that could be created in the post-crisis period. Greek and Portuguese are also concerned with the increasing borrowing costs. German firms believe in possible opportunities in the post-crisis era, while Italian firms do not.

Low-tech firms place greater emphasis than firms from other sectors in increasing borrowing costs, and the problems with suppliers/customers.

Table 3.31 Financing and creation of new opportunities in the post-crisis period

	% of positive answers
Liquidity will be significantly restricted in my sector (N = 3,833)	57.5
Borrowing costs will significantly increase (N = 3,702)	56.5
A lot of my customers/suppliers will face significant liquidity problems which may cause problems for my firm (N = 3,894)	64.7
Bankruptcies and restructuring in my sector might create new opportunities for my firm (N = 3,880)	56.7

Source: Aegis Survey, data processing by LIEE/NTUA.

Mixed signals are evident in the KIBS sectors, as only half the sample agrees with the proposed statements. Furthermore, it is the sector where only 53% believe in possible opportunities, when some 60% of the firms in the other two groups are more optimistic.

4 Policy implications

Some key messages that arise from the survey results are the following:

Provide better access to finance
Results show that entrepreneurs have difficulties in raising finance during the early stages of their businesses. Therefore, the financing of their ventures is highly dependent on their own savings while other sources of finance such as venture capital or national and EU subsidies are rather scarce. Therefore, better awareness and access to finance at both European and national level are required. Venture capitals and business angels that provide seed and first round equity investments should be strengthened through fiscal incentives. In addition, new alternative forms of financing for start-ups (e.g. crowd sourcing) should be facilitated. European structural funds resources could be used to set up microfinance support schemes under the respective EU investment priorities.

Support young firms in crucial phases of their lifecycle and help them grow
The starting-up phase of a firm is a highly risky phase, as a significant part of new firms fail to survive within the first five years of their life. New businesses often lack an appropriate or favourable ecosystem that will help them grow. Policy support actions/measures aiming at increasing the success rate of newly established firms could include:

- facilitation of networking with peers, potential customers and suppliers;
- provision of advice and support in dealing with resource shortages and supply insecurity through strategic investment and product development;
- reduction in high tax rates as well as the reduction in the cost of tax compliance arising from complex and frequently changing tax legislation and cumbersome tax reporting procedures;
- setting up an efficiently functioning financial system that allows access to various sources and types of financing;
- setting in place a transparent and well-functioning intellectual property protection regime (which is instrumental for KIE firms).

Access to innovative public procurement
Empirical findings suggest that the role of public demand in promoting and supporting innovative activity is extremely weak. Enhancement of the role of public procurement in the innovation production and KIE can be

attained through a mix of policy measures. Specifically, during the first stages of the innovation lifecycle pre-commercial procurement practices are more suitable to provide incentives to young firms for R&D activities and the development of highly innovative products/services. Thus the aim of this practice would be to initially create technological opportunities and mitigate risk by providing favourable conditions for knowledge creation and innovation production. At a later stage market opportunities can also be created by ensuring that the products/services that successfully meet the pre-commercial stages will be procured by a public organization. For the latter phases of the innovation cycle, policies should be more focused on the diffusion of innovations and the development of market and institutional opportunities for KIE. For this purpose, public procurement policies should focus on strengthening the demand of already existing innovative products/services.

Access to scientific knowledge networks

Our findings suggest that the most important knowledge sources for young firms are related to customers, suppliers and competitors. However, empirical evidence also shows that only a few of the AEGIS survey firms have international presence in international markets while 36% of them do not have any kind of innovative activity. National policy measures facilitating networking with universities and research institutes as well as EU policy measures promoting the young firms' participation in EU-funded research networks may help young companies complement and expand their limited technological resource and knowledge bases and support (new) business projects being able to innovate, grow and improve their presence in international markets.

Leverage entrepreneurial experience

The AEGIS survey results suggest that firm founders have a relatively limited entrepreneurial experience. Therefore, policy makers should strive to promote serial entrepreneurship as a way to leverage entrepreneurial experience. A failure in entrepreneurship should not be regarded as a 'stigma' but should be seen as an opportunity for learning and improving. Thus, legal obstacles such as personal credit and bankruptcy laws, and policy tools such public financing schemes should clearly consider the importance of not focusing only on de novo entrepreneurs.

Reach out to underrepresented groups within founding teams

Specific demographic groups which are underrepresented within the early stage entrepreneurs in Europe are young people, women and migrants (European Commission, 2013). These facts are also confirmed by the AEGIS survey data, indicating the need to address the needs of each group by specific policy actions.

Women represent a large pool of entrepreneurial potential. However, as entrepreneurs they usually face more difficulties than men mainly in access to finance, training, networking, and in reconciling business and family. Thus, potential women entrepreneurs should get aware of business support programmes and funding opportunities. In addition, policies allowing women to achieve satisfactory work-life equilibrium should be implemented, for example, by establishing appropriate and affordable care for children and/or elderly dependents.

Young people, especially high-potential would-be entrepreneurs, should be encouraged to set up their own businesses. In particular, by enriching the human capital of a social group that is most exposed to scientific and technological knowledge, early enough (i.e. during their undergraduate studies), towards entrepreneurship will increase the specific weight of a particular kind of opportunity entrepreneurship, i.e. technological entrepreneurship. Therefore, European higher educational systems could contribute towards this direction by developing the appropriate competences, stimulating the entrepreneurial spirit of the young students and providing initial assistance in their entrepreneurial activities (incubating activities, coaching and mentoring activities, etc.).

Moreover, the encouragement of early-stage entrepreneurial activity should be further enhanced by promoting the process of turning new research results into innovations by supporting spin-offs from research institutes and universities.

Notes

1 See Chapter 1.
2 In OECD countries 10–25% of the new employer firms disappear during the first year after their birth. On average, survival rates after one year are around 85–90% in manufacturing and a little lower in services, and they continue to drop constantly in the following years (OECD, 2009, 2012).
3 The Amadeus database contains information on public and private companies that publish financial statements developed by Bureau Van Dijk. It does not include sole proprietary firms.
4 This does not imply that there is a bias towards large firms in terms of employment, as more than 30% of all firms included in Amadeus employ up to five employees. Actual survey results confirmed this.
5 For the rest of this chapter, the combination of high- and medium-technological sectors will be referred as 'high-technology' and the combination of low- and medium-to-low- tech as 'low-technology' for reasons of simplicity.
6 Clearly the problem was mainly in the high-tech sectors, where data availability was low.
7 www.gdcc.com/.
8 Pilot interviews were also undertaken to fine-tune the questions. Interviews were conducted in the native languages.
9 In some cases the Amadeus sample was not sufficient in order to achieve the desired number of interviews. Additional sample (~10% of the population) was purchased from other sources (Kompass/D&B) in order to achieve targets per country/sector.
10 Despite efforts, the minimum of 40 responses was not possible to achieve in some high-technology manufacturing sectors in certain countries.

11 The 5% trimmed average employment is seven people.
12 Of course this does not represent their actual age at the time of the founding. In any case and judging by the year of establishment, the majority of them were definitely above 32 years old.
13 An explanatory note was provided to interviewers, indicating that 'many' refers to over five competitors and 'few' refers to 3–5 competitors, but it was strongly suggested to leave respondents to assess the terms 'many/few' in their market. This is a variable that has been used for ten years in the Global Entrepreneurship Monitor.
14 Twenty-one European countries were used for this result which is a non-weighted average. Although data for 2009–2010 were used, this trend is robust in more recent surveys as well.
15 Average % of sales during 2007–2009.
16 As GEM results reveal, almost the majority of new firms that are created each year have as direct customers the final consumers. This is explained by the fact that most of these ventures are in retail. More specifically in GEM 2010, 44% of the start-ups for the same countries participating in the AEGIS survey are consumer oriented (GEM 2010 Global report).
17 Includes respondents that could not clearly identify their most important customer.
18 The report of 2010–2011 was used.
19 KIBS are able to develop their own knowledge base (Muller and Zenker, 2001). Thus they can create learning opportunities and enable accumulating learning experiences (Miles *et al.*, 1995).
20 The Oslo Manual definition was used as a guidance to the interview.
21 The proportion of innovative firms according to CIS 2008 in EU-27 is almost 50%.
22 The Oslo manual definitions for these two types of innovation were used.
23 Of the firms, 8.6% reported the introduction of all types of innovation within the specific time period.
24 It is not unreasonable to assume that the greatest part of these firms may actually consist of respondents who didn't feel confident to respond that they were on the negative side.
25 This is therefore the trimmed mean, including 96% of the sample in the specific calculation.
26 As the sample includes some micro firms, it may well be a result like this: a firm with four employees can double its size when reaching eight employees. Still however it is an important improvement, since most micro firms usually remain at this micro level for a long period of time.
27 The concept of profits may also include losses, meaning that when a firm reports an increase in losses, this is classified as significant decrease of profits.

References

Allen, I. E., Elam, A., Langowitz, N., & Dean, M. (2007). Global entrepreneurship monitor (GEM). 2007 Report on Women and Entrepreneurship. Babson Park, MA: Babson College.

Amason, A.C. and Sapienza, H.J. (1997). The effects of top management team size and interaction norms on cognitive and affective conflict. *Journal of Management*, 23(4), 495–516.

Besanko, D., Dranove, D., Shanley, M. and Schaefer, S. (2009). *Economics of strategy*. New York: John Wiley & Sons, Inc.

Bird, B.J. (1989). *Entrepreneurial behavior.* Glenview, IL: Scott, Foresman.

Bygrave, W.D. and Hunt, S. (2004). *Global entrepreneurship monitor 2004, financing report.*

den Hertog, P. (2000). Knowledge-intensive business services as co-producers of innovation. *International Journal of Innovation Management*, 4(4), 491–528.

European Commission (2013). *Entrepreneurship 2020 Action Plan: Reigniting the entrepreneurial spirit in Europe.* Communication from the Commission to the European Parliament, the Council, The European Economic and Social Committee and the Committee of the Regions, Brussels, 9.1.2013 COM(2012) 795 final.

Global Entrepreneurship Monitor, Global reports.

Hsu, D.H. (2004). What do entrepreneurs pay for venture capital affiliation? *The Journal of Finance*, 59(4), 1805–1844.

Janz, B.D., Colquitt, J.A. and Noe, R.A. (1997). Knowledge worker team effectiveness: The role of autonomy, interdependence, team development, and contextual support variables. *Personnel Psychology*, 50(4), 877–904.

Miles, I., Kastrinos, N., Flanagan, K., Bilderbeek, R., den Hertog, P., Huntink, W. and Bouman, M. (1995). *Knowledge-intensive business services: users, carriers and sources of innovation.* Luxembourg: EC (DG13 SPRINT-EIMS available at: www.mbs.ac.uk/research/centres/engineering-policy/publications/reports.htm).

Mosakowski, E. (1998). Entrepreneurial resources, organizational choices, and competitive outcomes. *Organization Science*, 9(6), 625–643.

Muller, E. and Zenker, A. (2001). Business services as actors of knowledge transformation: the role of KIBS in regional and national innovation systems. *Research Policy*, 30, 1501–1516.

OECD (2009). *Measuring entrepreneurship: a digest of indicators.* Paris: OECD.

OECD (2012). *Entrepreneurship at a glance.* Paris: OECD. DOI: http://dx.doi.org/10.1787/entrepreneur_aag-2012-en.

Päällysaho, S. and Kuusisto, J. (2011). Informal ways to protect intellectual property (IP) in KIBS businesses. *Innovation: Management, Policy & Practice*, 13(1), 62–76.

Reagans, R., Argote, L. and Brooks, D. (2005). Individual experience and experience working together: Predicting learning rates from knowing who knows what and knowing how to work together. *Management Science*, 51(6), 869–881.

Santarelli, E. and Vivarelli, M. (2007). Entrepreneurship and the process of firms' entry, survival and growth. *Industrial and Corporate Change*, 16(3), 455–488.

Schivardi, F. and Torrini, R. (2008). Identifying the effects of firing restrictions through size-contingent differences in regulation. *Labour Economics*, 15(3), 482–511.

Shane, S. and Stuart, T. (2002). Organizational endowments and the performance of university start-ups. *Management Science*, 48(1), 154–170.

Shane, S.A. (2004). *Academic entrepreneurship: University spinoffs and wealth creation.* Cheltenham, UK: Edward Elgar Publishing.

Toivonen, M. (2004). Expertise as business: Long-term development and future prospects of knowledge-intensive business services (KIBS). (Doctoral dissertation series 2004/2), Finland: Helsinki University of Technology, Department of Industrial Engineering and Management, Espoo.

World Economic Forum's Global Competitiveness report, 2010–2011.

4 Knowledge-intensive entrepreneurship

Exploring a taxonomy based on the AEGIS survey

Yannis Caloghirou, Aimilia Protogerou and Aggelos Tsakanikas

1 Introduction

Heterogeneity is an interesting problem that this chapter tackles, but it can also be a challenge in developing a general model in entrepreneurship. Firms are found by highly heterogeneous processes, their founding teams are diverse in terms of preferences, founding motivations, entrepreneurial ability and demographic characteristics. Furthermore, firms grow in different political, institutional, industrial, cultural and social environments, have dissimilar access to resources and ultimately achieve various performance outcomes (Delmar and Wennberg, 2010). This diversity among firms, and especially among young ones, cannot be easily reduced to a general model. Their variability calls for a taxonomy or a classification system in order to identify the many variables that can be at play and in turn provide distinct patterns of entrepreneurial behaviour.

This chapter takes up the challenge of studying patterns of entrepreneurship in Europe following the definition of knowledge-intensive entrepreneurship (KIE) provided by the conceptual framework of the AEGIS research project (Malerba and McKelvey, 2010) and analysed in Chapter 2 of this book. This definition suggests that knowledge-intensive entrepreneurship, which is considered as a high-potential entrepreneurship with significant impact on economic growth and social well-being, is associated with *four* basic characteristics. In particular, it refers to *new* firms that have significant *knowledge intensity* in their activity and develop and exploit *innovative* opportunities in *diverse sectors* (both high-, medium- and low-tech manufacturing and knowledge-intensive business services). In addition, it should be stressed that the AEGIS model adopts an approach which focuses on the new firm as the unit of analysis and emphasizes the importance of context (systems of innovation, networks, groups of industrial sectors, etc.).

The proposed taxonomy is based on empirical evidence and measured observations emerging from the large-scale *AEGIS survey* which was conducted in the context of the AEGIS research project and covered ten European countries. Our analysis consists of two steps. First we applied cluster analysis techniques to build a firm taxonomy of entrepreneurial behaviour based on the four predefined characteristics of KIE, next we examined how new ventures exhibiting different degrees of knowledge intensity and innovative performance are distributed across diverse institutional and industrial contexts.

The results of our research provide a snapshot of the knowledge intensity and the innovative performance of young ventures by classifying them into groups or clusters that share common traits. In particular, the empirical taxonomy identifies three types of entrepreneurial ventures which exhibit distinct KIE characteristics: (a) *all-around* KIE;[1] (b) *world-class KIE* (focusing on product innovation); and (c) a third 'mixed bag' category which can be labelled as '*modest KIE*', where firms co-exist with different degrees of 'knowvation' (a term which combines knowledge intensity and innovative performance). The 'all-around KIE' group shows a balanced emphasis on knowledge-seeking activities (both in-house and from external sources), on new-to-market product innovation, and on process and organizational innovation. On the other hand 'world-class KIE' emphasizes new-to-world product innovation drawing from in-house knowledge which in turn draws from high quality human capital (both in terms of founders and workforce). The 'modest KIE' group focuses on new-to-firm product innovation drawing from external industry knowledge sources. In general, it appears there are smaller degrees of knowledge intensiveness and innovation compared to the other two groups.

Moreover, our results suggest that although the strategic preferences of firms are up to a certain extent determined by their environment, within a particular institutional setting (e.g. a particular National Innovation System) or industrial sector, there are variations in firms that can be explained as a function of the diverse models of action chosen by entrepreneurs through the acquisition, combination and recombination of resources to exploit profit opportunities.

This work adds to the literature in several ways: (a) it operationalizes and measures KIE by testing its applicability in a large number of firms, thus opening up new ways for a better understanding and further refinement of this concept; (b) it provides a way of reducing the heterogeneity identified in the entrepreneurial behaviour of new firms into a few meaningful categories; (c) it shows that these categories of firms run across countries and sectors rather than coinciding with them; (d) it may assist in targeting and refining policies for promoting entrepreneurship and innovation.

The chapter begins with a theoretical discussion on the definition of knowledge-intensive entrepreneurship, gives some hints on how the AEGIS survey is differentiated from other large-scale surveys on entrepreneurship and attempts to show why a taxonomy of newly established firms exhibiting variations in their knowledge intensity and innovative outcome might be useful for better understanding knowledge-intensive entrepreneurship. In the third section we present the survey design and introduce the experimental setting. We then document the empirical results and discuss major findings. The chapter ends with our concluding remarks.

2 Theoretical background

2.1 Defining knowledge-intensive entrepreneurship

It is well established that investments in knowledge generation and dissemination and in human capital generate innovation, economic growth both directly and indirectly via knowledge spillovers (for a review see Rosegger, 1996; Freeman and Soete, 1997; Fagerberg *et al.*, 2005; Malerba and Brusoni, 2007). Nonetheless, large investments in knowledge generation such as research and development (R&D) do not lead automatically to innovation and economic growth. New knowledge does not always result in new economic activity. Even a higher degree of entrepreneurship and new business creation does not guarantee innovation, enhanced economic performance and faster rates of economic growth (Wong *et al.*, 2005).

Contemporary entrepreneurship research appears to be moving from a view that 'all forms of entrepreneurship are good' towards a more nuanced view where 'high-potential entrepreneurship' is an important driver for economic development (Autio and Acs, 2007; Henrekson and Johansson, 2010).

Knowledge-intensive entrepreneurship can be considered as a type of high potential entrepreneurship and indicates ventures whose initiation or expansion is based on the dynamic application of new knowledge. Also, new knowledge-intensive firms can play an important role in sectoral, local and national innovation systems by operating as problems solvers, knowledge brokers, knowledge-intensive service providers or specialized suppliers.

The definition of knowledge-intensive entrepreneurship adopted in this study (Malerba and McKelvey, 2010) is associated with new ventures that draw upon and integrate knowledge (both in-house and externally generated) in order to pursue and exploit innovative opportunities; moreover, they are ventures operating in diverse industries (including low-tech industries and services).

The notion of innovative opportunities, as used here, is broader than the pursuit of opportunities stemming from scientific and/or technological knowledge; it also involves the creative process of identifying the potential for delivering value for hitherto unserved market needs, mobilizing and/or creating the requisite resources for realizing the opportunity and, finally, devising ways by which at least part of the generated economic value can be appropriated by the firm.

Perhaps the best way to understand the notion of KIE is to compare it with related but distinct concepts. First, a KIE venture is not simply a new venture or start-up firm; it is a new venture that, as described above, pursues innovative opportunities by purposefully and systematically utilizing knowledge in its operational activities. Second, a distinction should be made with the related concept of new technology-based firms (NTBFs). The literature here focuses on new firms that either transform generic (basic science) research into basic technologies (i.e. science-based NTBFs) or new firms that apply basic technologies to develop new products/services for particular market needs (i.e. engineering-based NTBFs). The key difference between these two types of NTBFs and KIE ventures is that for the latter the transformation of science and technological knowledge is not the sole element in the innovation process. This is because for KIE new ventures technological assets are but one class of resources and capabilities needed for the successful commercialization of innovation. The ultimate goal here is *market success*, not 'simply' the development of a radical innovation.

The broader context (i.e. knowledge sources, markets, institutions and opportunities) within which ventures are embedded assumes a major role in our understanding of KIE. Specifically, it is assumed that the context affects directly and/or indirectly the ways and mechanisms by which KIE ventures are formed in the first place, as well as the management and strategic behaviour of these firms in pursuit of innovation and growth. Whatever effect KIE venture performance has in terms of the dynamics of market structure and wider economic and societal impacts feeds back to the broader institutional context, thus closing the loop. Put differently, KIE and the surrounding context find themselves in a state of constant dynamic interaction.

Beyond the immediate industry specificities (e.g. the existing technological regime in terms of opportunities and appropriability conditions) and factors of demand that make entry of KIE ventures more or less possible in the first place, the broader institutional and policy context also plays an important role in the supply and performance of KIE (Delmar and Wennberg, 2010). More specifically, depending on context, entrepreneurial ambitions will differ as the demand for specific types of entrepreneurship changes. This practically means that the opportunities identified and exploited, the people involved in self-employment and the firms that are eventually created, grow up and die depending on contextual conditions. National and sectoral systems of innovation are widely held to play a prominent role in this respect.

2.2 *The AEGIS survey*

The AEGIS survey, conducted in the first half of 2011, is the main instrument of the AEGIS project, as it supports the empirical investigation of knowledge-intensive entrepreneurship in Europe in different sectoral, country and socioeconomic contexts.

The AEGIS survey differs from other relevant surveys, both in its context and scope. It could be positioned between Community Innovation Survey (CIS) and Global Entrepreneurship Monitor (GEM). However, it is distinct from both, but also from other relevant surveys such as the KfW-ZEW Start-up Panel, the Kauffman Firm Survey and OECD. More precisely:

- The CIS investigates the innovative activity of all firms across sectors in order to produce important R&D and innovation indicators, which are widely used by the European Commission in policy design.
- The GEM project, on the other hand, is a general population annual survey undertaken across a wide range of countries. It explores the behaviour and characteristics of nascent entrepreneurs, new entrepreneurs and established business owners, within the total population of a country.
- The AEGIS survey also differentiates from other recent survey studies, such as the KfW-ZEW study. The latter covers only one country (Germany), while the AEGIS survey takes into consideration different groups of countries (out of ten in total) according to their size (large, medium, small countries) and the socioeconomic model they belong to. However, most importantly the KfW/ZEW survey is a panel survey which intends to track the development of newly founded firms over the first years after firm formation. It focuses on firm strategies, innovation, financing/capital investment and labour demand.

The Kauffman firm survey is undertaken in the US and is similar to the KfW/ZEW Start-up Panel as it also tracks down newly established firms for over six years and covers more or less the same topics (Robb *et al.*, 2009). More specifically, the Kauffman survey focuses on the nature of new business formation activity; characteristics of the strategy, offerings and employment patterns of new businesses; the financial and organizational arrangements of these businesses; and their founders' characteristics.

- The OECD's project on entrepreneurship, the 'Entrepreneurship Indicators Programme' (EIP) is mostly a secondary data approach building on existing national statistical sources. Hence, it suffers from the usual limitations in the availability of indicators.

Nevertheless, AEGIS takes into consideration most of the above mentioned surveys and incorporates all elements that support its unique aim: to examine the multi-dimensional concept of knowledge-intensive entrepreneurship. In this way we will be able not only to identify motives, characteristics and patterns in the creation and growth of new firms, but also pinpoint those key elements that will help us distinguish between discrete types of entrepreneurial new ventures. It will, therefore, be the first time, at least to our knowledge, that empirical data will be used to identify different patterns of entrepreneurial behaviour by classifying young firms based on their knowledge-based intensity and innovative performance (knowvation).

2.3 Why an empirical taxonomy of knowledge-based entrepreneurship might be useful

New firms have been identified as engines for growth, innovation and wealth creation (Audretsch and Turik, 2000). Young small firms are usually short-lived exiting the market within a few years from their formation. Empirical evidence shows that only a small proportion of young firms accounts for a significant share of new job creation (employment). However, those firms that do innovate successfully increase their chances of survival and growth and are therefore a key element for economic development and growth (de Jong and Marsili, 2006). High-potential young firms are described as 'the kind that create value and stimulate growth by bringing new ideas into the market, be they new technologies, new business models, or simply new and better ways of performing routine tasks' (Schramm, 2005, p. 163).

New firms are also highly heterogeneous. For example, the process by which firms are found is heterogeneous itself (Delmar and Davidson, 2000), entrepreneurs have different preferences, and demographic characteristics, firms evolve in different contexts, with different access to resources, and they strive for different performance outcomes (Gartner and Carter, 2003). Thus heterogeneity is a challenge for entrepreneurship and the diversity among young firms cannot be easily reduced into a universal model.

Having in mind the definition of KIE presented in the previous section we are interested in understanding the variability of newly established firms in terms of both their innovative performance and their knowledge assets. Indeed, research indicates that the innovative performance and behaviour of young firms can vary substantially. Some small firms survive by competing in a market niche, while others may pursuit radical innovations and eventually become new market leaders (de Jong and Marsili, 2006). Furthermore, young firms exhibit heterogeneity in terms of their knowledge assets (e.g. educational background and experience of founders, education of employees or employment training) and the knowledge-seeking activities they are involved in (for instance some are more extrovert and invest in collaboration with third parties such as universities and research centres while others obtain new knowledge mainly through their own R&D activities) (Gartner, 1988; Landstrom and Astrom, 2011).

The diversity among new firms cannot be easily reduced into a single model of entrepreneurial venture. Their variability calls for a taxonomy that can be used to identify the many variables that might play a role. Taxonomies of new entrepreneurial ventures that display different degrees of 'knowvation' might provide an empirically based framework to test the theoretical model of knowledge-intensive entrepreneurship built in the context of the AEGIS project as well as to provide useful policy guidelines.

Taxonomies are meant to classify phenomena with the aim of maximizing the differences across groups. A proposed taxonomy is considered useful if it helps in reducing the complexity of empirical phenomena into a few and easy to recall macro-classes (categories) (Pavitt, 1998; Archibugi, 2001; de Jong and Marsili, 2006). Thus a broadly accepted and usable taxonomy is an essential element in the development of a scientific body of knowledge and can serve as an empirically based framework to theory development and hypothesis testing. According to Rich (1992) organizational taxonomies provide a basis for strong research, permit parsimony without simplicity, and the ability to recognize fundamental structure and relationships by comparing organizations and clustering them into categorical types. Moreover, taxonomy is more than a simple classification of items into separate groups. It is rather a specific classification scheme that labels many different items into groups or clusters with common characteristics.

3 Data and variables

3.1 Data

The large-scale AEGIS survey was carried out in the first half of 2011 by means of computer-assisted telephone interviewing using a structured questionnaire. All respondents were usually the founder/entrepreneur or members of the founding team. The survey focus was on young firms established between 2001 and 2007 in ten European countries, namely France, Italy, UK, Germany, Sweden, Denmark, Sweden, Greece, Portugal, Croatia and Czech Republic. In order to interview actually newly established firms the survey instrument included a set of screening questions to detect: (a) firms that were just new legal entities resulting from legal transformation of already existing firms; (b) subsidiaries of existing companies; (c) mergers, acquisitions or joint ventures. These firms were characterized as non-eligible for the survey.

The primary data source for the survey population was the Amadeus database. However, additional data sources were used (Kompass, D&B) as during the interview process (screening questions) it was found out that a large number of firms recorded as new were not the case.

An initial sample of 23,405 firms was randomly drawn from the entire population of firms as available at the above mentioned databases. Among them 10,581 were judged as not eligible for the survey during the screening part of the questionnaire mostly because they were not actually new entities but just legal transformations of already existing companies. The final sample of eligible firms was 12,824 firms and 4,004 of them accepted to respond to the questionnaire, thus the survey obtained an average response rate of 31.2 per cent across countries.

Our choice of sampling was guided by the adopted definition of KIE and the need to limit unobservable heterogeneity, which plagues many contemporary entrepreneurship studies (Shane, 2003). New ventures are largely heterogeneous, ranging from 'mom and pop' retail stores to venture capital backed firms in high-tech industries. Random samples of new firms indicate that only one out of ten young firms can be characterized as 'innovative', while most new businesses are created as replications or marginal variations of already existing products or services (Delmar and Wennberg, 2010). The ventures of our sample are active in a wide variety of industries, including low- and high-tech manufacturing and knowledge-intensive business services (KIBS). Thus our understanding of KIE allows us to select not only traditional knowledge-intensive sectors (i.e. high-tech manufacturing and KIBS) but also low- and medium-tech industries suggesting that increased knowledge-seeking activities and innovation can also be found in sectors that are not necessarily heavy R&D spenders. In any case the specific sample selection enables us to focus on firms that exhibit some degree of 'knowvation', i.e. they can be characterized up to a certain point as knowledge-intensive entrepreneurial ventures (see Table 4.1).

3.2 A first step towards establishing a KIE taxonomy

3.2.1 Clustering variables

For the construction of the taxonomy we used cluster analysis techniques. These techniques are sensitive to the selection of the variables used meaning that the addition of irrelevant variables can affect clustering results (Milligan and Cooper, 1987). Therefore we employed a set of 'core variables' by 'translating' our general understanding of the KIE phenomenon into empirical indicators. In the theoretical background we have already stated that in the context of the AEGIS project, KIE is related to

Table 4.1 Industry coverage in the AEGIS survey

Selected sectors	NACE Rev. 1.1 codes
Manufacturing	
High-tech manufacturing	35.3, 30, 32, 33, 24.4
Medium high-tech manufacturing	31, 29, 24 (excl. 24.4)
Low-tech manufacturing	21, 22, 17, 18, 19, 15, 16
Medium low-tech manufacturing	27, 28
KIBS sectors	
High-tech services	64.2, 72, 73
Market services	74.1, 74.2, 74.3, 74.4, 74.5, 74.8*

four fundamental characteristics: it concerns new ventures; new ventures that are not to be found solely in high-tech industries (they may well be active in industries with medium- or low-tech characteristics or in services); new ventures that are innovative; and finally, new ventures engaging in activities that are knowledge intensive. The first and second conditions are satisfied a priori in our sample. We have collected data from new ventures (from four to a maximum ten years of age), and these ventures are sampled from a wide array of industries, including both high- and low-tech industries. We therefore need variables for the remaining two conditions: knowledge-intensive activities and innovation performance which point to the 'knowvative' content of KIE (i.e. the combination of knowledge intensity and innovative performance).

Table 4.2 presents the dimensions and variables that formed the basis of the proposed taxonomy. As it can be seen in the table, four classes of variables were employed as distinguishing features of KIE. The three first, as in the AEGIS survey, reflect what might be understood as the venture's *knowledge assets or knowledge intensity* dimension, while the last one represents the *innovation output* dimension.

3.2.2 Knowledge intensity

A firm's knowledge-intensity dimension includes measures of 'knowledge-seeking activities', 'initial knowledge capital' and 'human capital and innovation input'. *Knowledge-seeking activities* are related to specific linkages that can act as sources of information and knowledge for the young firm. These activities are measured by a Likert-type scale and confirmatory factor analysis revealed the following five dimensions.

- *External knowledge sources related to industry*: reflects the importance of knowledge sourced from clients, suppliers and competitors.
- *External knowledge sources related to science actors* such as public research institutes and universities.
- *In-house R&D knowledge*: knowledge generated from internal sources (single item).
- *External-open sources*: knowledge sourced from trade fairs, conferences and exhibitions, scientific journals and other trade or technical publications.
- *Participation in collaborative R&D:* participation in nationally funded or EU-funded research programmes.

The remaining two groups of indicators are 'initial conditions' and 'human capital and innovation input'. Beginning with 'initial conditions', average educational attainment of the founding team can be thought of as representing the initial stock of knowledge founders bring with them when starting the venture. For each individual member of the founding team we

Table 4.2 KIE variables that formed the basis of the proposed taxonomy

KIE variables

Knowledge intensity
Knowledge-seeking activities
External knowledge sources from industry (clients or customers, suppliers, competitors)
External sources of knowledge (public research institutes, universities, external commercial labs/R&D firms, technical institutes)
Internal knowledge sources/in-house R&D
External knowledge from 'open' sources (trade fairs, conferences, exhibitions, scientific journals and other trade or technical publications)
Participation in research collaborative activities funded by national or EU sources

Initial knowledge capital
Founding team educational attainment
% of initial funding from venture capital

Human capital and innovation 'input'
% of full-time employees with graduate degree
% of full-time employees with PhD degree
Employee training
R&D intensity

Innovation performance
Product innovation
Introduction of new goods/services during the last three years
New goods/services were new to the firm
New goods/services were new to the market
New goods/services were new to the world

Process innovation
Introduction of process innovation during the last three years

Organizational innovation the last three years
Introduction of logistics innovation
Introduction of innovation in support activities
Improvement of management systems
Changes in management structure

IPR protection methods during the last three years
Patents
Trademarks
Copyrights
Confidentiality agreements
Secrecy
Lead time advantages on competitors
Complexity of design

measure educational attainment using an ordinal variable taking the values: 1 – elementary education; 2 – secondary education; 3 – Bachelor degree; 4 – Postgraduate degree; 5 – PhD degree. We average across team members to derive an overall measure of founders' education.

The percentage of funding coming from venture capital may be seen to reflect the quality or ingenuity of the original idea that led to the formation of the venture. One would normally expect that, ceteris paribus, the higher the contribution of venture capital the higher the originality and innovation potential of the firm. Taken together, these two variables may be argued to represent the 'initial' knowledge capital available to the venture at start-up. As regards the next four variables, the positive role of human capital (percentage of employees with advanced qualifications, i.e. percent over full-time employment of employees with a graduate/PhD degree respectively), employee training (single five-point Likert-type question) and R&D intensity (the *average* percentage of R&D expenditures over sales for the last three years) as inputs for knowledge creation and innovation is self-evident.

Naturally, we do not pretend that the aforementioned variables are the only, or even the best, measures that could be used as indicators of knowledge intensity; we simply contend that, within our particular context and data at hand, they represent reasonably faithfully the latent concept of interest.

3.2.3 Innovation performance

The definition and measurement of *innovation performance* dimension is based on fairly standard variables similar to those employed in the Community Innovation Survey (CIS). Taken together they capture various aspects of innovation performance, including product, process and organizational innovation, and methods of intellectual property protection.

Product innovation is measured with variables capturing both the presence and degree of novelty of product innovation that had occurred in the three years previous to the survey. All innovation performance variables are binary (yes/no) ones.

3.3 Variables used for validation

In order to assess the validity of the proposed taxonomy of KIE derived from the above variables, we rely on a set of variables that have not been used in building the firm clusters but are expected to vary across them. For this reason we use variables indicative of various aspects of a firm's founding motives, capabilities and competitive strategy (internal factors) and performance. These variables can be assumed to vary across groups of KIE firms. For example, if a cluster is made up of young firms exhibiting high knowledge assets and innovative performance we would expect that its firms will develop to a greater extent R&D, product development and networking capabilities compared to their less KIE counterparts. Furthermore, such a cluster is expected to exhibit better performance in terms of growth, sales and exports.

The specific variables used to validate the clusters are as follows:

Founding motives are measured using a Likert-type scale (1: Not important; 5: Extremely important) that asks respondents to '*indicate the importance of various factors related to the formation of the venture*'. Confirmatory factor analysis revealed the following three dimensions (see Annex for CFA results):

- *Founding motive-technical knowledge*: this dimension is related with technical/engineering and design knowledge in the field.
- *Founding motive-market knowledge and networking*: this sub-scale reflects the importance of knowledge of the market and of networks built in the past.
- *Founding motive-opportunity*: perception of opportunities deriving from technical change and new market needs.

Following is a set of variables measuring various aspects of the firm's competitive behaviour. First, we measure the firm's dynamic capabilities using multi-item Likert type scales as reflected in three constructs:

Product development capability represents the firm's capacity to offer novel products, adapt its offerings to the needs of specific market segments and effective marketing and promotion.

R&D and alliance-related related capability captures the importance of R&D activities as well as of partnerships and networking with scientific research organizations.

Networking capability was measured by operations regarding market processes such as collecting information about competitors, accessing distribution channels, exploring export opportunities, advertising and promotion. Regarding the technology side of the networking capability we employed variables assessing the network's impact on the development of new products/services, the management of production and operations, as well as the easy access to skilled personnel. Finally in order to catch the economic and more generic value of networking we used variables assessing networks' assistance in obtaining business loans and attracting funds or providing support on legal issues.

The three multi-item scales pertaining to dynamic capabilities were tested following Confirmatory Factors Analysis (CFA) in order to confirm that particular items relate to a specific dynamic capabilities construct.

Next, we used two variables to measure strategic behaviour: *strategy* and *sales in international markets*. Strategy is an indicator variable showing whether the firm follows a low-cost, differentiation or focus strategy. Sales in international markets is a continuous variable measuring the percentage of sales obtained in international markets in the last three years. It reflects the degree to which a firm pursues opportunities beyond domestic markets.

Third, we measured venture performance with two variables. The first is a subjective, single item measure that asks respondents to indicate their venture's *average profit* over the past three years. The response scale ranges from 1 (losses) to 8 (more than €5 million). The second is a continuous variable measuring *average sales growth* over the past three years. Because the empirical distribution was highly non-linear with extreme skewness and kurtosis, we transformed this variable to range between 1 (negative growth) and 10 (corresponding to the 10–90 per cent percentiles of the empirical distribution).

4 Empirical results and discussion

Our analysis consists of two steps. We first applied cluster analysis techniques to build a firm taxonomy based on the characteristics of KIE and then we used analysis of variance and χ^2 tests in order to: (a) further test the validity of the proposed taxonomy using additional variables to those originally used to form the proposed clusters or groups; (b) examine how new ventures of different knowledge intensity and innovative performance are distributed across different institutional and industrial contexts.

4.1 Empirical taxonomy

Two remarks are in order here. First, all variables used for clustering (see below) are binary, including those that are originally operationalized as Likert-type scales (e.g. employee training) or as continuous (e.g. percentage of full-time employees with PhD degrees). This is due to technical reasons. Recall that most of our measures on innovation performance are binary. Clustering algorithms require a measure of (dis)similarity among cases (in our case: new ventures), and this typically necessitates that all variables are on the same metric. Since it would not be possible to transform binary variables into interval ones, we opted for the opposite. For interval variables (i.e. those ranging from 1 to 5) the transformed dichotomy took the value of one when the original value was greater or equal to 4 (and zero otherwise), whereas for continuous variables the lower threshold for one was a value greater or equal to the 75 per cent percentile of the empirical distribution (and zero otherwise).

Second, the reader may notice that some variables that might seem obvious to include in the clustering procedure are missing from Table 4.3 below. This basically concerns two measures of innovation performance (i.e. percentage of innovative sales and percentage of innovative services). Again the reason for not including these two variables is technical. There are simply too many missing values for these variables, and therefore their inclusion would greatly reduce the sample size. With the variables described in the above section, we have 3,226 firms with complete data.

We are interested to determine whether there exists a meaningful grouping in our observations on the basis of their similarity in knowledge assets and innovation performance as reflected by the (binary) variables identified above. We performed Kmeans cluster analysis with the STATA 12 software, employing the simple matching binary similarity coefficient (Sokal and Michener, 1958). Kmeans is a partition method that attempts to break the observations into a distinct number of non-overlapping groups (clusters). The main problem with cluster analysis is to decide on the number of clusters, to balance the need to represent the data appropriately and, at the same time, to keep the data manageable. Determining the 'correct' number of groups in one's data is an inherently subjective exercise. We set out to examine solutions comprising between two and six clusters. As an aid to the researcher, STATA provides two indexes: the Calinski and Harabasz (1974) pseudo-F index and the Duda-Hart (2001) index. Both these statistics favoured the two-cluster solution, suggesting the three-cluster as the second best (the remaining 4-, 5- and 6-cluster solutions provided much worse indexes). Upon inspection, we decided that the most meaningful grouping in our data is given by the 3-cluster solution. The descriptive statistics on each of the three groups are given in columns (2) to (4) of Table 4.3. Column (5) gives the sample means.

As can be seen from Table 4.3, we distinguish between 'modest KIE', 'all-around KIE' and 'world-class KIE' firms. The 'modest KIE' group is the most highly populated in our sample (i.e. 2,012 firms). Its main characteristic is that none of the means of the variables used in cluster analysis is greater than the respective sample average.[2] Apparently, this group of firms do engage in knowledge-intensive activities and innovation. For instance, they are the second best group in terms of process and organizational innovations outperforming the 'world class' KIE ventures. However, they generally lag behind in most variables compared to the other two groups. For example, only 44 per cent of firms belonging into this group have introduced product innovation in the last three years compared to 100 per cent for both remaining groups.

'All-around KIE' (AaKIE) firms are distinguished by their balanced emphasis on knowledge-seeking activities (both in-house and from external sources), on new-to-market product innovation, and on process *and* organizational innovation. Interestingly, initial knowledge stock, as reflected in founders' average educational attainment, does not seem exceptional; only 20 per cent of these firms report founders with graduate degrees or higher compared to 57 per cent in the last group. The all-around KIE group of firms also do not patent as much as world-class KIE, and more generally they do not emphasize much intellectual property protection, again as compared to the last group, except for lead-time advantages.

Table 4.3 Cluster analysis results

KIE variables	Modest KIE	All-around KIE	World-class KIE	Total sample
Knowledge-intensive activities				
Knowledge/External-Industry (0/1)	0.428	**0.642**	0.279	0.454
Knowledge/External-Science (0/1)	0.059	**0.186**	0.066	0.088
Knowledge/In-house R&D (0/1)	0.415	**0.736**	0.706	0.531
Knowledge/External-Open sources (0/1)	0.177	**0.421**	0.240	0.242
Knowledge/Participation in collaborative (0/1)	0.069	**0.241**	0.117	0.115
'Initial conditions'				
F-team avrg edu attainment (0/1)	0.249	0.199	**0.567**	0.285
% capital from venture capital (0/1)	0.012	0.016	**0.068**	0.0214
Human capital and innovation 'input'				
% ft employees: Graduate degree (0/1)	0.124	0.058	**0.246**	0.127
% ft employees: PhD degree (0/1)	0.061	0.116	**0.246**	0.101
Employee training (0/1)	0.360	**0.600**	0.464	0.430
RD intensity (0/1)	0.167	0.470	**0.548**	0.293
Innovation performance				
Introduced new goods/services last 3 years	0.440	**1**	**1**	0.651
New-to-firm (0/1)	0.206	0.283	0.168	0.218
New-to-market (0/1)	0.178	0.476	0.433	0.284
New-to-world (0/1)	0.057	0.241	0.398	0.150
Introduced process innov last 3 years	0.350	**0.817**	0.292	0.446
Introduced logistics innov last 3 years	0.275	**0.795**	0.113	0.368
Introduced innov in support activities last 3 years	0.406	**0.935**	0.331	0.514
Improved knowl mngmt systems last 3 years	0.414	**0.869**	0.417	0.517
Changes in mngnt structure last 3 years	0.258	**0.583**	0.228	0.327
IPR last 3 years: patents	0.026	0.213	**0.304**	0.110
IPR last 3 years: trademarks	0.117	0.519	**0.536**	0.271
IPR last 3 years: copyrights	0.072	0.311	**0.405**	0.176
IPR last 3 years: confidentiality	0.134	0.642	**0.932**	0.369
IPR last 3 years: secrecy	0.056	0.510	**0.799**	0.270
IPR last 3 years: lead_time	0.138	0.757	**0.692**	0.361
IPR last 3 years: complexity	0.088	0.612	**0.704**	0.299
Observations	2012	727	487	3226

In contrast, new-to-world product innovation, IPR protection and knowledge creation stemming from highly educated founders and human capital seem to be the distinguishing marks of the last group, hence the label 'world-class KIE' (WcKIE). WcKIE ventures appear to lag behind the other two groups in terms of process innovation implying a distinctive prevalence of product over process and organizational innovation. It is interesting to note that in this group, firms depend mainly on in-house knowledge creation and less so on knowledge from external sources (the latter characterizing AaKIE). It is perhaps no coincidence that this group is the least populated in terms of number of firms: 487 compared to 727 for 'all-around KIE' and 2,012 for the 'modest KIE'.

What is the general picture emerging from these results? Are there KIE ventures in our sample? The answer, we believe, is yes; in fact we find three clear varieties of ventures that are exhibiting different degrees of 'knowvation'. The AaKIE group appears to have a more balanced emphasis on different dimensions of innovation and relies basically on external knowledge seeking, while the WcKIE emphasizes new-to-world innovation drawing from in-house knowledge which in turn draws from high quality human capital (both in terms of founders and workforce). In addition, we find a third group of new ventures that although involved in diverse knowledge seeking and innovative activities, generally demonstrates a lower degree of both knowledge intensity and innovation performance as compared to the other two. In terms of product innovation, the 'modest KIE' group, focuses mainly on new-to-firm products and draws on external knowledge sources such as customers and suppliers. At the same time it is close to the average sample and well above WcKIE ventures as regards process and organizational innovations.

A further assessment of the validity of clusters and the proposed KIE taxonomy can be achieved by exploiting variables not used to form the clusters, but known or expected to vary across them (Milligan and Cooper, 1987; Hair *et al.*, 1998, p. 501).

Specifically, we examine differences with respect to three sets of external variables used for this purpose: (a) motives related with forming the venture; (b) a host of internal factors (e.g. dynamic capabilities, strategy, etc.); and (c) firm performance.

We performed simple analysis of variance to produce the results shown in Table 4.4. We report the means of interval or continuous variables (column percentages for nominal variables) for each venture type, together with the sample means. The last column shows the number of observations available for each comparison, together with the probability level of significant difference. Notice that because the number of available observations is generally large (minimum 1,911; maximum 3,226) even small differences across venture types are statistically significant. In general, the analysis of variance indicates significant differences across the three groups in all variables. The nature of these differences is consistent with the characterization of clusters in our taxonomy.

Table 4.4 Comparative analysis of venture types

	Modest KIE	All-around KIE	World-class KIE	Total	Observations
Factors important for firm formation					
Technical knowledge	3.305	3.758	3.603	3.452	3,224(***)
Market knowledge and social networks	3.855	4.071	3.884	3.908	3,223(***)
Identification of opportunities	2.738	3.360	3.058	2.926	3,224(***)
Internal factors					
Capability/product related	3.545	4.105	3.924	3.728	3,226(***)
Networking capability	2.832	3.475	2.966	2.997	3,226(***)
Capability/RD and alliance related	2.458	3.203	3.136	2.728	3,226(***)
Strategy: low cost	19.28%	12.24%	7.19%		
Differentiation	58.00%	55.43%	60.57%		
Focus	22.71%	32.32%	32.24%		
Total	100%	100%	100%		
% sales in international market	11.55	18.06	25.06	15.05	3,226(***)
Performance					
Avrg. profit (2007–2009)	2.380	2.677	2.538	2.470	2,859(***)
Avrg. growth sales (quartile)	5.042	5.853	6.088	5.385	2,979(***)

In terms of founding motives and other internal factors, such as those characterizing competitive behaviour more KIE ventures also stand out compared to 'modest KIE' somewhat more clearly. The results in Table 4.4 show founding motives – originating in technical knowledge, market knowledge and networking, and in the perception of opportunities to be more strongly associated with KIE firms exhibiting a higher degree of knowledge seeking and innovative activities. It may be argued that 'modest KIE' are more 'traditional' ventures in the sense that they are not found on the basis of discovery of some form of latent opportunity to be exploited. Notice that founding motives, as measured in our survey, reflect both 'technology push' and 'demand pull' conditions. However, it also be noted that the average score on market knowledge as a founding motive is not significantly different between 'modest KIE' and WcKIE firms indicating that both groups are equally motivated by this type of expertise. More-over, and perhaps surprisingly, we also find that technical knowledge as a motive for founding is stronger for AaKIE than WcKIE (but again the pair-wise difference is not significant). Overall, however, the general impression is that these two groups of KIE ventures are driven more towards exploit-ing opportunities than the 'modest KIE' group, which is what we would expect, given our definition of KIE.

Turning to dynamic capabilities and strategic behaviour, the results are again as we would expect. Our findings suggest that more knowledge-intensive firms, i.e. firms that have more knowledge assets and exhibit better innovative performance (characterized as 'world-class KIE' or 'all-around KIE') have developed to a greater extent all types of dynamic cap-abilities as compared to their less knowledge-intensive counterparts. They have built more strongly their product-related capabilities, they engage more strongly in networking activities and, of course, spend significantly more on R&D. In addition, more KIE ventures tend to pursue differenti-ation and focus strategies more intensively as compared to the 'modest KIE' group, which shows more emphasis on low cost strategies. Similarly, 'world-class' and 'all-around' KIE ventures are more heavily geared towards international markets, presumably based on their more innovative profile and they seem to enjoy higher performance both in terms of average profits and average sales growth rate.

4.2 How are KIE ventures distributed across different sectors and National Innovation Systems?

In this section we will examine whether the three new venture groups iden-tified using the proposed taxonomy are distributed evenly across different types of institutional context. Our main interest lies in examining preval-ence rates across different types of industries and different National Innovation Systems (NIS). Should we find statistically significant differ-ences in the concentration of ventures in specific types of institutional (and industry) settings, that would mean context does indeed influence the presence of KIE.

Table 4.5 presents the results of simple Chi-square tests, where we show the prevalence rates of the three types of ventures identified with cluster analysis (i.e. 'modest KIE', AaKIE and WcKIE) across: (a) different NIS, and (b) different types of industries (classified according to their technological content).

To construct a *NIS indicator* we used the Innovation Union Scoreboard (IUS, 2011)[3] classification of NIS, which is based on a wide variety of innovation-related measures at the national level of analysis. Given the countries present in our sample, the indicator takes the following values: (1) 'Modest' innovators (i.e. Croatia[4]); (2) 'Moderate' innovators (i.e. Czech Republic; Greece; Italy; and Portugal); (3) 'Followers' (i.e. France and UK); and (4) 'Leaders' (i.e. Denmark; Sweden; and Germany).

The Chi-square tests show that, within the institutional and industry settings examined, the distribution of firms across the clusters is not uniform. Hence, context does seem to matter, but how exactly? We begin with the distribution of KIE ventures across different NIS (panel A).

The best way to interpret the results presented in Table 4.5 is by comparing the percentage in any given cell (e.g. 66.5 per cent for low-tech and 'modest KIE') against the corresponding 'total' (i.e. 62.4 per cent). What does this 66.5 per cent tell us? It says that 66.5 per cent of the sample firms belonging to the low-tech group of sectors are found in the 'modest KIE' group, and this is higher than the 62.4 per cent of all firms in the sample that are classified as 'modest KIE'. It appears that there is a higher concentration of 'modest KIE' firms in the low-tech industry than would be expected should the firms be distributed evenly across categories.[5] To ease reading the results in Table 4.5, figures higher than expected are in bold characters, whereas percentages lower than expected are in italics.

Looking at panel A, which shows the association between KIE and NIS, we find statistically significant differences. The results show that: (a) world-class KIE are mostly found in 'leader' economies (i.e. Denmark, Germany and Sweden) as would be expected; (b) in contrast, in these countries we find fewer all-around KIE than expected; (c) these firms are found mostly in modest (i.e. Croatia) and moderate (i.e. Czech Republic, Greece, Italy and Portugal) economies; (d) and – surprisingly, there is a higher than normal concentration of 'modest KIE' firms in 'follower' economies (follower economies are second only to leader economies in terms of their National Innovation Systems). *The general message therefore is that ventures exhibiting higher degrees of 'knowvation' are mostly to be found in leading economies and (surprisingly) in modest and moderate (in terms of NIS classification) countries. On the other hand, 'modest KIE' firms can also be found in the UK and France which are economies closely following the innovation leading countries.*

Table 4.5 Distribution of KIE venture types across different types of context

	Modest KIE (%)	AaKIE (%)	Wc KIE (%)	Total (%)	Observations
National Innovation Systems					
CR	47.4	**42.9**	9.7	100.0	175
CZ/GR/IT/PT	58.3	**33.4**	8.3	100.0	1230
FR/UK	**72.9**	11.6	15.4	100.0	868
DK/GER/SV	60.8	14.7	**24.6**	100.0	953
Total	62.4	22.5	15.1	100.0	3226
Pearson $\chi^2(6) = 291.5104$ Pr $= 0.000$					
Technology class					
Low-tech manufacturing	**66.5**	25.5	8.0	100.0	1066
Medium low-tech manufacturing	**67.0**	28.8	4.2	100.0	212
Medium high-tech manufacturing	53.8	30.2	16.0	100.0	262
High-tech manufacturing	45.6	23.3	**31.1**	100.0	103
KI high-tech services	48.4	24.3	**27.3**	100.0	506
KI market services	**67.6**	15.6	16.8	100.0	1077
Total	62.4	22.5	15.1	100.0	3226
Pearson $\chi^2(10) = 191.891$ Pr $= 0.000$					

Finally, panel B shows results in connection to the association between KIE and industry type. Again the findings show significant differences in prevalence rates across industries. Specifically, we find that: (a) 'modest KIE' firms are more concentrated in low-tech manufacturing, medium-low manufacturing and KI market services; (b) world-class KIE are basically to be found in high-tech manufacturing, KI high-tech services and in KI market services (and correspondingly are less concentrated than expected in low-tech and medium-low manufacturing); and (c) all-around innovators are more prevalent than expected in almost all types of industries, except for high-tech manufacturing. *In general, therefore, industry context also seems to play a role in KIE, with the qualification that all-around innovators appear to be spread in somewhat higher proportions than expected across all industries except in high-tech manufacturing.*

5 Concluding remarks

In this study we were interested in developing a useful taxonomy of young ventures on the basis of entrepreneurial behaviour. More specifically, we have attempted to shed new light on questions related to the phenomenon of knowledge-intensive entrepreneurship, which is understood here to involve new ventures that are highly innovative as a consequence of their being engaged in knowledge-intensive activities. A useful taxonomy is one that reduces the complexity of empirical phenomena to a few and easy to remember categories. Thus a taxonomy of young firms taking into account their knowledge intensity and innovation performance provides an empirically based framework that may help to refine and further build a theory of knowledge-intensive entrepreneurship as well as to guide related policies.

Using data from more than 4,004 new ventures, we first sought to identify firms in our sample that could be characterized by similar traits in terms of their entrepreneurial behaviour. Specifically, employing cluster analysis we investigated whether there exists a meaningful grouping in our observations on the basis of their similarities in various measures of knowledge assets and innovation performance. The results obtained showed the presence of three unique groups of firms. The first of these, termed 'world-class KIE', emphasizes new-to-world innovation drawing from in-house knowledge which in turn is based on high quality human capital (both in terms of founders and workforce), while the second, labelled 'all-around KIE', shows a more balanced emphasis on different dimensions of innovation and relies basically on external knowledge seeking. The third group, called 'modest KIE', appears to be mainly pursuing new-to-firm innovation drawing from industry knowledge sources while it generally lags behind the other two groups both in terms of knowledge seeking and innovative activities.

Our results confirm that the proposed taxonomy of ventures that is based on differences as defined by their knowledge intensity and innovative output can also be extended to map differences in founding motives, capabilities, business strategies and firm performance. These particular variables are important not only because they confirm the validity of the explored taxonomy but also because we find that differences in these variables can systematically be linked to differences in knowledge intensity and innovative performance helping us better understand additional aspects of KIE and refine its measurement.

Our taxonomy suggests that different sources of knowledge, different innovation strategies and, thus, different pathways of development of KIE ventures can be identified. All too often entrepreneurship and innovation policy that overlooks the diversity of paths toward successful innovation and growth slips into myopic strategies related to oversimplified quantitative targets such as R&D spending and the like (Srholec and Verspagen, 2012). However, such a policy framework for KIE is likely to neglect the essence of innovation process in many ventures. For instance, as external knowledge sources appear to be conducive to the identification of new technology and market opportunities for young firms, policy measures should focus on the development of organizational capabilities and management skills that enable the companies to recognize important external knowledge, combine it with already existing internally generated knowledge and exploit it in a beneficial way (Hirsch-Kreinsen and Schwinge, 2011). In practice, this can be achieved by introducing and promoting advanced management methods and work methods conducive to innovation and at the same time upgrading already existing R&D-related activities or even introducing limited internal R&D capacity.

Next we examined whether our three varieties of firms are distributed evenly across different types of institutional settings. Our main interest here lies in the notion of National Innovation Systems (NIS), which denotes different socioeconomic configurations that, in theory, provide distinct types of institutional comparative advantages to firms operating within their boundaries. Simple analysis of variance, categorizing our sample countries on the basis of their national innovation systems, showed that world-class KIE ventures are mostly concentrated in leading economies (leading in the sense of having developed an advanced innovation system). Somewhat surprisingly, all-around innovators are basically found in countries with modest and moderate innovation systems. However, it should be taken into account that while the strategic preferences of firms are up to a certain extent determined by their institutional environment, within a particular setting (e.g. a particular NIS type or a variety of capital) there are variations in firms that can be explained as a function of the diverse models of action chosen by entrepreneurs through the acquisition, combination and recombination of resources to exploit profit opportunities (Allen, 2006; van der Walt, 2010). This practically means that even in countries characterized as moderate or modest innovators, i.e. countries with unbalanced research and innovation systems, entrepreneurs are certainly able to pursue opportunities for developing knowledge-intensive activities. At the same time, the modest and moderate innovators exhibit the highest innovative performance growth rates among the EU 27 indicating a clear catch-up to the higher performance level of both the innovation leaders and innovation followers (IUS, 2011), justifying, at least partly, the increased presence of all-around innovators in these two NIS groups.

Finally, we examined the distribution of young ventures across different types of industries, categorized according to their technological content. The findings indicate that industry context also plays a significant role, but this concerns mainly world-class KIE. This type of venture is basically concentrated in high-tech manufacturing, and knowledge-intensive services industries. On the other hand, all-around innovators are more or less equally spread across all different types of industries. According to these results, KIE is only partly industry specific. Our findings point out that knowledge-intensive does not equate with high-tech manufacturing. Therefore, contrary to the stereotypical view that low-tech sectors offer limited opportunities for KIE activities and innovation (von Tunzelmann and Acha, 2005) our analysis indicates that knowledge-intensive firms can also be found in services and most importantly in low-tech manufacturing sectors. These findings are in line with the case study work undertaken in the context of the AEGIS project which confirms that KIE opportunities do exist in traditional sectors arising from the fact that competitive pressures force actors to modify their role and to adopt an increasingly reflective position towards established practices seeking at the same time to break new ground regarding innovations. Furthermore, the AEGIS case study findings indicate that impact of KIE on existing mature sectoral structures can be quite significant, offer new possibilities for further entrepreneurial activities and in consequence lead to the sustainable improvement of the competitive position of European traditional sectors and firms (Hirsch-Kreinsen and Schwinge, 2011). In addition, our findings also suggest that 'modest KIE' firms (at least in terms of the proposed taxonomy) can also be found in high-technology sectors. Thus, our findings suggest that an aggregate sectoral perspective does not take into consideration important differences at the firm level. It is worth noting that within an industry there tends to be a wide variation across firms in terms of their R&D intensities, so that it is common to find low-tech firms in high-tech industries and vice versa (Kirner *et al.*, 2009).

Our findings suggest that policy makers should increase their awareness with respect to low-tech industries. They emphasize that measures towards promoting KIE should not only be focused on high-tech industries as low- and medium low-tech sectors and firms – contrary to the established scientific and popular beliefs – appear to get heavily involved in knowledge-seeking activities and exhibit innovation potential. Effective entrepreneurship and innovation policy needs to take into account the firm-level variety and at the same time the specific environmental conditions in which companies operate.

Annex I

Table 41.1 Description of key constructs (CFA results)

	Items
CONSTRUCTS	
Knowledge intensity	
Knowledge/External-Industry	Clients or customers Suppliers Competitors
Knowledge/External-Science	Public research institutes Universities External commercial labs/R&D firms/technical institutes
Knowledge--In-house R&D	In-house (know-how, R&D laboratories in your firm)
Knowledge/External-Open sources	Trade fairs, conferences and exhibitions Scientific journals and other trade or technical publications
Knowledge/Participation in collaborative...	Participation in nationally funded research programmes Participation in EU funded research programmes (Framework Programmes)
Important factors for firm formation	
Technical knowledge	Technical/engineering knowledge in the field Design knowledge
Market knowledge and social networks	Knowledge of the market Networks built during previous career
Identification of opportunities	Opportunity deriving from technological change Opportunity deriving from a new market need Opportunity deriving from new regulations or institutional requirements
Firm dynamic capabilities	
Product development capability	Capability to offer novel products/services Capacity to adapt the products/services to the specific needs of different customers/market niches Marketing and promotion activities
R&D and alliance capability	R&D activities Establishment of alliances/partnerships with other firms Networking with scientific research organizations (universities, institutes, etc.)
Networking	Selecting suppliers Recruiting skilled labour Collecting information about competitors Accessing distribution channels Assistance in obtaining business loans/attracting funds Advertising and promotion Developing new products/services Managing production and operations Assistance in arranging taxation or other legal issues Exploring export opportunities

Notes

1 The term 'all-around' is a metaphor drawn from basketball. The all-around basketball players have a combination of speed, agility, jumping ability, strength, power and conditioning. The combination of these skills allows them to be all-around players, able to perform the various actions required during the game-shooting, dribbling, playing defence and grabbing rebounds.
2 Note that in Table 4.3, means are in bold when they are greater than the overall mean. Also note that because variables are binary their means represent the percent of firms *within each group* that score one in any given variable.
3 Innovation Union Scoreboard, 2011, http://ec.europa.eu/enterprise/policies/innovation/files/ius-2011_en.pdf.
4 Croatia is not included in the Innovation Union Scoreboard report. We assume that Croatia's innovation system falls within the 'Modest' category.
5 Statistically speaking, 'evenly' means: according to the marginal percentages. Put differently, since 62.4 per cent of the sample belongs to the 'modest KIE' group, we would expect the percentage of modest KIE groups *for each industry* to be around 62 per cent.

References

Allen, M.C. (2006), *The Varieties of Capitalism Paradigm: Explaining Germany's Comparative Advantage?* New York: Palgrave Macmillan.
Archibugi, D. (2001), 'Pavitt's taxonomy sixteen years on: a review article', *Economic Innovation and New Technology*, 10, pp. 415–425.
Audretsch, D.B. and Turik, A.R. (2000), 'Capitalism and democracy in the 21st century: from the managed to the entrepreneurial economy', *Journal of Evolutionary Economics*, 10, pp. 17–34.
Autio, E. and Acs, Z. (2007), 'Individual and country-level determinants of growth aspiration in new ventures', (interactive paper), *Frontiers of Entrepreneurship Research*, 27(19), Article 2. Available http://digitalknowledge.babson.edu/fer/vol27/iss19/2.
Calinski, T. and Harabasz, J. (1974), 'A dendrite method for cluster analysis', *Communications in Statistics*, 3(1), pp. 1–27.
De Jong, J.P.J. and Marsili, O. (2006), 'The fruit flies of innovation: a taxonomy of innovative small firms', *Research Policy*, 35, pp. 213–229.
Delmar, F. and Davidsson, P. (2000), 'Where do they come from? Prevalence and characteristics of nascent entrepreneurs', *Entrepreneurship and Regional Development*, 12(1), pp. 1–23.
Delmar, F. and Wennberg, K. (2010), 'The knowledge intensive sector: theoretical concerns, research design and data'. In: F. Delmar and K. Wennberg (eds) *Knowledge Intensive Entrepreneurship: The Birth, Growth and Demise of Entrepreneurial Firms*, Cheltenham, UK: Edward Elgar.
Duda, R.O., Hart, P.E. and Stork, D.G. (2001), *Pattern Classification and Scene Analysis*, USA: A Wiley Interscience Publication.
Fagerberg, J., Mowery, D.C. and Nelson, R.R. (eds) (2005), *The Oxford Handbook of Innovation*, Oxford: Oxford University Press.
Freeman, C. and Soete, L. (1997), *The Economics of Industrial Innovation*, 3rd edn, Cambridge, MA: MIT Press.
Gartner, W.B. (1988), 'Who is the entrepreneur? is the wrong question', *American Journal of Small Business*, 12(4), pp. 11–32.

Gartner, W.B. and Carter, N.M. (2003), 'Entrepreneurial behavior and firm organizing processes'. In: Z.J Acs and D.B. Audretsch (eds) *Handbook of Entrepreneurship Research*, New York: Springer.

Hair, J.F., Anderson, R.E., Tatham, R.L. and Black, W.C. (1998), *Multivariate Data Analysis*, 5th edn, Englewood Cliffs, NJ: Prentice Hall.

Henrekson, M. and Johansson, D. (2010), 'Gazelles as job creators: a survey and interpretation of the evidence', *Small Business Economics*, 35(2), pp. 227–244.

Hirsch-Kreinsen, H. and Schwinge, I. (2011), 'Knowledge-intensive entrepreneurship and innovativeness in traditional industries: conceptual framework and empirical findings', Deliverable 1.3.1, AEGIS project funded by FP7.

Kirner, E., Kinkel, S. and Jaeger, A. (2009), 'Innovation paths and the innovation performance of low-tech firms: an empirical analysis of German industry', *Research Policy*, 38(3), pp. 447–458.

Landstrom, H. and Astrom, F. (2011), 'Who's asking the right question? Patterns and diversity in the literature of new venture creation'. In: K. Hindle and K. Klyver (eds) *Handbook of Research on New Venture Creation*, Cheltenham: UK: Edward Elgar.

Malerba, F. and Brusoni, S. (eds) (2007), *Perspectives on Innovation*, Cambridge: Cambridge University Press.

Malerba, F. and McKelvey, M. (2010), 'Conceptualizing knowledge-intensive entrepreneurship: concepts and models', Deliverable 1.1.1, AEGIS project funded by FP7.

Milligan, G.K. and Cooper, M.C. (1987), 'Methodology review: clustering methods', *Applied Psychological Management*, 11(4), pp. 329–354.

Pavitt, K. (1998), 'Technologies, products and organization in the innovating firm: what Adam Smith tells us and Joseph Schumpeter doesn't', *Industrial and Corporate Change*, 7, pp. 433–452.

Rich, P. (1992), 'The organizational taxonomy: definition and design', *Academy of Management Review*, 17(4), pp. 758–781

Robb, A.J. Ballou, J., DesRoches, D., Potter, F., Zhao, Z. and Reedy, E.J. (2009), *An Overview of the Kauffman Firm Survey – Results from the 2004–2007 Data*, Kansas City: Ewing Marion Kauffman Foundation.

Rosegger, G. (1996), *The Economics of Production and Innovation*, 3rd edn, Oxford: Butterworth-Heinemann.

Schramm, C.J. (2005), 'Building entrepreneurial economies', *Transition Studies Review*, 12(1), pp. 163–171.

Shane, S. (2003), *A General Theory of Entrepreneurship: The individual-Opportunity Nexus*, Cheltenham, UK and Northampton, MA, USA: Edward Elgar Publishing.

Sokal, R.R. and Michener, C.D. (1958), 'A statistical method for evaluating systematic relationships', *Univ. Kans. Sci. Bull.*, 38, pp. 1409–1438.

Srholec, M. and Verspagen, B. (2012), 'The Voyage of the Beagle into innovation: exploration on heterogeneity, selection and sectors', *Industrial and Corporate Change*, 21(5), pp. 1221–1253.

van der Walt, J. (2010), 'Entrepreneurship and the varieties of capitalism paradigm'. Working Paper No. 10–10, Mercatus Center at George Mason University.

von Tunzelmann, N. and Acha, V. (2005), 'Innovation in "low-tech" sectors'. In: J. Fagerberg, D.C. Mowery and R.R. Nelson (eds) *The Oxford Handbook of Innovation*, Oxford: Oxford University Press.

Wong, P.K., Ho, Y.P. and Autio, E. (2005), 'Entrepreneurship, innovation and economic growth: evidence from GEM data', *Small Business Economics*, 24(3), pp. 335–350.

5 Managing risk in new entrepreneurial ventures[1]

Nicholas S. Vonortas and YoungJun Kim

1 Introduction

Risk is pervasive in human activity. The most commonly accepted definition is that risk is the potential that a certain action will lead to an undesirable effect. While the word risk has a negative connotation in the English language, undesirable effects can be either positive or negative (Leitch, 2010). In the business sector, risks have real monetary and operational impact. Every enterprise, by joining the market, implicitly agrees to carry risk as a matter of business. Risks vary by sector, by type of organizational structure and by (perceived) severity. Experts seem to agree on two broad types of risk: diversifiable and systematic. The former type a firm can hedge away, or reassign (outsource); the latter it cannot and must be dealt explicitly within a firm's business plan. Both kinds of risk must be taken into account in a management plan, but are treated differently. New ventures typically carry higher risks for investors.

Organizations have stakeholders and customers. A stakeholder is 'any individual whose personal welfare is affected by the success of the organization' (Culp, 2001). Customers are the demand side of the equation. Depending on the structure of the firm, customers and stakeholders have slightly different roles in the running and risk assessment of a business. The customers and stakeholders themselves can also add to the risk incurred by doing business. For example, if customers expect a certain level of service or quality of product, and the product is not up to expectations, the business may expect a high level of returns and dissatisfaction. This does not bode well for the future of the venture. Stakeholders usually have a financial stake in the company. Depending on the financial structure (Ben-Ari and Vonortas, 2007), stakeholders may require a portion of the returns on a certain schedule. Without an adequate discussion of the firm's risk and realistic projections for economic success, these obligations to stakeholders may not be met.

Aligning the goals of stakeholders is critical to determining the level of risk the organization is willing to take, and how it will be managed. It would be fair to say that the literature is still undecided on a robust list of well-defined risks for businesses: definitions and specific types of risk abound. Ebben (2005), for example, lists five types:

- Market risk: Is the market ready for entry? Is there demand for the product?
- Operational risk: Is the business set up effective internally to deliver its goods?
- Financial model risk: Possibility the business won't work due to the numbers.
- Financial risk: Tangible value the investors lose if the business fails.
- Opportunity risk: The opportunity cost of the entrepreneur: What's the alternative to setting up the business in question?

In essence, such lists try to replicate business-making processes and capture the obstacles to a successful, profit-making business. For instance, even if the business is run well, has plenty of funding and makes a quality product, the market may be already saturated and carving a niche for your product is nearly impossible. This is an example of market risk, one that requires a skilled entrepreneur from the very beginning to realize the right moment to introduce a product or start a business.

This chapter investigates aspects of risk management in young entrepreneurial companies. In particular the chapter empirically relates various types of risk to risk-mitigation strategies of newly established knowledge-intensive enterprises (KIEs). We use a new important set of information on 4004 young businesses in ten European countries (AEGIS survey) to understand the important factors in their efforts to mitigate risk.

Straightforward data tabulation and t-tests indicate that a prevalent risk management procedure is the start-up of new companies in areas in which the entrepreneur has had significant prior experience. Extensive financial risk obliged the vast majority of our entrepreneurs to fund their new ventures through own funds. The vast majority of survey respondents reported heavy competition risk. Competition is present in terms of both quality and price. When rating the different factors that shape competitive advantage, the clear winner was the capacity to adapt products/services to customer needs, followed by product/service quality and novelty. Market risk/uncertainty was an important perceived obstacle to company growth, followed by funding difficulties (financial risk) and difficulties in recruiting high-skill employees (recruiting risk). Lack of technological know-how and technology risk/uncertainty were rated at the bottom of the obstacle list. A slew of external factors were considered important barriers for operating the company, including frequently changing taxation regulations, high tax rates, bureaucracy for permits and licences, poorly enforced competition legislation and weak intellectual property protection. These make up systematic risks that must be considered in the business plan.

Our empirical analysis indicated that the lesser obstacle, technology risk, is also the easiest to deal with. Companies treat technology risk as unsystematic (diversifiable), manage it actively and try to decrease it through networking. Timing risk is also diversifiable – depends largely on company circumstances – and is, thus, actively managed too. On the other hand, we find competition risk, market risk, financial risk and IPR risk apparently being considered systematic. Consequently they do not lend themselves easily to management. One should observe here that market risk and financial risk were placed (in that order) at the top of the list of the obstacles to a successful company operation. Networking appears to be a way companies try to defend against them as well as against IPR risk.

Within the examined population of relatively small KIEs, growing size is associated with higher/better risk management and, in conjunction to better educational background of the entrepreneurs, higher likelihood of networking.

Three important policy implications arise from this analysis. First, the government should primarily concentrate in assisting young entrepreneurial companies with factors that underlie systematic risks, i.e. risks that the companies cannot hedge or diversify. These include financial risk and IPR risk. Market risk and competition risk, on the other hand, while also perceived by companies as systematic, do not lend themselves easily to government intervention. Second, contrary to popular belief, on the basis of self-reported information there seems to be little perceived need for direct government intervention in alleviating technology risk for young KIEs. Finally, the government should also concentrate on the factors underlying recruitment risk, reportedly one of the most important obstacles for our firms' growth. This specifically refers to the availability of skilled personnel for hire.

The rest of the chapter is organized as follows. Section 2 deals with the concept of risk management and its significance for newly established companies. Section 3 uses the data of the AEGIS survey to reflect on certain aspects of risk and risk management in new knowledge-intensive enterprises in the European Union. Section 4 proceeds to the empirical analysis on the basis of this data. Finally, Section 5 concludes.

2 Concepts

2.1 Risk management

Risk management is the 'identification, assessment, and prioritization of risks followed by coordinated and economical application of resources to minimize, monitor, and control the probability and/or impact of unfortunate events or to maximize the realization of opportunities' (Hubbard, 2009: 46). Managing risk responsibly means developing a framework that is not too far on either side of cautiousness or carelessness (see Culp,

2001). It also means considering risk an integral part of corporate strategy and financing. Risk cannot be eliminated; rather, it must be managed. Three fallacies must be avoided: (1) risk is always bad; (2) some risks are so bad that they must be eliminated at all costs; and (3) playing it safe is the safest thing to do. If risk is thought of along the lines of any one of these fallacies, or even in combination, the value of risk management is lost.

Risk is neither good nor bad. It just exists, and depending on how it is managed, the outcome *becomes* either a hindrance or a boon. Eliminating certain risks at all costs probably creates more complications than if the risk had been managed properly in the first place. According to Culp (2001), risk must be viewed within the context of probability of the event happening *and* its consequences. The benefit and costs of risk reduction must be equalized, or at least the benefit must come out ahead. Deciding on a risk management concept that is woven throughout a business will facilitate such cost-benefit analysis. Firm values and priorities will drive the conceptualization of risk management in the firm.

The Geneva-based International Organization for Standardization addresses the issue of risk management standardization. In 2009, it published a new standard ISO 31000: Risk Management-Principles and Guidelines. ISO 31000 is designed to be the international standard for enterprise risk assessment (ERM) and functions as a best management practices document (Baker, 2011). ISO 31000 highlights the need for a formal internal process for identifying risk and then ways to assign that risk with a value (essentially risk triage).

Figure 5.1 illustrates the model risk management process as prescribed by ISO 31000. Note that (most of) the arrows connecting the various parts of the diagram point in both directions. Additionally, the process of risk assessment is continuous, with communication, consultation, monitoring and review throughout a firm's life. Risk management does not just identify risks; instead, it actively manages them.

Criticism has followed quickly. Some have said that the system turns a multifaceted conceptual issue into a numbers-oriented process. Others see discussion on human and cultural factors as not specific enough. In his analysis of the impacts of ISO 31000 Leitch (2010) tends to agree with many of these assessments. He finds many faults with the language used in the standard, citing them as too vague and not helpful for organizations seeking to improve upon their current risk management efforts. The consequences of risks can be *both* positive and negative and indeed the ISO 31000 attempts to craft a definition that addresses both sides. While this is an admirable attempt, the process is considered less successful when it comes to risk treatment. According to Leitch, a central problem with the new reference is that while it acknowledges that each organization is unique, it is trying to standardize to a fault.

A well-thought-out risk management plan can be critical to the future of either a current or forthcoming venture (Longenecker *et al.*, 2010). The

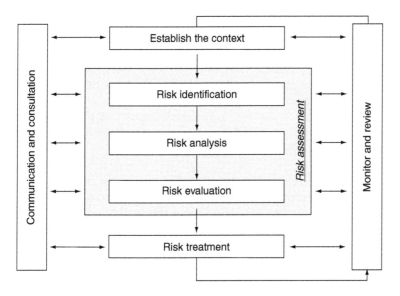

Figure 5.1 The risk management process of ISO31000:2009 (Purdy, 2010).

plan must concentrate on risk control – minimizing loss through prevention, avoidance and/or reduction. Learning from undesirable experiences is valuable to a venture's overall risk management plan. Showing progress in the way a firm thinks about and deals with risk (as evidenced by an updated risk management scheme) may attract more (and unique) investors (Ebben, 2005). The plan is one way to make a favourable impression on investors, who in turn may introduce entrepreneurs to their investor network (Haar *et al.*, 1988). This is of utmost importance when dealing with new entrepreneurial ventures.

2.2 New entrepreneurial ventures

Even successful established entrepreneurs can be hesitant to invest in new ventures they consider risky. The perception of risks by all parties related to a venture (entrepreneurs, investors, customers, partners, etc.) can vary widely. These variations can prove to be troublesome for funding purposes. Janney and Dess (2006) argue that traditional measures of risk do not work for new ventures. Conventional measures create the illusion that the entrepreneur is a greater risk-taker than others, which can scare off potential investors. Forlani and Mullins (2000) found that entrepreneurs were less likely to choose ventures that had high levels of variability but were more willing than average to take a greater (perceived) risk for the projection of a greater reward.[2]

There is a widespread perception among investors that investing in early stage technology-based firms carries higher risks than investing in non-technology ventures. This could in turn translate into lesser funding potential for the former firms (Ben-Ari and Vonortas, 2007; Macmillan *et al.*, 1985, 1987). If all the proposed value of a venture is contained in the head of one of its founders, prospective investors have a hard time projecting this knowledge into real profits.

In their analysis, Mason and Harrison (2004) argue that the perception of higher risks in technology-based ventures rests on the consideration of the following sources of risk:

- *Management risk*: technology entrepreneurs are likely to have excellent science/engineering credentials but be inexperienced in the commercial exploitation of technological innovations.
- *Agency risk*: Investors will encounter greater difficulties in undertaking due diligence and incur higher costs, on account of the newness and complexity of the technology, products and markets and, as a consequence, the greater scale of information gathering.
- *Market risk*: it is difficult for investors to assess the market potential for products that may not exist or which may create a new market.
- *Technological risk*: the technology is likely to be unproven and the application yet to be demonstrated; development may take longer than expected, it may not work or it may be superseded by competitors.
- *Valuation risk*: evaluation of new technology-based firms may be difficult because it is heavily dependent on the potential value of soft assets, notably patents, trademarks and human capital. Traditional financial-based valuation methods are likely to be inapplicable in such circumstances.
- *Project risk*: the speed of technological trajectories often requires rapid rate of commercial exploitation – and hence large injections of finance – before the advent of competitor products and/or redundancy.
- *Growth risk*: technology-based firms need to grow, internationalize and develop new products in a short time horizon. This places exceptional managerial, financial and technical demands on a new business.
- *Timing risk*: technology-based firms are often characterized by short 'windows of opportunity' such that they might be unsuccessful if they enter the market too late, or too early.

(Mason and Harrison, 2004: 317–318)

Some of these risks are more manageable (diversifiable) than others in the sense that they depend heavily on internal firm decisions. Such can be managerial risk, technology risk and growth risk. Others depend more on external factors to the company and may be described as systematic such as market risk, project risk and timing risk. To the best of our knowledge, no official classification exists reflecting the fact that a lot depends on the specific business of a company.

The interaction of various such sources of risk creates significant uncertainties about the outcomes of the new business (Gompers and Lerner, 2001) which leaves investors in technology-based firms facing high adverse selection risk. For instance, a combination of technology risk, project risk and timing risk often proves deadly. Or a combination of agency risk and growth risk can leave a prospective investor aghast with a scale problem of large costs of investment appraisal and monitoring (arguably a largely fixed cost) compared to the relatively small initial rounds of financing for new ventures.

Trying to diversify, investors will seek to invest a portion of their capital in seemingly high-risk ventures to capture 'high risk, high reward' payoffs. Those entering the high-tech field are more likely to be risk-takers and willing to assume higher risk for greater reward (Agarwal *et al.*, 2004). Entrepreneurial quality will play as big a role as any other factor in considering the possibilities of success of a start-up high-tech venture. Start-ups require the principal to invest time and resources into the product and push it through the market. Their entrepreneurial skill matters because successful strategies will differ between high- and low-tech ventures (Kataki, 2003). A firm's flexibility and ability to deliver product tailored to the client is a strong indicator of long-term survival. It is not a unique product that solely determines success. As globalization becomes more prevalent, the services attached to the product, unique or not, are the sought-after goods.

While there has been progress in thinking about business risk, however, its appraisal arguably remains more of an art than a science. Thus, in innovative ventures risk must be assigned at least partly subjectively. Reid and Smith (2008), for instance, suggest that mere categories such as 'high', 'medium' or 'low' may suffice. Moreover, risk appraisal must be customized: to some extent at least, risk should be conceptualized to match the specific firm in the specific sector.

In this chapter we take an explorative step in attempting to use self-reporting information from a recent business survey to point out evidence of risk management efforts in young knowledge-intensive enterprises. We do not examine these efforts in any great detail.

3 Data

3.1 AEGIS survey

The data used in this chapter comes from the AEGIS survey. The survey was launched in an attempt to identify motives, characteristics and patterns in the creation and growth of new firms which are based on the intensive use of knowledge and operate in both knowledge-intensive and low-tech sectors. It was carried out during Autumn 2010 and Spring 2011.

The survey recovered 4,004 fully completed questionnaires (about 300 variables) from an equal number of newly established knowledge-intensive enterprises (KIE) spread out in ten European countries (Croatia, Czech Republic, Denmark, France, Germany, Greece, Italy, Portugal, Sweden and the United Kingdom). Both manufacturing and service sectors were covered, including fourteen high- and low-tech manufacturing sectors and four knowledge-intensive business service sectors (KIBS).

The population of companies in these preselected sectors was created from the Amadeus business database with additional criteria of allocation among the ten countries in rough accordance to their relative size and income.[3] The starting population of 338,725 firms was allocated among high-tech manufacturing (4.9 per cent), low tech manufacturing (19.1 per cent) and KIBS (76 per cent). Multiple screenings left us with a sample of 12,824 companies that satisfied all criteria. All were contacted by telephone and completed the questionnaire online in their local language under the tutelage of expert interviewees. Of those contacted, the overall achieved response rate was 31.3 per cent (4,004 companies) which varied from 19.5 per cent in Sweden to 63.9 per cent in Croatia. Table 5.1 shows the final distribution of responding companies across the ten countries within the major sector groups. Table 5.2 shows the frequency distribution of the companies across sectors. These 4,004 companies were very young at the time of the survey, established between the years 2002 and 2007.

3.2 First brush with data

About two-thirds of the founders were employed in another company just before establishing the one surveyed in AEGIS. Their previous employer

Table 5.1 Frequency distribution of surveyed firms, by aggregate sector and country

Country	Sector			Total
	High-tech	*Low-tech*	*KIBS*	
Croatia	35	115	50	200
Czech Republic	25	92	83	200
Denmark	34	69	227	330
France	68	196	306	570
Germany	67	160	330	557
Greece	22	184	125	331
Italy	57	316	207	580
Portugal	31	170	130	331
Sweden	34	108	192	334
United Kingdom	47	192	332	571
Total	420	1,602	1,982	4,004

Table 5.2 Frequency distribution of surveyed firms, by sector

Industry[a]	Number of sample firms
High-technology manufacturing sectors	
Aerospace	1
Computers and office machinery	20
Radio-television and communication equipment	35
Manufacture of medical, precision & optical instruments	67
Medium to high-technology manufacturing sectors	
Manufacture of electrical machinery and apparatus	45
Manufacture of machinery and equipment	201
Chemical industry	51
Medium to low technology manufacturing sectors	
Basic metals	31
Fabricated metal products	214
Low-technology manufacturing sectors	
Paper and printing	618
Textile and clothing	209
Food, beverages and tobacco	297
Wood and furniture	233
Knowledge Intensive Business Services (KIBS)	
Telecommunications	24
Computer and related activities	518
Research and experimental development	71
Selected business services activities	1,369
Total	*4,004*

Note
a OECD classification based on R&D intensity.

was in the same sector with a factor 2:1. In other words, about 40 per cent of the founders in the surveyed companies brought with them fresh and directly relevant experience.[4] Large majorities considered market knowledge, technical/engineering knowledge and networks built during their previous career highly important. No fewer than half of the company founders reported technical and engineering knowledge as their main area of expertise. An additional quarter reported general management as the main area of expertise. When asked about the factors that prompted them to establish the companies in question, more than four-fifths graded work experience in the current activity field as of high or very high importance, while three-quarters graded market knowledge similarly, and more than two-thirds graded technical/engineering knowledge and networks built during previous career similarly.

Experience seemed, then, an obvious risk management procedure: many entrepreneurs were establishing companies in fields in which they had had significant prior experience. We ran *t*-tests comparing the average growth of sales (2007–2009, end of 2010) between firms whose owners' last occupation before the establishment of the company in question are still in

Table 5.3 Two sample t-test: comparison of mean of average growth of sales (2007 2009, end of 2010)

	Mean (sales growth, 2007–2009)	Mean (sales growth, 2010)
Owner still in existence	42.80	19.53
New owner	13.48	−8.62
Diff	29.32	28.15
	$t=2.14$	$t=1.50$
	$P>t=0.02*$	$P>t=0.05*$

Note
* Significant at 5% significance level.

existence and firms led by a first-time entrepreneur. Table 5.3 indicates that sales growth of the former firms is higher on the whole than that of firms established by a new owner (statistically significant).

Interviewees reported funding the new ventures by and large with own financial resources: more than nine in ten using own resources extensively. Pointing at the perception of high risks by external investors, very few of the surveyed entrepreneurs accessed venture capital (5 per cent) or bank funding (28%), public funding (7 per cent) or funding from EU sources (3 per cent). Yet, in those relatively few companies that benefited from them, venture capital made up 45% of all available funds and bank funds made up 52%.

About 60 per cent of the respondents reported having many business competitors, compared with 34 per cent reporting few competitors and 7 per cent reporting no competition. Innovation was considered key: about half responded that a company in their sector can succeed only if it is able to launch new products and/or services frequently. Competition comes in terms of both quality and price: almost two-thirds of the respondents considered quality competition prevalent; more than half answered similarly for price competition. When rating the different factors that shape competitive advantage, the clear winner is capacity to adapt products/services to customer needs. It is followed at close distance by product/service quality and novelty.

Market risk/uncertainty was perceived as an important obstacle to company growth: three-quarters of the respondents opined it is at least of moderate importance and at least two-fifths that it is of great importance. Market risk was followed by two other factors, funding difficulties and difficulties in recruiting high-skill employees: 60 per cent of respondents thought each of these obstacles as of moderate importance for company growth, with 40 per cent considering them of high importance. Interestingly, lack of technological know-how and technology risk/uncertainty were the two factors at the bottom of the obstacle list: only about 15 per cent or respondents considered them of high importance.

Moreover, a slew of externally determined factors were considered important barriers for operating the company, including taxation, bureaucracy, and legislation for competition and property rights. Listed in terms of importance: frequently changing taxation regulations, high tax rates, bureaucracy for permits and licences, poorly enforced competition legislation and weak intellectual property protection.

Simple tabulations and *t*-tests of self-reported information of relatively young entrepreneurial KIEs across sectors and several European countries indicate:

1   Market risk is viewed as the most important obstacle for company growth and must be reflected clearly in the risk management plans of new KIEs. Securing external funds for growth and recruiting skilled employees also rank very high.
2   Important operating risks relate to taxation, government bureaucracy, and legislation for competition and intellectual property protection. These are all externally determined.
3   Competition risk tends to be high. Both quality and price competition are present and must be dealt with. Adaptation to customer needs and product/process novelty underline competitive advantage.

We build our empirical model in the next section on the basis of these findings.

4 Empirical model

In order to manage risk effectively, it is important for the KIE to sense technical and market opportunities and to seize them strategically. That is, a KIE can manage risk through (a) actively observing and adopting best practices; (b) responding rapidly to competitive moves; (c) changing practices based on customer feedback; (d) actively and regularly considering the consequences of changing market demand in terms of new products and services; and (e) being quick to recognize shifts in the broader market (e.g. competition, regulation, demography). All these factors were reflected in the survey.

A quite extensive and diverse literature has extensively referred to these issues and offered advice for accessing the requisite capabilities (e.g. Culp, 2001; Ebben, 2005; Nocco and Stulz, 2006; Perez-Luno and Cambra, 2013). Extant literature has by and large focused on large incumbent companies, however, leaving much to be desired in terms of systematic empirical evidence addressing young small companies (Verbano and Venturini, 2013).

Another way of managing risk may be networking with other firms. Through networking, a firm can obtain the necessary complementary assets/resources and valuable information that are required to manage risk effectively. The KIE can form networks with other firms through strategic alliances such as R&D agreements, technical cooperation agreements, licensing agreements, subcontracting, marketing/export promotion and/or research contract-out. A large volume of literature on alliances and networks has arisen over the past three decades but interest in small business and start-ups is much more recent. On the whole, this literature indicates cooperative agreements and network strategy as a critical element in determining survival and prosperity of young and small companies (Colombo *et al.*, 2006; Street and Cameron, 2007; Schoonjans *et al.*, 2013).

4.1 Model specification

We run probit models for internal risk management and networking where the dependent variable is a binary construct.

$$Strategy_i/Network_i = \beta_1 + \beta_2 \, Technologyrisk_i + \beta_3 \, Market \, risk_i + \beta_4 \, Financial \, risk_i + \beta_5 \, Operation \, risk_i + \beta_6 \, Competition \, risk_i + \beta_7 \, IPR \, risk_i + \beta_8 \, Timing \, risk_i + \beta_9 \, Recruiting \, risk_i + \beta_{10} \, Firm \, size_i + \beta_{11} \, Firm \, age_i + \beta_{12} \, Education_i + \varepsilon_i,$$

For $i = 1, \ldots, N$ firms

The error term is assumed to be normally distributed.

4.1.1 Dependent variables

i   **Strategy.** The firm was asked to indicate to what extent it agrees or disagrees with the strategic actions to sense and seize opportunities. *Strategy* is coded as 1 if the firm uses at least one type of strategy above: (a) actively observing and adopting best practices; (b) responding rapidly to competitive moves; (c) changing practices based on customer feedback; (d) actively and regularly considering the consequences of changing market demand in terms of new products and services; and (e) being quick to recognize shifts in the broader market (e.g. competition, regulation, demography). *Strategy* is coded as 0 otherwise.

ii   **Network.** The firm was asked to indicate the types of formal agreements it has engaged in. *Network* is coded as 1 if the firm has often or very often participated in at least one of the different types of formal agreements mentioned earlier including: R&D agreements, technical cooperation agreements, licensing agreements, subcontracting, marketing/export promotion and/or research contract-out. *Network* is coded as 0 otherwise.

4.1.2 Independent variables

Technology risk. The technology is likely to be unproven and the application yet to be demonstrated. Development may take longer than expected, may not work or may be superseded by competitors. Respondents were asked to indicate to what extent technology risk and uncertainty has been an obstacle to setting up and operating the company. Responses were weighed through a five-point Likert-type scale ranging from 1 ('not at all') to 5 ('to a great extent'). Higher values represent higher levels of perceived financial risk.

Market risk. It is difficult for investors to assess the market potential for products that may not exist or which may create a new market. Respondents were asked to indicate to what extent market risk and uncertainty has been an obstacle to setting up and operating the company. Responses were weighed through a five-point Likert-type scale ranging from 1 ('not at all') to 5 ('to a great extent'). Higher values represent higher levels of perceived market risk.

Financial risk. Fears of losing significant amounts of money on the part of prospective investors in a new company results in unwillingness to provide funding. Respondents were asked to indicate to what extent difficulty in finding the necessary funding has been an obstacle to setting up and operating the company. Responses were weighed through a five-point Likert-type scale ranging from 1 ('not at all') to 5 ('to a great extent'). Higher values represent higher levels of perceived financial risk.

Operation risk. Operation risk relates to external factors that operate as barriers to setting up and operating the company. Respondents were asked to indicate to what extent changing taxation regulations, high tax rates, time-consuming regulatory requirements for issuing permits and licences, rigid labour market legislation, and corruption (government officials' favouring well-connected individuals) were felt to create such barriers. Responses for each item were weighed through a five-point Likert-type scale ranging from 1 ('not at all') to 5 ('to a great extent'). Responses to the various items were combined to create this variable. Higher values represent higher levels of perceived operation risk.

Competition risk. The presence of many business competitors with uncertain behaviour creates difficulties for the firm. Respondents were asked to indicate to what extent the activities of their competitors are unpredictable and competition is very intense. Responses were weighed through a five-point Likert-type scale ranging from 1 ('completely disagree') to 5 ('completely agree'). Higher values represent higher levels of perceived operation risk.

IPR risk. Having appropriate legislation property rights protection in the books does not suffice to appease entrepreneurs when enforcement is lagging. Respondents were asked to indicate to what extent poorly enforced property rights, copyrights and patent protection operate as barriers to setting up and operating the company. Responses were weighed through a five-point Likert-type scale ranging from 1 ('not at all') to 5 ('to a great extent'). Higher values represent higher levels of perceived IPR risk.

Timing risk. KIEs are often characterized by short 'windows of opportunity' such that they might be unsuccessful if they enter the market too late, or too early. Our assumption here was to approximate the window of opportunity with the product cycle. Respondents were asked to indicate whether in their core industry the life cycle of products is typically short. Responses were weighed through a five-point Likert-type scale ranging from 1 ('completely disagree') to 5 ('completely agree'). Higher values represent higher levels of perceived timing risk.

Recruiting risk. It is quite frequently argued by industry, and small knowledge-intensive companies in particular, that a major problem is to locate well-qualified personnel. Respondents were asked to indicate to what extent difficulty in recruiting highly skilled employees has been an obstacle to setting up and operating the company. Responses were weighed through a five-point Likert-type scale ranging from 1 ('not at all') to 5 ('to a great extent'). Higher values represent higher levels of perceived recruiting risk.

4.1.3 Control variables

Firm size. The number of workers measures a firm's size. This variable controls for the possibility that bigger firms might have different attitudes toward risk management.

Firm age. The number of years since the firm's establishment. This variable controls for the unobserved firm characteristics because firms that have survived long in the market may be qualitatively different in terms of managing risk from those that have not.

Education. The first founder's educational attainment with higher values indicating higher levels of education is included (i.e. elementary = 1, secondary = 2, bachelor = 3, postgraduate = 4, Ph.D. = 5). This variable controls for the possibility that the educational attainment of the entrepreneur may be associated with decisions to behave strategically and the decision to participate in networks when the KIEs perceives risk.

Sector and country dummy variables are included to control for potential sector and country specific effects.

Table 5.4 shows the descriptive statistics for the independent variables and controls. Table 5.5 presents the econometric results.

4.2 Discussion

4.2.1 Strategically sensing and seizing opportunities

The results of this analysis are presented in column 1 of Table 5.5. Both technology risk and operation risk affect the firm's propensity to act strategically positively. That is, the higher the perceived technology and operational risk, the higher the firm's incentive to actively try to manage it by

Table 5.4 Descriptive statistics of the variables

Variables	Mean (std. dev.)
Dependent variables	
Strategy	0.98 (0.13)
Network	0.85 (0.3)
Independent and control variables	
Technology risk	2.28 (1.21)
Market risk	3.23 (1.20)
Financial risk	3.02 (1.50)
Operation risk	0.90 (0.30)
Competition risk	3.29 (1.27)
IPR risk	2.33 (1.39)
Timing risk	2.62 (1.51)
Recruiting risk	2.99 (1.42)
Firm size	10.90 (37.73)
Firm age	7.12 (2.17)
Education	

Note
***, **, *: Standard errors are in parentheses.

Table 5.5 Econometric results

Estimation method	(Column 1) Probit	(Column 2) Probit
Dependent variable	Strategy	Network
Technology risk	0.113* (0.0662)	0.0859*** (0.0244)
Market risk	−0.1813*** (0.0679)	0.0679*** (0.0229)
Financial risk	−0.0868* (0.0459)	0.053*** (0.0182)
Operation risk	0.5444** (0.2763)	0.0598 (0.0857)
Competition risk	−0.285* (0.1571)	−0.2279*** (0.0529)
IPR risk	−0.2478*** (0.0609)	0.0237 (0.0205)
Timing risk	0.0388 (0.0491)	−0.0467*** (0.0167)
Recruiting risk	0.0547 (0.055)	0.0298* (0.0182)
Firm size	0.0119* (0.0068)	0.0032** (0.0015)
Firm age	−0.0325 (0.0346)	−0.0087 (0.0118)
Education	−0.0707 (0.0615)	0.1282*** (0.0221)
Constant	1.832 (0.8843)	−7.2527 (0.57)
N	3,917	3,917
Pseudo R-squared	0.1319	0.0533

Notes
***, **, *: Significant at 1%, 5% and 10% significance levels. Standard errors in parentheses. Coefficients on sector and country dummies are not reported.

adopting good practices, responding rapidly to competitive moves, reacting to customer feedback, and/or observing and reacting quickly to changing market conditions.

In contrast, the coefficients on market risk, competition risk and IPR risk are negative and statistically significant. They indicate that higher market uncertainty, strong perceived competition and inability to break through competitors' practices, and poor IPR protection are inversely related to active risk management efforts. In the presence of such factors firms may become more conservative and defensive of established strategy.

The positive and statistically significant coefficient on firm size indicates that relatively bigger firms are more likely to manage risk strategically. Given that the companies in our sample are all on the smaller side – established in the past 2–8 years – this result essentially shows a rapid increase in awareness as companies evolve from micro to small to medium size.

4.2.2 Networking

The results of this analysis are reported in column 2 of Table 5.5. The perceived technology risk, market risk, financial risk and recruiting risk positively affect the likelihood of the firm engaging in networks. High technology, market, financial and recruiting risk will increase the general level of uncertainty in the market. Firms will try to check these risks and overcome such market uncertainty by entering into collaborative agreements of various kinds.

The coefficients on competition risk and timing risk are negative and statistically significant. Severe and unchecked competition and commercial success perceived to be highly dependent on market timeliness raise uncertainty and make companies less likely to cooperate under fear they might lose their competitive advantage and not be able to move quickly.

The positive and statistically significant coefficient on firm size and education indicates that bigger firms as well as firms with better educated entrepreneurs are more likely to participate in networking.

4.3 Summing up

The findings reported above can be summarized as follows:

1   Technology risk is positively related with both strategic reaction to mitigate risk and with networking.
2   Competition risk is negatively related with both cases strategic reaction to mitigate risk and with networking.
3   Market risk, financial risk and IPR risk are negatively related with strategic reaction to mitigate risk while they are positively related with networking.
4   Timing risk is positively related with strategic reaction to mitigate risk while it is negatively related with networking.
5   Firm size is positively related with both cases strategic reaction to mitigate risk and networking.
6   Education of the entrepreneur is positively related to networking.

The clearest message comes with technology risk: companies treat it as unsystematic (diversifiable) and, consequently, manage it actively and try to decrease it through networking. Timing risk is also diversifiable and thus actively managed. On the other hand, competition risk, market risk, financial risk and IPR risk as defined herein appear to be considered systematic and do not lend themselves easily to management. Networking emerges as a tool companies use in trying to defend against them, with the exception of excessive and unchecked competition.[5]

5 Conclusion and policy implications

'Innovation without risk is paradoxical because the process by which risk is most naturally addressed quite often *is* innovation – replacing the old with the new often makes the world a safer place' (Culp, 2001: 4). A better place too, we would add. Entrepreneurs enter the market with innovative ideas and products designed to fix a problem or make something better or make something altogether new. To ignore risk is foolhardy and for those who consider themselves able to think outside the box, embarrassing. Starr *et al.* (2003) and IBM (2011) discuss the global links that make a firm resilient. Having a sound risk management strategy goes a long way toward the long-term success of a venture, especially a new one.

The literature provides little specific information on risk management in new entrepreneurial ventures. This chapter addressed this topic and presented an attempt to empirically relate the influence of various types of risk on risk mitigation strategies of young knowledge-intensive enterprises (KIEs). The analysis was based on a new extensive database of KIEs spanning ten European countries and eighteen sectors. The KIEs in question had been formed within the 8–9 years prior to the undertaking of the extensive survey that provided extensive detailed information on 4,004 of them. Some of the important results are worth recounting here.

An obvious risk reduction procedure was the establishment of new companies in areas in which the entrepreneur has had significant experience prior to establishing the company. More than four-fifths of the surveyed entrepreneurs graded prior work experience in the current activity field as of high or very high importance, while three-quarters graded market knowledge similarly, and more than two-thirds graded technical/engineering knowledge and networks built during previous career similarly.

They funded the new ventures by and large with own financial resources: more than nine in ten using own resources extensively. Few of the surveyed entrepreneurs had accessed venture capital or bank funding. The large majority reported having strong competition in terms of both quality and price. Competitive advantage was created by the capacity to adapt products/services to customer needs, followed by product/service quality and novelty. Market risk/uncertainty was the most important perceived obstacle to company growth, followed by funding difficulties (funding risk) and difficulties in recruiting high-skill employees (recruiting risk). Lack of technological know-how and technology risk/uncertainty were the two factors at the bottom of the obstacle list.

A slew of factors were considered important barriers for operating the company, including taxation, bureaucracy, and legislation for competition and property rights. Listed in terms of importance: frequently changing taxation regulations, high tax rates, bureaucracy for permits and licences, poorly enforced competition legislation and weak intellectual property protection. These make up systematic risks that must be considered in the business plan.

Interestingly, then, our empirical analysis associates the clearest message with the factor that interviewed entrepreneurs considered the easiest risk to deal with: technology. Companies treat technology risk as unsystematic (diversifiable) and, consequently, manage it actively and try to decrease it through networking. Timing risk is also diversifiable – depends largely on company circumstances – and is, thus, actively managed too. On the other hand, competition risk, market risk, financial risk and IPR risk seemed to be considered systematic – largely depending on external factors – and, consequently, do not lend themselves easily to management. There was an inverse relationship between this set of four risks and active risk management. One should observe here that market risk and financial risk were placed (in that order) at the top of the list of the obstacles to a successful operation. Networking appears to be a way companies try to defend against them as well as against IPR risk.

The only risk category that did not give us statistically significant results regarding risk management was recruiting risk which had been reported as one of the most important obstacles in the survey. Positive signs for the coefficients were the expected ones – the risk is diversifiable and, thus, positively manageable. But the companies apparently attributed part of their difficulties in the absence of qualified personnel for hire, a problem they could not rectify on their own easily. Seemingly, this risk led them to more cooperative agreements.

Finally, within this population of relatively small companies, growing size is associated with higher/better risk management and, in conjunction to better educational background of the entrepreneurs, increases the likelihood of networking.

Important policy implications arise from this analysis. They are predicated on the view that the public sector (a) concentrates on the gaps/weaknesses of the private sector and (b) selects areas of intervention for maximum impact. Three clear messages emerge:

- The government should primarily concentrate in assisting young entrepreneurial companies with factors that create systematic risks, i.e. risks that the companies cannot hedge or diversify.

These include financial risk and IPR risk. In particular, setting up an efficiently functioning financial system that allows young entrepreneurial companies access to various sources and types of financing is key. Moreover, setting in place a transparent and well-functioning intellectual property protection regime is instrumental for knowledge-intensive enterprises.

On the other hand, market risk and competition risk, while also perceived by companies as systematic, do not lend themselves easily to government intervention. This is because the public sector is notoriously incapable of assessing the market potential of new products (beyond those that it itself utilizes such as for defence). It is also difficult to see how the government can alleviate competition risk for a company without falling back into practices of picking winners. Of course, there is a lot of legitimate role for public policy in maintaining well-functioning markets and healthy competition.

- Seemingly there is little room for direct government intervention in alleviating technology risk for young KIEs.

Such risk appears the easiest for individual companies to deal with: they treat it as unsystematic, manage it actively and decrease it by networking. Needless to say, there is a very important role for the public sector in supporting the scientific and technological context within which firms pursue their specific goals.

- The government should also concentrate on the factors underlying recruitment risk, reportedly one of the most important obstacles for our firms' growth.

Availability of skilled personnel is key. This points at the necessity of well-functioning educational systems at all levels, also including vocational and other professional training.

Notes

1 A modified version of this chapter entitled 'Managing risk in the formative years: Evidence from young enterprises in Europe' by the same authors appeared in *Technovation* (2014), 34(8): 454–465.
2 Essentially thus differentiating between uncertainty and risk, a 'bad' and a 'good' for business.
3 In order to avoid three-quarters of the sample coming just from three large countries, a minimum of 200 responses was set for Croatia and the Czech Republic, about 330 responses for each of Denmark, Greece, Portugal and Sweden, and 570 responses for each of France, Germany, Italy and the UK.
4 The average professional experience prior to establishing the companies in the AEGIS survey was 12 years. Seven out of ten founders were over 40 years old when establishing the firm.
5 To the best of our understanding, there is no broadly accepted distinction between diversifiable and systematic risks in the literature. Our distinction in this

chapter is based on the regression results reported in Table 5.5 regarding company efforts to actively manage.

References

Agarwal, R., Echambadi, R., Franco, A.M. and Sarkar, M. (2004), 'Knowledge transfer through inheritance: Spin-out generation, development and survival', *The Academy of Management Journal*, 47(4), 501–522.

Baker, N. (2011), 'Managing the complexity of risk', *Internal Auditor*, 68(2), 35–38.

Ben-Ari, G. and Vonortas, N.S. (2007), 'Risk financing for knowledge-based enterprises: Mechanisms and policy options', *Science and Public Policy*, 34(7), 475–488.

Colombo, M.G., Grilli, L., and Piva, E. (2006), 'In search of complementary assets: The determinants of alliance formation of high-tech start-ups', *Research Policy*, 35, 1166–1199.

Culp, C.L. (2001), *The Risk Management Process: Business Strategy and Tactics*. New York: John Wiley & Sons, Inc.

Ebben, J. (2005), 'Managing risk in a new venture', *www.Inc.com*. Retrieved from www.inc.com/resources/startup/articles/20050301/risk.html.

Forlani, D. and Mullins, J.W. (2000), 'Perceived risks and choices in entrepreneurs' new venture decisions', *Journal of Business Venturing*, 15(4), 305–322.

Gompers, P.A. and Lerner, J. (2001), *The Money of Invention: How Venture Capital Creates New Wealth*. Boston: Harvard Business School Press.

Haar, N.E., Starr, J. and Macmillan, I.C. (1988), 'Informal risk capital investors: Investment patterns on the east coast of the U.S.A.', *Journal of Business Venturing*, 3(1), 11–29.

Hubbard, D.W. (2009), *The Failure of Risk Management: Why It's Broken and How to Fix it*. New York: John Wiley & Sons, Inc.

IBM (2011), *Key Trends Driving Global Business Resilience and Risk*, Report Retrieved from http://public.dhe.ibm.com/common/ssi/ecm/en/rlw03004usen/RLW03004USEN.pdf.

Janney, J.J. and Dess, G.G. (2006), 'The risk concept for entrepreneurs reconsidered: New challenges to the conventional wisdom', *Journal of Business Venturing*, 21(3), 385–400.

Kakati, M. (2003), 'Success criteria in high-tech new ventures', *Technovation*, 23(5), 447–457.

Leitch, M. (2010), 'ISO 31000:2009 – the new international standard on risk management', *Risk Analysis: An International Journal*, 30(6), 887–892.

Longenecker, J.G., Petty, J.W., Palich, L.E. and Moore, C.W. (2010), *Small Business Management: Launching & Growing Entrepreneurial Ventures* (15th edn). Mason, OH: South-Western.

Macmillan, I.C., Siegel, R. and Subbanarasimha, P.N. (1985), 'Criteria used by venture capitalists to evaluate new venture proposals', *Journal of Business Venturing*, 1(1), 119–128.

Macmillan, I.C., Zemann, L. and Subbanarasimha, P.N. (1987), 'Criteria distinguishing successful from unsuccessful ventures in the venture screening process', *Journal of Business Venturing*, 2(2), 123–137.

Mason, C.M. and Harrison, R.T. (2004), 'Does investing in technology-based firms involve higher risk? An exploratory study of the performance of technology and non-technology investments by business angels', *Venture Capital*, 6(4), 313–332.

Nocco, B. and Stulz, R. (2006), 'Enterprise risk management: Theory and practice', *Journal of Applied Corporate Finance*, 18, 8–20.

Perez-Luno, A. and Cambra, J. (2013), 'Listen to the market: Do its complexity and signals make companies more innovative?', *Technovation*, 33, 180–192.

Purdy, G. (2010), 'ISO 31000:2009 – setting a new standard for risk management', *Risk Analysis: An International Journal*, 30(6), 881–886.

Reid, G.C. and Smith, J.A. (2008), *Risk Appraisal and Venture Capital in High Technology New Ventures*. New York: Routledge.

Schoonjans, B., Van Cauwenberge, P. and Vander Bauwhede, H. (2013), 'Formal business networking and SME growth', *Small Business Economics*, 41, 169–181.

Starr, R., Newfrock, J. and Delurey, M. (2003), 'Enterprise resilience: Managing risk in the networked economy', *Strategy+business*, 30. Retrieved from www.boozallen.com/media/file/Enterprise_Resilience_Report.pdf.

Street, C.T. and Cameron, A.-F. (2007), 'External relationships and the small business: A review of small business alliance and network research', *Journal of Small Business Management*, 45(2), 239–266.

Verbano, C. and Venturini, K. (2013), 'Managing risks in SMEs: A literature review and research agenda', *Journal of Technology Management & Innovation*, 8(3), 1–17.

6 Structuring the process of knowledge intensive entrepreneurship

Empirical evidence and descriptive insights from 86 AEGIS case studies

Maureen McKelvey, Daniel Ljungberg and Astrid Heidemann Lassen

1 Introduction

This chapter provides insights about the process of venture creation, which is structured through a conceptual process model. These insights should help business managers, students, researchers, public policy officers and others to understand knowledge intensive entrepreneurship (KIE) during the management and development phase of the venture especially. These insights are based upon 86 case studies.[1] We use the multiple independent case studies in order to draw out patterns, which are structured according to the model of the KIE venture and according to theoretical insights about opportunities. In doing so, the quotes provide insights about the views and perceptions of specific entrepreneurs. The focus here is upon the perspectives of the founder and of the venture, where 'KIE venture' refers to the new company, business project or new organizational form. A KIE venture is defined as a specific type of start-up firm, with four characteristics: It is (i) a new firm; which (ii) is innovative; (iii) has a significant knowledge intensity; and (iv) exploits innovative opportunities in several sectors (Malerba and McKelvey, 2011; Chapter 2 of this book).[2]

This chapter thus provides empirical insights regarding how knowledge intensive entrepreneurs structure, perceive and describe the processes of developing and managing new ventures, as well as the major factors influencing them from the surrounding innovation system. The case studies have been conducted in the AEGIS project, at a high level of detail, and as analysed below these cases describe different firms, sectors and countries, and they provide evidence that KIE does indeed exist across sectors and countries in the way argued in the conceptual framework in Chapter 2. The interested reader can find specific and more detailed case studies in later chapters of this book, at the AEGIS website[3] and in *How Entrepreneurs Do What They Do* (McKelvey and Lassen, 2013b).[4]

The KIE processes – as discussed in this chapter and throughout the book – are highly dynamic with strong feedback loops between the individuals, the company and society. In this chapter we apply a conceptual model of the KIE venture to help structure the insights of specific individuals and ventures into a larger understanding of the overall process. The model outlines three main phases, namely Inputs, Development and Outputs, and each phase consists of a set of second order dimensions (Lassen and McKelvey, 2012; McKelvey and Lassen, 2013a). Illustrations of each phase, and its corresponding variables, are provided, by drawing from the longer, historical studies of the 86 specific cases. Thus, the empirical insights from analysed cases studies are specifically placed relative to phases and key dimensions. And in doing so, the focus here is upon the processes of creating, developing and managing the KIE venture.

The second section provides an overview of the methodological considerations behind the analysis of the 86 cases. The following three sections provide the case study evidence, structured according to the three KIE phases of Inputs, Development and Outputs. The final two sections respectively discuss implications of the methodology for further research and address public policy.

2 Methodology for structuring the empirical evidence and descriptive insights

The main contribution of the current chapter is to structure and aggregate the responses from the 86 case studies. The chapter is focused upon descriptive insights, but these are organized and structured relative to the analytical generalization as found in our model of the phase of developing and managing a KIE venture.[5] The methodological considerations applicable to this chapter thus involve both consideration on the conceptual model, the research design of the 86 case studies, and the relationship between the model and the case studies.

The research presented in this chapter is developed following a design science approach. The design science paradigm is fundamentally a problem-solving paradigm (Hevner *et al.*, 2004; van Aken *et al.*, 2012; Wieringa, 2009), thus distinguishing itself from the purely explanatory or exploratory paradigms that have customarily been applied in organizational and economic research. Design Science builds on an abductive reasoning (which integrates both deductive and inductive phases) and is appropriate in circumstances where new knowledge and understandings are so complex in nature that gradual and iterative development is necessary. The key activities (phases) in a design science research include (a) problem identification, (b) solution design, (c) implementation and (d) evaluation. In this research these phases are addressed through the following activities:

a   The fundamental argumentation behind the Aegis project of the need for further understanding of the dynamics of KIE.

b   Development of the conceptual model of KIE which synthesizes contemporary understandings of KIE, and suggests dynamic relationship between phases and knowledge developments.

c   Exploration of 86 case studies following the suggested conceptual model, with the purpose of reflecting the appropriateness of the model as well as developing it further based on the empirical insights.

d   Discussion on the findings in relation to the model and how this advances our understanding of KIE.

The proposed three-phase model of KIE venture management and development is based upon an extensive literature review, detailed in Lassen and McKelvey (2012) and further refined in McKelvey and Lassen (2013a). This chapter uses the model in Lassen and McKelvey (2012), as this served as a foundation for the original case data collection throughout all cases conducted in Aegis. Our focus is upon the KIE venture, and how they interact with the wider innovation system.

The model synthesizes and structures research relevant to specifying the particular nature of KIE. As KIE has only recently become an established topic of research, the review also includes numerous pieces of work on adjacent topics, which are influential to the understanding of KIE. The review includes work from the fields of entrepreneurship, innovation management and knowledge management. The search-strings used were: academic spin-off; corporate spin-off; corporate venturing; high-tech entrepreneurship; knowledge-based entrepreneurship; knowledge-intensive entrepreneurship; knowledge-intensive innovation; knowledge-intensive start-up; knowledge-intensive ventures; R&D* and knowledge-intensive*; R&D* and venturing*; science-intensive entrepreneurship; technology-based entrepreneurship; university spin-off; venture creation; venture creation* and R&D*. In total 1044 distinct citations were identified based on the initial keyword search.

This approach allows for the capturing of emerging themes and understandings relevant to KIE. Conceptually, the literature review and model of KIE venture development is useful to identify three unique phases, which we here illustrate through case study evidence. This literature review helped us generate (a) the three phases and (b) the key dimensions (or second-order variables), that existing theory postulates exist and which specifically ought to affect KIE ventures. From the literature review, we propose that the three main phases of KIE are: Inputs, KIE Development and Outputs. For each phase, existing literature on related concepts was found to cluster around a set of dimensions or variables – such as financing for inputs and patents for outputs – as the key explanatory factors. The KIE venture model is visualized in Figure 6.1.

This model is also used in this chapter as a device to structure insights from the 86 reviewed case studies into what is actually going on inside KIE

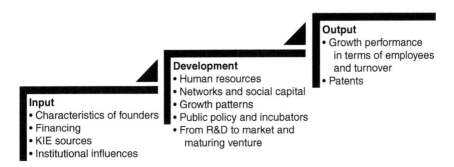

Input
• Characteristics of founders
• Financing
• KIE sources
• Institutional influences

Development
• Human resources
• Networks and social capital
• Growth patterns
• Public policy and incubators
• From R&D to market and
  maturing venture

Output
• Growth performance
  in terms of employees
  and turnover
• Patents

Figure 6.1 KIE model (Lassen and McKelvey, 2012).

ventures. The 86 case studies conducted during the AEGIS provide empirical evidence on the dynamics of KIE proposed and discussed through the
conceptual model. From the beginning, the empirical work in AEGIS has
been explicitly linked to definitions, theory development and conceptual
frameworks, albeit broad ones. All the selected cases this way deal with the
phases of Input, Development and Output in our model. This allows us to
organize and structure the analysis relative to these three phases and key
dimensions. In accordance with the design science approach such initial
conceptual structuration of the empirical data not only serves the purpose
of validating the appropriateness of the model, but also allows for further
developments based on the empirical insights. We use the model in order
to classify and code the case studies, which allows us to understand much
more about perceptions of how and why KIE ventures are able to develop,
over time. Thus, it provides a way to structure the insights into how these
processes 'work in practice' – and through this refine our understanding
of KIE.

Still, definitions may be ambiguous in what exactly should be studied,
because one often needs to study proxies or related phenomena since so
little is known empirically. There are always differences and gaps between
the definition and operationalization, and different research designs lead to
somewhat different operationalization, even within the same project.
Developing this chapter and the companion chapter in this book thus
required much additional analysis of the existing case studies, though
guided by the overall conceptual model (see Chapter 2 of this book).

The authors of the current chapter read each descriptive case study –
and where possible, we also read the more analytical case study or report.
We coded the material into the three phases, and the key dimensions, in
accordance with the model. From the rich empirical evidence, this chapter
presents evidence and insights into how the entrepreneurs and ventures
perceive the processes, so as to understand how they perceive what is
going on.

Naturally, there will be many feedback loops among phases and variables. This is also reflected by the case studies. Case studies are by definition at a high level of detail. So, depending upon how the case is written up descriptively and analytically, one can focus on a few variables in detail or on many inter-related and complex processes at the same time. This chapter does not provide full and detailed case studies for the 86 KIE ventures. The chapter instead limits the descriptive insights to understanding in relation to the model of a KIE venture. This gives us a better understanding of these three phases and second-order variables, from the perspective of the people engaged in entrepreneurship.

3 Inputs to the KIE ventures

The first phase we consider in the KIE model addresses inputs to KIE ventures. By input we refer to prerequisites and existing structures affecting the formation of this type of new venture. Each one reflects a broad topic in its own rights in the general entrepreneurship literature, but of particular importance to KIE ventures, found to affect firm formation and performance. The systematic literature review by Lassen and McKelvey (2012) identified four types of inputs, which are used to guide our understanding in relation to the model:

- Characteristics of founders
- Financing
- Sources of KIE
- Institutional influences.

3.1 Characteristics of the founders

The first type of input to the KIE venture is the characteristics of the founder(s). Here, the study of the characteristics of the individual focuses on specific traits, such as cognitive and behaviour studies on how KIE entrepreneurs differ from individuals, as well as the underlying motivations for pursuing an entrepreneurial opportunity and starting a KIE venture.

The majority of KIE ventures studied in these cases are independent start-ups. Among these KIE ventures, a prevalent feature of the founders is that they often have extensive prior experience of the industry of their start-ups, which is commonly also accompanied with related technical and market knowledge. This is in line with the findings from the AEGIS survey study, which found prior industry experience and market knowledge to be the most salient and frequent characteristics of the surveyed entrepreneurs (Caloghirou *et al.*, 2011).

Here, we can exemplify this by the following case of a Portuguese KIE venture operating within the textile industry, which illustrates founders with different, but complementary, prior knowledge and industrial and market experience:

> [The firm's] initial knowledge base can be identified by the complementary knowledge (both formal and practical) from the three entrepreneurs/company's founders. That is, Mr PP's textile and clothing industry sectoral knowledge (attained by his University degree plus 20 years of working experience) was complemented by the (more oriented) management competencies of both Mr CC and Mr AM.

Having prior industrial experience is more likely for founders of independent start-ups and corporate spin-offs. However, all new ventures do not have founders with industry knowledge, especially not academic spin-offs. The founders of academic spin-offs tend to have a more narrow experience and prior knowledge, usually limited to scientific and technical knowledge but with sparse or non-existing management and market knowledge, as illustrated by the following quote taken from a case study of a Danish academic spin-off:

> The education of the entrepreneurs and the subsequent PhDs are causes of great specialization within the technology development area that is not easily transferred to managerial competences.

Another common characteristic of KIE founders is prior entrepreneurial experience. In the AEGIS survey, it was found that in approximately 15 per cent of the KIE firms, the founder had previous entrepreneurial experience (see Caloghirou *et al.*, 2011). The same finding appears in the cases studies analysed in this chapter, where in approximately 10 per cent of the cases, the founders were experienced entrepreneurs, having set up at least one firm before and in many cases founding several start-ups over the years.

Entrepreneurial experience can be exemplified by two cases, the first being a Greek start-up within the food industry, and the second being a German academic spin-off in the textile industry.

> Mr KS was an entrepreneur long before the establishment of [the case firm]. He actually has been an experienced entrepreneur for more than 40 years. He is an economist. He was running a construction company, when in 1974 he turned to tomato processing, since it was one of the region's main cultivations. In 1982 he engages a young chemist who later marries his daughter and becomes partner – Mr T. Meanwhile his son KJ takes his diploma in Economics and enters the firm in the end of the decade of the 1990s. In 2000, they all decide to abandon the tomato product foreseeing its slow death. In 2001 a cooperative grain mill went to auction. The family bought it and in June 2002 the first conventional wheat flour was produced.

Mr L has been an experienced entrepreneur for 36 years. He has already founded 14 companies in different sectors like IT, electronics or leasing services but had no business experience in the textile industry so far. Mr L has no formal education. He broke off the secondary education and a professional education as a mechanic, worked as a vendor and purchaser without any formal commercial apprenticeship. He picked up his commercial know-how on the job. At the age of 22 he founded his first company. Before the establishment of [the firm] Mr L sold a former company in the electronics sector to a leading company for metal fittings and took a timeout from business. Mr L is considered as creative and as a professional in marketing and sales. He widened the business strategy for consumer products which is supposed to lead to the main volume of sales in a few years by licensing to big manufacturers. Moreover, he organized the investors for commercializing the new fibres from his social network. The motivation of Mr L can be described as intrinsic.

These cases illustrates why one important characteristic of entrepreneurs is experience, from the industry and market, the technology or the experience of starting other ventures.

Moreover, this first type of input to the KIE venture is not only about the traits and prior knowledge of the entrepreneurs but also their underlying motivations for pursuing an entrepreneurial opportunity. The motivations for starting a company can be quite different, as illustrated by the following four separate cases from Denmark, Germany and Sweden.

'I was 39 years and could not get a higher position in the industry. I could not reconcile myself with sitting back in the chair.' He felt the urge for creating a new business and had to try it for himself.

All three entrepreneurs got to know each other from their work in the joining technology group at a private research centre. According to Mr S. they all felt intrinsically motivated by the work for the research centre but at the same time too restricted by the general conditions so that they were encouraged in looking for new challenges and solutions. Above all they are interested in implementing their own ideas and think of themselves as less being in employment. Moreover, there were no career options at the research centre for the three entrepreneurs since the positions of department chiefs are limited and mainly assigned to the period of employment.

It turned out that both researchers were interested in commercializing the idea. There were two reasons. First, they wanted to see that the knowledge could be put into practical use. Second, they were also interested in having their own commercial project or company to work with. The results obtained so far had been promising and a range of possible applications in life science had been identified.

At this time he was 51 years old and had earned enough money through his entrepreneurial activities to retire. He was fascinated by the platform technology and its numerous fields of application and felt challenged by this risky situation that no one else of the sector felt encouraged to join this venture.

The motivations to start a KIE venture thus include a range of motives, which may be micro or macro related. Starting a venture ranges from the sense of necessity to do something interesting ('could not get a higher position') and lack of career options, to implementing ideas in practice. The quotes also convey a sense of risk-taking and desire to do something unusual or different, as compared to existing occupations and technologies.

3.2 Financing

Financing entrepreneurship is an area that has received much attention in the field of entrepreneurship as well as in research focusing on policy issues. Thus, financing represents another important input to the KIE venture creation. Financing issues refer to e.g. different types of finance, their effect on the venture, when in the process and which types are needed, etc.

The frequency and importance of different sources of financing found in these case studies are overall consistent with the findings from the AEGIS survey, where, in the majority of the cases (approximately 70 per cent), the studied ventures relied on the founders' own resources. In the analysed case studies, founders' own resources were indeed the most common type of financing, present in the majority of cases. In several instances resources from family members were also used for (initially) financing the start-ups. Using own financial resources does not require contacts outwards.

An interesting topic to focus upon is therefore when and how those that do obtain other sources of financing manage to do so. Especially in the case studies from the Western European countries, the case studies show that seed capital, venture capital and bank loans are also quite common. However, in many of the cases where venture capital was part of the financing, getting access to this type of funding seems to be linked with personal contacts of the founders, as illustrated by the following quote:

By mid-2007, [the original founder] and Mr CC met through common friends. 'I immediately got interested in the idea. It seemed very interesting', says Mr CC. But he thought the project needed a strategic plan and a financial partner. From his network he knew Mr AM who owned a venture capital company and who got interested in the project, both as an investor and as a partner.

In this illustration, the venture capitalist was outside the initial network, but was encouraged to join the founding team and provide part of the start-up capital. Thus, resources were moved from the level of the innovation system through venture capital to the entrepreneur.

Other types of financing may come through universities and technology transfer offices. Simply getting access to initial financing in many cases seems to have played an important role for the entrepreneurs to choose to pursue the venture foundation, as illustrated by the following case of a German start-up in the food industry:

> The company made use of a funding program called EXIST-SEED for academic start-ups in 2006/07 kick starting formal establishment as a legal entity and building up production facilities. This program is the standard tool of the technology transfer office of the University of Kassel. It has a competitive selection process of the applicants which guarantees a certain quality of the funded ideas. According to the founders the grant was vital for the firm and they do not know if they would have pursued establishment of the firm without it.

In this illustration, public policy played a part. Different types of public grants in terms of seed financing from public actors like agencies, universities and regional actors can play a role. When they are involved in the analysed cases, the founders report that they play an important role in starting the firms.

EU grants appear less often in the case studies, and when they do, they are often linked to corporate entrepreneurship rather than the start-up of independent KIE ventures. However, in some cases and countries EU grants were found to play an important role for developing the ventures, especially in Eastern Europe.

> As many innovative firms in Poland are currently successful partially thanks to EU grants they did not have enough money e.g. to do good marketing of the innovation without the grant.

The case studies analysed in this chapter thus illustrate the different means of obtaining financing. They also suggest that available financing is crucial for KIE ventures, which suggests that financing remains a difficult challenge for these types of firms and that they are dependent both upon internal resources (own, family) and external resources (venture capital, public policy).

3.3 Sources of KIE

The third type of input identified as central to the understanding of the antecedents of KIE venture creation is the variety of sources from which KIE arises, and the impact each of these have on the development and success of the new venture.

The literature on the sources of KIE ventures relates to many aspects, and these are different from the individual characteristics described above. However, when we analyse these inputs in depth, it turns out that the most common source of the KIE is closely related to the KIE ventures' founders. They are identified generally as being the persons that identify potential opportunities based on their prior knowledge (and experience) of industry, market and/or technology.

In this way, the different sources of KIE, at an aggregated level, are highly related to the three different categories of KIE ventures: independent start-ups, academic and corporate spin-offs. As such the most common driver of firm formation (i.e. sources of KIE) in the cases are the prior work experience of founders of independent start-ups that through their knowledge and experience of an industry and its market(s) identify opportunities leading to the foundation of a KIE venture. This is in line with the results from the AEGIS survey (see Caloghirou *et al.*, 2011), and can be exemplified by the following case of a Danish firm within the food industry.

> All three entrepreneurs had knowledge of the industry from former work experience and the major investor, who is also the chairman of the board, also had many years of experience in convenience food market. Their insight in the market helped them identify the niche market and the potential products.

In the case of academic spin-offs, the source of KIE is naturally most often the research conducted at the university where the academic founders are, or prior to the KIE foundation were, employed. In this way, academic spin-offs are mostly driven by the scientific and/or technical knowledge and experience of founders. The following case of a Danish spin-off illustrates this point.

> The source of knowledge is the research environment at Aalborg University ... [The firm] has commercialized the ideas that emerged during the research. The competencies acquired from the research are mainly technical.

However, in a few cases, academic spin-offs were not founded by academic researchers but by recent graduate students, which identified an opportunity, leading to a venture foundation, during their university studies.

The firm was founded by two graduates (labelled 'Mr X' and 'Ms Y' below) of the University of Kassel, who had studied international agriculture there. Mr X wrote his thesis on quality issues in the drying process of fruits and vegetables, while Ms Y investigated the production of cocoa in South America. Both worked together on an internship in fruits drying in India and already decided there that starting a company in this business would be an option after graduating from the university. One of their professors (labelled Prof. Z below) offered interested students to work on an experimental solar dryer. Ms Y and Mr X decided to sign up as volunteers.... The entrepreneurial process started in 2006. The founders were asked by the university in 2005 to represent their department at a regional event where they were supposed to sell experimentally produced dried fruits. Both were astonished how fast they sold 400 packages of dried cherries. The next day the local newspaper ran an article about the not-yet-existing firm and people started to phone the two students. After careful consideration they decided to give the idea a try.

Thus, public policy should remember that students also represent a driving force for commercializing science and technology.

In the case of corporate spin-offs, the sources of the KIE is an established firm, which has either (i) identified a business opportunity that is deemed to lie outside the scope of the current business of the firm; or (ii) decided to narrow down the scope of its business. This latter case can be illustrated by the following example of a Swedish MedTech firm.

[The firm] decided to form a separate business area for the non-dental products. It was called Cranio-Facial Reconstruction and Audiology ('CFRA') ... In 1997, the top management decided that [the firm] should become 'a dentistry company' with two complementary businesses, viz., implants and prosthetics. The Chief Financial Officer therefore got the assignment to find a new environment for the CFRA business area. As preparation for sale a business plan for a conceivable new company was made.

In this illustration, the established firm transfer knowledge and experience regarding industries, markets and technologies, to a new firm. Thus, the resulting venture is during the KIE process able to rely on the resources and competences of the parent company. This often creates favourable circumstances for the survival of the venture.

To summarize, the sources of KIE are quite important for classifying the venture as independent start-up, corporate spin-off or academic spin-off. More interesting, perhaps, is that these sources tend to be closely tied to the individual founders or founding team, and thus are closely related to the traits and characteristics of the individuals.

3.4 Institutional influences

The fourth dimension within the input phase is the institutional influences. Amongst such influences we find for example the influence of counselling and business planning in incubator settings; the impact of Triple Helix programs; and the effect of institutional training of entrepreneurs.

In the case studies analysed in this chapter, institutional influences primarily concerned academic spin-offs and took the form of public policy initiatives, which influenced the KIE venture.

> As for the second phase, [the firm] would go a step further and invest in research and development (R&D), with a strong emphasis in research. 'We want to be in the [technology] forefront. We know the [technology] state of the art ... but we want [to develop new products] based on scientific research', says Mr CC. This strategic (long term) goal allowed the entrepreneurial team to submit its business idea to the Technology Transfer Office of the local University and obtain the spin-off statute from this University. Three other factors were important to obtain the spin-off seal: Mr PP was a former student of this University, the project was textile related which was relevant as the University has a strong Textile Engineering Department, and the business idea was innovative ... the University has been mostly a service provider (laboratory tests, industrial property and quality certification) of [the firm].

> The financing of the previously developed new scientific knowledge embodied in the innovations of [the firm] before its foundation is mainly based on different supporting programmes during a period of ten years. One of them is due to a regional supporting programme for the Eastern German Economy.

In both cases above, public policy has played an important role, and in a very long-term perspective. The first illustration is organized around the technology transfer office of a university, while the second refers to regional support for developing the underlying knowledge, which occurred over a decade.

The main findings illustrated in relation to Inputs to KIE ventures are:

- Characteristics of the founder: This has an important effect on the founding and development of the KIE ventures, in terms of motivation and incentives, but also in terms of access to resources and knowledge in the innovation system.
    - The characteristics of the founder have been found to bring in resources and networks that matter for the development of the KIE

venture. These are found generally in relation to market knowledge or in relation to scientific, technological and creative knowledge. Few cases demonstrated the importance of business knowledge. The academic spin-offs in particular are dependent upon scientific and technological knowledge, and have low market and business knowledge. This matters for later stages of KIE venture development, when they need to combine different types of knowledge into the venture to identify and mobilize resources to pursue the innovative opportunity.

- Financing: These resources are primarily based upon own financial resources from the individual and their family, with surprisingly little reliance upon external resources initially for financing. This suggests that at least in the start-up phase, there is less interaction between the individual founder and innovation system than what the literature on financing has focused upon. In later stages, however, the KIE venture usually relies more on external sources of financing, and often of different types.
- Sources of KIE: The most common source of KIE is closely related to the founders, who generally are the persons that identify potential opportunities based on their prior knowledge (and experience) of industry, market and/or technology.
  - In this way, the different sources of KIE, at an aggregated level, are highly related to the three different categories of KIE ventures, the most common being:
    - The prior work experience of founders of independent start-ups that through their knowledge and experience of an industry and its market(s) identify opportunities;
    - The scientific and/or technical knowledge and experience of founders of academic spin-offs;
    - Corporate spin-offs are founded by established firms, which have either i) identified a business opportunity that is deemed to lie outside the scope of the current business of the firm; or ii) decided to narrow down the scope of its business.
- Institutional influences: Primarily concerned academic spin-offs and took the form of public policy initiatives.

4 Development and management phase of KIE ventures

The second phase of knowledge intensive entrepreneurship concerns the different aspects related to the management and development processes of KIE ventures. By 'processes' we refer to the internal competences, resources and approaches affecting the management and growth of the new venture after formation, i.e. the process of venture development. The dimensions described are:

- Human resources
- Networks and social capital
- Growth patterns
- Public policy and incubators
- From R&D to market and maturing venture.

4.1 Human resources

This dimension reflects which types of personnel the ventures employ as well as the impact of the founders' prior knowledge and experience on the venture development. This topic has been addressed in management literature at large, but remains an issue of great interest to entrepreneurship, due to its direct correlation to growth and survival. Human resource issues cover a range of different aspect related to entrepreneurship, such as, e.g. types of personnel hired in KIE, problems related to availability of knowledgeable employees, impact of prior experience of employees, and the challenges faced when occupying different roles, such as founder, owner and manager.

The cases illustrate the necessity of having multiple competencies, amongst a founding team. This can be exemplified by the following case of a Danish firm operating in the food industry.

> The entrepreneurs had professional competences in different fields such as business management, baking, logistic and finance, but they all had basic knowledge of the food processing industry. With the common knowledge as solid foundation, they could contribute with the expert knowledge in the respective fields to build up the new business.... Internal knowledge base was solid within the field of bread and convenience food manufacturing.

In this illustration, when it comes to the impact on the venture development of the founders' prior knowledge and experience, one issue that is evident from the cases is the impact of diversified knowledge of the founding team. Developing and managing the team once the KIE venture is started affects how human resources influence the development of the firm.

Human resources also illustrate the challenges facing small KIE startups. This challenge is especially evident for academic spin-offs. As mentioned earlier, founders of academic spin-offs tend to have a more narrow experience and prior knowledge, usually limited to scientific and technical knowledge but with sparse or non-existing management and market knowledge. They need to solve this in some way.

> The entrepreneurs hold respectively Master and PhD degrees with knowledge and experience within the cubesat technology. Since the industry [the firm] is involved in is extremely technological the focus

of [the firm] is primarily technological.... The education of the entrepreneurs and the subsequent PhDs are causes of great specialization
within the technology development area that is not easily transferred
to managerial competences. Thus, in the early years of [the firm] the
focus on sales and business development was limited. This is not necessarily a deliberate choice, but rather a natural consequence, reflected
by the backgrounds and experiences of the founders ... added managerial competencies to their field of expertise ... since its conception has
moved from a company with a strong technological focus to a
company capable of both developing and commercializing on its
products.

This case study illustration shows how limited human resources can lead
to initial restriction on the venture development, especially in terms of
market development. Thus, there is not uncommonly a need for this type
of venture to enhance their managerial competencies in order to be able to
develop the venture further than allowed by their technological competencies. They need new managerial talent, in order not to be locked solely to
their technical focus.

4.2 Networks and social capital

Networks and social capital are important concepts in order to understand
the entrepreneurial process and how the social networking affects
knowledge-intensive firms' performance. In terms of the KIE framework,
this dimension is about issues such as the formal and informal relationships the KIE venture has with different actors like academia, industry,
investors and customers. Another question is how such relationships are
used, and at which stages of the development of the KIE venture.

Just as the AEGIS survey found, the case studies show that one of the
more common and important network links are those to customers. While
it in the survey mostly seems to be related to finding new customers, this is
not always the only reason for networking with customers in the cases
studied here. To some extent, these links are also utilized for gaining feedback and aiding in for instance product development. This can be seen
among others in the following case of a Polish IT start-up.

The firm's most important relationships are those with its customers.
These relationships and its internal resources are the most important
resources in product development. Relationships with suppliers and
research institutes play a minor role as well. The knowledge gained as
a result of these relationships relates most importantly to finding new
customers; other important areas include information about the competition and tax and legal advice. To some extent the relationships are
also useful for product development (note that this form of profit from

relationships is of secondary importance), operations management and finding new distribution channel.

In this illustration, note that interaction with customers is not only to identify potential new customers, but also related to finding out about product development and other aspects of developing the KIE venture. Overall, we can see from the case studies that networking is a very important dimension of the venture development process.

This need for customer feedback is especially important for firms that to a large extent provide customized solutions to their customers. This is nicely illustrated by the following case of a Danish firm operating within the metal industry.

> Since [the firm] is a custom-made product manufacturer, it is important to cooperate closely with the customers. To satisfy customers' specific needs, the company has to involve customers in the development phase. It was also the case when the company was developing the remote-controlled vehicle ... has given feedbacks on the prototypes so that they could make modifications accordingly.

This illustration from Denmark stresses the importance of customer links for customization of the product.

Networks can also be used for production, especially links to suppliers and manufacturers, when the KIE venture has outsourced production.

> As a micro sized company the strategy was to exploit available external resources.... In house [the firm] focused on product development and communication activities.... To overcome limited financial resources [the firm] took advantage of local manufacturing capacity and implemented a business model based on production outsourcing ... almost all [the firm's] activities are outsourced.... This strategy allowed for the company to (almost) eliminate fixed costs, to gain production flexibility (responding easier to demand fluctuations) and for the company to concentrate on its core competencies (which in a broad sense are more commercial oriented activities). Moreover, the outsourcing strategy extended the internal knowledge base of the company.

This quote suggests that networks in low-tech industries may also relate to manufacturing. Interestingly enough, similar results about the importance of networks can be seen in high-tech industries, but for slightly different reasons, where they are more likely to stress the role of networks for aspects such as access to scientific knowledge.

Somewhat other trends are visible in high-tech industries. The following three quotes come from three separate cases in the medical technologies in Sweden. The first one illustrates the possibility to cooperate with competitors who are also potential collaborators, yet also that the KIE venture may lose control to another firm, particularly if they collaborate with large firms in the industry.

> A MedTech start-up may need to involve other MedTech companies in its innovation process in order to innovate ... there is the importance of timing for explaining why two firms in a certain situation manage to establish a collaborative relationship ... how a small start-up can easily become single-sidedly dependent on large firms that it collaborates with. For example, Nobel Biocare's decision to discontinue the project was made outside the control of [the firm], but had serious consequences.

In other words, the KIE venture may choose to engage in a particular network and venture, but the decision about whether or not to continue the network is not always up to them. Sometimes, the large firm decides to end the agreement.

The second and third quotes show that the importance of networks may change over time. In particular, the linkages to the academic environment appear to decrease in importance over time.

> While the networking with users has become crucial for [the firm's] development, the relationship to the research environment from which Promimic was once spun off has lost much of its initial importance. The responsibility for developing the technology has been taken over by the company and it is no longer dependent on Chalmers for its competence development.

> This case nicely illustrates how a small MedTech start-up company needs to develop relationships to a broad range of external actors ... the incubator Chalmers Innovation as well as several public financing organizations (regional as well as national) played a crucial role before and after the company was formed (2003). Now, eight years later, some of these relationships remain but are no longer central for the company's development ... the most important and challenging task for a start-up company is to build relationships to potential users and customers.... This case exemplifies how a local technical university (Chalmers) has supported [the firm's] product development. As newly formed, [the firm] had scarce internal resources but could gain access to valuable manpower (mainly master students and their supervisors) as well as certain equipment.

This illustration shows that even though academic spin-offs may be initially quite reliant upon the university environment, later on they tend to change and shift their relationships to the customers and potential users.

Thus, an interesting result found from the case studies about the importance of networks is not only that they are important, but that different types are likely important at different phases of the KIE venture.

4.3 Growth patterns

In relation to the process of managing KIE ventures, this dimension covers factors influencing the growth patterns of the KIE in different ways.

In particular, there are interesting questions about the size of KIE ventures studied, seen in terms of number of employees. Figure 6.2 shows the distribution per size in the 86 case studies.

The majority of the case studies are of small or medium-sized firms, if one employs the OECD definition of less than 250 employees. KIE ventures between one and nine employees constitute 24 per cent of the case studies and KIE ventures between ten and 49 employees another 32 per cent.

Furthermore, a significant number of case studies were conducted on the KIE processes in large firms (>250 employees), with a focus upon renewal through corporate entrepreneurship. These case studies differ somewhat from the AEGIS survey, which is primarily oriented to micro-firms. The large firms in the case studies were studied due to recently having established new organizational forms, usually in connection with privatization in Eastern Europe. Thus, the relatively large share of cases from these countries can to some extent explain the difference between our results and those of the AEGIS survey. The potential differences in types and sizes of KIE ventures across Europe are likely an interesting topic for future research, but also an element that public policy makers need to take into consideration.

Turning to other aspects of growth patterns studied in the cases, a clear pattern emerges in terms of internationalization. Many of the cases study

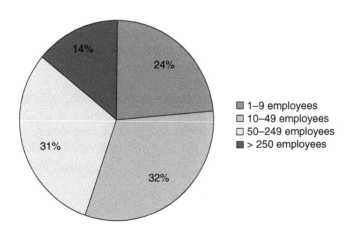

Figure 6.2 Distribution of size of KIE ventures in the case studies (employees).

KIE ventures which cater to customers internationally and have a large share of its market abroad. In fact, there seems to be two dominant, although not exclusive, patterns here: The cases to a large extent study firms that either only serve customers in their own region or that have a predominantly international approach. The firms focusing upon the region tend not to conduct any export, while those that are international tend to be what is sometimes called 'born globals', having a high share of sales coming from exports from the very beginning.

> In the very early years of the venture [the firm] experienced problems of liquidity, in spite of rapid growth (700 per cent over a two-year period). But last year's positive result, along with the high expectations to the demand from NASA, is strengthening their position. This enables positive search for the necessary investors to support the development of the company.

The above example illustrates the high reliance on international market demands in order to generate sales as well as credibility in the eyes of potential investors. As seen in several of the case studies, the example also illustrates how the growth patterns are characterized by several fluctuations; periods of liquidity problems followed by extreme growth which in return creates renewed challenges to the financial investments. These findings support the conclusion that growth patterns of KIE venture are highly influenced by the managerial ability to overcome the liability of smallness and liability of newness experienced by the venture.

4.4 Public policy and incubators

This dimension addresses the effect of incubators on the development of KIE, how to manage the incubator, academia and industry technology transfer, and so forth. Here, we focus on the relationships between the KIE and the various mechanisms for technology transfer or for firm growth, such as incubators. This is similar to the institutional influences found in the start-up phase, but here we are focused upon their influence during managing and developing the KIE venture after foundation.

In the cases studied here incubators are not at all common, and only six case firms are incubator ventures. The most common effect of incubators on venture development is that it provides support, in terms of activities like business coaches, for developing the idea and opportunity seeking as well as ideas for funding and other strategic issues. This is illustrated in an academic spin-off.

> After careful consideration they decided to give the idea a try and contacted the incubator of the University of Kassel. The incubator helped in developing the idea further (including a 20-pages grant proposal)

and gave advice to the entrepreneurs on strategic and administration issues.

However, as illustrated by a case of Swedish medical technology venture, incubators can also support KIE ventures by aiding in developing their academic (and business) networks.

> [The firm] is not a spin-off from Chalmers but the establishment of fruitful relationships with various departments was facilitated by [the firm's] location at Chalmers Innovation. This illustrates one way in which an incubator can effectively help new companies to develop their networks.

So, in the first illustration, the incubator helps with the business development and in the second illustration, the incubator helps by facilitating networks, in this case, with additional technological experts.

4.5 From R&D to market and maturing the venture

One of the topics often highlighted in entrepreneurship literature and innovation management literature alike, is related to the difficulties experienced by many firms in creating balance between R&D activities and activities focusing on bringing products efficiently to market.

One aspect is that in shifting to the market focus, the KIE ventures rely particularly upon external sources related to users and markets, as shown in the AEGIS survey. For KIE ventures, however, the literature suggests there are very specific and particular difficulties in balancing R&D and market foci, and this is what this dimension tries to capture in the following quote.

> Specialization within the technology development area is not easily transferred to managerial competences. Thus, in the early years of GomSpace the focus on sales and business development was limited. This is not necessarily a deliberate choice, but rather a natural consequence, reflected by the backgrounds and experiences of the founders ... added managerial competencies to their field of expertise.

This is not the least common among academic spin-offs where the founders tend to have very limited market and management knowledge, which makes this problem apparent and warrants the need for searching externally for this type of knowledge and employing new co-workers in order to be able to shift away from a pure technical focus to market development. For particularly the academic spin-offs, the shift from a focus upon R&D to a shift upon a focus to market is often related to hiring new competences, and is thus highly related to both the human resources dimension and to the growth pattern dimension (for illustration see example under the section 'Human resources').

4.6 *In summary*

The main findings illustrated in relation to processes of developing and managing the KIE venture are:

- Human resources: The KIE venture has an advantage when they hire skilled employees, who have had experience in similar industries. However, human resources also entail many challenges, given the small size of the ventures and the need to balance both managerial and technological experiences and knowledge.
- This is especially important for academic spin-offs, whose founders tend to be limited to scientific and technical knowledge and experience, but with sparse or non-existing management and market knowledge.
- Networks: Customers are often identified as the most important link to the innovation system, suggesting that many opportunities require access to additional market knowledge. Hence, even KIE ventures started based upon technological opportunities are highly dependent upon networks to access market and business knowledge. This is particularly true in the phase after start-up, as demonstrated in the case study of a medical technology firm (see Chapter 11).
    - Networks also influence the initial set-up of the KIE venture. These are usually related to scientific, technological and creative knowledge or to market knowledge. Over time, though, the focal networks of the KIE venture often change, in order to focus more upon market and business knowledge.
    - These networks involve linkages both in high-tech and low-tech sectors. This suggests that innovative opportunities are developed in interaction between the KIE founder and venture with the innovation system, in multiple types of firms and industries.
    - Networks can be international, and related to market expansion. This is a way for the KIE venture to combine entrepreneurial opportunities, technological opportunities and possible productive opportunities through internationalization.
- Growth patterns: The KIE ventures included in the case studies are quite small, with more than 50 per cent of them having less than 50 employees. Despite the small size, these KIE ventures could grow either through only serving companies in their regions or else by going global from the beginning.
    - There seems to be two dominant patterns here – basically, internationalization or not. Essentially, the KIE ventures either have a deeply integrated international approach, which affects their

development of innovative opportunities and access to knowledge, or else they serve a domestic market primarily and this national approach means that their networks are more limited.

- Public policy and incubators: They provide support, which can help through identifying ideas and opportunity seeking, as well as providing valuable networks.
- According to the case studies, incubators are not commonly used by KIE ventures.
- From R&D to market and maturing the venture: The KIE venture often starts out with a focus upon scientific and technological knowledge such as R&D and skilled human capital, but must shift to focusing upon demands of the market, and this often entails challenges for the venture.

5 Outputs

The third and final overall KIE phase identified through the literature review by Lassen and McKelvey (2012) is related to the different types of outcomes generated through KIE.

Basically, the fundamental interest in KIE is based on the understanding that KIE creates positive and above-average output. When public policy is focused upon KIE, it is generally because there is a view or belief in the ability of KIE to stimulate economic growth and development. Here we focus on outcomes in terms of the following two commonly used dimensions:

- Growth performance in terms of employees and turnover
- Patents.

5.1 Growth performance

The first dimension of outcomes of KIE ventures is the actual performance created through growth. There are a variety of measures to assess growth performance and future potential. The most common ones include: Annual sales; Number of employees; Return on sales; Growth in sales; Growth in employees; Financing obtained, such as venture capital.

Collecting data on the performance of new ventures is often difficult due to a lack of historical information and accessibility. There are also major differences in what is defined as growth, including a variety of proxy measures such as sales, employees, venture capital obtained, etc. Moreover, as demonstrated above in the analysis of growth patterns of KIE ventures, the case studies demonstrate sharp shifts between good and bad periods, rendering the predictability of growth performance low.

However, we would like to point out that the problems of measuring the performance of new ventures is of interest because they are a major source of job creation and because improvement in performance is critical to their survival and growth. In the case studies, the focus has been on growth performance in terms of employees as well as turnover.

As already shown under growth patterns above, the majority of the KIE ventures studied are relatively small firms. Generally, the majority of case firms (64/84) have had at least moderate growth during recent years at the time of the interviews, in terms of turnover and/or employees. However, several of the case studies illustrate that growth and performance is often considered in a longer-term perspective than the annual sales/employment increase. As seen in the quote below sales growth is in focus, but emphasis is placed on increase in ability to reach future potential.

> [The firm] has grown 16.5% in sales and 10% in employment over the past 3 years. This is a good result. More importantly however is that we are moving successfully towards our vision of being an innovative and flexible development partner that delivers high quality products to the convenience food market. Innovation is placed at the top of our agenda and the goal is to generate 10% of turnover with the new products introduced within the last 12 months.

As many KIE ventures experience high fluctuations in sales, employment and profitability during the early stages of organizational maturity, this focus on the development of appropriate abilities which will allow the venture to develop towards a future potential, seems to capture the essence of evaluating the performance of the venture to a better degree than traditional measures.

5.2 Patents

The second dimension identified as a measure of output is patenting and intellectual property rights (IPR). Patenting is a commonly employed proxy used for measuring the output of innovation and entrepreneurship alike.

Similarly, the analysis of the case studies indicates that patenting is not a common method for protecting IPRs. However, some patents do exist in the case studies, and Figure 6.3 shows the number of KIE ventures that have taken out patents per sector.

Figure 6.3 shows that 13 studied case firms owns one or more patent, which is approximately 15 per cent of the cases. This is almost an identical finding as in the AEGIS survey, which reported that less than 20 per cent of firms hold patents. Hence, KIE firms prefer other ways of protecting their knowledge.

Interestingly enough, the majority of the case firms owning patents are found in traditionally low-tech industries, such as textiles and food. This is

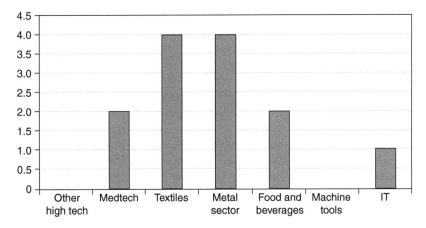

Figure 6.3 Patenting KIE ventures per sector.

probably for the reason pointed out earlier, that many of the firms operating within these low-tech industries in fact provide applications with a high-tech nature.

5.3 In summary

The main findings illustrated in relation to output of the KIE venture creation processes are:

- Growth is common, if measured in terms of turnover/employees during the last three years (64/84 cases). Generally, the majority of case firms seem to have had at least moderate growth during the three latest years at the time of the interviews, in terms of turnover and/or employees. Their growth patterns may also be quite volatile, with sharp up-turns and down-turns. These patterns are generally not related to sales, as they have few in the early stages. Instead, the volatility is related to interactions with the innovation system, such as access to external sources of financing, the acquisition and utilization of business knowledge, and the foci of networks.
- Patenting is very uncommon (only 19/84 case firms have patents). This is a type of scientific and technological knowledge which is protected through patents, which allows appropriability of (part of) the economic value.
- This suggests that the use of patenting data is not a suitable measure for evaluating the true value of KIE. Moreover, the case studies show that many of the patents were in low-tech sectors, again suggesting that the technological opportunities may be more extensive in these sectors than previously understood.

6 Conclusions and policy implications

The end of each section has synthesized the findings of the 86 AEGIS case studies, relative to our model of venture creation in terms of the main dimensions identified in the literature review as particularly important for understanding KIE venture creation and development.

These syntheses illustrate how the KIE founder and venture, on the one hand, depend upon and interact with the innovation system, on the other hand, in the identification and realization of innovative opportunities. These are thus analytical generalizations (Yin, 2003) in the sense that we identify the main results that either confirm or question existing theory which underlies the model of KIE venture as presented in Figure 6.1. In line with the design science approach analytical generalizations allow for discussion on the findings in relation to the model and how this advances our understanding of KIE.

Note that the role of networks is highly visible in all the cases, in that the different types of opportunities and knowledge discussed above are accessed through networks. The knowledge networks link the KIE venture and innovation system. These networks are of different types and diversity. Three main points can be summarized here: (1) Network diversity is important for identifying and acting upon both market and technological and scientific opportunities; (2) Being part of a network means that the partner can contribute knowledge through the network; (3) Networks for KIE ventures are often emerging from previous experience, work place, etc. So the origins of founders (and of firms) influence probabilities of accessing appropriate networks. This suggests that institutional context may play a larger role in KIE venture development than previously understood. In later phases, the role of networks for the KIE development seems to affect development processes and output (performance) in the longer run.

The institutional context of the innovation system seems to influence probability of venture creation through the following mechanisms:

- SMEs often rely upon public policy for growth later on, but initially primarily upon their own sources of financing and networks.
- Empirically, few firms studied as KIE ventures in detail have taken patents. This suggests that public policy ought to focus upon other mechanisms for appropriation, based upon the rich literature available that suggests that patents are only minor (but measurable) inputs into the innovation process (see Winter, 2006).
- Interaction with market (customers, NGOs, business) and with research helps define where firms can develop market and technical opportunities.

This means that the institutional context influences probability of venture creation, and probably their later success or failure. It also allows us to focus upon the dynamic aspect in the range and necessity of developing innovative opportunities through a process that combines entrepreneurial, technological and productive opportunities. This in turn requires that the KIE venture is able to acquire and use market knowledge; scientific, technological and creative knowledge; and business knowledge. From the perspective of the KIE venture, neither opportunities nor knowledge are 'out there' waiting to be discovered per se. Instead, they report on an interactive, dynamic process involving the creation of opportunities across many dimensions.

Public policy that focuses exclusively on one source of opportunities or that assumes a linear process may not help these firms combine the opportunities, knowledge and resources together into innovations. The discussion is more about how to think about public policy based upon this analysis, and where public policy may need more direct inputs and information to make informed decisions. In several cases, the complexity of the case studies suggest that 'intermediary' policy-actors may be needed, whereby the policy instruments and goals do not directly influence venture creation and management but via other mechanisms that affect KIE ventures.

A key issue for KIE ventures is financing. However, financing is not a one-off need of the company, nor does it rely only upon market instruments for these types of firms. This raises public policy issues. There is a need to differentiate different types and sources of financing – such as venture capital, corporate investments and personal and family savings. Obtaining new or repeated sources of financing may be influenced by organizational changes that affect whether the firm exists, and in what ways. Other types of financing are public, where complementary policy instruments like incubators, can affect the performance of firms, which indicates a need to address the interactions amongst different domains of policy. A related issue is about how long, and who should finance both the first round of financing but also later rounds of financing. This suggests that there may be a need to stimulate intermediary policy goals, such as reviewing regulatory conditions for buy-outs or bankruptcy.

A more intangible public policy implication is whether it is possible to create new opportunities, and whether one can develop better instruments and goals that indicate how to bring together (entrepreneurial) opportunities and resources. One goal could be to stimulate (or increase the likelihood) of serial entrepreneurship, i.e. the launching of multiple ventures by the same entrepreneur, which would enable knowledge spillovers across a portfolio of start-ups.

Another important question for policy is how to develop instruments to promote entrepreneurial learning. A clear issue is the need to develop learning not only about technological knowledge but also, or even especially, about market knowledge, such as the demands of customers. An issue is especially how to balance between a focus on knowledge-intensive development and a focus on bringing the knowledge efficiently to market in terms of product, processes or services, and thereby creating wealth. Policy might intervene in order to promote a perspective that is more market oriented – and less technology oriented – for the firm. This could be done, for example, through introducing subsidies for demonstration projects or soft loans for products to be introduced into markets. These types of policy instruments try to provide incentives and resources for firms that are more oriented towards the market, and market opportunities.

Based upon the insights and perspectives of entrepreneurs in KIE ventures, more information is needed to conduct public policy initiatives. Public policy instruments must clearly identify specific goals and targets of different forms of start-ups, to be effective. This suggests the need to obtain more distinct tools and analysis of especially university spin-offs but also of corporate spin-offs. One could also further develop intermediary policy that stimulates knowledge development and diffusion. For example, the evaluation of public policy could more focus upon mechanisms that increase the knowledge intensity of existing companies through technology transfer such as consultancy rather than focusing upon the formation of ventures per se.

There is also a need for public policy to reconsider what venture creation and firm growth means. Venture creation as a proxy is often taken as given, e.g. as a useful and relevant measure of the impact of policy upon entrepreneurship. The research outlined above suggests that the process of new firm formation is somewhat more complex than previously imagined. Policy may thus need different measures of what constitutes a high level of firm formation, in different regions or different types of technologies. Public policy needs to keep in mind both the expected effects of growth and performance, as well as the expected timeline. This matters in terms of policy evaluation, because many effects may take a long time and also because the performance may vary widely in different time periods.

Notes

1 The analysis of these 86 case studies was developed during the European Union research project AEGIS (Advancing Knowledge-Intensive Entrepreneurship and Innovation for Economic Growth and Well-being in Europe), project number 225134. IMIT has administered the project, and our work has been funded by IMIT and by the University of Gothenburg. We appreciate all the comments during the AEGIS project on this work. In addition, we would like to thank participants at the following conference. This paper presented at the ZEW conference 'International conference on the Dynamics of Entrepreneurship' Center for European Economic Research (ZEW) and Mannheim Center for Competition and innovation (Macci). Mannheim University, Germany, 3–5 September, 2012. For an overview of the case studies, see Ljungberg *et al.* (2012). Note that AEGIS also included case studies of sectors, regions and countries. These are at different levels of aggregation, and include studies of high-tech, low-tech and services. However, they are not included for analysis here, because this chapter is focusing upon the level of aggregation of the KIE venture.

2 This definition has also been used to develop the AEGIS survey of KIE ventures (see Chapter 3, Chapter 4 and Caloghirou *et al.*, 2011).
3 www.aegis-fp7.eu.
4 A few later chapters in this book also follow the typical case study format, that is, they give a detailed and historical case description of one or a set of companies, which allows analysing in detail how the KIE process unfolds.
5 The companion chapter is more focused upon analytical generalizations, relative to how the novel empirical work enables us to further expand our conceptual (and possibly our theoretical) knowledge as well.

References

Caloghirou, Y., Protogerou, A. and Tsakanikas, A., 'Final report summarizing survey methods and results', AEGIS – 7th Framework Programme for Research and Technological Development, Deliverable 7.1.5, 2011.

Hevner, A.R., March, S., Park, J. and Ram, S., 'Design science in information systems research', *MIS Quarterly*, 28(1), 2004, 75–105.

Lassen A.H., and McKelvey, M., 'Conceptualizing knowledge-intensive entrepreneurship: a literature review for analyzing case studies and defining policy implications', AEGIS – 7th Framework Programme for Research and Technological Development, Deliverable 7.2.2, 2012.

Ljungberg, D., McKelvey, M. and Lassen, A.H., 'Final report on case studies: emerging trends, lessons and methodological issues'. AEGIS – 7th Framework Programme for Research and Technological Development, Deliverable 7.2.3. 2012.

Malerba, F., and McKelvey, M., 'Conceptualizing knowledge-intensive entrepreneurship: concepts and models', AEGIS – 7th Framework Programme for Research and Technological Development, Deliverable 1.1.1, 2011.

McKelvey, M., and Lassen, A.H., *Managing Knowledge Intensive Entrepreneurship*. Cheltenham, UK: Edward Elgar Publishers, 2013a.

McKelvey, M., and Lassen, A.H., *How Entrepreneurs Do What They Do: Case Studies of Knowledge Intensive Entrepreneurship*. Cheltenham, UK: Edward Elgar Publishers, 2013b.

van Aken, J. E., Berends, H. and Van der Bij, H., *Problem Solving in Organizations: A Methodological Handbook for Business and Management Students*. Cambridge: Cambridge University Press, 2012.

Wieringa, R., 'Design science as nested problem solving', paper presented at the Proceedings of the 4th international conference on design science research in information systems and technology, 2009.

Winter, S., 'The logic of appropriability: from Schumpeter to Arrow to Teece', *Research Policy*, 35(8), 2006, 1100–1106.

Yin. R., *Case study research*, 3rd edition, Thousand Oaks, CA: Sage, 2003.

7 Opportunities and knowledge intensive entrepreneurship

A meta-analysis of 86 case studies of ventures

Maureen McKelvey, Daniel Ljungberg and Astrid Heidemann Lassen

1 Introduction

Knowledge is increasingly seen as vital for economic growth and societal development, including a specific focus upon the role of technological knowledge in stimulating certain types of entrepreneurship.[1] This book, the AEGIS project and Malerba and McKelvey (2011, and see Chapter 2 of this volume) go further. A key issue here is that knowledge intensive entrepreneurial (KIE) ventures can exist in many different sectors, drawing upon different types of opportunities and knowledge, and how those dynamics occur.

In this chapter we present and discuss the results of 86 case studies, with the aim to further the understanding of venture creation as a specific process of opportunity identification and exploitation, which can be seen as a process view of development over time.[2] Hence, this chapter addresses an important issue, namely the dynamics of knowledge intensive entrepreneurship in different sectors, and specifically how the process of venture creation occurs in relation to external knowledge networks and innovation systems.[3] This book as a whole makes the argument that KIE venture creation must be understood as a developmental process, which involves the interaction between the 'micro' events around individuals, ventures and firms with the 'macro' events around opportunities, markets and technologies. The KIE processes are highly dynamic with strong feedback loops between the individuals, the company and society.[4] This chapter addresses how such dynamics occur at the level of the firm in relation to different types of opportunities and knowledge, when we take a process view.

The purpose of this chapter is to consider in detail what different types of opportunities and knowledge are identified during the start-up phase and realized through the management and development phase. Networks are an aspect of management. Malerba and McKelvey (Chapter 2 in this volume) argue that the process and innovation system play a particular role in KIE entrepreneurship, because networks for knowledge help create innovative opportunities.

A major aspect of the context can be called innovation systems. Networks including actors other than firms are highly influential and affect entrepreneurship, interpreted from an innovation system perspective. Networks influence access to resources for the KIE and also influence their perception of which innovative opportunities can be developed through science, technologies and markets.

(Malerba and McKelvey, Chapter 2 in this volume)

While the concept of networks and relations to innovation systems should help us understand the broad picture, this chapter focuses on more specific details about the different types of opportunities and knowledge that are actually used by KIE ventures.

Based on 86 case studies of KIE ventures, this chapter provides empirical insights and analytical generalizations about how the process of venture creation occurs in relation to external knowledge networks and innovation systems. Following the approach of e.g. Eisenhardt (1989) and Yin (2003), the current chapter uses these 86 case studies to generate analytical generalizations, which allow for in-depth insights as well as validity through generalizability.

In Section 2 we first provide a literature review, focusing upon different types of opportunities and how knowledge networks represent linkages between the KIE venture and the innovation system. Hereafter, Section 3 presents the empirical findings, analysis and conclusions, while Section 4 provides a discussion of implications for public policy.

2 Literature review

Entrepreneurship is a broad field. Indeed, research in entrepreneurship may well be a 'catch-all' term, carried out by scholars in many different disciplines (Davidsson and Wicklund, 2001). Nevertheless, there is consistency in the literature in that the concept 'entrepreneurship' refers in a broader sense to a phenomenon of novelty and change, often considered and analysed in terms of opportunity and change in the economy (Shane, 2000, 2004). Recent research calls for us to understand entrepreneurship and opportunities as the nexus between action and interaction (Venkataraman *et al.* 2012). This means that actions at the individual and organizational level need to be understood in relation to opportunities.

To understand such processes, Carlsson *et al.* (2013: 914) provide a useful definition of entrepreneurship in general, in such a way as linking the micro and macro levels:

Entrepreneurship refers primarily to an economic function that is carried out, by individuals, entrepreneurs, acting independently and within organizations, to perceive and create new opportunities and to introduce their ideas into the market, under uncertainty, by making decisions about location, product design, resource use, institutions, and reward systems. The entrepreneurial activity and the entrepreneurial ventures are influenced by their socio-economic environment, and they result ultimately in economic growth and human welfare.

This definition provides a broad framework for trying to understand the interactions between the micro level and the meso and macro levels.

This chapter focuses upon the specific type of entrepreneurship, called knowledge intensive entrepreneurship (KIE). In order to identify the phases and key dimensions in the cases, we apply the McKelvey and Lassen KIE venture creation model, as developed extensively in McKelvey and Lassen (2013a, 2013b). An earlier version of the model (Lassen and McKelvey, 2012) is in Chapter 6 of this book applied for detailed analysis of the 86 case studies, which in turn also enabled the further development of the model as used in the present chapter. This chapter uses the model to help focus, and help us better understand the process of entrepreneurship, from the perspective of the founder and firm, in relation to the innovation system and knowledge.

Figure 7.1 presents the three main processes of Inputs, Development and Outputs, as well as the underlying dimensions that need to be analysed for a process view. The model and underlying theories represent a useful focusing device, in order to discuss how societal organizations (like firms) can translate ideas and opportunities through their internal organization and their external networks into profits and new products and services.

Our proposition is that the KIE venture can access resources and realize opportunities, through a series of decisions, balancing alternative logics between business planning and identification and exploitation of unexpected opportunities generated externally during these processes. Thereby, we can enrich the model by explaining how the KIE venture obtains resources, ideas and translates ideas into innovative opportunities during these phases (McKelvey and Lassen, 2013a, 2013b). This enables detailed yet structured understanding of how the founders and ventures involved in KIE manage the process of venture creation.

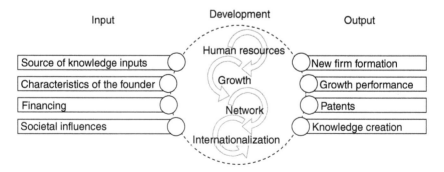

Figure 7.1 KIE model (McKelvey and Lassen, 2013a).

Meta-analysis of 86 case studies is used to examine how the KIE entrepreneur and venture can identify and exploit opportunities, and generate economic value in specific situations, whereby they can gain access to knowledge and resources through their interactions with the innovation system. In doing so, we consider the different phases and key dimensions of KIE venture creation, including observing the role of different types of knowledge networks and of opportunities. The different sources of opportunities identified include entrepreneurial, technological and productive.

2.1 Innovative opportunities and the different sources of opportunities

This chapter is based upon a process view of opportunities, which arise in interaction between the individual, organization and innovation system. Because we are discussing a dynamic process, the initial idea that is considered an opportunity will most likely be modified over time, in order to better fit the firm strategy and external environment.

The concept of 'innovative opportunities' was explicitly developed to address the strengths and shortcoming of the existing discussions of opportunities as arising from different sources. Holmén *et al.* (2007) develop the argument that 'innovative opportunities' arise from the systemic interaction between three types of opportunities – namely entrepreneurial, technological and productive ones.

The implication for analysing how a KIE venture realizes an innovative opportunity is that we should be able to identify the following three conceptual elements. They are necessary in order for actors to have the possibility to identify, act upon and realize the potential inherent in an idea:

- an economic value for someone;
- a possibility that the resources needed to realize the opportunity can be mobilized;
- a possibility that at least some part of the generated economic value can be appropriated by the actor pursuing the opportunity.

These constitute the conceptual elements that occur throughout start-up and development of the KIE venture. For the purposes of this chapter, we have structured the summary of this process, through the model of the KIE venture, as found in Figure 7.1.

For the KIE venture, the innovative opportunity can be driven by different sources of opportunities – which we define as entrepreneurial, technological and productive. Holmén *et al.* (2007) and McKelvey and Lassen (2013a) have reviewed existing literature from different fields, in order to help specify how different sectors and national institutional contexts may be driven by different sources of opportunities.

Within entrepreneurship literature, a dominant line of thought is 'entrepreneurial opportunities'. The main idea is that market imperfections create the possibility for the entrepreneur to capture price differentials and thereby introduce non-equilibrium as an emergent property of the economy (Carlsson *et al.*, 2013).

The idea of 'entrepreneurial opportunities' can be traced back to the Austrian school of economics (Hayek, 1945). According to this perspective, the role of the entrepreneur is to observe market imperfections, and to eliminate differences in prices through introducing products and services. The entrepreneur exploits market imperfections, due to the possibility of gaining arbitrage profits (Kirzner, 1973). Much of the more recent literature focuses upon the specific and idiosyncratic patterns. Ardichvili *et al.* (2003) argue that the individual entrepreneur is more or less able to identify these market opportunities and develop a venture, based upon: (a) entrepreneurial alertness, (b) information asymmetries and prior (individual) knowledge, (c) social networks, (d) personality traits and (e) the type of opportunity. Hence, the main structural explanation for entrepreneurial opportunities can be seen to be the 'market', especially how market imperfections enable arbitrage profits. However, given that these market imperfections could in principle be visible to all entrepreneurs, much of the literature stressing this type of opportunity tends to try to find explanations at the level of characteristics and traits of the individual entrepreneur. This has also led to a central discussion in entrepreneurship research about the origin of opportunities as related to specific characteristics of the founder (Eckhardt and Shane, 2003; Sarason *et al.*, 2006; Shane and Venkataraman, 2000; Vaghely and Julien, 2010).

A second concept, which is important within evolutionary and Schumpeterian economics, is 'technological opportunities'. This has been seen as a key concept of how science and technological knowledge help drive economic development, which may differ in different sectors and nations. Scherer (1965) put forth the argument that technological opportunities help explain the differential propensity of firms in different sectors to patent and innovate. He argues that 'differences in technological opportunity – e.g. differences in technical investment possibilities unrelated to the mere volume of sales and typically opened up by the broad advance of knowledge – are a major factor responsible for inter-industry differences in inventive output' (Scherer, 1965: 1121).

This literature often identifies and explains major differences amongst industries, and the role of technological knowledge in stimulating growth. Breschi *et al.* (2000: 390–391) argue that

> observed sectoral patterns of innovative activities are related to the nature of the relevant technological regimes ... defined by the specific combination of technological opportunities, appropriability of

innovations, cumulativeness of technical advance and the properties of the knowledge base underlying firms' innovative activities.

This concept of technological opportunity thus places the firms' own investment into research and development activities into an idea that their probability of finding an invention and later innovation is dependent not only on the firm per se, but upon the likelihood of discovering new knowledge and the overall rate of change in this type of knowledge (Klevorick *et al.*, 1995). The firm's willingness to invest in R&D and innovation is often explicitly tied to a discussion of appropriability, that is, about whether the firm will secure the rewards for themselves, in contrast to the spill-over effects upon competitors (Winter, 2006).

The concept of 'productive opportunities' is used within theories of the firm from a resource-based and knowledge-based perspective. Moran and Ghosal (2006) presents an argument that productive opportunities within existing firms are those resource combinations (possibilities for resource deployment) that an actor can perceive and is able and willing to act upon and exploit.

This concept of 'productive opportunities' refers to the firm's internal organization of resources and competencies and how creative reconfiguration of such resources lead to success in the market. Penrose (1959), who is often seen as the pioneer in these theories, stressed that opportunities are not a market imperfection, but arise from the possibilities to combine the internal resources of a firm in various ways. How those resources are deployed will affect the firm's growth and profitability, but these are limited by the managers' capacity to envision alternative modes.

More modern literature, like Hamel and Prahalad (1989), takes into account factors that are internal and external to the firm, through the concept of strategic intent, whereby the internal resource base should not limit the growth possibilities. Teece *et al.* (1997) stress that firms can develop dynamic capabilities, consisting of positions, paths and processes. These authors stress that the possibility to re-configure the firm is limited by the firm's historical development, in terms of paths that it has followed over time, and by the organizational and managerial processes used to leverage existing resources and access new ones.

Taken together, this discussion of different sources of opportunities can lead us to expect that different types of KIE ventures are started. Four main types have been identified empirically in the 86 case studies, namely: independent start-ups, academic spin-offs, spin-offs and internal corporate entrepreneurship. The latter type is specifically related to existing firms, whereas the other types assume more independent start-ups. Academics spin-offs can be defined in different ways, such as ones started by employees at universities or ones started by students. For many different types of KIE ventures, the founder is expected to play a key role, although in relation to existing resources in companies or in the network in the innovation system.

The bulk of the studied KIE ventures (38 cases) are what we label as independent start-ups, meaning firms that are neither corporate nor academic spin-offs. Fourteen cases concerned corporate entrepreneurship[5] within existing firms, in that the founders start new organizations and business units but still linked to the established firm. From the case studies analysed here, these are generally in low-tech sectors, and often in Eastern Europe.

This leads us to a number of propositions, based on the literature, about how the sources of opportunities will lead to different categories of KIE ventures.

> Entrepreneurial opportunities have been defined relative to the market, resulting in the creation of a new venture. This source of opportunity ought to have as its primary mode of entry as 'independent' entrepreneurs or independent start-ups. However, the dynamics of the relationship between the KIE venture and innovation system suggests that relevant knowledge is also transferred in other cases. Therefore, we argue that the KIE ventures resulting from this source of opportunity should correspond to the categories of academic spin-offs, corporate spin-offs and independent start-ups.

> Technological opportunities correspond to sources that rely upon new scientific results and technologies which renew the technological pool (cf. Klevorick *et al.*, 1995). The literature primarily discusses R&D intensity as a measure of the pool of technological opportunities. Therefore, we argue that the KIE ventures resulting from this source of opportunities are either academic spin-offs or corporate spin-offs.

> Productive opportunities have to do with re-configuring the internal resources of an existing firm. The primary category is therefore corporate entrepreneurship, but this may also entail corporate spin-offs.

In summary, this section has identified three conceptual elements that need to occur in order for innovative opportunities to be identified and realized within the model of KIE venture (Inputs, Development and Outputs). Within these processes, the KIE founder and venture needs to interact with the innovation system in relation to defining economic value, mobilizing resources and appropriating returns.

Moreover, a brief overview of different streams of literature suggests that innovative opportunities may primarily arise from entrepreneurial opportunities (related to the market); from technological opportunities (related to scientific and technological knowledge) and from productive opportunities (related to internal business resources and management vision). Because we are using a process view, the opportunities may be relevant both in relation to the inputs needed for venture creation as well as in the phases of development and management.

2.2 Different types of knowledge

The above discussion of innovative opportunities and different sources of opportunities has not explicitly addressed the different types of knowledge involved. Given that knowledge is a key part of KIE in general, an understanding of knowledge and especially the relevance of different types of knowledge is a key part of our overall discussion.

The broader literature suggests that knowledge is distinct from data and information. Data is described as having no meaning, a series of inputs, providing the raw material from which information is produced. Information is the next level and is defined as data that has been organized into patterns enabling the extrapolation of meaning (Antonelli, 1999). Cook and Brown (1999) take the concept of knowledge a step further by differentiating between knowledge and knowing. They suggest that knowledge is about possession and knowing is about interaction between the knower and the world.

This suggests that the KIE venture needs to find relevant types of knowledge – what we can call knowledge acquisition – and they also need to use what we can call knowledge utilization. The firm must both acquire appropriate information and utilize the knowledge within the firm.

Information *acquisition* refers to the capability to identify and acquire information. Effort in information acquisition routines has mainly three attributes: intensity, speed and direction (Zahra and George, 2002). The intensity, speed and direction of a firm's attempts to identify and collect relevant information can determine the quality of a firm's acquisition capabilities. These activities vary in their richness and complexity, highlighting a need to have different areas of expertise within a firm to successfully internalize knowledge from externally generated information.

Knowledge utilization refers to the assimilation, transformation and exploitation of new knowledge (Zahra and George, 2002). Hence, for KIE ventures, it covers the routines and processes that allow the entrepreneur to analyse, process, interpret and understand the information obtained from external sources, as well as the actual implementation of new knowledge. Knowledge *utilization* is also emphasized as an important factor in innovation activities (von Hippel, 1988; Cockburn and Henderson, 1998; Cohen *et al.*, 2002; Chesbrough, 2003). For example, according to Chesbrough (2003), openness to using external sources of information and ideas in the firm's innovation processes, as well as interaction among different partners is of high importance when creating value through innovation activities.

This has implications for our analysis. Throughout the model of venture creation, the KIE founder and venture needs to be active in terms of acquiring knowledge and utilizing it inside the firm. In doing so, we postulate that the three sources of opportunities outlined above can be used to identify three types of knowledge needed by the KIE venture. Due to the particular characteristics of knowledge, all three types of knowledge are to some extent held (or understood) inside the firm but they are also to some extent information that can be obtained from the innovation system.

A first source of opportunity discussed above is 'entrepreneurial opportunities', which are related to the market per se and also to how the founder could acquire and use this type of knowledge related to the market. Hence, we propose that a first category is market knowledge.

Market knowledge refers to information gathered from past and current customers and markets – but also an idea of what future buyers may want. KIE ventures are engaged in entrepreneurship and turning an idea into value, and a business proposition, someone or some organization must be willing to buy the product, licence or service at sale for a price. This is sometimes called a 'business model', in relating what the firm makes or does to what the customers want. If the customers or buyers do not buy the offer, then something is incorrect in what the KIE ventures thought they knew about the market. Many things could be wrong, including their overall interpretation of the market. The price may be too high (or more occasionally, too low in the case of some services like consultancy where high price may be thought to signal high quality). The customers may want different technologies or performance attributes. The competitors may be offering something that is better, cheaper or more useful for other reasons. Hence, market knowledge includes understanding of what customers want or are willing to buy, but also includes an understanding of the market dynamics and industrial dynamics over time.

Another source of opportunity discussed above is 'technological opportunities', which are related to how different types of scientific and technological knowledge stimulate different types of sectors. Moreover, creativity matters such as in services, which may not be included in traditional definitions of scientific and technological knowledge. The literature on services suggests that 'creativity' is key and not captured by scientific and technological knowledge (Gallouj and Djellal, 2011). Hence, creativity needs to be added specifically, and we propose that a second category is scientific, technological and creative knowledge.

This type involves *scientific, technological and creative knowledge*. This type of knowledge is generally gained as the result of many years of study, and so the experts here are often natural scientists and engineers as well as creative artists and design specialists. They like to develop things and to apply their expertise to solve problems and offer solutions (e.g. Stephan, 1996). These individuals may or may not have had previous work experience. They do, however, have specialized knowledge that can be gained in different manners, such as through experience, work experience and education.

Another type of opportunity discussed above is 'productive opportunities', and literature on this is related to reconfiguring internal firm resources (and capabilities) to use them the most effectively in a competitive situation. Hence, we propose that a third category is *business knowledge*. Business knowledge has to do with running the company, both internally and externally. Internally involves things like running the company through organizational design and management techniques and externally through things like networks, relating to government regulations, and so on. Much of this type of knowledge cannot be codified as laws and principles in the way that scientific and technological can be codified and taught. Business knowledge has to do with facing uncertainty and risk, trying reasonably right solutions and finding new paths forward. Hence, this business knowledge has to do with both 'knowing' and 'doing' business.

In summary, this section proposes that one can study three types of knowledge as key for KIE ventures, namely: market knowledge; scientific, technological and creative knowledge; and business knowledge. These three domains of knowledge may be useful to understand many different types of firms, but here, we state that they seem especially important, to KIE ventures, during the processes identified in the KIE venture creation process.

3 An overview of the 86 KIE ventures

The case studies of 86 KIE ventures can be described in different ways. One way is to consider whether the KIE venture has strong linkages to new organizational forms within companies (corporate entrepreneurship); emerged from universities (academic spin-off); emerged from existing companies (corporate spin-offs) or were independent start-ups. Figure 7.2 demonstrates the distribution in the 86 case studies. This categorization of the cases is based on the sources of the KIE, i.e. the sources of the ideas, knowledge and opportunities leading to the foundation of the venture.

Seventy-two case studies concerned the start-up and development of different types of KIE ventures, which includes academic and corporate spin-offs as well as independent start-ups. Moreover, 14 cases have been conducted on new organizational forms within large companies, i.e. corporate entrepreneurship.

Another way to classify the KIE ventures is the distribution of cases over types of sectors, defined as low tech, high tech or service. Figure 7.3 shows the distribution, when the KIE ventures are classified into their industrial sector.

Figure 7.3 shows that the majority of cases concern firms within industries that traditionally can be characterized as low tech, which includes industries such as textiles and food. Moreover, 35 cases relate to firms within high-tech industries, which in the analysed case studies means

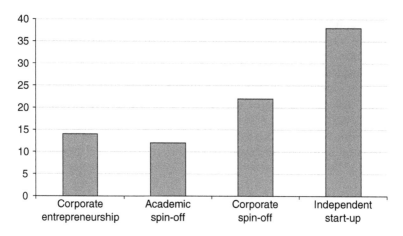

Figure 7.2 Distribution per type of KIE venture.

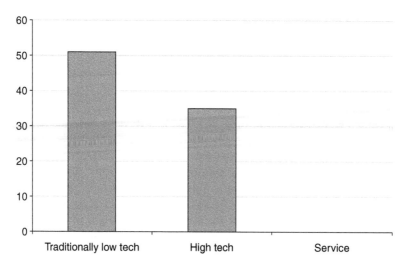

Figure 7.3 Distribution of case studies over type of sector (low tech, high tech and service).

primarily IT and Medical technologies (Medtech). Note that no case studies were conducted on KIE ventures that were a priori classified in service industries. However, this is not actually a correct representation at the firm level. When reading the detailed case studies, it is clear that the firms classified as primarily belonging to low-tech or high-tech industries often had a business model based at least partly on service provision. Thus, there are many case studies where services play a very important part of the venture development, although no case studies of KIE ventures cover firms only focused upon services. Figure 7.4 provides a more detailed overview of the sectors.

The figure demonstrates a range of industries that can be considered high-tech (IT, Medtech) and low-tech (Machine tools, Food and beverages). Note that many case studies were concentrated within the Machine tool and IT industries. This distribution reflects that one of the AEGIS work-packages delivering case studies was aimed at comparing certain low-tech industries.

Figure 7.5 shows the distribution of cases across countries. More case studies were done in Eastern than in Western Europe. The reported case studies often had a different character in terms of depth of the cases. The Eastern European case studies were often short and to the point, providing valuable insight into national contexts, which may offer different types of opportunities for entrepreneurship. The case studies in the Western Europe countries were often quite detailed and extensive, following the KIE venture in more detail and usually over longer periods of time.

Our analysis of the case studies demonstrates two very interesting methodological observations. Technological opportunities appear to be wider spread than only in the academic spin-offs or only in high-tech industries. The first is that the detailed material provided by the analysed case studies in the traditionally low-tech industries demonstrates that the focus is upon the application of science-based and high-tech knowledge into these industries. So, even though these case studies are explicitly chosen to illustrate KIE ventures in low-tech industries, the case studies themselves relate to the development and application of advanced technology and knowledge.

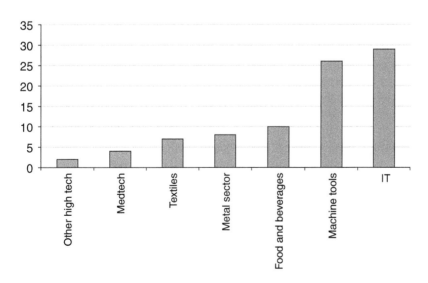

Figure 7.4 Distribution per specific industry.

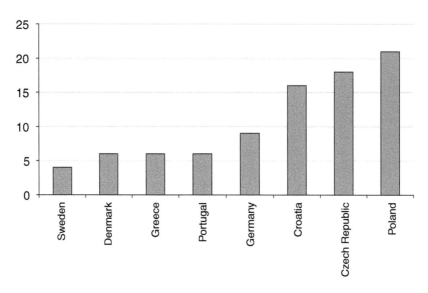

Figure 7.5 Distribution across countries.

More specifically, the majority of cases within traditional low-tech industries focus on high-tech applications, meaning that there is an overlap between these two categorizations, which is not visible by only looking at the industry classification.

The second methodological observation is that although no case study concerns firms that are specifically dedicated to service industries, in many cases, especially for firms within the IT sector, the firms also provide their customers with service offers, in terms of e.g. maintenance, support and training. Hence, services are definitely represented in the case studies. This leads us to raise questions about the value of using pre-defined industrial classifications. The results demonstrate that the idea of low-tech, high-tech and services is much more complex at the level of the KIE venture than can be captured by industry classifications and thus supports the notion that these innovative opportunities can also be stimulated by technological opportunities in sectors other than high-tech ones.

4 Opportunities and knowledge in the 86 case studies of KIE venture creation and development

This section provides an analysis of the different types of opportunities and knowledge that are identified during the start-up phase and realized through the management and development phase. More specific context details are provided, including industry and country, to better understand how and where these three types of opportunities can be found in the case studies.

A first aspect is that the type of spin-off can be related to the sources of opportunities. Based upon our meta-analysis, we can relate what we expected, relative to what we find through the case studies as summarized in Table 7.1.

Table 7.1 shows the expectations from the literature and that these are confirmed in the empirical findings from the meta-analysis. In addition, we found entrepreneurial opportunities in corporate entrepreneurship; we found technological opportunities could be present in all four types of spin-offs.

Twelve cases concern academic spin-offs, which are firms founded by researchers employed at universities or research institutes, but in a few cases also by recent graduates that established the case firm based on ideas and knowledge gained during their academic studies. Corporate spin-offs are similarly firms founded based on knowledge and opportunities identified by existing firms, but where they have been actively spun off by the parent company. This means that the established firm has played some role in the process of venture creation.

A second aspect is that the type of sector can be related to the sources of opportunities relative to different types of sectors (see Table 7.2). This may affect the availability of opportunities.

Table 7.2 again relates the expectations from the literature to the empirical findings, and the confirmation from the meta-analysis. In addition, for entrepreneurial opportunities, they were found in low-tech and service sectors; and, in addition, for technological opportunities, they were found

Table 7.1 Type of spin-off and sources of opportunities as expected from literature and in the empirical findings

	Expectations based upon our analysis of literature	*Empirical findings*
Entrepreneurial opportunities (EO)	Academic spin-offs Corporate spin-offs Independent start-ups	Confirmed that found in these three types of spin-offs. In addition, found in corporate entrepreneurship.
Technological opportunities (TO)	Academic spin-offs Corporate spin-offs	Confirmed that found in these two types of spin-offs. In addition, it is found that technological opportunities can be one driver for all four types.
Productive opportunities (PO)	Corporate spin-offs Corporate entrepreneurship	Confirmed that found in these two types of spin-offs.

Table 7.2 Sector and sources of opportunities as expected from literature and in the empirical findings

	Expectations based upon our analysis of literature	Empirical findings
Entrepreneurial opportunities (EO)	High-tech sectors	Confirm high tech In addition, low tech In addition, services
Technological opportunities (TO)	High tech	High tech In addition, low tech
Productive opportunities (PO)	All sectors could benefit from more strategic use of resources	Not found across sectors Primarily in low tech

in low-tech sectors. For productive opportunities, these were primarily found within firms in low-tech sectors, and not across all sectors as was predicted.

As shown in Table 7.3, the meta-analysis suggests that KIE ventures are widely distributed across Europe, and they have reasonably similar patterns. Finding similarities across European Union countries is an interesting result, given the wide diversity in countries studied here. The sectoral aspects as related to the type of opportunity appear to be more important than the country context per se.

4.1 Implications for public policy

This section will briefly summarize the results of this chapter, and then discuss the broader implications of the findings for public policy. To

Table 7.3 Country and sources of opportunities as in the empirical findings

	Empirical findings
Entrepreneurial opportunities (EO)	Found in many different countries The KIE are found across many different sectors in the different countries. This supports the proposition that low-tech and service sectors can also engage in KIE across different countries.
Technological opportunities (TO)	KIE ventures often use TOs in relation to both universities and to the industry. This means that both universities and large firms stimulate and renew the pool of TO, and depending upon which country where they are located, this may influence the propensity for KIE venture creation.
Productive opportunities (PO)	Most common in Eastern Europe. Appears to relate more to ownership, restructuring of existing businesses more than the development of new ideas.

impact public policy, further work should be done to elaborate each implication in terms of goals, relevant information to analysis, and instruments to be effective tools of policy.

The purpose of this chapter is to consider in detail what different types of opportunities and knowledge are involved. The discussion of opportunities and knowledge was discussed in detail. The analysis linked the three types of opportunities to an overview of the KIE ventures analysed, as summarized in Table 7.4.

Table 7.4 synthesizes our results relative to the pattern identified in terms of the type of KIE venture exploiting that opportunity, the type of sector, and the country. Several results – which strengthen the overall notion of KIE – are reported, especially as the idea is extended to other types of spin-offs and start-ups and to new industries and countries.

Indeed, creating the opportunities and the importance of knowledge networks can be seen as much in 'high-tech' as for 'low-tech' sectors. The patterns are surprisingly similar between high-tech and low-tech firms but different in different sectoral and national institutional contexts. These contexts appear to influence the propensity and direction of KIE development.

One issue is the scope of public policy, given that different sources of opportunities, different types of knowledge and different pathways of development of KIE ventures can be identified. Public policy decision-makers need to choose whether to try to support all KIE or whether to try to support the ones that they evaluate as more likely to succeed. This is a difficult issue to evaluate. On the one hand, clearly, the ventures that receive support will report that they feel it is important to the development of the firm, and this seemed particularly true in Eastern Europe as reported here. On the other hand, there are always counter arguments about other

Table 7.4 Summary of the new evidence (i.e. not predicted from theory) that has been generated through meta-analysis

	Type of KIE venture	Industry	Country
Entrepreneurial opportunities (EO)	Also corporate entrepreneurship	Also in low tech and services	Uneven distribution
Technological opportunities (TO)	Holds for all four types of KIE ventures	Also in low tech	KIE ventures often relate to the country's university and industry structure
Productive opportunities (PO)	Also corporate entrepreneurship	Primarily low tech	More common in Eastern Europe

uses of public money, and other sources of financing and advice. Therefore, there is a clear contradiction between the two opposing ways to evaluate policy – that the public money was put to the most efficient uses or that the public money influences KIE venture creation in geographical areas and sectors that would not have been started otherwise.

Notes

1 The case study was developed during the European Union research project AEGIS (Advancing Knowledge-Intensive Entrepreneurship and Innovation for Economic Growth and Well-being in Europe), project number 225134. IMIT has administered the project, and our work has been funded by IMIT and by the University of Gothenburg. We appreciate all the comments during the AEGIS project on this work.
2 We refer to 'opportunities' in relation to identification and exploitation. There is a large debate on whether opportunities are created or developed. Here, we follow Short *et al.* (2010: 54): 'A reasonable middle ground position is that some opportunities are discovered whereas others are created. Our expectation is that the literature will move towards this position in the future'. Hence, we consider that the identification of opportunities may include either creation or discovery.
3 The analysis of these 86 case studies were developed during the European Union research project AEGIS (Advancing Knowledge-Intensive Entrepreneurship and Innovation for Economic Growth and Well-being in Europe), project number 225134. IMIT has administered the project, and our work has been funded by IMIT and by the University of Gothenburg. We appreciate all the comments during the AEGIS project on this work. In addition, we would like to thank participants at the following conference. This paper presented at the ZEW conference 'International conference on the Dynamics of Entrepreneurship' Center for European Economic Research (ZEW) and Mannheim Center for Competition and innovation (Macci). Mannheim University, Germany, 3–5 September, 2012. Earlier work with co-authors Mats Magnusson and Magnus Holmén in related to the opportunities concept is also acknowledged.
4 We will use the term 'KIE venture' for the company, business project or new organizational form created in this way.
5 Corporate entrepreneurship is

> the process of entrepreneurship within an existing organization of any size or age. The process refers to emergent, behavioural intentions and behaviors of an organization that are related to departures from the customary. Corporate entrepreneurship processes not only refer to the creation of new ventures, but also to the innovative activities and orientations, such as development of new products, services, technologies, administrative techniques, strategies and competitive posture.
>
> (Lassen, 2007: 93)

References

Antonelli, C., 'The evolution of the industrial organisation of the production of knowledge', *Cambridge Journal of Economics*, 23(2), 1999, 243–260.
Ardichvili, A., Cardozo R. and Ray, S., 'A theory of entrepreneurial opportunity identification and development', *Journal of Business Venturing*, 2003.

Breschi, S., Malerba, F. and Orsenigo, L., 'Technological regimes and Schumpeterian patterns of innovation', *The Economic Journal*, 110, 2000, 388–410.

Carlsson, B., Braunerhjelm, P., McKelvey, M., Olofsson, C., Persson, L. and Ylinenpää, H., 'The evolving domain of entrepreneurship research', *Small Business Economics*, 41, 2013, 913–930.

Chesbrough, H.W., 'The logic of open innovation: Managing intellectual property', *California Management Review*, 45(3), 2003, 33–58.

Cockburn, I.M., and Henderson, R.M., 'Absorptive capacity, coauthoring behavior, and the organization of research in drug discovery', *The Journal of Industrial Economics*, 46, 1998, 157–182.

Cohen, W., Nelson, R.R. and Walsh, J., 'Links and impacts: The influence of public research on industrial R&D', *Management Science*, 48, 2002, 1–23.

Cook, S.D.N., and Brown, J.S., 'Bridging epistemologies: The generative dance between organizational knowledge and organizational knowing', *Organization Science*, 10(4), 1999, 381–400.

Davidsson, P., and Wicklund, J., 'Levels of analysis in entrepreneurship research: Current research practice and suggestions for the future', *Entrepreneurship Theory & Practice*, 2001, 81–100.

Eckhardt, JT., and Shane, S.A., 'Opportunities and entrepreneurship', *Journal of Management*, 29, 2003, 333.

Eisenhardt, K., 'Building theories from case study research: Academy of Management', *The Academy of Management Review*, 14(4), 1989, 532–550.

Gallouj, F., and Djellal, F., *The Handbook of Innovation and Services*. Cheltenham, UK: Edward Elgar Publishers, 2011.

Hamel, G., and Prahalad, C.K., 'Strategic intent', *Harvard Business Review*, May/June, 1989, 63–76.

Hayek, F.A., 'The use of knowledge in society', *The American Economic Review*, 35(4), 1945, 519–530.

Holmén, M., Magnusson, M. and McKelvey, M., 'What are innovative opportunities?' *Industry and Innovation*, 14(1), 2007, 27.

Kirzner, I.M., *Competition and Entrepreneurship*. Chicago: University of Chicago Press, 1973.

Klevorick, A., Levin, R., Nelson, R.R. and Winter, S., 'On the sources and significance of interindustry differences in technological opportunities', *Research Policy*, 24, 1995, 185–205.

Lassen, A.H., *Corporate Entrepreneurship: Towards an Understanding of the Importance of Radical Innovation in Knowledge Intensive Firms*. Aalborg University, 2007.

Lassen, A.H., and McKelvey, M., 'Conceptualizing knowledge-intensive entrepreneurship: A literature review for analyzing case studies and defining policy implications', *AEGIS – 7th Framework Programme for Research and Technological Development*, Deliverable 7.2.2, 2012.

Malerba, F., and McKelvey, M., 'Conceptualizing knowledge-intensive entrepreneurship: Concepts and models', *AEGIS – 7th Framework Programme for Research and Technological Development*, Deliverable 1.1.1, 2011.

McKelvey, M., and Lassen, A.H., *Managing Knowledge Intensive Entrepreneurship*. Cheltenham, UK: Edward Elgar Publishers, 2013a.

McKelvey, M., and Lassen, A.H., *How Entrepreneurs Do What They Do: Case Studies of Knowledge Intensive Entrepreneurship*. Cheltenham, UK: Edward Elgar Publishers, 2013b.

Moran, P., and Ghoshal, S., 'Markets, firms, and the process of economic development', *Academy of Management Review*, 24, 2006, 390–412.

Penrose, E.T., *The Theory of the Growth of the Firm*. Oxford: Oxford University Press, 1959.

Sarason, Y., Dean, T., and Dillard, J.F., 'Entrepreneurship as the nexus of individual and opportunity: A structuration view', *Journal of Business Venturing*, 21(3), 2006, 286–305.

Scherer, F.M., 'Firm size, market structure, opportunity and the output of patented inventions', *The American Economic Review*, 55, 1965.

Shane, S.A., 'Prior knowledge and the discovery of entrepreneurial opportunities', *Organization Science*, 11, 2000, 448–469.

Shane, S.A., *Academic Entrepreneurship: University Spinoffs and Wealth Creation*. Cheltenham, UK: Edward Elgar, 2004.

Shane, S.A., and Venkataraman, S., 'The promise of entrepreneurship as a field of research', *Academy of Management Review*, 25, 2000, 217–226.

Short, J.C., Ketchen, D.J., Shook, C.L. and Ireland, R.D., 'The concept of "opportunity" in entrepreneurship research: Past accomplishments and future challenges', *Journal of Management*, 36, 2010, 40–65.

Stephan, P., 'The economics of science', *Journal of Economic Literature*, 34, 1996, 1199–1235.

Teece, D.J., Pisano, G.P., and Shuen, A., 'Dynamic capabilities and strategic management', *Strategic Management Journal*, 18, 1997, 509–533.

Vaghely, I.P., and Julien, P.A., 'Are opportunities recognized or constructed?: An information perspective on entrepreneurial opportunity identification', *Journal of Business Venturing*, 25(1), 2010, 73–86.

Venkataraman, S., Sarasvathy, S., Dew, N. and Forster, W.R., 'Reflections on the 2010 AMR Decade Award: Whither the promise? Moving forward with entrepreneurship as a science of the artificial', *The Academy of Management Review* (AMR), 37, 2012, 21–33.

Von Hippel, E., *The Sources of Innovation*. New York: Oxford University Press, 1988.

Winter, S., 'The logic of appropriability: From Schumpeter to Arrow to Teece', *Research Policy*, 35(8), 2006, 1100–1106.

Yin, R., *Case Study Research*, 3rd edition. Thousand Oaks, CA: Sage, 2003.

Zahra, S.A., and George, G., 'Absorptive capacity: A review, reconceptualization, and extension', *The Academy of Management Review*, 27, 2002, 185–203.

Part II
Sectors

8 Knowledge intensive entrepreneurship in different sectoral systems

A taxonomy

Roberto Fontana, Franco Malerba and Astrid Marinoni

1 Introduction

Knowledge intensive entrepreneurship (KIE) takes place in sectors, which may differ along several relevant dimensions. Several studies on innovation in sectors have examined these dimensions and these differences. In this chapter, we use the concept of sectoral system in order to identify and measure some key differences across sectors that affect KIE. By using the AEGIS Survey we identify several dimensions of a sectoral system which lead us to propose five different sectoral contexts in which KIE takes place, and which encompass both manufacturing and services. The outcome of our empirical analysis is a taxonomy. On the basis of this taxonomy we provide insightful implications about the impact of public policies on entrepreneurship.

The chapter is organized as follows. In Section 2 we discuss the literature on the sectoral differences of innovative activities and industrial dynamics and on sectoral systems. In Section 3 we introduce the data and the methodology used, and in Section 4 we present the results obtained. Finally in Section 5 some general and policy conclusions are advanced.

2 Differences in innovative activities and industrial dynamics across sectors

2.1 The Pavitt taxonomy and beyond

Efforts aimed at capturing stylized facts and regularities in the patterns of innovation across industrial sectors have characterized the research agenda of numerous scholars of innovation and technological change for more than two decades.

The Pavitt taxonomy (1984) is perhaps the best example of this type of effort and one that surely has the merit of having inspired a new trajectory of research. Relying upon a dataset of more than 2,000 innovative firms in the UK, Pavitt classified firms in four major categories: science-based, specialized suppliers, supplier-dominated and scale-intensive firms depending on firms' positioning with respect to some dimensions such as: sources of technology, type of user, means of appropriation, nature of innovation, firm size and rate of technological diversification. Underneath this conceptualization lies the idea that firms' innovative behaviour is to a certain extent constrained by the technological setting they operate in, predicting feasible paths of innovation activities for each firm belonging to a specific regime.

Starting from Pavitt's seminal work, empirical research has moved along two research trajectories. On the one hand, one field of research has explored further the Schumpeterian suggestions of the taxonomy. Malerba and Orsenigo (1995) proposed a framework that conceives the presence of two alternative patterns of innovation across industrial sectors. In the 'Schumpeter Mark I' (the entrepreneurial regime) pattern, innovation is mainly produced by the entrepreneurial activity and creativity of small and newly born firms. Instead, in the 'Schumpeter Mark II' (the routinized regime) pattern, innovation originates in the formal R&D activity of larger and already established firms.

On the other hand, researchers have attempted to extend Pavitt's original contribution to new sectors or to refine it by adding new dimensions. This approach has given rise to a considerable number of empirical contributions. A newer version of the taxonomy was proposed by Tidd *et al.* (1997), with the aim of giving a better representation of service-based firms in the overall picture as these firms were arbitrarily confined in the 'supplier dominated' category in the original version. This effort led to the addition of an extra group, the 'information intensive' group, to the original classification.

Other scholars tried to build on Pavitt's work by taking into account additional aspects of firms' innovative patterns. An example can be found in Kristensen (1999) that focuses on the analysis of organizational learning and knowledge management within the boundaries traced by Pavitt. A further example is the work of Bodas Freitas (2011) who establishes a link between the Pavitt industry classification, technological learning regimes and the adoption of innovative management practices. Souitaris (2002) instead draws attention on the different rates of technological innovation across sectors while Marsili and Verspagen (2002) focused on deepening the analysis of the determinants shaping technological regimes.

One of the reasons why Pavitt's taxonomy turned out to be so appealing is that it has largely confirmed its soundness and validity in a variety of environments and contexts.

A large number of studies undertaking empirical analysis at different levels have indeed produced results closely resembling those found by Pavitt. An example is Archibugi *et al.* (1991) who examined a sample of Italian firms at the business unit-level focusing especially on the role played by the sources of technical knowledge. Similarly, Evangelista (2000) has found support for the taxonomy in the case of service-based firms. Looking at Italian firms active in the service sectors he identified four main categories that can be differentiated along several dimensions such as type of innovative output, overall innovative performance, technological source for innovation, patterns of interactions in innovation and objectives pursued with innovation. Eventually, four groups of sectors are identified. Technology users, which closely resemble 'suppliers dominated' firms; S&T based, which are endowed with the typical characteristics of 'science based' firms, and finally 'interactive and IT based' as well as 'technical consultancy' which instead exhibits innovative patterns not resembling any of the previous categories.

Evangelista's study represents only but one of the works that extended the original taxonomy to service sectors. One of the early attempts in this respect is attributable to Soete and Miozzo (1989), whose work aimed primarily at decomposing Pavitt's category of 'supplier dominated' firms. Through a bottom-up exercise, the authors identified a novel group 'scale-network intensive' firms whose activity is heavily dependent on the presence of large physical networks and information networks (mostly transport and financial services) and highlighted how these firms should not be considered as simple adopters of technology, as they were in Pavitt's, but rather firms trying to pursue their own innovative efforts. In addition, the authors attempted for the first time to analyse the innovative behaviour of 'interactive-network-based' enterprises.

Their pioneering effort notwithstanding, Soete and Miozzo (1989) were criticized (see for instance Gallouj and Gallouj, 2000). In particular, most scholars began to consider inappropriate the application of theoretical and empirical tools formerly used in a manufacture-based context to services. This view, commonly known in the literature as the 'demarcation approach', regarded service sectors as highly peculiar, incomparable to most manufacturing industries because of the presence of exclusive characteristics such as intangibility, and high levels of interactions among actors.

Along these lines, Den Hertog and Bilderbeek (1999) proposed a new taxonomy based on seven types of innovation patterns each one exhibiting a combination of relationships among three main actors in the system: suppliers of inputs, the (innovating) service firm and the users (i.e. the customers) of the innovative service product. By examining these three roles, the authors identified seven categories of innovative patterns: 'supplier-dominated innovation', 'innovation within services', 'customer-led innovation', 'innovation through services', 'paradigmatic innovation', 'innovation in a firm's internalized service function' and 'innovation in an outsourced service function'.

Sundbo and Gallouj (2000) proposed that different innovative patterns can be found within the same firm, depending on the type of innovation pursued. Moreover, as Miles (2001) and Castellacci (2008) will later confirm, they observed for the first time the emergence of convergent innovation tendencies between manufacturing and sectors where manufacturing and services are treated as interrelated activities. This evidence will later lead to the development of another research perspective, namely the 'synthesis approach' (Gallouj and Weinstein, 1997; Djellal *et al.*, 2003; Drejer, 2004; Hipp and Grupp, 2005; Gallouj, 2010).

The analysis of innovative patterns at the sectoral level and the consequent attempts to refine and redefine existing taxonomies represented only one of the research paths pursued by scholars. A number of empirical works aimed instead at extending the investigation to the relationship between the newly born taxonomies and existent sectoral classifications, in both manufacturing and service context. The purpose was to verify whether innovative behaviours are 'endemic' to specific sectors or are indeed able to co-exist in the same setting. This latter case would imply that firms are given a larger room of discretionality when designing and implementing their innovative strategies, therefore allowing for the presence of different 'strategic groups of firms' within the same industry.

Analysing the Swiss service sector, Hollenstein (2003) aimed at identifying shared 'innovation modes' among firms. Discriminating on factors such as innovation-related indicators, demand and supply-side determinants of innovative activity, firms' position in knowledge networks, structural characteristics of firms, and performance, the analysis highlighted the presence of five main innovative behaviours: 'Science-based high-tech firms with full network integration', 'IT-oriented network-integrated developers', 'Market-oriented incremental innovators with weak external links', 'Cost-oriented process innovators with strong external links along the value chain', 'Low-profile innovators with hardly any external links'. Concerning the sectoral distribution of innovation modes, the study suggests that, while most innovation modes are somewhat evenly distributed in several industries, three out of five are heavily concentrated in specific industries, thus hinting at a tendency of innovative patterns to be coupled with specific sectoral configuration.

De Jong and Marsili (2006) instead focused their analysis on small and micro firms in the Netherlands in both manufacturing and services. They identified four categories of firms which share common traits with Pavitt's taxonomy. 'Science-based', 'specialized suppliers', 'supplier-dominated' and 'resource-intensive' are the categories identified by the use of variables related to numerous innovative aspects such as innovative output and input, sources of innovation, managerial attitudes, innovation planning and external orientation. Alongside this similarity with the Pavitt taxonomy, they also found the presence of great variety in the pattern of innovation *within* the categories. In addition to this, the authors did not find a clear-cut correspondence concerning the relationship among industrial sectors and clusters of firms. Rather, results pointed at the co-existence of several and different 'strategic groups' within industries.

These results are somewhat confirmed by additional works. Looking at both manufacturing and service sectors in Finland and Denmark, Leiponen and Drejer (2007) suggest that firms within industries do indeed follow multiple patterns of innovation behaviour, since the majority of sectors considered do not present a dominant innovation regime. Heterogeneity is found to be prevalent in both high and low technology industries, as well as in both manufacturing and service industries in both countries analysed, thus also excluding the fact that multiple regimes could be a country-specific phenomenon.

Findings that challenge the economic view that industries consist of relatively homogeneous organizations are also put forward by Shrolec and Verspagen (2012). Using data on 13 countries from the Community Innovation Survey, the purpose of their work is to analyse heterogeneity of innovative behaviour at the lowest possible level of aggregation, i.e. the firm level, and discover how subsequent aggregations affects the loss of this variety. The study investigated enterprise innovative activity along a variety of dimensions such as innovative engagement, benefit stemming from the innovative activities, sources of information, cooperative agreements, intellectual property protection and the nature of changes in the firm. Their results suggest that differences among firms' innovative patterns remain relevant and largely independent of both sectoral and national contexts. On the contrary, the analysis of firms' strategies distribution among countries and sectors seems to highlight the presence of a rather regular pattern that cut across traditional breakdown categories such as countries and industries thus challenging the basic idea underlying the original work of Pavitt that patterns of innovation are industry specific.

2.2 Sectoral systems

A radical move beyond the Pavitt taxonomy and the contributions discussed above in order to include a larger set of factors is to consider differences across sectors in terms of systems. In this respect, drawing from the innovation system literature (Edquist, 1997) which focuses on learning and interaction among agents and from the evolutionary literature in which knowledge, dynamics, innovation processes and economic transformation are considered, the framework of sectoral systems has been introduced.

This framework encompasses, at the sectoral level, concepts such as national systems of innovation (which is delimited by national boundaries and examines the role of non-firms organizations and institutions), regional/local innovation systems (in which the boundary is the region), technological systems (in which the focus is on technologies and not on sectors) and distributed innovation systems (in which the analysis is on specific innovations). The concept of sectoral systems also develops evolutionary notions at the sectoral level. In fact evolutionary theory stresses the presence of major sectoral differences in opportunities related to science

196 R. *Fontana* et al.

and technologies, in the knowledge base underpinning innovative activities, and in the institutional context. Thus for evolutionary theory heterogeneous firms facing similar technologies, searching around similar knowledge bases, undertaking similar production activities and 'embedded' in the same institutional setting, share common strategic and organizational features and develop a similar range of learning patterns.

More specifically a sectoral system framework focuses on the nature, structure, organization and dynamics of innovation and production in sectors. In a sectoral system, firms with their related capabilities and learning processes are indeed the major drivers of innovation, production and change. However, a sectoral system framework also considers other relevant factors in a sector: the type of knowledge that characterizes the sector, the variety of actors other than firms, the relationships and networks among actors, customers and demand, and institutions. In particular, a sectoral system approach examines innovation as the result of both firm-specific variables (such as firms' learning and capabilities, R&D and production investments, strategies and organizational structure) as well as other variables related to knowledge, networks and institutions. In synthesis, a sectoral system can be seen as composed of the following elements: (a) the knowledge base of a sector; (b) firms; (c) other actors (in addition to firms) such as suppliers, universities and public research organizations, financial organizations, government and public agencies; (d) demand in terms of users and consumers users; (e) networks of agents that interact in a formal or informal ways; (f) institutions such as standards, IPR systems, regulations. A more general discussion of sectoral systems can be found in Malerba (2002, 2004).

Up to now, the work on sectoral systems has concerned mainly developed countries (Malerba, 2004; Malerba and Adams, 2013) and developing countries (Malerba and Mani, 2009; Malerba and Nelson, 2012). No detailed taxonomies of sectoral systems have been proposed yet, also because firm level data have not been available until recently. The only attempts in that direction have been the ones by Castellacci (2004, 2009) and Peneder (2010) based on the availability of firm level data from national innovation surveys and on other large databases such as the Community Innovation Survey. Castellacci (2004) aimed at identifying differences in innovative activities among manufacturing sectors. Considering both aspects related to the concept of technological regime and technological trajectories, he identified four sectoral patterns of technological change namely: 'advanced users-based', 'systemic', 'investment intensive' and 'embodied diffusion' industries. Peneder (2010), combining the Schumpeterian distinction between creative and adaptive behaviour with the three characteristics of technological regimes (i.e. opportunities, appropriability and cumulativeness), provided a classification of industries on the basis of their NACE code (both manufacturing and services) along these dimensions. Finally, Castellacci (2009) looked at how national systems interact with sectoral patterns of innovation. His work highlights the powerful interrelatedness between country-based factors and Pavitt's sectoral classification, especially when considering the intensity of vertical sectoral linkages with external sources of information for innovation such as suppliers, customers, universities and Public Research Organizations (PROs).

In the remaining sections of this chapter we directly take on the challenge of providing some initial taxonomy of sectoral systems that matter for KIE survival and performance. Indeed, KIE intrinsically embeds peculiar characteristics that are worthwhile to explore under a sectoral system perspective. First and foremost, KIE is a knowledge intensive activity. Second, knowledge intensive entrepreneurs who exploit opportunities from diverse sectors are embedded in different knowledge contexts and networks and their activities are deeply affected by the surrounding institutional context. Therefore, how the type of sectoral system affects KIE in terms of sources of opportunities, type of networking, agreements and appropriability is worth exploring. From a sectoral systems perspective we will argue that, the presence of firm level heterogeneity notwithstanding, the way firms undertake their innovative activity presents some characteristics that remain by and large industry specific. Our aim is to highlight these specificities by proposing a profile of sectoral systems.

3 Data and method

Our analysis is based on data coming from the AEGIS survey, whose aim was to understand the determinants of KIE in Europe in different sectoral, country and socioeconomic contexts. For this purpose, relying on a sample drawn mostly from the Amadeus database (Bureau Van Dijk), 4004 founders of newly established firms in the period 2001–2007 in ten EU countries were interviewed. The survey intended to capture several environmental and firm level dimensions such as demand, institutional factors, strategies to understand the returns to innovation, dynamic capabilities and many others as well as founder-specific dimensions.

Using this survey our analysis was carried out in four main steps. First, we selected specific questions in the survey which could be used to capture the main characteristics of sectoral systems as summarized above in Section 2.2. These questions and a brief summary of the items are reported in Table 8.1.

Second, on each question a factor analysis has been performed in order to pinpoint the main characteristics of the sectoral systems. Factor analysis is commonly used to analyse relationships among a given number of variables. Its purpose is to summarize the information contained in the original variables (i.e. the 'items' of the question) into a smaller set of variates (factors) minimizing the loss of information (Hair *et al.*, 2006).

As most of our variables were not continuous, we had to rely upon polychoric and tetrachoric correlation matrices, which assume ordinal

Table 8.1 List of variables used in the analysis

Macro-variables capturing characteristics of sectoral systems	Variables	Type
Funding sources for the establishment of the company	Own financial resources Family members Previous employer (CVC, university incubator) Venture capital Bank National government or local authorities European Union funds	Continuous (%)
Sources of knowledge for exploring new business opportunities	Clients or customers Suppliers Competitors Public research institutes Universities External commercial labs, R&D firms, technical institutes In-house (know-how, R&D lab) Trade fairs, conferences and exhibitions Scientific journals and other technical publications Nationally funded research programmes EU funded research programmes	Likert (1–5)
Operations in which the firm's network is involved	Contacting customers Selecting suppliers Recruiting skilled labour Collecting information about competitors Accessing distribution channels Assistance in obtaining business loans/funds Advertising and promotion Developing new products/services Managing production and operations Assistance in arranging taxation and other legal issues Exploring export opportunities	Likert (1–5)

Types of agreements in which the firm participates	Strategic alliance R&D agreement Technical cooperation agreement Licensing agreement Subcontracting Marketing and export promotion Research contract-out	Likert (1–5)
Methods to protect firm's intellectual property	Patents Trademarks Copyrights Confidentiality agreements Secrecy Lead-time advantages on competitors Complexity of design	Dummy

variables to reflect the underlying continuous variables (Bartholomew *et al.*, 2002). The factors were extracted using the principal components method, which has the advantage of not requiring a specific assumption concerning the distribution of the variables under examination. An oblimin oblique rotation was then applied to relax the orthogonality assumption and allowing factors to be correlated to each other (Basilevsky, 2009). The final number of factors to be retained was mainly chosen by applying the Kaiser criterion as a cut-off guideline. However, as numerous scholars suggest, the Kaiser method has many shortcomings (see for instance Velicer and Jackson, 1990). As a consequence, we based our final decision also on scree plot test result. In addition to this, following Manly (2004), the number of retained factors was also evaluated accordingly to its plausibility and interpretability in the economic context.

The third step aimed at constructing profiles of sectoral systems on the basis of the factors identified in the previous step. To achieve this purpose we conducted a cluster analysis using both hierarchical and non-hierarchical techniques, in order to obtain a robust clustering solution (Milligan and Sokol, 1980; Punj and Stewart, 1983). Empirical studies on the performance of clustering algorithms often points at non-hierarchical methods as the best performing ones. In particular, K-means partitioning algorithm exhibits the best recovery of cluster structure.[1] However, this procedure requires a given number of clusters to be specified a priori. Thus, following Hartigan (1967) and Milligan (1980) we decided to perform a hierarchical, explorative analysis using Ward's method (Ward, 1963) in order to roughly define some candidate numbers of clusters. Homogeneous groups are built with the purpose of minimizing the distance in scores of firms within a given cluster and maximizing the distance in scores among companies from different clusters. Subsequently, in order to improve the accuracy of the analysis, we used as starting points for the K-means partition Ward-derived centroids. The final cluster solution was identified also through the use of Duda-Hart and Calinski-Harabasz stopping rules (Duda and Hart, 1973; Calinski and Harabasz, 1974). The outcome of this step was a profile of sectoral systems.

The final step was aimed at making sense of the profiles. In order to achieve this aim we associated the profiles with the actual sectoral distribution of the firms in our sample based on the NACE (Rev. 1.1) classification. The approach used was the 'simple correspondence analysis', which has proven to be an increasingly popular interdependence technique for dimensional reduction and perceptual mapping. In particular, it allows to examine the pattern of relationships of categorical variables decomposing the total variation of the data matrix which is measured by the Chi-squared statistic for row-column independence.

4 Results

4.1 Identifying the characteristics of sectoral systems: the factor analysis

The first characteristic of a sectoral system that we analysed concerned the sources of knowledge which are considered fundamental to the firm for exploring business opportunities. In this respect, the factor analysis returned three factors (see Table 8.2).

The first factor includes respondents that score high on items such as public research institutes, universities and external commercial labs, R&D firms, technical institutes as well as national and EU funded programmes as major sources for detecting potential novel sources of business. They score low on other items such as clients, suppliers or competitors. These are firms that use 'non market based' and 'horizontal' links as sources of knowledge to explore business opportunities and neglect other sources such as clients, suppliers or competitors.

The second factor includes respondents that score high on items such as: clients, suppliers and competitors as sources of knowledge. These are firms that use 'market based' and 'vertical' links. The third factor includes instead firms that source for knowledge from business events (i.e. trade fairs, conferences, exhibitions) and publications (i.e. scientific journals).

The second characteristic that we analysed referred to the embeddedness of a firm in a network as captured by the tendency of the firm to rely upon

Table 8.2 Factor analysis on: sources of knowledge for exploring business opportunities

	(1) Non mkt horizontal	(2) Mkt and vertical	(3) Events and publications
Clients or customers	0.04	**0.78**	0.07
Suppliers	0.24	**0.75**	0.04
Competitors	0.28	**0.61**	0.08
PROs	**0.87**	0.08	0.03
Universities	**0.88**	0.04	0.02
External R&D	**0.82**	0.10	0.07
In-house R&D*	0.36	0.08	0.39
Trade fairs, conferences	0.33	0.17	**0.77**
Scientific journals	0.41	−0.02	**0.72**
Participation in national research programmes	**0.87**	−0.00	0.13
Participation in EU funded research programmes	**0.84**	0.03	0.11

Notes
Number of observations is 3,835; three factors were retained, which explain 64.8 per cent of total variance.
* In-house R&D not well explained (exhibits high uniqueness).

Table 8.3 Factor analysis on: benefits from involvement in networking

	(1) Network to access complementary assets/mkt	(2) Network for production
Contacting customers/clients	0.34	**0.79**
Selecting suppliers	0.52	**0.62**
Recruiting skilled labour	0.52	0.50
Collecting information about competitors*	0.59	0.33
Accessing distribution channels	**0.68**	0.15
Assistance in obtaining business loans/attracting funds	**0.77**	−0.11
Advertising and promotion	**0.70**	0.05
Developing new products/services	**0.67**	0.22
Managing production and operations	**0.69**	0.27
Assistance in arranging taxation or other legal issues	**0.69**	−0.00
Exploring export opportunities	**0.73**	−0.06

Notes
Number of observations is 3,835; two factors were retained, which explain 54.7 per cent of total variance.
* Collecting information about competitors not well explained (exhibits high uniqueness).

other actors in order to carry out certain operations. In this case, our analysis unveiled two main factors (see Table 8.3).

The first factor includes firms that score high on items such as networking for assistance in attracting financial resources, for establishing marketing cooperation, for obtaining legal assistance, but also for developing new product and services, managing production, opening new distribution channels and exploring of export opportunities. We identify these respondents as firms that benefit from networking through access to complementary assets and markets. The second factor includes firms that score high on items such as networking for contacting customers and clients and selecting suppliers. We identify these respondents as firms that do networking for obtaining advantages that are more production-based.[2]

The third characteristic that we analysed, which can be considered complementary to the previous one, refers to the types of formal agreements that firms underwrite (Table 8.4).

Our factor analysis in this case identified only one factor that has the ability to explain alone the majority of the variance. Two items resulted poorly represented, namely 'Subcontracting' and 'Marketing/export promotion'. These two items refer to agreements aimed at establishing production-related and market-based relationships, in contrast to the other items which clearly highlight the presence of some technological reasons as underlying purpose of the deals. As we are mostly interested in technology-based agreements, we decided to neglect these two items and consider a

Table 8.4 Factor analysis on: participation in types of formal agreements

	(1) Agreements for technological reasons
Strategic alliance	0.69
R&D agreement	0.81
Technical cooperation agreement	0.79
Licensing agreement	0.72
Subcontracting*	0.51
Marketing/export promotion*	0.66
Research contract-out	0.76

Notes
Number of observations is 3,835; one factor were retained, which explains 51 per cent of total variance.
* Subcontracting and marketing/export promotion competitors not well explained (exhibit high uniqueness).

single factor solution that was labelled 'agreements for technological reasons'.

The last characteristics of the sectoral systems concern the methods used by firms to appropriate the rents from innovation. In this case, results from our factor analysis are straightforward (Table 8.5).

Three factors were identified. The first factor, that we label 'tacit method of IP protection', scores high on items like 'confidentiality agreements' and 'secrecy'. The second factor, that we label 'codified and formal methods of IP protection' scores high on items like patents, trademarks and copyrights. The third factor, that we label 'informal methods of IP protection', scores high on both 'lead times advantages' and 'complexity of design'. This last tendency, dubbed 'Informal', tends to gather those mechanisms which are directly reflected in the firm's supply chain strategy or products.

Table 8.5 Factor analysis on: methods of IP protection

	(1) Tacit	*(2) Codified and formal*	*(3) Informal*
Patents	0.10	0.72	0.32
Trademarks	0.04	0.89	0.02
Copyrights	0.46	0.62	−0.13
Confidentiality agreements	0.91	0.10	0.05
Secrecy	0.85	0.06	0.28
Lead time advantages on competitors	0.22	−0.04	0.79
Complexity of design	0.18	0.23	0.77

Note
Number of observations is 2,452; three factors were retained, which explain 72 per cent of total variance.

4.2 *Constructing profiles of sectoral systems: the cluster analysis*

Using factor scores as a starting base, we performed a cluster analysis to investigate possible patterns of behaviours which are cross-sectional to our previously identified perspectives. Five main profiles can be defined, as can be seen from Table 8.6.

The first profile can be labelled 'Diffused sectoral system'. In terms of our four key dimensions it does not present any specificity. It has been labelled diffused because KIE in this sectoral system does not exhibit any specific source of knowledge for business opportunity, benefit from networking, type of formal agreement or method of IP protection.

The second profile can be labelled 'Vertical with production asset sectoral system'. It has some specific features. The sources of knowledge for business opportunities come from customers and suppliers (as well as from competitors), highlighting a vertical relation in knowledge flows and opportunities. At the same time the benefits from the involvement in networking with customers and suppliers (as it is obvious from the result regarding the source of knowledge) concern production activities. Therefore this profile is very much production related, with flows of knowledge and links which are mainly vertical.

The third profile has been labelled 'Vertical with complementary assets sectoral system'. Also in this case the sources of knowledge for business opportunities come from customers and suppliers, but the main benefits from the involvement in networking relates to the access to distribution channels and to networking for a variety of activities: assistance in obtaining funds, advertising and promotion, developing new products and services, managing production and operations, arranging taxation and exploring export opportunities. In addition, the main methods of IP protection regard patents, trademarks and copyrights and to a certain extent also informal methods. Therefore this profile is vertical in terms of knowledge flows but with a variety of both codified and uncodified instruments of IP protection and with benefits from networking that come for the access to complementary assets needed for KIE activities.

The fourth profile can be characterized as 'Distributed information sectoral system'. This profile reveals features that are quite different from the previous ones. In this case, the sources of knowledge for business opportunities are related to trade fairs, conferences as well as external R&D. Networks provide benefits to KIE through the involvement in relationships with customers and suppliers, the types of formal agreements refer to R&D agreements, research contracted out, technical cooperation or licensing agreement. The methods of IP protection concern confidentiality agreements and secrecy. Therefore this profile is distributed in terms of knowledge and information and agreements for technological reasons play a major role. In order to counterbalance the quite distributed information and knowledge sources, the way to protect information relies on tacit instruments.

Table 8.6 Cluster analysis on the factor scores

Questions	Factors	Profiles				
		Diffused	Vertical production. assets	Vertical compl. assets	Distributed information	Distributed S&T knowledge
Sources of knowledge for business opportunity	Non mkt and horizontal	-0.16	-0.52	0.35	-0.31	**1.43**
	Mkt and vertical	-0.84	**0.56**	**0.58**	-0.21	0.03
	Events and publications	-0.13	-0.51	0.38	**0.67**	0.10
Benefits from network	Network to access complementary assets	-0.53	-0.37	**0.91**	-0.07	**0.94**
	Network for production	-0.83	**0.92**	-0.14	0.17	-0.15
Types of formal agreements	Agreements for technological reasons	-0.51	-0.36	-0.09	0.28	**1.52**
Methods of IP protection	Tacit	-0.52	-0.31	-0.86	**0.95**	0.49
	Codified and formal	-0.09	-0.27	0.48	-0.31	0.31
	Informal	-0.38	-0.26	0.41	0.03	0.24

Note
Cells report the average factors score on the factors identified in the previous analysis; columns identify the five profiles of sectoral systems.

Finally, the fifth profile presents yet a different combination of dimensions, so that it can be labelled 'Distributed science and technology knowledge sectoral system'. Here the sources of knowledge for business opportunities are universities, public research organizations and external R&D and the benefits from networking come from accessing complementary assets related distribution channels, assistance in obtaining funds, advertising and promotion, developing new products and services, managing production and operations, arranging taxation and exploring export opportunities. Formal agreements are quite common and refer to R&D agreements, research contracted out, technical cooperation and licensing. Relatedly, the methods of IP protection cover a wide range of instruments, ranging from tacit, to codified and formal (such as patents, trademarks and copyrights) to informal (such as lead time advantages and complexity of design). Therefore this profile is characterized by reliance upon scientific and technological knowledge and on extended distributed external knowledge, with a wide method of IP protection.

4.3 Making sense of the profiles: the correspondence analysis

Correspondence analysis (CA) is a technique that facilitates the perceptual mapping of objects on a set of non-metric attributes (Hair *et al.*, 2006). It aims at providing a multivariate representation of qualitative data based on the analysis of contingency tables and Pearson's Chi-square statistics. In our case, we apply the CA to find an association between the profiles identified above, capturing the main features of sectoral systems, and the industries firms belong to as identified by their NACE (Ver. 1.1) classification. A preliminary analysis confirms the presence of association among row and column profiles.[3] As far as the number of dimensions to consider is concerned, we might have retained only the first two, capable of explaining more than 85 per cent of total inertia. However, in order to provide a satisfactory representation of most profiles, we decided to consider three dimensions (that account for 95 per cent of total variance).

Figure 8.1 maps the profiles along the two most important dimensions identified by the CA. The subsequent involvement of a third dimension will have a substantial explicative power exclusively on those profiles that are neglected by these two dimensions.

The horizontal axis highlights a clear opposition among three profiles. On the left hand side we find the *'Vertical with complementary assets'* profile. In opposition to this, we find on the right hand side the *'Distributed information'* and the *'Distributed science and technology knowledge'* profiles.

The *'Vertical with complementary assets'* profile attracts *traditional manufacturing* industries related to the production of textiles and clothing (NACE 17 and 18), wood and furniture (NACE 20 and 36.1), fabricated metal product (NACE 28), alongside paper manufacturing (NACE 21) and electrical machinery manufacturing (NACE 31). The former sectors are

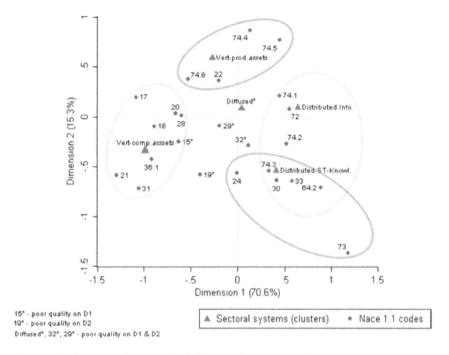

Figure 8.1 Correspondence analysis biplot (dimensions 1–2).

'supplier dominated' while the latter are considered to be 'scale intensive' according to the Pavitt's taxonomy. In both cases, firms belonging to these categories rely upon interactions with external actors (such as suppliers and/or customers) for innovation. The '*Distributed information*' and the '*Distributed science and technology knowledge*' profiles are instead associated with much less reliance upon a variety of knowledge sources for their innovative activities and much more reliance upon formal agreements. They include mostly knowledge intensive based *services* (KIBS) such as computer related activities, management, architectural as well as engineering consulting and telecommunications (NACE 72, 74.1, 74.2, 64.2 respectively) alongside 'science based' *manufacturing* industries such as medical, precision and optical instruments (NACE 33).

Along the second dimension (vertical axis) the opposition is instead between the '*Vertical with production assets*' profile and the '*Distributed science and technology knowledge*' profile. The former profile attracts mainly service-based industries such as advertising (NACE 74.4), labour recruitment (74.5), publishing (NACE 22), but also call centres, photographic, graphic and secretarial activities (NACE 74.8). The second profile is instead highly associated with manufacturing activities as shown by the inclusion of manufacture of chemicals and chemical products (NACE 24),

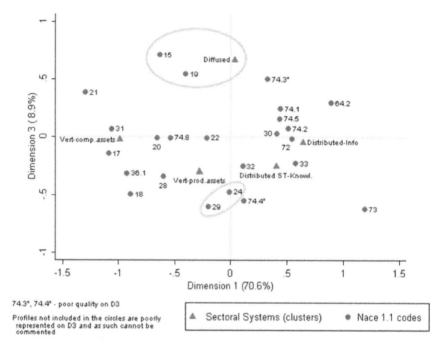

Figure 8.2 Correspondence analysis biplot (dimensions 1–3).

technical testing and analysis (NACE 74.3), computer and office machinery (NACE 30) and R&D (NACE 73).

Most of the sectors not fully explained along the two main dimensions can be explained in Figure 8.2 by considering an additional dimension.

Along this third dimension we find an opposition between the '*Diffused*' profile, including manufacture of food products and beverages (NACE 15) and footwear, luggage, handbags, harness (NACE 19), and two sectors such as manufacture of machinery and equipment (NACE 29) and manufacture of chemicals and chemical products (NACE 24).[4] A more straightforward picture of the results can be found in Table 8.7 where associations between the profiles and the sectors are summarized.

5 Conclusions and policy implications

This chapter has examined whether KIE is affected by the type of sectoral systems in which entrepreneurship takes place. Starting from the framework of sectoral system, several dimensions have been isolated: knowledge and its sources, the benefits coming from relationships and networks, the type of participation in formal agreements and the instruments of IP protection. The statistical analysis has shown that one can identify more than

Table 8.7 Summary of main associations among sectoral systems and industries

Sectoral system	Sectors (NACE code)	Sector (description)
Diffused	15	Manufacture of food products and beverages
	19	Tanning and dressing of leather; manufacture of luggage, handbags, saddlery, harness and footwear
Vertical with production assets	22	Publishing, printing and reproduction of recorded media
	74.4	Advertising
	74.5	Labour recruitment and provision of personnel
	74.8	Call centres, graphic, photographic, secretarial activities
Vertical with complementary assets	17	Manufacture of textile
	18	Manufacturing of wearing apparel; dressing and dyeing of fur
	20	Manufacture of wood and of products of wood and cork, except furniture; manufacture of articles of straw and plaiting materials
	21	Manufacture of pulp, paper and paper products
	28	Manufacture of fabricated metal products, except machinery and equipment
	31	Manufacture of electrical machinery and apparatus n.e.c.
	36.1	Manufacture of furniture
Distributed information	72	Computer and related activities
	74.1	Legal, accounting, book-keeping and auditing activities; tax consultancy; market research and public opinion polling; business and management consultancy; holdings
	74.2	Architectural and engineering activities and related technical consultancy
Distributed S&T knowledge	24	Manufacture of chemicals and chemical products
	74.3	Technical testing and analysis
	30	Manufacture of office machinery and computers
	33	Manufacture of medical, precision and optical instruments, watches and clocks
	64.2	Telecommunications
	73	Research and development

210 *R. Fontana* et al.

one profile of sectoral systems in which KIE operate. This result means that the environment in which entrepreneurs are active can be very diverse, and provides different sources of knowledge, types of networks and means of appropriability of innovation.

In particular, five different profiles of sectoral systems have been identified. The first one is the 'diffused sectoral system', in which knowledge diffusion is quite high and the structure of the system is quite atomistic. Footwear and food are examples of this type. The second profile is the 'vertical with production asset sectoral system', in which knowledge sources and networks relate mainly to suppliers and customers to deliver *services* within a context characterized by low R&D intensity. Adverting, publishing, labour recruitment and call centres are example of that. The third one is 'vertical with complementary asset sectoral system', in which knowledge sources and networks again relate to suppliers and users, but in which networks are related to the access to complementary assets. Several so-called *traditional manufacturing* sectors as well as of machinery are examples of this type of sectoral system. The fourth profile is the 'distributed information sectoral system', in which problem-solving service KIE relies on a variety of sources of information as well as on technological alliances, and in which secrecy is a relevant form of protection. Several KIBS sectors such as engineering and computer activities and accounting are examples of this type. Finally, the fifth profile is the 'distributed science and technology knowledge sectoral system', in which a wide variety of knowledge sources are present and in which networks complement firms' internal activities in order to create, integrate and distribute knowledge within a context characterized by medium-high R&D intensity. Here many *high technology manufacturing* sectors such as telecommunications, computers, medical devices and chemicals, are present.

This new taxonomy encompasses both manufacturing and services and represents the first step at identifying the specific role of the sectoral environment in terms of knowledge and systems in affecting KIE and its evolution. This result strongly points to the fact that the strategies of knowledge access, networking and IPR that KIE have to use in their activities have to take into account also the specific dimensions of the sectoral system.

This analysis has some clear implications for public policy supporting KIE. The main implication is that specific policies supporting entrepreneurship must be aware of the sectoral influence on the way they look for knowledge, the benefits of networking and the agreements they make which consequently affect the performance of knowledge intensive entrepreneurship. Therefore the understanding of the relationship between specific dimensions of a sectoral system and KIE becomes a prerequisite for any policy addressed to entrepreneurship. This does not necessarily imply that policies need to be sector specific. It means however that even general policies aiming at affecting entrepreneurship should at least acknowledge that the actual impact of horizontal policies on entrepreneurship may drastically differ across sectors, because the channels and ways through which policies exert their effects on KIE differ from sector to sector and/or from groups of sectors to other groups of sectors as those identified in the five profiles of the sectoral systems.

In addition, a sectoral system view of KIE identifies not just one, but systems of policies that affect entrepreneurship in sectors. This point highlights on the one hand the importance of interdependencies, links and feedbacks among policies (that will be discussed in Chapter 15), but on the other that these interdependencies may greatly differ from sectoral system to sectoral system. Thus the most effective policies may differ according to the type of knowledge, actors and networks and institutions that knowledge intensive entrepreneurs face in their activities.

Notes

1 The K-means approach executes a variance minimizing non-hierarchical cluster analysis. It can be thus considered the non-hierarchical counterpart of Ward's method.
2 The item variable 'capturing recruitment of skilled labour' is problematic. Although its explanatory power can be considered sufficient for the purpose of this analysis, this variable does not exercise a driving thrust in any of the two depicted factors, playing an equally marginal role in both of them.
3 Pearson Chi-square of 356.9 $(p > x^2 = 0.00)$.
4 Few industries remain unexplained in our analysis and as such they cannot be affiliated to any profile. Among these we find firms involved in the manufacture of machinery and equipment n.e.c. (NACE 29), that, although they surely do not belong to the '*Diffused*' profile, they are not entirely attracted by any of the others and firms involved in the production of radio, television and communication equipment (NACE 32) that does not find full representation in any profile.

References

Archibugi, D., Cesaratto, S. and Sirilli, G. (1991). Sources of innovative activities and industrial organization in Italy. *Research Policy*, 20(4), 299–313.

Bartholomew, D.J., Steele, F., Moustaki, I. and Galbraith, J.I. (2002). *The analysis and interpretation of multivariate data for social scientists*, Boca Raton, FL: Chapman & Hall/CRC.

Basilevsky, A.T. (2009). *Statistical factor analysis and related methods: theory and applications*, New York: Wiley-Interscience.

BodasFreitas, I.M. (2011). Technological learning environments and organizational practices: Cross sectoral evidence from Britain. *Industrial and Corporate Change*, 20(5), 1439–1474.

Calinski, T. and Harabasz, J. (1974). A dendrite method for cluster analysis. *Communications in Statistics-theory and Methods*, 3(1), 1–27.

Castellacci, F. (2004). A neo-Schumpeterian approach to why growth rates differ. *Revue économique, Presses de Sciences-Po*, 55(6), 1145–1169.

Castellacci, F. (2008). Technological paradigms, regimes and trajectories: Manufacturing and service industries in a new taxonomy of sectoral patterns of innovation. *Research Policy*, 37(6), 978–994.

Castellacci, F. (2009). The interactions between national systems and sectoral patterns of innovation. *Journal of Evolutionary Economics*, 19(3), 321–347.

De Jong, J.P.J., and Marsili, O. (2006). The fruit flies of innovations: A taxonomy of innovative small firms. *Research Policy*, 35(2), 213–229.

Den Hertog, P., and Bilderbeek, R. (1999). Conceptualising service innovation and service innovation patterns. *Thematic essay within the framework of the Research Programme Strategic Information provision on Innovation and Services (SIID) for the Ministry of Economic Affairs, Directorate for General Technology Policy.*

Djellal, F., Francoz, D., Gallouj, C., Gallouj, F., and Jacquin, Y. (2003). Revising the definition of research and development in the light of the specificities of services. *Science and Public Policy*, 30(6), 415–429.

Drejer, I. (2004). Identifying innovation in surveys of services: A Schumpeterian perspective. *Research Policy*, 33(3), 551–562.

Duda, R.O., and Hart, P.E. (1973). *Pattern classification and science analysis*, Oxford: Wiley.

Edquist, C. (1997). *Systems of innovation: technologies, institutions and organizations*, London: Pinter/Cassell.

Evangelista, R. (2000). Sectoral patterns of technological change in services. *Economics of Innovation and New Technology*, 9(3), 183–222.

Gallouj, C., and Gallouj, F. (2000). Neo-Schumpeterian perspectives on innovation in services. In M. Boden and I. Miles (eds), *Services and the Knowledge Based Economy*, London: Continuum, 21–37.

Gallouj, F. (2010). *The handbook of innovation and services: a multi-disciplinary perspective*, Cheltenham, UK: Edward Elgar Publishing.

Gallouj, F., and Weinstein, O. (1997). Innovation in services. *Research Policy*, 26(4), 537–556.

Hair, J.F., Black, W.C., Babin, B.J., Anderson, R.E. and Tatham, R. (2006). *Multivariate data analysis*, 6th edn, Upper Saddle River, NJ: Pearson.

Hartigan, J.A. (1967). Representation of similarity matrices by trees. *Journal of the American Statistical Association*, 62(320), 1140–1158.

Hipp, C., and Grupp, H. (2005). Innovation in the service sector: The demand for service-specific innovation measurement concepts and typologies. *Research Policy*, 34(4), 517–535.

Hollenstein, H. (2003). Innovation modes in the Swiss service sector: A cluster analysis based on firm-level data. *Research Policy*, 32(5), 845–863.

Kristensen, F.S. (1999). Towards a taxonomy and theory of the interdependence between learning regimes and sectorial patterns of innovation and competition: An empirical analysis of an elaborated Pavitt taxonomy applying Danish data. *The DRUID 1999 Winter conference Seeland, Denmark, 7–9 January, 1999.*

Leiponen, A., and Drejer, I. (2007). What exactly are technological regimes? Intra-industry heterogeneity in the organization of innovation activities. *Research Policy*, 36(8), 1221–1238.

Manly, B.F.J. (2004), *Multivariate statistical methods: a primer*, Boca Raton, FL: Chapman & Hall/CRC.

Malerba, F. (2002). Sectoral systems of innovation and production. *Research Policy*, 31(2), 247–264.

Malerba, F. (ed.) (2004). *Sectoral systems of innovation: concepts, issues and analyses of six major sectors in Europe*, Cambridge, UK: Cambridge University Press.

Malerba, F., and Adams, P. (2013) Sectoral systems of innovation. In: M. Dodgson, D. Gann and N. Phillips (eds), *Oxford handbook of innovation management*, Oxford: Oxford University Press.

Malerba, F., and Mani, S. (ed.) (2009) *Sectoral systems of innovation and production in developing countries*, Cheltenham, UK: Edward Elgar.

Malerba, F., and Nelson, R. (eds) (2012). *Economic development as a learning process: variation across sectoral systems*, Cheltenham, UK: Edward Elgar.

Malerba, F., and Orsenigo, L. (1995). Schumpeterian patterns of innovation. *Cambridge Journal of Economics*, 19(1), 47–65.

Manly, B.F.J. (2004). *Multivariate statistical methods: a primer*, Boca Raton, FL: Chapman & Hall/CRC.

Marsili, O., and Verspagen, B. (2002). Technology and the dynamics of industrial structures: An empirical mapping of Dutch manufacturing. *Industrial and Corporate Change*, 11(4), 791–815.

Miles, I. (2001). Services innovation: A reconfiguration of innovation studies. *PRES Discussion Paper 01–05, Manchester*.

Milligan, G.W. (1980). An examination of the effect of six types of error perturbation on fifteen clustering algorithms. *Psychometrika*, 45(3), 325–342.

Milligan, G.W., and Sokol, L.M. (1980). A two-stage clustering algorithm with robust recovery characteristics. *Educational and Psychological Measurement*, 40(3), 755–759.

Miozzo, M., and Soete, L. (2001). Internationalization of services: A technological perspective. *Technological Forecasting and Social Change*, 67(2), 159–185.

Pavitt, K. (1984). Sectoral patterns of technical change: Towards a taxonomy and a theory. *Research Policy*, 13(6), 343–373.

Peneder, M. (2010). Technological regimes and the variety of innovation behaviour: Creating integrated taxonomies of firms and sectors. *Research Policy*, 39(3), 323–334.

Punj, G., and Stewart, D.W. (1983). Cluster analysis in marketing research: Review and suggestions for application. *Journal of Marketing Research*, 20(May), 134–148.

Soete, L., and Miozzo, M. (1989). Trade and development in services: a technical perspective. Maastricht Economic Research Institute on Innovation and Technology.

Souitaris, V. (2002). Technological trajectories as moderators of firm-level determinants of innovation. *Research Policy*, 31(6), 877–898.

Srholec, M., and Verspagen, B. (2012). The Voyage of the Beagle into innovation: Explorations on heterogeneity, selection, and sectors. *Industrial and Corporate Change*, 21(5), 1221–1253.

Sundbo, J., and Gallouj, F. (2000). Innovation as a loosely coupled system in services. *International Journal of Services Technology and Management*, 1(1), 15–36.

Tidd, J., Bessant, J., and Pavitt, K. (1997). *Managing innovation: Integrating technological, market, and organizational change*, Chichester, UK: Wiley.

Velicer, W.F., and Jackson, D.N. (1990). Component analysis versus common factor analysis: Some issues in selecting an appropriate procedure. *Multivariate Behavioral Research*, 25(1), 1–28.

Ward Jr, J.H. (1963). Hierarchical grouping to optimize an objective function. *Journal of the American Statistical Association*, 58(301), 236–244.

9 Knowledge-intensive entrepreneurship in low-technology industries

Hartmut Hirsch-Kreinsen and Isabel Schwinge

1 Introduction[1]

The starting point of this chapter is the recent discussion in innovation research on knowledge-intensive entrepreneurship (KIE). This discussion highlights the following dimensions of KIE (Malerba, 2010; Malerba and McKelvey, 2010): First, KIE is related to new ventures that introduce innovation in the economic system based on an intensive use of knowledge. Second, the term knowledge-intensity points to the fact that entrepreneurial activity is to a significant extent based not only on the use of existing knowledge like existing experiences and skills but also on the integration and coordination of different knowledge assets and the creation of new knowledge. Thus, it is a constitutive feature of knowledge-intensive processes that they call for more than the already existing and established procedural and scientific knowledge of the firm. Third, the dimension of knowledge is primarily related to scientific, engineering and design knowledge, especially to systematic, problem solving knowledge. In this sense knowledge-intensive entrepreneurs are considered as 'knowledge operators' (Malerba, 2010) aiming at the development of new products and technologies. Fourth, KIE is mostly characterized by the foundations of new companies, i.e. start-ups or spin-offs. Fifth, this concept refers to innovation system approaches. Their embeddedness in the institutionalized conditions of a system of innovation is regarded as crucial prerequisites for economic success. In general, the term KIE is narrowly linked to the discourse on the growing significance of knowledge for societal development and on the emerging 'knowledge economy' (Foray, 2002). Consistently, the debate on KIE has mainly focused on firms or start-ups in new technology-based high-tech industries (Cohendet and Llerna, 2010; Malerba, 2010; Audretsch *et al.*, 2011).

Therefore, this chapter aims at an understanding of KIE phenomena in the context of so-called low-technology industries. As is well known, the terms 'low-tech' and 'medium-low-tech' denote those industrial branches that have a R&D intensity below 3 per cent. Both categories are subsumed under the term 'low- and medium-technology' (LMT). Regarding the industrial branches, primarily 'mature' industries such as the manufacture of household appliances, textiles and footwear, the food industry, the paper, publishing and print industry, the wood and furniture industry and the manufacture of metal products as well as the manufacture of plastic products are regarded as LMT industries (OECD, 2005). Due to their mature character it seems very plausible that so far the ongoing debate on entrepreneurship has not focused at all on these industries. In other words, KIE in LMT industries can be regarded as a contradiction in itself.

Nonetheless, in this chapter the question will be examined whether KIE activities can be identified in LMT industries, and which specific characteristics they have. To answer this query, this chapter proceeds as follows: In Section 2 we will discuss the constraints and opportunities for KIE in LMT sectors and will draft an analytical framework as a guideline for the interpretation of empirical findings. Section 3 deals with methodological questions and the empirical base of the investigation. Section 4 comprises the empirical findings, namely four empirical patterns of KIE in the LMT sector. In Section 5 the findings will be summarized and policy-oriented conclusions will be outlined.

2 KIE in LMT industries

2.1 Constraints

The main features of KIE consider unexploited opportunities, dealing with uncertainties, the creation of new knowledge and overcoming of established routines at the company and at the sectoral level (Cohendet and Llerena, 2010). However, it must be assumed that these opportunities are rare in LMT sectors.

The findings of LMT research support this:[2] On the one hand, findings emphasize the specific innovation ability of LMT industries (Arundel *et al.*, 2008; Hirsch-Kreinsen, 2008; Huang *et al.*, 2010). On the other hand, these findings show a dominance of incremental, mostly process innovations and disruptive innovation activities are in contrast very seldom. Generally, the dominant pattern of technological development in LMT industries runs along the given technological paths and is based on a relatively slow accumulation of capabilities around previously known technological specialization. In other words, the LMT innovativeness is characterized by a high path-dependency which is continuously stabilized by incremental innovation activities, by increasing returns as the result of the continuously optimized processes of the existing technologies and the therefore basically emerging momentum of these developmental paths.[3] Unlike high-tech industries with their prevailing technological contingency, the technologies of the LMT industries are well known and established and the processes and products are not only highly routinized but also at an advanced stage. The same holds for the knowledge base, which includes mostly codified, transferable and well-known elements such as design methods, engineering routines or the know-how about markets and customer preferences. Therefore, technological norms, methods and leitmotifs as well as occupations and skills are well developed and have existed for many generations. Furthermore, normal sales market conditions force companies to continuously optimize their processes and technologies than to pursue risky innovation activities. They do not trigger KIE-based activities at all. Rather, the economic success of LMT companies is linked to professionalized managers whose job is to optimize, to rationalize and to streamline the processes of their companies along the given trajectories in order to meet the needs of the intensive price competition on the sales markets. Considering this situation, entrepreneurial activities have only limited chances due to the fixed LMT technological trajectories and the costly uncertainties they may produce.[4]

2.2 Opportunities

However, contradictory tendencies that go along with opportunities for KIE in LMT should not be overlooked (see also Schwinge, 2014). Based on conceptual considerations of entrepreneurial research this situation can be traced back to two interlinked determining factors.

First, the activities of individual agents or firms can go beyond the borders of an established sectoral system; it may be argued that a majority of actors involved may look at new ideas and inventions as a cul-de-sac whereas for a minority of economic actors a situation of stable path-dependency offers opportunities with a high potential for economic success (Garud and Karnøe, 2003; Garud et al., 2007). It may also be argued that competitive pressure will force managers to change their role by adopting an increasingly reflective approach towards established practices and by looking for breakthrough innovations (Beckert, 1999). This reflective approach may be triggered by a situation when formerly increasing returns may cease to increase or may even turn into decreasing returns (Deeg, 2005). Generally, the intensive competitive pressure in LMT industries forces actors not only to adopt managerial strategies of cost cutting and optimizing existing routines but may also compel them to adopt a reflective stance towards the established practices in order to overcome this situation. Especially because of the high persistence and stability of LMT industries, entrepreneurial activities and a successful deviation from established practices and technological paths promise competitive advantages and a high profitability. As research on entrepreneurship shows (Shane, 2003; Grichnik, 2006) such activities are based on two distinct abilities: the ability to take up given opportunities for KIE activities based on existing information about these opportunities, and the ability to look actively for possible opportunities and to create a beneficial situation for a KIE process based on a specific 'alertness' of the entrepreneurial actor.[5]

Second, these arguments refer to the concept of entrepreneurial opportunities presented in the entrepreneurial literature (Shane, 2003). This highlights that entrepreneurial activities can only be understood as a nexus of entrepreneurial activities on the micro-level of individual companies and valiable opportunities on the macro-level of economic, institutional and technological structures (for a summary see Radosevic, 2010). This argument can also be linked with conceptual findings in LMT research which emphasized the particular relevance of a 'distributed knowledge base' for the innovativeness of companies from LMT firms, i.e. the relevance of sector-external knowledge stocks, especially scientifically created knowledge in high-tech industries for LMT firms (Robertson and Smith, 2008). In other words, individual actors or firms cannot be the drivers of KIE processes if they only rely on their specific individual capabilities and knowledge; instead they have to build up relationships with actors, resources and sense opportunities from outside the sector. Hence, LMT industries should basically not be understood as a closed and 'ultra-stable' system, as it is influenced by the conditions of various other systems to which it is linked; e.g. it is embedded in regional, national and supra-national innovation systems.

2.3 An analytical framework

Based on these considerations an analytical framework for the empirical analysis of KIE processes in LMT industries will be sketched out. The purpose of this framework is to guide the analysis of the empirical results in order to identify typical patterns of KIE processes in LMT industries. Its basic dimension refers to knowledge. It is a constitutive feature of KIE processes that they call for more than the already existing and established procedural and scientific knowledge of the firm and its specific industrial sector. This means that scientifically created knowledge may play a major role in KIE processes (Malerba, 2010). However, due to the specific mature situation of LMT industries also knowledge of operative or practical character may be of larger importance (Hirsch-Kreinsen, 2008).

To analyse KIE process in LMT industries the aforementioned concept of the 'distributed knowledge base' will be taken up and used as an analytical heuristic for the empirical analysis. Following Robertson and Smith a distributed knowledge base is a set of knowledges and knowledge sources maintained across an economically and socially integrated set of agents and institutions.[6] Referring to this concept, firms do not depend on a single technology or on single sources of technological knowledge. Rather, they must blend knowledge that is distributed among various knowledge bases according to such factors as industrial source, geographical location, scientific or technical location, social location and chronology (Robertson and Smith, 2008: 100). This specific ability to combine different sources of established and new knowledge has to be regarded not only as the main prerequisite for innovativeness in general but in particular for successful KIE processes in the context of technologically mature LMT sectors.

Following this concept and the conceptual considerations about the constraints and opportunities of KIE processes in LMT industries (sector 2) three levels of knowledge can be distinguished:

- First, the level of firm-specific knowledge which has a localized character and is specific to very specialized product characteristics in firms which they understand well; on this level especially the capability to purchase new knowledge and the capability to combine existing and new knowledge to a new level of knowledge has to be regarded as an important determining factor for KIE activities (Bender and Laestadius, 2005).
- Second, sector or product-field-specific knowledge; at this level there are shared scientific and technological understandings concerning e.g. the functions, performance characteristics, use of materials of products. This level constitutes a body of knowledge and practice which shapes the performance of all firms in an industry.[7] As aforementioned, it has to be assumed that this sectoral situation is characterized by a strong path dependency and competitive pressure.
- Third, generally applicable knowledge which includes to a larger extent to generally available mostly scientific knowledge which is basically new for established industrial sectors. However, following entrepreneurial research (Shane, 2003, Radosevic, 2010) this level encompasses also market, technological and institutional opportunities beyond the specific and restrictive situation of the LMT firms and sectors. Therefore, this level of globally available knowledge may constitute an important determining factor for successful KIE processes in LMT sectors.

It can be argued that these three levels of knowledge, their characteristics and specific combination constitute the *determining factors* of KIE processes in LMT industries. However, additional *intervening factors* have to be taken into consideration. These factors cannot be regarded as core dimensions of KIE rather they may modify the KIE process. Referring to the literature on LMT innovativeness such factors are of minor significance, e.g. innovation policy and aspects of regional proximity (Jacobson and Heanue, 2005).

The interplay of these factors leads to the outcome of the KIE process which has to be defined in terms of *technological innovation*. Due to the KIE perspective of this analysis one has to exclude the type 'incremental innovation' which may be regarded as typical for LMT industries. This innovation type is typical for and widespread in LMT branches but it does not affect and overcome the established industrial situation. Thus, oriented on the well-known taxonomy of Henderson and Clark (1990) and research findings on LMT innovation, one can conclude that 'architectural' and 'modular' innovations can be regarded as relevant for KIE-LMT. But due to the connotation of KIE, radical innovation cannot be completely excluded either.

Finally, one has to emphasize – unlike the general debate on KIE (Malerba, 2010) – that the focus on KIE in LMT has to include not only newly founded companies (start-ups and spin-offs) but also change processes in established companies, termed as corporate entrepreneurship.[8] The reason for this extended definition of KIE is that in traditional manufacturing sectors with mature technologies newly founded companies based on new technological knowledge may be more unusual than in high-tech sectors with their technologically less established situation. Besides, they would probably face high entrance barriers due to the strong path dependency of LMT industries. Therefore, already existing firms have also to be taken into consideration and it should be asked whether they are able to overcome the restricted situation of LMT industries. As discussed in a conceptual perspective (see Section 2.2) competitive pressure may force managers of established firms to change their role by adopting an increasingly reflective approach towards established practices and by looking for breakthrough innovations. Generally, the intensive competitive pressure in LMT industries may force firms not only to adopt managerial strategies of cost cutting and optimizing existing routines but may also compel them to adopt a reflective stance towards the established practices in order to overcome this situation.

3 Methodology

3.1 Database

The intention of this chapter is to analyse processes of KIE in LMT industries in an *exploratory* manner. It is based on the findings of case study research and it aims at a first understanding of a not yet investigated issue and the development of hypotheses which should stimulate further research. In other words, based on the outlined analytical framework the empirical analysis aims at a preliminary identification of the opportunities and patterns of KIE processes in LMT industries. Methodologically, these opportunities and patterns are of a hypothetical nature which should stimulate further research.

The exploratory analysis is based on the results of 27 qualitative case studies that were conducted in selected LMT companies in 2009 and 2010.[9] The case studies were conducted in the LMT branches food, beverages & tobacco (NACE 15/16), textiles, apparel & leather (NACE 17/18/19) and metalworking (NACE 27/28). The case study companies were either established or newly founded companies; the KIE process of established companies is termed as *corporate entrepreneurship*; newly founded companies include foundations by already existing companies or individual entrepreneurs termed as *industrial start-ups* or foundations from academic institutions termed as *academic spin-offs* (see Table 9.1 below).

The selection criteria for the case study companies were: New companies founded between 2000 and 2006 and implementation of innovations in established companies between 2000 and 2006. Furthermore: The company should evidently be a first mover or be reckoned among the most innovative companies in the market or product field. The case study companies should be SMEs, i.e. have less than 250 employees. The innovation implemented by the investigated company can be either a new product or a new, not previously applied, process technology (i.e. generally more than only incremental innovation activities). The case study companies are located in Southern Europe (Greece) and Western Europe (Portugal, Denmark and Germany). Because of the exploratory character of this study the different national settings of the companies and sectoral differences will not be considered systematically. The case study companies are summarized in Table 9.1.[10]

For allowing comparability of the results, the common methodological basis of all case studies was a standardized questionnaire and a structured interview guideline. The items of the common interview guideline included the following dimensions: general information about the entrepreneur and the firm, the entrepreneurial innovation process, the determining factors of this process, the outcome and performance of this process. On the basis of the structured interview guideline, one or two interviews per case study were conducted with company experts from different hierarchical levels and from different functions. Normally, the managing director or the

Table 9.1 The AEGIS LMT case studies

Sector KIE-Modus	Textile	Food	Metal
Corporate entrepreneurship	CTGR1 CTGR2 CTGE2 CTGE3	CFDK2 CFGR2 CFGR3 CFGE1 CFGE3 CFP2	CMDK2 CMGE1 CMP2
Industrial start-up	CTDK2 CTP2	CFDK1 CFGR1 CFP1	CMDK1 CMGE2 CMGR1 CMP1
Academic spin-off	CTDK1 CTGE1 CTP1	CFGE2	CMGE3
Total (N=27)	9	10	8

founder, or the owner of the firm was interviewed. The expert interviews were often supplemented by a company tour and the analysis of accessible company documents. The data collected were summarized in case study reports based on a standardized structure. These reports were evaluated systematically by a qualitative content analysis.

3.2 KIE patterns

On the basis of the case study results four patterns of KIE processes in LMT industries will be outlined in the following. The generation of these patterns is based on the dimensions of the analytical framework (see section 2.3). They differ in the following respects: Each KIE pattern represents a specific expression and combination of the various dimensions of the framework, i.e. the different levels of knowledge. Additionally, the patterns differ due to the most influencing factor; i.e. one of the knowledge levels proves to be the main determining factor for the KIE pattern. Hence, the description of the different KIE pattern is centred on two features: First, the dominant determining factor leading the course of the KIE process. Second, complementary factors which are – in comparison – of less importance. Third, further common intervening factors have to be taken into consideration. As outlined above, these intervening factors cannot be regarded as core dimensions of KIE, rather they may modify the KIE process in a general way.

The estimation of the importance of the various influencing factors for the analysed KIE processes is based on a combination of several indicators referring to conventional methodological steps of qualitative analysis (Kelle and Kluge, 2010): First, the direct statements of the interviewees and their self-estimation of their entrepreneurial activities have been regarded as the main indicator. Second, a comparative 'cross examination' of the various data of the whole case study analysis (standardized data, interview results, secondary sources as documents) and their 'plausible' interpretation had been regarded as a second important indicator. Third, the criterion whether the distinction between the different KIE patterns is convincing and clear-cut has to be regarded as a further indicator for the estimation of which factors are of utmost, minor or only intervening importance for the KIE process. Methodologically, the KIE patterns have to be regarded as ideal types. Their development is data-driven but also guided conceptually. That means they are formed from characteristics and elements of the given phenomena, i.e. the case study findings phenomena. Due to this methodological status, they do not correspond to all of the features of any one particular case.

4 Empirical findings: four patterns of KIE-LMT

Bearing this methodological approach in mind, four patterns of KIE-LMT can be distinguished on the basis of the case study findings: *a demand-driven*

Table 9.2 KIE-LMT patterns and classification of case study companies

Pattern KIE-Modus	Market-driven	Science and technology-driven	Capability-driven	Competitive pressure
Corporate entrepreneurship	CMDK2 CTGR1 CFGR2 CFGR3	CFGE3	CFDK2 CFGE1 CTGE2 CMP2	CMGE1 CTGE3 CTGR2 CFP2
Industrial start-up	CMDK1 CFDK1 CMGR1 CTP2	CFP1	CTDK2 CFGR1 CMGE2	CMP1
Academic spin-off		CTDK1 CFGE2 CMGE3 CTGE1 CTP1		
Total (N=27)	8	7	7	5

pattern, a science- and technology-driven (S&T-) pattern, a capability-driven pattern and a fourth pattern termed competitive pressure (see Table 9.2).

These four patterns will be described in detail in the following sections.

4.1 Demand-driven

4.1.1 Market knowledge as determining factor

This pattern of KIE-LMT is characterized by the fact that its KIE processes are mainly driven by available knowledge about market opportunities. This means that new market segments emerge due to an increasing variety of customer demands or that already existing and so far unexploited market segments are tapped. Nine of the examined case study companies can be regarded as this KIE pattern. Five of these can be termed as corporate entrepreneurship, i.e. enterprises with extended business activities and four are start-up companies. They come from all three examined branches. There are no case study companies which can be characterized as academic spin-offs. It may be assumed that the identification of new market opportunities is easier for established companies or industrial oriented entrepreneurs compared to entrepreneurs stemming from academia who are only loosely coupled with markets and customer demand.

The common feature of these market opportunities is that they usually do not constitute an element of traditional LMT industries; instead they tend to be of global character and are sources of generally applicable knowledge beyond the specific sectors' LMT situation. They offer new sales opportunities and high profits compared to the established restrictive sectoral market situation of the individual LMT firms. The empirical material shows that in many of the examined cases the new market opportunities resulted from socio-structural changes, in particular changed ways of life, new role structures and – hence – new customer preferences. Outstanding examples for this are changed customer preferences with regard to foods and eating habits as well as a notable increase in demand for sophisticated convenience products or functionally sophisticated textiles (CFGR2; CFDK1; CTGR2). Moreover, in two cases the market opportunities resulted from direct customer requests and the therewith associated innovation impulses. Thus, a Danish manufacturer of sintered components reported that the development process for the innovation was triggered by a customer who wanted to make wear plates from a new material. The customer's role in the development of the new product was to motivate the company to start testing and prototyping different material blending (CMDK2).

All in all, the companies investigated are exposed to a significant 'market pull', which offers excellent prerequisites for the successful market launch of new products. Furthermore, new market opportunities were to some extent also accelerated by political and institutional influences. Thus one of the examined companies profited from the liberalization of the national telecommunications market which opened up a completely new market segment for newly developed technical components for communication systems (CMGR1). In other cases, stricter environmental protection regulations influenced indirectly customer preferences (CMDK2).

4.1.2 Complementary factors: transformative capabilities of the actors

As the research findings show, at the level of the individual firm and/or entrepreneur, the existing stock of firm-specific knowledge and set of capabilities to acquire new knowledge and to combine existing and new knowledge to a new level of knowledge plays an additional and indispensable role for this KIE pattern. To begin with, the research findings show that a key prerequisite for this is a broad firm-specific knowledge base regarding the specific situation of the firm and the own achievement potential. This is essential to be able to evaluate the extent to which the respective companies can take advantage of market opportunities. In all studied cases, this knowledge base comprised a high degree of accumulated knowledge about and manifold experiences in markets, management and organizational issues as well as the potentials of the given technology. This knowledge base is only to some extent the result of own research efforts in in-house R&D departments (CFGR3). In fact, it is to a high degree of a practical nature. In the case of the established companies, it was acquired in the running process and in the case of new foundations it is the result of previous business activities. A typical example for this is the foundation of a food business with convenience and bread products (CFDK1). The founder had acquired the necessary management and technological skills during his earlier business activities for industrial bakeries.

In all of the examined cases belonging to the market-driven pattern of KIE, the capability to transform and absorb external knowledge proved to be of utmost importance. First, the company's ability to manage and effectively co-ordinate network relations across company borders with other companies within the value chain, research institutes and universities or specialized consultants, is a central precondition for successful KIE-LMT. According to the research findings, the co-operation with customers or potential customers and with competitors too proved to be of great significance in these cases (e.g. CMGR1; CMDK1). Evidently, these co-operation relations are the precondition for the ability of enterprises and founders to gain the necessary knowledge about the given market. In addition, co-operation relations with technology suppliers from other sectors, such as machine manufacturers or research institutions, also played a large role for the realization of planned innovations. These relations enabled the companies to obtain the necessary additional technological and scientific knowledge, e.g. new machine designs, new materials or design competencies.

Second, the companies had to be able to synthesize and combine the available and the new knowledge if they wanted to profit from the given opportunities. In this regard, the established firms point to an established learning culture or to very open organizational routines that facilitate the integration and utilization of new knowledge (CMDK1; CTGR2). This specific capability of the actors can be termed as 'bricolage' capability, i.e. the ability to synthesize knowledge from many fields and hence to derive long-term company goals.

4.1.3 Outcome: architectural innovations

In a nutshell, knowledge intensification in the examined enterprises stands for a considerable expansion of the local knowledge base, primarily by means of referring to generally applicable knowledge about markets and application possibilities of new products beyond the given sectoral constraints. This knowledge intensification leads to innovations that can be mostly referred to as architectural. Compared with the established situation of LMT sectors, these innovations represent a new type of technology which has been not in use so far. The new products or processes are based not only on new combinations of existing local or sectoral available knowledge resources and technologies but also on globally available technologies and corresponding components which are new to the local level LMT firms and the sectoral level of LMT industries. An example is the flexible process innovation of the described Danish start-up from the food industry. Although this innovation is referred to as 'unique' with regard to its flexibility, it is of an architectural nature, i.e. the development of new process design by a recombination of already available machine technologies and components (CFDK1). The innovation of a Greek metal company follows a similar mode: It is featured by the redesign of an existing product technology to increase its functional efficiency. In doing so, they systematically made use of globally available technological components and changed already existing ones without changing the products in their basic design (CMGR1).

4.2 Science and technology-driven

4.2.1 Science and technology as determining factors

This pattern is characterized by the fact that scientific and technological opportunities and the interlinked generally applicable knowledge are the main driving factor of the KIE process. These opportunities facilitate the development of new products or processes that open up possibilities for overcoming the restrictive LMT situation and for gaining new business perspectives. One can speak of a situation that can be characterized as 'technology push': The entrepreneurial activities of this pattern fall back on technologies that are globally available but which application is completely new to the LMT industry. Seven of the examined case study companies can be assigned to this pattern. The large majority of six companies includes newly founded firms, some as start-ups but most as spin-offs of scientific research (Table 9.2). This distribution is quite obviously no coincidence. Newly founded enterprises normally aim at the implementation of technological opportunities that are new in relation to the established technology paths. The empirical evidence shows that the examined enterprises drew on new and above all obviously utilizable technological opportunities. Thus the start-ups of the textile industry used the opportunities of electronic technologies, especially of new fiber technologies to combine these with traditional textile and clothing concepts and, by way of example, to develop smart textiles. The situation in the examined companies from the food industry is comparable. These companies drew on globally available research findings as knowledge about the use of eatable films in foodstuffs, knowledge about fruit drying and methods of a specific drying technology. The importance of globally available technological opportunities is plainly demonstrated by the example of a German metal start-up. Its foundation is based on the use of a process technology that has been available for a long time, a specific welding technology, by means of which the scope of applications of established welding technologies could be significantly expanded.

4.2.2 Complementary factors: technological knowledge of the actors and new market niches

Following the case study results, this pattern of KIE activities is also to a certain extent based on a sound technological knowledge which the founders of the academic spin-offs acquired in their previous scientific fields of work. This factor can be classified as a complementary factor for this KIE pattern. A German spin-off company that developed systems for the drying of fruits is a good example for this: Both founders had gained great expertise and experience with fruit drying in general and the solar drying system in particular during their times at the university (CFGE2). Similar evidence can be found, for example, in the case of a start-up metal company that developed new welding technologies. Here, the precise knowledge of traditional welding technologies and their possibilities and limitations was cited as an essential precondition for the innovations.

Another essential influencing factor is the extension and intensification of this knowledge base by means of co-operation relations with external partners. The enhancement of application-oriented technological knowledge and a broadening of the product-field-specific (sectoral) knowledge is an important objective of these co-operative activities in which the often technology-savvy founders are not well versed. Especially the examined start-ups cultivated close formal and informal co-operation relations with diverse organizations from various fields to obtain the necessary basic knowledge for the active business. The missing application-oriented competencies were e.g. obtained by the targeted recruitment of technology specialists such as electronic and software engineers. A prerequisite for this was the close contact to a scientific institute that trains such specialists (CTP1). In another case, the lacking process technology was secured within the framework of a close co-operation with a mechanical engineering company. The more practice-oriented business-competencies were acquired within the scope of network relations with suppliers of primary products, future clients as well as industry associations (e.g. CTGE1; CMGE3; CFGE3; CFP1).

The utilization of the technological opportunities was additionally spurred on by the given market opportunities and existing limitations of the traditional markets. Both factors urged the companies and the entrepreneurs to actually convert the pressing technological opportunities into marketable technologies. All in all, the market niches were new and resulted from new customer preferences that are generally due to changed lifestyles and high disposable incomes. In the cases of the start-ups from the textile sector, these changes entailed a growing demand for sophisticated and functionally enhanced clothing. In the case of the enterprises from the food industry, growing expectations with regard to healthy and high-quality products played an important role. In several cases, the emerging market opportunities can also be ascribed to stricter institutional-political regulations. Most notably, to be mentioned here are stricter EU standards regarding the shelf life of food, which has led to a growing demand for effective preservation methods.

4.2.3 Outcome: towards 'radical' innovation

To sum up, this KIE pattern is characterized by a process of knowledge intensification based on the expansion of the already available technologically oriented competencies by generally applicable, mostly scientifically created knowledge which is fundamentally new to the local and sectoral knowledge base. Therefore, the innovations implemented within this context have at least a partially more far-reaching character, or, putting it tentatively: Measured by the traditional technologies of LMT industries, they approach the type 'radical innovations': Often a new dominant design of a product or a process can be discerned that results from the combination of various technological components. In the case of the technology-driven KIE pattern this is highly plausible. It seems obvious that the use of globally available technological opportunities leads to completely new product and process technologies and that these are especially implemented in the context of academic spin-offs. Thus, this pattern is characterized by the use of technologies that were not used before by LMT firms. As described above, this involved specific and newly developed IT and software components, the use of completely new textile fibres and the deployment of new process technologies. Compared with the previous technological development paths these innovations often have a fundamentally novel character.

4.3 Capability-driven

4.3.1 Company's capabilities as determining factors

A third pattern of KIE-LMT can be termed 'capability-driven'. This pattern is not propelled by globally available market or technological opportunities; instead the driving forces for the innovative process can be primarily found at the local level of individual companies. On the basis of the ability to extend systematically the available knowledge stock, the company management or the individual entrepreneur implemented an idea that was considered promising and thus lastingly improved his economic situation. This idea has not only the character of an everyday innovation activity. Rather, it can be understood as KIE because it exceeds the given technological limitations of LMT industries. In a nutshell, this is a classic case of the Schumpeterian entrepreneur. Of course, this KIE process cannot be seen in isolation from the overall situation, i.e. the given sectoral specific constraints and opportunities. Seven of the examined case study companies can be allocated to this KIE pattern. Four companies of these cases can be termed corporate entrepreneurship and three companies have the character of industrial start-ups (Table 9.2). This empirical pattern is plausible because this KIE pattern is based on accumulated capabilities may it be within an established company or may it be based on the sector and product-field-specific experiences and knowledge of individual entrepreneurs. On the contrary, entrepreneurs from academia normally lack such capabilities.

In all examined cases, the starting point of these KIE activities was a profound knowledge base about the given industrial structures and the development potentials of the available technologies. In addition, the key actors, especially the management of the existing LMT firms, have extensive management and organizational experience. The KIE activities of a Danish dairy products manufacturer are an instructive example for this pattern. The precondition for these activities was a strong knowledge base about cream production dating back 20 years and sound knowledge about and experience with competitors, suppliers and customers (CFDK2). The situation in a more than 100-year-old family enterprise, a brewery, is described in similar terms: It has outstanding brewery knowledge at its disposal (CFGE1).

Additionally, the interview partners pointed almost unanimously to a long culture of innovation and an entrepreneurial tradition in their companies, which e.g. finds its expression in interdisciplinary development teams that continually drive innovations. In the case of the Portuguese met-alware manufacturer the innovation process was based on the existence of a qualified, interdisciplinary team which acted in each of the projects or in consultations with clients, and which embraced the commercial, market-ing, design, engineering, production, procurement and quality departments (CMP2). These activities were accompanied by continuous internal learn-ing and training of the workforce. The interview results point to a similar situation in one of the two spin-offs. Here the typical low-tech innovation culture: 'tinkering around' is highlighted by the founder (CMGE2).

4.3.2 Complementary factors: market opportunities

The knowledge about market opportunities has to be regarded as an important complementary factor that the companies tapped by means of their KIE activities. This is often linked to market niches beyond the sec-toral and product-field-specific structures that developed in the context of changing market structures and demand preferences. First, the growing demand for high-quality products has to be mentioned here. For the manu-facturers of foodstuff and a textile manufacturer, this trend opened up the possibility of creating actively new market segments (CFGR1; CFDK2; CTDK2). Second, the opportunity of expanding given markets played an important role. In one of the examined cases, the company's objective was to expand its regional market outlet in order to reach the national market (CFGE1) and in the other case the company aimed at entering foreign markets (CMP2). Third, the innovation of the aforementioned mentioned textile manufacturer was aimed at the creation of new market segments; the conveyor belts with advertisements printed on them were intended for supermarket cash registers and thus created a so-far non-existent field of application. Opportunities offered by globally available technologies have to be regarded as a further influencing factor; these are e.g. packaging tech-nologies (CFGR1), materials technologies (CMP1; CMGE2), and transport technologies have to be mentioned which offer promising innovation per-spectives in most of the entrepreneurial activities belonging to this KIE pattern (CFGE1).

4.3.3 Outcome: mostly modular innovations

With regard to this KIE pattern, knowledge intensification signifies the use and expansion of the accumulated firm-specific knowledge base by a recombination of the elements on hand and the systematic integration of pertinent generally available knowledge about market opportunities. The innovations pursued by firms belonging to this KIE pattern are mostly of a modular nature. The firms belonging to this pattern make systematic use of globally available technological components and change already existing ones without changing the products in their basic design. Examples are a new label for children's fashion (CTDK2), high-quality, health-oriented food and beverages (CFGR1; CFDK2; CFGE1) and new metal and textile products (CMP2; CTGE2; CMGE2).

4.4 Competitive pressure

4.4.1 Competitive pressure as determining factor

A fourth pattern of KIE-LMT can be termed 'competitive pressure'. The innovation driver of this pattern is the particularly strong competitive pressure of the specific sectoral situation. The representatives of the companies belonging to this pattern have pronounced knowledge about the economically and technologically severe situation of their firms. This knowledge is of a firm-specific and sector-specific nature. The interviewees expressed this knowledge convincingly and emphasized that if the enterprises did not act or were not successful in their innovation efforts, their existence could be in jeopardy. Five of the examined case study companies belong to this KIE pattern. Four of these can be referred to as corporate entrepreneurship; one of them can be regarded as an independently founded start-up (Table 9.2). Similar to the demand-driven KIE pattern it may be assumed that the identification of a severe industrial situation is primarily possible for established companies or industrial-oriented entrepreneurs compared to entrepreneurs stemming from academia who are only loosely coupled with the industrial situation.

If one summarizes the research material, two basic aspects of competitive pressure can be distinguished: First, the overall economic situation is extremely difficult, due to the growing cost pressure by competitors from low-cost countries. As has been shown, this is a central feature of the whole LMT sector with its mature technologies. This problem, however, proves to be particularly pressing in the case of the examined enterprises. Second, technological product or process bottlenecks are a weak point. These bottlenecks frequently result from new requirements on the companies that often thwart attempts to increase efficiency and lower costs. Or they hamper the further incremental development of products which is needed to help to secure the company's market share. Both instances have to be resolutely tackled to avoid risky situations.

An example of a difficult economic situation is the situation of a German manufacturer of customized fireplaces and steel-made goods (CMGE1). The market situation was described as follows: 'It is becoming thinner and thinner.' There was increasing competition from abroad and from bigger firms in general, which were able to provide cheaper products because of scale economies for this relatively simple kind of product, which, according to the interviewed manager, 'anyone can build'. The company has depended on occasional orders from customers who need products at short notice. However, these orders are subject to high volatility.

The firm has been in a permanent state of hustling for customers. Therefore, the management has been systematically seeking for possibilities to become more independent of this market segment. A further example is the very difficult situation of a Greek textile manufacturer, which was confronted with a highly internationalized and fragmented market and high competitive pressure (CMGR2). Apparently there were hardly any opportunities for innovation for specific market niches. However, the examined enterprise is an exceptional case within its sector, as it has been addressing this situation. Within the framework of a corporate entrepreneurship, a new process for the dyeing and finishing of textiles was developed. This process was vertically integrated into the whole value chain. Therewith, this company could achieve a good competitive position despite the difficult situation.

The situation of an enterprise of the food industry that treats fruit and vegetables for wholesale is an instructive example of a bottleneck trade (CFP2). Because of the growing quality requirements of the wholesale trade, the company was confronted with a high number of rejects, i.e. unmarketable apples. To avoid related losses due to this, the idea arose to use the apples of lesser quality for the production of apple juice in order to avoid costs and to establish a new product line. This situation is succinctly described by the interviewed company representative as follows: 'Of course, the rationalization of the company's resources – namely, the fruit that couldn't be commercialized – was the underlying motivation for the new business' (ibid.).

4.4.2 Complementary factors: specific innovation culture

A distinct knowledge base and special innovative capabilities of the companies have to be interpreted as complementary factors also important for the success of initiatives to overcome the competitive pressure. For one of the examined cases (CMGE1), the interviewees pointed to the 'typical low-tech innovation culture' – a situation similar to the aforementioned KIE pattern competitive pressure. It is characterized by innovation activities during and besides the daily work, furthermore innovative ideas are developed by individual actors; structured and systematic search processes seem to be less common. For all of the examined companies, the case study findings moreover make the point that their management or founders have a good stock of knowledge – accumulated in the course of many years – about technological opportunities, the sales market situation as well as management requirements. This knowledge stock enabled them to systematically and purposefully establish co-operation relations with machine manufacturers, suppliers, marketing experts and other external partners as well as to integrate and use new knowledge.

Furthermore, one has to inquire the market opportunities that the companies opened up with their KIE activities and with which they could markedly improve their competitive position. According to the research material these opportunities arose solely due to generally emerging market trends. By means of their KIE activities, the enterprises tapped these markets and created their own market niches. A typical example of this is a German metal company that is described as follows (CMGE1): The firm benefitted from a discernible shift of interest in society towards environmental issues in general and green technologies in particular. With its early focus on these issues the company had a head start in comparison to competitors. Having the most efficient and environmentally friendly product has been a major sales argument for the firm.

4.4.3 Outcome: far-reaching innovations

In summary, knowledge intensification in this KIE pattern signifies the use and expansion of the firm-specific and product-field-specific knowledge base, most notably by purposefully rounding it off with generally applicable knowledge about new technologies and market opportunities. The innovations pursued by the firms of this KIE pattern aim at innovations of a far-reaching or even radical nature. In doing so, they attempt to overcome their situation of a strong competitive pressure and to exceed the technological limitations of LMT industries. The case of a completely new production facility for the production of apple juice, based on a likewise new process (CFP2), the development of an elastic and conductive textile fibre based on the use of completely new materials (CTGE3) or the development of a purlin that does not only have a completely new design but is also characterized by the use of new materials (CMP1) are empirical examples in the sample of the case study companies.

4.5 Intervening factors

As outlined above (Section 3), additional intervening factors have to be taken into consideration in order to analyse a KIE process as completely as possible. However, the empirical material indicates that there is no clear correlation between certain intervening factors and the various KIE patterns that have been sketched. In fact, such factors can only be identified on the basis of the whole research sample in a general perspective, i.e. they prove to be occasionally important for individual KIE cases. According to the empirical material, there are at least three factors of major significance:

First, the issue of funding and financing the KIE processes proved to be of great importance in nearly all cases, independently of the KIE pattern. However, no companies obviously suffered from a crucial lack of financial resources. Most of the KIE companies and start-ups investigated made use of internal funds to finance their activities. Some of the companies took out a loan for smaller parts of the needed funding (CMGE2). Only a few successfully applied for funding by the state or by public support programmes. In fact, many of the interviewed company representatives emphasized that such programmes have not been attractive for the companies because e.g. of the bureaucracy and the programme manager's lack of knowledge about the specific situation of LMT firms (CMP1; CTP1). These and similar comments refer to both national funding programmes[11] as well as European programmes.

Second, for some of the companies, regional embeddedness seems to be beneficial for their KIE process. The local proximity to e.g. suppliers, scientific organizations or banks and investors makes it easier to gain new technological knowledge, additional capacities or financial resources. An example of this is the Portuguese firm from the metalworking sector and its network with local 'rivals' (CMP2). This local network has two functions: For one thing, the production capacities were levelled out between the different metalware manufacturers; for another thing, this co-operation facilitated the opening up of 'unfriendly' markets such as the Chinese market.

Third, there are also constraining conditions for the KIE process which can be summarized as follows: The interviewees, often from Southern Europe, referred to an 'unfriendly environment for entrepreneurial activities' and the lack of a clear institutional framework promoting such activities; furthermore they highlighted the existence of many political and institutional obstacles (e.g. CTGR2). They also mentioned a lack of support from industry associations and poor professional guidance by consultants (CMGE3). Furthermore, they criticized the limited or even lacking availability of venture capital that was needed especially in the high-risk initial phases of foundations (e.g. CFP1).

5 Conclusion: theoretical and policy implications

To sum up, four patterns of KIE-LMT can be distinguished: a market-driven pattern, a science and technology-driven pattern, a capability-driven pattern and a pattern termed as competitive pressure. These patterns differ due to the configuration of the most important determining factor, complementary factors which step up the effects of the determining factors and the innovation modes resulting from the KIE processes. The main features of these four patterns are summarized below in Table 9.3:

The value of this typology is primarily of a conceptual nature because it advances the theoretical understanding about the opportunities for KIE activities in a technologically restricted industrial sector like LMT. The findings widen and overcome the positions of mainstream research and concepts of KIE that exclusively link this concept to high-tech and knowledge-intensive sectors and start-up firms. As the findings show, entrepreneurial activities can go beyond the borders of a highly path-dependent system; it may be that a majority of actors involved may look at new ideas and inventions as a cul-de-sac whereas for a minority of economic actors a situation of

Table 9.3 Main features of KIE-LMT patterns

KIE-pattern factors	Market-driven	Science and technology-driven	Capability-driven	Competitive pressure
Determining factor	Knowledge about new global market segments	New global technology opportunities and the corresponding knowledge	Broad and profound local knowledge base and an outstanding entrepreneurial and innovation culture	Knowledge about a severe sectoral situation, cost and competition pressure and technological bottlenecks
Complementary factors	Outstanding transformative capabilities of the firms	Sound local technological knowledge, close relations with external organizations	Local knowledge about new market opportunities	Accumulated local knowledge base and an outstanding entrepreneurial and innovation culture
Innovations	Mostly architectural innovations	Towards 'radical' innovations	Modular innovations	Far-reaching innovations
Intervening factors	• Available financial resources, mostly internal sources and loans • Regional embeddedness as an advantageous situation • Unfriendly environment to entrepreneurial activities as constraints			

stable path-dependency offers opportunities with a high potential for economic success. The intensive competitive pressure in LMT industries may force actors not only to adopt managerial strategies of cost cutting and optimizing existing routines but may also compel them to adopt a reflective stance towards the established practices in order to overcome this situation. Especially because of the high persistence and stability of LMT industries, entrepreneurial activities and a successful deviation from established practices and technological paths promise competitive advantages and a high profitability. As the findings show such activities are based on two distinct capabilities: The capability to take up given opportunities for KIE activities based on existing information about these opportunities and the capability to look actively for possible opportunities for KIE based on a specific 'alertness' of the entrepreneurial actor.[12]

However, the findings also show that KIE activities can only be understood as a nexus of entrepreneurial activities on the micro-level of individual companies and valiable opportunities on the macro-level of economic, institutional and technological structures. It constitutes an indispensable influencing factor of KIE activities to overcome the restrictions of the established LMT situation. Due to the strong path dependency of LMT industries firms and individual entrepreneurs cannot be the drivers of KIE processes if they only rely on their specific sectoral or local knowledge, instead they have to connect with actors, resources and opportunities from outside the sector. Furthermore, this argument can be linked with conceptual findings in LMT research which emphasized the particular relevance of a 'distributed knowledge base' for the innovativeness of companies from LMT firms, i.e. the relevance of sector-external knowledge stocks, especially scientifically created knowledge in high-tech industries for the innovativeness of LMT firms (Robertson and Smith, 2008).

The value of this typology is also of a practical political nature because the findings of this study point to several possibilities for policy measures which would foster KIE activities in LMT. These are e.g.:

- improving access to trans-sectoral knowledge especially for existing LMT firms and individual entrepreneurs with their often limited resources;
- improving the transfer processes of the globally available knowledge to the local knowledge stock of individual LMT firms and entrepreneurs;
- enhancing the local and firm-specific capabilities to integrate and utilize new knowledge, e.g. by improving management competences, especially the capability to co-operate and network in a global direction;
- considering the framework conditions, i.e. the moderating factors should be the object of policy measures, in particular with respect to

regional proximity and networking as well as the terms of corporate financing.

Without question, these policy recommendations are of major relevance for entrepreneurial activities in LMT industries. However, they need to be specified in further broad-based research on entrepreneurial activities in LMT industries. The outlined KIE patterns may be the conceptual starting point for further research. Additionally, a systematic comparison between KIE-LMT and KIE in the high-tech sectors will be of particular importance. The assumption is plausible that these differences may be only a matter of degree. One may speak of a spectrum with two extremes: On the one side KIE-LMT, on the other side KIE in high-tech, with a smooth transition in between the two ends. However, this comparative perspective has not been systematically applied yet and should also be a major issue of future research.

Notes

1 In particular, we wish to thank our project partners Ioanna Kastelli, Manuel Mira Godinho, Ricardo Mamede and Rick Woodward for comments and suggestions on draft versions of this chapter.
2 Recent years have seen a growing body of innovation literature devoted to the innovativeness of LMT industries. This research interest is mainly motivated by criticism of the mainstream of innovation research and innovation policy, which regards a high investment in R&D and advanced technologies as the key to growth and prosperity (for a summary see Robertson *et al.*, 2009).
3 The concept of path dependency in social sciences and innovation theory (Garud and Karnøe, 2003; Beyer, 2005). In this perspective incremental innovations can be regarded as 'small events' not changing but only stabilizing existing paths.
4 Whereas a manager orients his decisions on routines, adaptation and imitation, entrepreneurs are characterized by a reflective stance towards taken-for-granted scripts and existing institutional regulations – following Schumpeter's distinction between the manager and the entrepreneur (Schumpeter, 1997: 110).
5 The first aspect refers to Schumpeter's notion of innovative opportunities (Schumpeter, 1997), the second aspect to Kirzner who emphasized the discovering of opportunities (Kirzner, 1997).
6 As the authors emphasize, this concept is based on a long-standing discussion in innovation research (Robertson and Smith, 2008: fn 9).
7 See also the concept of Sectoral Innovation Systems which highlights knowledge as a main building block of a specific sector (Malerba, 2005).
8 Corporate entrepreneurship will be understood here 'as the presence of innovation plus the presence of the objective of rejuvenating or purposefully redefining organizations, markets, or industries' (Covin *et al.*, 1999: 60; see also Schwinge, 2014).
9 We would like to thank our work package partners Bram Timmermans, Christian Østergaard, Eun Kyung Park and Kenney V. Christiansen from Aalborg University (AAU); Guido Bünstorf, Christina Guenther and Matthias Geissler from Max Planck Institute of Economics (MPI); Glykeria Karagouni, Ioanna Kastelli and Yannis Caloghirou from National Technical University of Athens

(LIEE-NTUA); and Alexandra Rosa, Manuel Mira Godinho and Ricardo Mamede from Technical University of Lisbon (UECE) for their case study research. Each partner conducted at least six case studies in companies from typical low-tech sectors.

10 The abbreviations of the cases may be clarified by the following example: CFGR2 stands for Case, Food, Greece, Case Study No 2.

11 There are of course national specific divergences which cannot be discussed in the context of this chapter due to its limited scope.

12 The first aspect refers to Schumpeter's notion of innovative opportunities (Schumpeter, 1997), the second aspect to Kirzner who emphasized the discovering of opportunities (Kirzner, 1997).

References

Arundel, A., Bordoy, C. and Kanerva, M. (2008) Neglected innovators: How do innovative firms that do not perform R&D innovate? Results of an analysis of the Innobarometer 2007 Survey No. 215, INNO-Metrics Thematic Paper, MERIT 31 March.

Audretsch, D.B., Falck, O., Heblich, S. and Lederer, A. (eds) (2011) *Handbook of Research on Innovation and Entrepreneurship* (Cheltenham and Northampton, MA: Edward Elgar).

Beckert, J. (1999) Agency, entrepreneurs and institutional change: The role of strategic choice and institutionalized practices in organizations. *Organizational Studies*, 20(5), pp. 777–799.

Bender, G. and Laestadius, S. (2005) Non-science based innovativeness: On capabilities relevant to generate profitable novelty. In: G. Bender, D. Jacobson and P.L. Robertson (eds), *Non-Research-Intensive Industries in the Knowledge Economy. Perspectives on Economic Political and Social Integration*, Special Edition, XI(1–2), pp. 123–170.

Beyer, J. (2005) Pfadabhängigkeit ist nicht gleich Pfadabhängigkeit! Wider den impliziten Konservativismus eines gängigen Konzepts. *Zeitschrift für Soziologie*, 34(1), pp. 5–21.

Cohendet, P. and Llerena, P. (2010) The knowledge-based entrepreneur: The need for a relevant theory of the firm. In: F. Malerba (ed.), *Knowledge-Intensive Entrepreneurship and Innovation Systems. Evidence from Europe*, pp. 31–51 (London and New York: Routledge).

Covin, J., Miles, G. and Morgan, P. (1999) Corporate entrepreneurship and the pursuit of competitive advantage. *Entrepreneurship Theory and Practice*, 23(3), pp. 47–63.

Deeg, R. (2005) Change from within: German and Italian finance in the 1990s. In: W. Streeck and K. Thelen (eds), *Beyond Continuity. Institutional Change in Advanced Political Economies*, pp. 169–204 (Oxford: Oxford University Press).

Foray, D. (2002) The knowledge economy and society. *International Social Science Journal*, 54(171), pp. 1–169.

Garud, R. and Karnøe, P. (2003) Bricolage versus breakthrough: Distributed and embedded agency in technology entrepreneurship. *Research Policy*, 32(2), pp. 277–300.

Garud, R., Hardy, C. and Maguire, S. (2007) Institutional entrepreneurship as embedded agency: An introduction to the special issue. *Organization Studies*, 28(7), pp. 957–970.

Grichnik, D. (2006) Die Opportunity Map der internationalen Entrepreneurship-forschung: Zum Kern des interdisziplinären Forschungsprogramms. *Zeitschrift für Betriebswirtschaft*, 76(12), pp. 1303–1333.

Henderson, R.M. and Clark, K.B. (1990) Architectural innovation: The reconfiguration of existing product technologies and the failure of established firms. *Administrative Science Quarterly*, 35(1), pp. 9–30.

Hirsch-Kreinsen, H. (2008) Low-tech innovation. *Industry and Innovation*, 15(1), pp. 19–43.

Huang, C., Arundel, A. and Hollanders, H. (2010) How firms innovate: R&D, non-R&D, and technology adaption. The UNU-Merit Working papers series, 2010–027.

Jacobson, D. and Heanue, K. (2005) Policy conclusions and recommendations. In: G. Bender, D. Jacobson and P.L. Robertson (eds), *Non-Research-Intensive Industries in the Knowledge Economy. Perspectives on Economic Political and Social Integration*, Special Edition, XI(1–2), pp. 359–416.

Kelle, U. and Kluge, S. (2010) *Vom Einzelfall zum Typus* (Wiesbaden: VS Verlag).

Kirzner, I. (1997) Entrepreneurial discovery and the competitive market process. *Journal of Economic Literature*, 35(1), pp. 60–85.

Malerba, F. (2005) Sectoral systems: How and why innovation differs across sectors. In: J. Fagerberg, D. Mowery and R.R. Nelson (eds), *The Oxford Handbook of Innovation*, pp. 380–406 (Oxford: Oxford University Press).

Malerba, F. (2010) *Knowledge-Intensive Entrepreneurship and Innovation Systems: Evidence from Europe* (London and New York: Routledge).

Malerba, F. and McKelvey, M. (2010) Conceptualizing knowledge intensive entrepreneurship: Concepts and models. Paper presented at DIME – AEGIS – LIEE/NTUA Athens 2010 Conference: The emergence and growth of knowledge intensive entrepreneurship in a comparative perspective. Studying various aspects in different contexts, 29–30 April 2010.

OECD (2005) *Oslo-Manual, Proposed Guidelines for Collecting and Interpreting Technological Innovation Data* (3rd edn) (Paris: OECD).

Radosevic, S. (2010) What makes entrepreneurship systemic? In: F. Malerba (ed.), *Knowledge-Intensive Entrepreneurship and Innovation Systems: Evidence from Europe*, pp. 52–76 (London/New York: Routledge).

Robertson, P.L. and Smith, K. (2008) Technological upgrading and distributed knowledge bases. In: H. Hirsch-Kreinsen and D. Jacobson (eds), *Innovation in Low-tech Firms and Industries*, pp. 93–117 (Cheltenham: Edward Elgar).

Robertson, P. L., Smith, K. and von Tunzelmann, N. (2009) Innovation in low- and medium-technology industries. *Research Policy*, 38, pp. 441–446.

Schumpeter, J. (1997) (1934) *Theorie der wirtschaftlichen Entwicklung* (Berlin: Duncker & Humblot).

Schwinge, I. (2014) The paradox of knowledge-intensive entrepreneurship in low-tech industries – using the example of cases from the German textile industry. PhD dissertation. TU Dortmund University.

Shane, S. (2003) *A General Theory of Entrepreneurship* (Cheltenham: Edward Elgar).

10 Dynamic capabilities in young knowledge-intensive firms

An empirical approach

Aimilia Protogerou and Yannis Caloghirou

1 Introduction

Entrepreneurial firms create, discover and exploit opportunities. While there is an ongoing debate about the underlying processes of opportunity creation, discovery and successful exploitation, most researchers do acknowledge the significance of these processes in generating value for firms. However, up to now, research has not provided an adequate explanation for the ability of some new and established firms to constantly explore, discover and exploit entrepreneurial opportunities (Zahra *et al.*, 2006).

One source of this difference can be identified in these firms' developing and applying different 'dynamic capabilities' (Zahra *et al.*, 2006), a concept which Teece (2007) defines as the capacity to sense and shape opportunities, seize opportunities, and in turn to reconfigure and recombine assets and organizational structures as the firm grows and as markets and technologies change.

Dynamic capabilities have been mainly associated with relatively large, well-established companies operating in high-tech sectors and single national contexts. This stems from the fact that big, older enterprises are generally thought of as more eligible for the empirical study of dynamic capabilities (DCs) because it is assumed that their size and age ensure an adequate organizational structure and the required resources to develop and exercise dynamic routines. On the other hand, high-tech sectors are typically understood as synonymous to rapidly changing environmental conditions and therefore are considered as a suitable context for studying dynamic capabilities whose essence is related to change.

However, new entrepreneurial ventures often face resource base weaknesses and are confronted with subsequent performance loss if these weaknesses are not dealt with early enough. It is necessary for entrepreneurs to create and adapt the resource base of the new firm (Garnsey, 1998; West and DeCastro, 2001), and therefore newly established companies have to demonstrate dynamic capabilities to reconfigure or modify their resource base as required. Furthermore, a changing business environment should not be exclusively associated with high-tech sectors as conditions of relevant turbulence and volatility can also occur in low- and medium-technology industries especially in the midst of the financial crisis that most European countries have recently been experiencing. Thus dynamic capabilities may be beneficial to the firm in both high and low levels of environmental change and therefore can also play an important role even in less dynamic environments (Eisenhardt and Martin, 2000; Helfat *et al.*, 2007; Easterby-Smith *et al.*, 2009; Protogerou *et al.*, 2012).

This chapter attempts to bring more clarity to the dynamic capabilities notion by examining the role and impact of this core concept in the context of new ventures.

In particular, first we empirically test the applicability of dynamic capabilities in newly established firms by examining the impact of specific processes on the growth and international performance of 4,004 entrepreneurial ventures. The dynamic capabilities literature has given scant attention to younger enterprises as they create, scout out and exploit opportunities. However, young firms, especially knowledge-intensive ones, are considered to be of strategic significance as they are often at the leading edge of innovation and, therefore, can play an important role in economic development. In this way we advance the understanding of dynamic capabilities in young vs established firms.

Second, we attempt to link the dynamic capabilities notion with that of knowledge-intensive entrepreneurship by examining whether young firms dynamic capabilities' development is differentiated on the basis of their knowledge-seeking activities, knowledge assets and innovative performance.

Third, we empirically investigate the impact of different industrial sectors on the development of dynamic capabilities. In this way we suggest that dynamic capabilities can be useful not only in rapidly changing environments (e.g. high-tech manufacturing) but also in environments exhibiting low or moderate degrees of dynamism (e.g. low- and medium-tech sectors), while confirming that the dynamic capabilities involved could differ in their degree of development across these types of contexts.

The chapter begins with a theoretical discussion on the role of dynamic capabilities in newly established firms and their impact on new [ventures] growth and performance. In the third section we present the research design, introduce the experimental setting and measures used paying special attention to the dynamic capabilities processes. We then document the empirical results and discuss major findings. The chapter ends with our concluding remarks.

2 Theoretical framework

2.1 Dynamic capabilities and young entrepreneurial ventures

Dynamic capabilities and their role in firm strategy, value creation and competitive advantage have attracted a great deal of interest among scholars (e.g. Teece *et al.*, 1997; Eisenhardt and Martin, 2000; Winter, 2003; Helfat *et al.*, 2007; Teece, 2007). Since the concept of dynamic capabilities was first introduced by Teece *et al.* (1997), additional research has refined and expanded the original idea (e.g. Eisenhardt and Martin, 2000; Zollo and Winter, 2002; Helfat *et al.*, 2007; Teece, 2007). However, many questions remain open. The core concept still requires clarification and development of the theoretical underpinnings along with further empirical grounding (Helfat *et al.*, 2007; Barreto, 2010).

Helfat *et al.* (2007) define dynamic capabilities as 'the capacity of an organization to purposefully and systematically create, extend or modify its resource base' (p. 4). A firm's resource base includes tangible, intangible and human assets such as labour, capital, technology, knowledge, property rights, and also the structures, routines and processes that are needed to support its productive activities (i.e. organizational structures and capabilities). 'Creating' a resource includes all forms of resource formation, such as obtaining new resources through acquisitions and alliances, as well as through innovation and entrepreneurial activity. 'Extending' an existing resource base may result in promoting growth in an ongoing business, whereas 'modifying' a firm's resource base includes any reaction to change, e.g. response to external environment changes. Helfat *et al.* also highlight that creating, adapting to and exploiting changes in the business environment is an inherently entrepreneurial activity (not implying of course a lack in strategy and organization), for *large* firms and *small*, for *established* firms and *new* ones. However, they point out that almost by definition new ventures 'typically develop fewer patterned forms of behaviour that underpin a capability' (p. 6) compared to older companies.

Furthermore, Teece (2007) points out that the dynamic capabilities framework goes beyond traditional approaches in terms of understanding competitive advantage in that it does not only stress the characteristics and processes needed to achieve superior positioning in a munificent ecosystem, but it also attempts to elucidate new strategic considerations and the decision-making disciplines required to ensure that opportunities, once *sensed*, can actually be *seized* and how the firm's resources can be *reconfigured* as soon as the market and/or the technology changes. An important point in Teece's article on the microfoundations of DCs is that that maintaining dynamic capabilities requires 'entrepreneurial management'. Entrepreneurial management has little to do with analysing and optimizing but it is more about sensing and seizing and addressing the next promising technological opportunity while staying in alignment with customer needs. In conclusion, the implicit thesis advanced here by Teece is that in both *large* and *small* firms, entrepreneurial management is a necessary prerequisite to sustain financial success. He also advocates that the entrepreneurial management function embedded in dynamic capabilities applies both to *start-up* activities and established firms.

These two recent contributions connect the DCs concept with entrepreneurial management suggesting that these capabilities can be present both in young and established firms. This is particularly important if we take into account that the literature on dynamic capabilities has given limited attention to younger firms focusing mainly on large and established enterprises (Zahra *et al.*, 2006; McKelvie and Davidsson, 2009). However, researchers have recently begun to explore the birth and evolution of new ventures' dynamic capabilities (e.g. Zahra and Filatotchev, 2004; Arthurs and Busenitz, 2006) indicating that entrepreneurial ventures and their managers should identify their weaknesses and emerging problems and constantly hone and reconfigure their resources and capabilities accordingly or they will likely find themselves in a death spiral. For example, as a part of a venture's planning process specific markets may be targeted to the new products the young firm is offering. However, it is quite possible that the primary targeted market may not correspond as expected. In this case new market segments should be pursued and perhaps emerging market possibilities should be explored. Consequently, adjustments to a firm's resource base are necessary to accommodate such changes (Arthurs and Busenitz, 2006).

In addition, McKelvie and Davidsson (2009) show that whereas new firms may well get successfully started with extremely limited resources, their development and continued growth is contingent on the existence of dynamic capabilities to further extend and develop the existing resource endowments. For example, when a young firm experiences rapid growth, it faces the challenge of how to reconfigure its internal processes in order to achieve effective functional specialization and organizational integration (Zahra *et al.*, 2006).

Zahra *et al.* (2006) suggest that dynamic capabilities exhibit different attributes and are developed, used and updated in different ways in young companies compared to the older ones. In particular they propose that firms start with simple processes which become more complex as firms grow and add to their initially little knowledge or resources. Furthermore, they put forward that at an early age it is more likely that a firm's choice for developing and using dynamic capabilities is based on improvisation and trial-and error learning. In this line of argument Boccardelli and Magnusson (2006) advocate that early-stage dynamic capabilities reveal themselves as bricolage, that is, the capacity to re-interpret and re-combine already existing resources and thereby improve their fit with the demands of the market environment.

In conclusion, there is a growing interest among scholars related to the role of dynamic capabilities in the context of new ventures. Although there is little congruence in defining the exact nature of these capabilities, a literature review indicates that DCs can be important to young firms' survival and growth by expanding their limited set of resources and/or by reconfiguring their resources to adapt to technology changes, uncertain markets, better resourced rivals or even to internal organizational changes.

2.2 *Dynamic capabilities and young firms' organizational performance*

One of the most important issues in entrepreneurship concerns processes associated with firm survival and growth. A relatively small but increasing body of empirical research focuses on the way dynamic capabilities relate to the performance, survival and growth of new firms (e.g. Zahra and Fila-totchev, 2004; Arthurs and Busenitz, 2006; Stam *et al.*, 2007; McKelvie and Davidsson, 2009; Stam and Wennberg, 2009; Grande, 2011), while the grand majority involve high-tech sectors. For example, Stam *et al.* (2007) examined the impact of dynamic capabilities on high-tech start-ups' growth, resulting in initial R&D activities and inter-firm alliances as the dynamic capabilities most likely to accompany growth. The authors noted that in newly established firms, attempts to sustain and renew capabilities do not at first take the form of routines, but of trial and error efforts, for instance at R&D and alliances. Boccardelli and Magnusson (2006) use the dynamic capabilities framework of strategy trying to investigate how firms go about matching their resource bases with opportunities in the marketplace in the Swedish mobile Internet industry. They suggest the single entrepreneur as a source of dynamic capabilities, arguing that 'dynamic capabilities can exist already at the outset of a venture, then however residing primarily in the few individuals constituting the entrepreneurial team and not always throughout the organization'.

Research also suggests that dynamic capabilities are important for the evolution and successful entry and survival of new firms especially in international markets (Jantunen *et al.*, 2005; Sapienza *et al.*, 2006). Zahra *et al.* (2006) adds that the skills and competencies that 'these firms have, must be upgraded and new dynamic capabilities must be built to ensure successful adaptation for growth'.

Some researchers also address questions on the existence and importance of dynamic capabilities for the creation and evolution of new ventures. Newbert (2005), for example, based on a study of 817 US nascent entrepreneurs, sees firm formation process as a dynamic capability, defined as the 'organizational and strategic routines by which firms achieve new resource combinations'.

While a literature review indicates that the majority of existing empirical studies examining the link between dynamic capabilities and new firms are focused on high-tech sectors, a few researchers choose to explore this relationship in traditional, more stable sectors.

Yet, which business environment can be characterized as 'stable' or even as 'moderately dynamic' today? Helfat and Peteraf (2009) argue that the oil industry, which is normally classified as a low-medium tech (LMT) sector (following OECD's guidelines), is far from 'stable', since it 'has endured large price swings and several rounds of consolidation since the mid-1970s' (p. 98). Although mature, traditional industries are not dynamic by definition

(Sciascia *et al.*, 2009) they are characterized by environmental hostility and are also subject to major changes. Globalization and trade liberalization have raised interesting new problems and significant challenges for them, delineating a vulnerable, volatile and rapidly changing environment. Mature industries can even create environmental dynamism through cumulative knowledge which can provide options to expand to new markets and businesses (Penrose, 1959; Wall *et al.*, 2010), since this is the only way to survive.

It's also worth mentioning that a new research stream tries to explore dynamic capabilities within the crisis *extreme* high-velocity environment (Simon, 2010; Piva *et al.*, 2012) which can have a major impact on both high- and low-tech sectors.

Therefore, although dynamic capabilities can play a role in more mature, traditional industries there is limited empirical research on the dynamic capabilities' existence and role in low-tech firms either in their start-up stage or later on in their lifetime. Helfat (1997) was perhaps one of the first scholars to engage a medium-tech industry in her research and confirm R&D as a dynamic capability in the US petroleum industry. Since then a stream of empirical research has been slowly emerging trying to capture the impact of dynamic capabilities in LMT sectors. These research efforts, both qualitative and quantitative, address several issues such as the relationship between dynamic capabilities and firm performance, the role of DCs in achieving competitive advantage at the international level and their impact on innovative performance and change capability (Salvato, 2003; Telussa *et al.*, 2006; Borch and Madsen, 2007; Chirico, 2007; Grande, 2011). In addition, other studies explain how dynamic capabilities are actually developed and manifested in medium- and low-tech industries mostly in cases of internationalization (Evers, 2011; Kuuluvainen, 2011; Quentier, 2011).

In conclusion, despite the substantial body of work on dynamic capabilities, the DCs approach has so far been developed and empirically grounded mainly in highly dynamic contexts (especially in high-tech manufacturing) using as a unit of analysis large, established firms.

It is evident that further research of dynamic capabilities in young SMEs and micro firms is necessary and of great importance especially nowadays, since the pressures of increasing globalization and rapid technological and socioeconomic changes have major impacts on small and medium-sized entrepreneurial ventures, bringing up quite different issues than those of interest to large organizations. Consequently, the need to establish theoretically and empirically sound recommendations and policies on the creation and sustainment of strong competitive advantages is vital for the vast majority of the European business ecosystems.

3 Methodology

3.1 Research design

So far, the limited but gradually increasing research on DCs regarding newly founded firms is evident through a number of empirical studies, which indicate that new ventures need dynamic capabilities in order to survive, grow and thus enhance the potential for innovative entrepreneurial activity. This growing interest imposes the need for more empirical research to address the issue of the creation and importance of dynamic capabilities for the creation and evolution of new ventures.

First we have tried to develop a set of dynamic capabilities constructs that can be of value to young firms. The starting point of this attempt was Teece's (2007) recent work on dynamic capabilities, in which three processes are stressed: the capability of organizations and entrepreneurs to sense new opportunities and threats in the business environment, the capability to address the once sensed new opportunities through new products, processes or services, and the ability to recombine and reconfigure resources as the enterprise grows and the markets and technologies change. Having these core processes as a guide we proceeded to a literature review to search for similar processes and also to examine the need for including additional ones or dropping any of them. The next step was to reconcile the different labels and meanings of the processes found in the literature and to create distinctive categories that would best reflect both the original conceptualization advanced by Teece (2007) and our own understanding of the literature. As already mentioned the empirical and theoretical research on dynamic capabilities in new firms is quite limited and provides inconclusive results concerning the DCs underlying processes in such contexts. It is clear that the effort here is not designed to be comprehensive, but to provide an initial framework emphasizing key capabilities that can be empirically tested in the context of young entrepreneurial ventures. We identified four dynamic capabilities processes: (a) sensing capability which includes market and technology adaptation dimensions; (b) product development capability which can be understood as a proxy for seizing opportunities; (c) networking capability; and (d) participation in technology collaborations. The last two processes can be thought of as significant drivers for reaching and integrating technology, market and other types of knowledge which are developed outside their boundaries. In this way, various networking activities can support sensing opportunities but can also help firms build learning and knowledge-sharing procedures that are likely to be critical to business performance and a key foundation of dynamic capabilities (Teece, 2007).

Second, we have tried to empirically assess the applicability of the dynamic capabilities concept using the aforementioned processes in a large sample of young entrepreneurial ventures operating in various industrial sectors and in ten different European countries by examining their impact on growth, international sales and innovative performance.

Third, taking into consideration that: (a) dynamic capabilities can be important both in rapidly changing and more stable environments; and (b) that knowledge-intensive young firms are in a continuous need to recombine and transform their market and technology knowledge in order to address changing business contexts, we examined the impact of different industrial settings and different types of knowledge-intensive entrepreneurial (KIE) ventures on the development and use of dynamic capabilities.

In Chapter 4 of this book we proposed a taxonomy to capture the high heterogeneity observed among young entrepreneurial ventures. The firms' classification was developed on the basis of their knowledge assets and innovative performance and identified three types of KIE ventures: (a) *All-around KIE* (b) *World-class KIE*, and a third residual group or 'mixed bag' category which can be labelled as *'modest KIE'* compared to the other two types.

'World class KIE' emphasizes new-to-world product innovation drawing from in-house knowledge which in turn draws from high quality human capital (both in terms of founders and workforce). On the other hand, the 'all-around KIE' group shows a balanced emphasis on knowledge-seeking activities (both in-house and from external sources), on new-to-market product innovation, and on process and organizational innovation. The 'modest KIE' group focuses on new-to-firm product innovation drawing from external industry knowledge sources. In general, it appears to have smaller degrees of knowledge-intensiveness and innovation compared to the other two groups.

3.2 The sample

The data used in quantitative analysis originate from the AEGIS project survey. The AEGIS questionnaire was filled in by 4,004 firms during a telephone interview with one of the firm founders in ten European countries, namely, the UK, Germany, France, Italy, Sweden, Denmark, Greece, Portugal, Croatia and Czech Republic. The total response rate of the survey was 31.2 per cent, but rates ranged within countries from 19.5 per cent in the UK to 63.9 per cent in Croatia.

The sample firms are independent young entities founded between 2001 and 2007 with an average age of 7.1 years (min: 4; max: 10 years). All firms have been in operation at least four years, and therefore it can be assumed that they have managed to exceed the critical three-year survival threshold. The majority of them (63.6 per cent) are micro firms, i.e. they employ up to nine full-time persons, while 88.4 per cent can be qualified as small firms because they employ less than 50 persons. At the same time only a very small share of them can be regarded as large or very large firms

(0.28 per cent). The surveyed firms belong to different sectors: high and medium-to-high technology manufacturing, low and medium-to-low technology manufacturing, and KIBS.

3.3 The variables

The variables used to capture *dynamic capabilities* were: market and technical adaptation capability, new product development capability, networking capability and capability to participate in technology collaborations. Each of them was measured with specific items. Firm founders were asked to indicate in a five-point Likert type scale the extent to which the particular capabilities have been developed in their firms.

3.3.1 Sensing capability (market and technical adaptation)

Following Teece's (2007) terminology, sensing capabilities denote the firm's activities in scanning and monitoring changes in operating environments and identifying new opportunities. Sensing is an inherently entrepreneurial set of capabilities that involves exploring market and technological opportunities, probing markets and listening to customers.

Market adaptation, i.e. the capability to sense new market opportunities, involves understanding and responding to market intelligence (Pavlou and El Sawy, 2011) by observing, counteracting and capturing related opportunities. More specifically, customer feedback and processes of market-shift recognition are used to identify new market segments and changing customer needs. In addition, market observation and collection of information and knowledge on competitive moves, outstanding products, novel promotion methods and other relevant best practices is imperative in order to detect, interpret new opportunities and effectuate change as required.

However, sensing entails also processes to acquire knowledge about, and understand technology developments in the business environment. An organization that has a high level of technology sensing capability will continually scan for information about potential technological opportunities and threats (Srinivasan *et al.*, 2002) and respond to technological changes in its environment. Organizations develop systems and infrastructure such as formal technical and engineering departments to select and understand new technologies, and direct internal R&D. R&D activities can be thought of as a form of 'search' for new products and processes (Teece, 2007). Yet, technical adaptation extends to a blending of research and development activities with design and market oriented dimension needed to proceed with seizing and communication of products/services to markets.

In our research market adaptation was captured by employing items reflecting adaptation to best practices, response to competitive moves, and customer feedback, recognition of shifts in markets, consideration of the consequences of changing market demand and capturing of new opportunities. Technological adaptation was measured using three items, namely the existence of formal R&D and technical departments and the frequent exchange of practical experience among employees.

3.3.2 *New product development capability*

New product development (NPD) is considered to be a key source of competitive advantage and a strategic function of the organization which constitutes a major requirement for success (Teece, 2007). In today's competitive environment, firms have to cover latent needs, find new markets for novel products and diversify their markets adapting to specific needs of different customers.

New product development capability is commonly defined as organizational processes that purposefully change the firm's product portfolio. It is generally assumed that such routines lead to new product innovations that in turn result in competitive advantage (Danneels, 2008; Schilke, 2014). Several authors suggest that new product development is a prototypical dynamic capability and argue that innovation is the cornerstone of DCs (e.g. Iansiti and Clark, 1994; Helfat, 1997; Dosi *et al.*, 2000; Eisenhardt and Martin, 2000; Helfat *et al.*, 2007, Helfat and Winter, 2011). In an effort to better investigate the blurry line between DCs and operational capabilities, Helfat and Winter (2011) suggest that DCs such as new product development capability have very specific purposes and support very specific activities.[1]

New product development can be considered as an important dynamic capability not only for established firms but also for young ones (e.g. McKelvie and Davidsson, 2009; Piva *et al.*, 2012; Evers, 2011). In industries populated by entrepreneurial high technology firms, the rapid development of new products is a key factor of success. In dynamic environments young firms have to rely on a portfolio of new products to compete and survive. Developing a steady stream of innovative products is necessary to gain early cash flows, to enhance external visibility, attain early market share and to increase likelihood of survival (Deeds *et al.*, 2000). However, the development of new products can be critical to firms' competitive advantage in low-tech sectors as well. These industries are typically challenged more by globalization and their products can be easily imitable to a large extent (Hirshch-Kreinsen, 2008). In this context competitive and cost pressure forces firms to reflect on their established practices, identify new market segments and stimulate customer demand through introducing new or upgraded products (von Tunzelmann and Acha, 2005). The capability of young low-tech firms to develop and renew their product portfolios either by extending their product lines or by adding new ones also enables their international market growth through their expansion or penetration to new foreign markets (Evers, 2011).

Altogether, a new product development capability enables firms to better satisfy existing and potential customers' current and future needs, to better serve these needs and create new market niches as well as new business ecosystems. NPD was measured with three items, namely: capability to offer novel products, capacity to adapt the products to the specific needs of different customers and market niches, and capability to actively promote and market the developed products/services.

3.3.3 Networking capability

Networking refers to the formation of mutually beneficial personal or business relationships to expand and accelerate the acquisition of useful resources and skills. These resources include the exchange of information and knowledge, as well as the discovery and control of opportunities and it is also extended to various types of financial and institutional support.

Enterprises search not only the core but also the periphery of their business ecosystems by embracing potential collaborators which can be customers, suppliers and producers of complementary products or even competitors. Especially in KIE, firms recognize opportunities for profitable exchanges of knowledge and technology, identify the relevant knowledge sources or partners (Birkinshaw *et al.*, 2008), and develop different network types in order to sense market and technology opportunities. Networking can therefore be considered as a necessary (though not sufficient) condition for the existence of a sensing dynamic capability.

Knowledge acquisition, through networking, is positively related to new product development, technological distinctiveness and sales cost efficiency (Yli-Renko *et al.*, 2001). Furthermore, networking enhances the capturing of novel technologies and production methods, the access to skilled human capital and supports innovativeness.

Networking is shown to influence the viability and development paths of new firms (Yli-Renko *et al.*, 2001; Stam and Wennberg, 2009; O'Gorman and Evers, 2011).

Networks have been found important for firms to create competitive advantages (Littunen, 2000; Dahl and Pedersen, 2004). Common goals are shared by network members regarding markets, market shifts and customer needs, for example information sharing including competitor activities as well, and the establishment of best practice techniques in advertising and promotion. Nevertheless, incentives for participating in networks can also be of an economic nature such as financial assistance in loans or fund seeking or can start from the idea of 'safety', whereby associated firms are able to reduce uncertainty resulting from legal and other institutional issues related to new markets and access of new distribution channels or even export potential.

To operationalize the different underlying dimensions of networking capability we first used items related to market processes such as collecting information about competitors, accessing distribution channels, exploring export opportunities, advertising and promotion. To capture the technology side of the networking capability we employed variables assessing the network's impact on the development of new products/services, the management of production and operations, as well as the easy access to skilled personnel. Finally in order to grasp the economic and more generic value of networking we used variables assessing networks' assistance in obtaining business loans and attracting funds or providing support on legal issues.

3.3.4 Participation in technology collaborative agreements

Collaborations assist firms to use efficient and cost effective ways to access additional or complementary resources that can speed up progress and advance set targets. Firms develop various types of collaborations depending on the expected benefits: share the costs of R&D development, introduce new products in global markets, minimize costs, develop sales or gain access to rare or expensive resources.

A frequent type of collaboration which has gained considerable attention is strategic alliances. A review of the literature reveals a list of benefits derived by strategic alliances, such as enhancement of market power (Kogut, 1991) and access to new, rare or critical resources, skills and capabilities (Rothaermel and Boeker, 2008).

Especially R&D and technical cooperation agreements have become a strategically important part of business decision making in many industries in recent years in both high- and low-tech sectors. They include any agreed-upon cooperative R&D or technology arrangement between firms, such as joint ventures, technology partnerships and informal networking arrangements.

Contract R&D serves as an instrument to access knowledge resources that may subsequently be redeployed with existing resources in a way superior to a competitor's deployment (DeSarbo et al., 2005; Barthélemy and Quélin, 2006). Contractual forms of collaboration include also licensing agreements which, in contrast to strategic alliances, introduce rather passive relationships.

The various types of collaborations appear to play a special role when new firms try to develop competitive advantages. New product development and market introduction, although crucial for high technology new firms' successful performance, can be costly and time consuming processes with uncertain outcomes and this, according to Haeussler et al. (2012), constitutes a major reason for the employment of strategic alliances. Collaboration is important for start-ups to gain the knowledge necessary to develop or acquire the capabilities needed for NPD, R&D, innovation, design, manufacturing or even technical services (Park et al., 2002; Stam et al., 2007; Haeussler et al., 2012) as well as to gain higher rates of growth (Stearns, 1996).

Within the present research firms' collaborative activities were operationalized using four variables: participation in strategic alliances, agreements regarding R&D, technical cooperation and licensing.

All multi-item scales pertaining to dynamic capabilities were tested following Confirmatory Factors Analysis (CFA) in order to confirm that particular items relate to a specific dynamic capabilities construct. Therefore five different dynamic capabilities constructs or composite variables were produced. All of these composite variables were constructed as averages of multi-item Likert-type scales, where higher numbers pointed to a 'higher quantity' of what was measured. Annex I presents all relevant CFA details. As shown there, all multi-item scales representing dynamic capabilities were reasonably valid and reliable.

3.3.5 Dependent variables

Firms generally find unprofitable growth difficult to sustain over time. Therefore, growth in firm size provides an alternative basis for assessing patterns of firm performance over time. Growth of firms can be measured in terms of inputs (e.g. employees), value (e.g. assets) or outputs (e.g. sales revenues). Here, growth is measured by the variations in employees and sales. Indeed, these are the most widely used indicators in the empirical literature on firms' growth (Delmar, 1997; Weinzinmer *et al.*, 1998; Helfat *et al.*, 2007). More specifically, an emerging consensus exists on the use of sales variation as a measure of growth because it reflects widespread market acceptance of the firm's products and services. At the same time, it is widely agreed that measuring employees' growth is especially appropriate for new ventures, where the number of employees often grows before any sales occur (Piva *et al.*, 2012). In addition, human resources are among the most important assets a new firm has.

In addition we measured firm performance as the percentage of sales obtained in international markets during the last three years. Internationalization exposes young firms to multiple and diverse exogenous (e.g. competitive conditions) and endogenous stimuli (e.g. resource demand) (Sapienza *et al.*, 2006). It reflects the degree of young firms' success in pursuing opportunities beyond domestic markets. Finally, we measured innovative performance in terms of the radicalness of product innovation in the last three years as an ordinal variable taking the values of 0 (= no innovation); 1 (= new-to-firm); 2 (= new-to-market); and 3 (= new-to-world product innovation).

3.3.6 Controls

As control variables we use founders' human capital and firm size in terms of turnover during the last three years (2007–2009). Founding teams have a strong imprinting effect on the subsequent stages of a young firms firm's life cycle, thus critically influencing its survival (Geroski *et al.*, 2010) and growth (Eisenhardt and Schoonhoven, 1990). For each individual member of the founding team we measure educational attainment using an ordinal variable taking the values: 1 – elementary education; 2 – secondary education; 3 – Bachelor degree; 4 – Postgraduate degree; 5 – PhD degree. We average across team members to derive an overall measure of founders' education.

4 Empirical results and discussion

Regression analysis results in Table 10.1 indicate that dynamic capabilities have, in general, a significant impact on both growth measures used in our model. More specifically it appears that market adaptation and technology collaboration activities have a significant positive effect on average employment and sales growth. In addition, networking capability appears to influence positively and significantly average employment growth.

New product development and technical adaptation capabilities have a positive but insignificant effect on new firms' growth. This suggests that young firms tend to pursue growth through sensing the market environment and responding to emerging customers' needs rather than adapting their technologies and developing new products. Most interestingly, empirical research in young firms in Sweden has also shown that change in market focus usually takes place without any related change in the firms' technological resources indicating that a significant factor at this stage is the flexible use of resources in searching for an appropriate match between resources and market opportunities (Boccardelli and Magnusson, 2006).

When we explore the impact of dynamic capabilities on performance using as a dependent variable the percentage of sales in international markets we observe that technical adaption and participation in technology collaborations have a positive and significant sign, while market adaptation appears insignificant. This practically means that keeping up with technological developments and acquiring or subtracting technology resources appears to be more important for international markets presumably due to their requirements for highly innovative products.

Moreover, DCs appear to have a positive and significant effect on the innovative performance of young firms. Market and technology-sensing capabilities allow them to effectively look for new opportunities on both market and technology fronts and thus may play a catalytic role in innovative performance. Furthermore, participation in technology collaborations enables newly established firms to absorb external knowledge that might prove essential to identifying new product and process development opportunities. Finally, product-development capability appears to be significantly related to innovative performance, as both the potential for developing higher-quality products and new products can contribute to offering differentiated outcomes of increasing value and quality.

Table 10.1 The impact of DCs on young firms' performance

Independent variables	Average growth in sales (N=3,354)	Average growth in employment (N=3,367)	% of sales in international markets (N=3,573)	Innovative performance (N=3,573)
	B coefficients	B coefficients	B coefficients	B coefficients
Constant	2.797*** (0.330)	0.557*** (0.151)	−8.696 ** (2.926)	−0.931*** (0.114)
Product development capability	0.047 ns (0.067)	0.005 ns (0.031)	−0.277 ns (0.595)	0.203*** (0.023)
Market adaptation	0.205*** (0.063)	0.074** (0.028)	−0.243 ns (0.528)	0.051* (0.021)
Technical adaptation	0.028 ns (0.048)	0.002 ns (0.022)	2.191*** (0.424)	0.191*** (0.017)
Networking	0.041 ns (0.063)	0.118*** (0.029)	0.353 ns (0.566)	0.031 ns (0.022)
Participation in technology collaborations	0.338*** (0.065)	0.152*** (0.030)	2.578*** (0.575)	0.161*** (0.022)
F-team avrg educational attainment	0.192*** (0.050)	0.056* (0.023)	2.334*** (0.451)	0.068*** (0.018)
Avrg turnover	0.084* (0.036)	0.200*** (0.016)	2.979*** (0.304)	0.052*** (0.012)
R^2	0.170	0.279	0.254	0.405
Adjusted R^2	0.027	0.076	0.063	0.162

Notes
B values significance level:* $p<0.05$, ** $p<0.01$, *** $p<0.001$, ns: not significant.
Standard errors in parentheses.

254 A. Protogerou and Y. Caloghirou

To examine the impact of the different types of KIE ventures as well as the effect of different industrial sectors on dynamic capabilities we have employed two-way analysis of variance (ANOVA). This technique allows us to examine the individual and joint effect of sector and KIE type (independent variables) on one dependent variable, namely product development capability, technical adaptation, market adaptation capability, networking capability and participation in collaborations.

A two-way ANOVA was conducted that examined the effect of KIE type and sector on the firm's capability to adapt to market changes. There was a significant main effect of KIE type on the firm's capability to sense changes in market and consumer needs [$F(2, 3208) = 37.576$, $p < 0.001$]. Post-hoc tests indicate that there is a statistically significant difference in the means of firms considered as 'modest KIE' and those classified as 'all-around KIE' and 'world-class KIE'. This is an expected result as 'modest KIE' ventures have apparently developed to a lesser extent the required knowledge assets that would enable them to better understand and respond to market transformations. In addition, 'all around innovators' appear to adapt to a greater extent to market changes than 'world class innovators' possibly as a result of their ability to rely more on the use of external knowledge sources to capture value and mobilize resources in order to address market opportunities and achieve competitive advantage.

The main effect of sector is found insignificant and thus there is no significant difference in market adaptation across groups. This finding indicates that the ability of a firm to sense market and customer needs and seek to respond to them is an important dynamic capability which may affect the competitive advantage of young firms irrespective of their sector classification.

Empirical results related to the impact of KIE type on the firms' capability to adapt to technical changes indicate that there is a significant main effect [$F(2,3208) = 153.136$, $p < 0.001$]. Post-hoc tests reveal that the mean scores for 'world-class KIE' and 'all-around KIE' groups are significantly different from the 'modest KIE' group indicating that that the first two groups have developed technical adaptability to a greater extent than the less knowledge-intensive group. This finding may be related to the fact that 'world-class' and 'all-around' KIE firms are involved more intensively in activities that allow them to acquire knowledge and understand technology advancements better than 'modest KIE' ventures. The main effect for sector is also statistically significant [$F(2,3208) = 16.950$, $p < 0.001$]. In addition, post-hoc comparisons showed that the high-tech group of firms has developed technical adaptability to a higher degree than low-tech firms and KIBS. This may be attributed to the fact that high-tech firms should be able to continuously scan for information about potential opportunities and threats as they are usually active in dynamic environments where rapid response to technological changes is vital for their survival and growth.

There was a statistically significant main effect for KIE type [F(2, 3208) = 73.164, $p < 0.01$] on product development capability. Post-hoc comparisons[2] indicated as expected that the firms characterized as 'all-around KIE' and 'world-class KIE' have developed to a greater extent their product development capability compared to the 'modest KIE' ones. Most interestingly, 'all-around KIE' firms appear to create and offer novel goods and services to a higher degree than 'world-class'. This may be attributed to the fact that 'all-around KIE' ventures, being more extrovert in terms of the mechanisms they use to collect new knowledge and information, can identify more rapidly new product development opportunities compared to 'world-class KIE' firms which mainly rely on their own resources (in-house R&D efforts). Sector classification does not appear to have a significant effect on product development capability suggesting that the specific capability is equally important across sector groups.

Empirical results show a significant effect for KIE type on networking capability [F(2,3208) = 72.648, $p < 0.001$]. Post-hoc comparisons indicate that more knowledge-intensive firms ('world class KIE' and 'all-around KIE') tend to be more involved in different types of networks than their less knowledge-intensive counterparts. This finding results from the fact that more knowledge-intensive firms have also developed more advanced knowledge-seeking capabilities which practically allows them to participate more easily and efficiently in different types of interpersonal and inter-organizational networks. Furthermore 'all-around KIE' firms appear to develop a more intensive networking activity than 'world-class KIE' due to the fact that they follow a different innovation model, i.e. they innovate primarily based on their external knowledge-seeking activities as opposed to the group of 'world-class' which base their innovative capacity mainly on their internal new knowledge generation ability.

In addition, there was also a significant main effect of sector on networking capability [F(2,3208) = 10.141, $p < 0.001$]. Post-hoc tests reveal that either low- or high-tech manufacturing firms appear to be more involved in networks than KIBS. However, we should note that this is perhaps a counterintuitive finding which would require further research, e.g. taking also into account the heterogeneity of the KIBS firm group.

Finally the results of the two-way ANOVA conducted to examine the impact of KIE type and sector on a firm's capability to participate in collaborations indicate that there was a statistically significant main effect for KIE type [F(2, 3208) = 120.844, $p < 0.001$]. Furthermore, knowledge-intensive firms seem to get more actively engaged in different types of formal technological agreements than those characterized as 'modest KIE'. Empirical results also confirm a significant main effect of firm sector on the participation in collaborations [F(2, 3208) = 19.060, $p < 0.001$]. This practically means that irrespectively of whether a firm is knowledge-intensive or not, its capability to form collaborative agreements is influenced by the sector it belongs to. More specifically, young firms that belong to low- and medium-tech sectors seem to participate less in technology collaborations compared to high-tech firms and KIBS. This finding can be attributed to the fact that young firms engaged in high-tech manufacturing and KIBS are presumably more prone to participate in technology collaborative agreements aiming at sharing knowledge and mitigating risk because of the technological content and complexity of the products they are offering.

5 Concluding remarks

In this chapter we have attempted to empirically explore the applicability of the dynamic capabilities concept in a large sample of newly established firms using the large data set of the AEGIS survey. In order to measure dynamic capabilities we have used the following constructs: market adaptation, technical adaptation, product development capability, networking capability and capability to form collaborative technology agreements.

Our findings suggest that, in general, dynamic capabilities have a positive relationship with new firms' growth, international sales and innovative performance. In particular, the young firms' growth is dependent on market adaptation rather than technology adaptation showing that at this stage of their life new ventures are more focused on scanning business environment, addressing customer needs and matching their resources with market requirements. However, due to their liability of newness and limited resources their effort related to adapting their technologies (radical change in their resource base in terms of acquisition or transformation) is less intensive indicating they are more likely to adopt an altered use of existing resources in order to address changing circumstances at the market side.

Nevertheless, a firm's presence in international markets is more dependent on technology adaptation than market adaptation indicating that to extend its scope of activity beyond national borders; a young firm has to readjust its technical resources and capabilities to fit the new conditions it faces in the foreign market. In addition, participation in technology collaborative agreements appears to have a positive impact on all performance measures. This may be attributed to the fact that new firms that establish technological collaborations/alliances can draw on complementary resources and capabilities provided by their partners and face their internal shortage of resources especially under the current economic crisis. In this way, they can possibly complement and expand their resource and knowledge base and support (new) business projects being able to innovate, grow and improve their presence in international markets.

In addition, almost all constructs of dynamic capabilities appear to have a strong effect on innovative performance suggesting a significant link between DCs and the innovative capacity of young firms which empowers them to successfully exploit new entrepreneurial opportunities.

Although dynamic capabilities can play an important role in new ventures their degree of development appears to differ in accordance to the firm's knowledge-intensiveness and their sector of economic activity.

It is important to note that our findings indicate that NPD and market sensing capability are equally important in high-tech and traditional markets as they are both considered as important drivers for sustaining profitability and business growth. It is rather sensible that especially new companies that are striving to earn and keep a piece of the pie by creating or entering markets develop both market sensing and NPD capabilities. Shorter life cycles of products and the aggressiveness of global markets intensify strategies of all types of companies towards translating market messages into new products ready to entice customers.

However, our results also advocate that high-tech manufacturing firms have developed technical adaptability to a greater extent than low-tech firms and KIBS. This may be attributed to the fact that high-tech firms should be able to continuously scan for information about potential opportunities and threats as they are usually active in dynamic environments where rapid response to technological changes is vital for their survival and growth. Furthermore, firms that belong to low- and medium-tech sectors participate less in technology collaborative agreements compared to high-tech manufacturing firms and KIBS. This finding indicates that participation in specific collaborative agreements is significantly related to the technological content and complexity of the products offered.

Our findings also suggest that the more knowledge-intensive firms, i.e. firms that have more knowledge assets and exhibit better innovative performance (characterized as 'world class KIE' or 'all around KIE' ventures) have developed to a greater extent all types of dynamic capabilities compared to their less knowledge-intensive counterparts. Therefore it appears that a firm's increased knowledge resources and endowments (i.e. knowledge-seeking activities, human capital and innovation inputs) support the creation and further development of dynamic capabilities which in turn may help the new firm survive and grow.

In sum, this chapter empirically supports the assertion that dynamic capabilities can be present in newly established firms that in their majority are micro and small firms. The degree of DCs development is dependent on the firm knowledge base pointing out that knowledge assets and human capital are important for DCs creation and further nurturing. DCs also exist in low-tech firms although capabilities such as technical adaptation and technology collaborative agreements are present in a smaller degree compared to high-tech firms.

Annex I

CFA analysis results

Table 10.A1 CFA analysis results: sensing capability

Sensing capability	Construct indicators	Standardized first-order loadings
Market adaptation	Our firm actively observes and adopts the best practices in our sector	0.650[a]
	Our firm responds rapidly to competitive moves	0.707*
	We change our practices based on customer feedback	0.676*
	Our firm regularly considers the consequences of changing market demand in terms of new products and services	0.750*
	Our firm is quick to recognize shifts in our market (e.g. competition, regulation, demography)	0.779*
	We quickly understand new opportunities to better serve our customers	0.770*
Technological adaptation	Employees share practical experiences on a frequent basis	0.524a
	There is a formal R&D department in our firm	0.640*
	There is a formal engineering and technical studies department in our firm	0.719*
	Goodness-of-fit statistics	
	χ^2(d.f.)	920.378(35) $p = 0.00$
	CFI	0.911
	RMSEA	0.79

Notes
a Loadings are fixed to 1 for identification purposes.
* All factor loadings are significant at $p < 0.05$ level.

Table 10.A2 CFA analysis results: firm capability

Firm capability	Construct indicators	Standardized first-order loadings
New product development capability	Capability to offer novel products/services	0.712a
	Capacity to adapt the products/services to the specific needs of different customers/market niches	0.484*
	Marketing and promotion activities	0.407*
R&D and alliance related capabilities	R&D activities	0.761a
	Networking with scientific research organizations (universities, institutes, etc.)	0.621*
	Goodness-of-fit statistics	
	χ^2(d.f.)	178.30(8) p=0.00
	CFI	0.942
	RMSEA	0.73

Notes
a Loading is fixed to 1 for identification purposes.
* All factor loadings are significant at $p < 0.05$ level.

Table 10.A3 CFA analysis results: networking capability

Construct indicators	Standardized first-order loadings
Selecting suppliers	0.592[a]
Recruiting skilled labour	0.565*
Collecting information about competitors	0.580*
Accessing distribution channels	0.612*
Assistance in obtaining business loans/ attracting funds	0.596*
Advertising and promotion	0.588*
Developing new products/services	0.621*
Managing production and operations	0.677*
Assistance in arranging taxation or other legal issues	0.559*
Exploring export opportunities	0.559*
Goodness-of-fit statistics	
χ^2(d.f.)	920.378(38)
CFI	0.919
RMSEA	0.79

Notes

a Loading is fixed to 1 for identification purposes.

* All factor loadings are significant at $p < 0.05$ level.

Table 10.A4 CFA analysis results: participation in collaborations

Construct indicators	Standardized first-order loadings
Strategic alliance	0.540[a]
R&D agreement	0.743*
Technical cooperation agreement	0.702*
Licensing agreement	0.523*
Research contract-out	0.549*
Goodness-of-fit statistics	
χ^2(d.f.)	160.688(5) $p = 0.00$
CFI	0.963
RMSEA	0.88

Notes

a Loading is fixed to 1 for identification purposes.

* All factor loadings are significant at $p < 0.05$ level.

CFI and RMSEA measures (CFI >0.9 and RMSEA <0.9) indicate an acceptable fit of the data to the constructs tested.

Table 10.A5 Reliability analysis for CFA constructs

Constructs	Cronbach's Alpha
Market adaptation	0.857
Technical adaptation	0.617
New product development capability	0.611
Networking capability	0.845
Participation in technological collaborations	0.742

Notes
All capabilities constructs can be considered as reliable based on Cronbach's Alpha indicator (>0.6).

Notes

1 Helfat and Winter (2011) consider as an example of DCs the new product development at Intel. They suggest that this dynamic capability did not only help the company create new semiconductor designs but it also involved the organization of a large number of scientists and engineers working on multiple interconnected tasks and the managing of complex relations with equipment suppliers and customers to address key issues of manufacturing feasibility and market acceptance. In other words, NPD at Intel did not only create new products but it also enriched and altered significantly its resource base.
2 Post-hoc comparisons included Tukey HSD and Games-Howell test. The mean differences between pairs of groups are significant at the 0.05 level.

References

Arthurs, J.A. and Busenitz, L.W. (2006) 'Dynamic capabilities and new venture performance: The moderating effects of venture capitalists', *Journal of Business Venturing*, 21, pp. 195–215.
Barreto, I. (2010) 'Dynamic capabilities: A review of past research and an agenda for the future', *Journal of Management*, 36(1), pp. 256–280.
Barthélemy, J. and Quélin, B.V. (2006) 'Complexity of outsourcing contracts and ex post transaction costs: An empirical investigation', *Journal of Management Studies*, 43, pp. 1775–1797.
Boccardelli, P. and Magnusson, M.G. (2006) 'Dynamic capabilities in early-phase entrepreneurship', *Knowledge and Process Management*, 13(3), pp. 162–174.
Borch, O. and Madsen, E. (2007) 'Dynamic capabilities facilitating innovative strategies in SMEs', *International Journal of Technoentrepreneurship*, 1(1), pp. 109–125.
Birkinshaw, J., Hamel, G. and Mol, M. (2008) 'Management innovation', *Academy of Management Review*, 33(4), pp. 825–845.
Chirico, F. (2007) 'The value creation process in family firms: A dynamic capabilities approach', *Electronic Journal of Family Business Studies (EJFBS)*, 1(2), pp. 137–167.
Dahl, M.S. and Pedersen, C.O.R. (2004) 'Knowledge flows through information contracts in industrial districts: Myth or reality?, *Research Policy*, 33, pp. 1673–1686.

Danneels, E. (2008) 'Organizational antecedents of second-order competences', *Strategic Management Journal*, 29(5), pp. 519–543.

Deeds, D.L., DeCarolis, D. and Coombs, J. (2000) 'Dynamic capabilities and new product development in high technology ventures: An empirical analysis of new biotechnology firms', *Journal of Business Venturing*, 15, pp. 211–229.

Delmar, F. (1997) 'Measuring growth: Methodological considerations and empirical results'. In: R. Donckels and A. Miettinen, eds. *Entrepreneurship and SME Research: On its Way to the Next Millennium*, Aldershot: Ashgate, pp. 199–216.

DeSarbo, W.S., Benedetto, C.A., Song, M. and Sinha, I. (2005) 'Revisiting the miles and snow strategic framework: Uncovering interrelationships between strategic types, capabilities, environmental uncertainty, and firm performance', *Strategic Management Journal*, 26, pp. 47–74.

Dosi, G., Nelson, R. and Winter, S. (2000) *The Nature and Dynamics of Organizational Capabilities*, New York: Oxford University Press

Easterby-Smith, M., Lyles, M.A. and Peteraf, M.A. (2009) 'Dynamic capabilities: Current debates and future directions', *British Journal of Management*, 20, pp. S1–S8.

Eisenhardt, K.M. and Martin, J.A. (2000) 'Dynamic capabilities: What are they?' *Strategic Management Journal*, 21(10–11), pp. 1105–1121.

Eisenhardt, K.M. and Schoonhoven, C.B. (1990) 'Organizational growth: Linking founding team, strategy, environment and growth among U.S. semiconductor ventures, 1978–1988', *Administrative Science Quarterly*, 35, pp. 504–529.

Evers, N. (2011) 'International new ventures in low-tech sectors – a dynamic capabilities perspective', *Journal of Small Business and Enterprise Development*, 18(3), pp. 502–528.

Garnsey, E. (1998) 'A theory of the early growth of the firm', *Industrial and Corporate Change*, 7, pp. 523–556.

Geroski, P.A., Mata, J. and Portugal, P. (2010) 'Founding conditions and the survival of new firms', *Strategic Management Journal*, 31(5), pp. 510–529.

Grande, J. (2011) 'New venture creation in the farm sector – critical resources and capabilities', *Journal of Rural Studies*, 27(2), pp. 220–233.

Haeussler, C., Patzelt, H. and Zahra, S.A. (2012) 'Strategic alliances and product development in high technology new firms: The moderating effect of technological capabilities', *Journal of Business Venturing*, 27(2), pp. 217–233.

Helfat, C.E. (1997) 'Know-how and asset complementarity and dynamic capability accumulation: The case of R&D', *Strategic Management Journal*, 18(5), pp. 339–360.

Helfat, C.E. and Peteraf, M.A. (2009) 'Understanding dynamic capabilities: Progress along a development path', *Strategic Organization*, 7(1), pp. 91–102.

Helfat, C.E. and Winter, S.G. (2011) 'Untangling dynamic and operational capabilities: Strategy for the (n)ever changing world', *Strategic Management Journal*, 32(11), pp. 1243–1250.

Helfat, C.E., Finkelstein, S., Mitchell, W., Peteraf, M.A., Singh, H., Teece, D.J. and Winter, S.G. (2007) *Dynamic Capabilities: Understanding Strategic Change in Organization*, Malden, MA: Blackwell Publishing.

Hirsch-Kreinsen, H. (2008) ' "Low technology": A forgotten sector in innovation policy', *Journal of Technology Management and Innovation*, 3(3), pp. 11–20.

Iansiti, M. and Clark, K.B. (1994) 'Integration and dynamic capability: Evidence from product development in automobiles and mainframe computers', *Industrial and Corporate Change*, 3(3), pp. 557–605.

Jantunen, A., Puumalainen, K., Saarenketo, S. and Kylaheiko, K. (2005) 'Entrepreneurial orientation, dynamic capabilities and international performance', *Journal of International Entrepreneurship*, 3, pp. 223–243.

Kogut, B. (1991) 'Joint ventures and the option to expand and acquire', *Management Science*, 37(1), pp. 19–34.

Kuuluvainen, A. (2011) 'Dynamic capabilities in the international growth of SME: Case study from Finland', *ICSB (International Council for Small Business)-Conference*, Stockholm, Sweden, 15–18 June.

Littunen, H. (2000) 'Networks and local environmental characteristics in the survival of new firms', *Small Business Economics*, 15, pp. 59–71.

McKelvie, A. and Davidsson, P. (2009) 'From resource base to dynamic capabilities: An investigation of new firms', *British Journal of Management*, 20, pp. S63–S80.

Newbert, S.L. (2005) 'New firm formation: A dynamic capability perspective', *Journal of Small Business Management*, 43(1), pp. 55–77.

O'Gorman, C. and Evers, N. (2011) 'Network intermediaries in the internationalisation of new firms in peripheral regions', *International Marketing Review*, 28(4), pp. 340–364.

Park, S.H., Chen, R. and Gallagher, S. (2002) 'Firm resources as moderators of the relationship between market growth and strategic alliances in semiconductor start-ups', *Academy of Management Journal*, 45, pp. 527–545.

Pavlou, P. and El Sawy, O. (2011) 'Understanding the elusive black box of dynamic capabilities', *Decision Sciences*, 42(1), pp. 239–273.

Penrose, E.T. (1959) *The Theory of the Growth of the Firm*, New York: John Wiley.

Piva, E., Colombo, M.G., Quas, A. and Rossi-Lamastra, C. (2012) 'Dynamic capabilities during the global crisis: Evidence from Italian new technology based firms', paper presented at the *DRUID 2012 Summer Conference*, Copenhagen, 19–21 June.

Protogerou, A., Caloghirou, Y. and Lioukas, S. (2012) 'Dynamic capabilities and their indirect impact on firm performance', *Industrial and Corporate Change*, 21(3), pp. 615–647.

Quentier, J.-M. (2011) 'International new ventures in the commodity sector: A dynamic capabilities perspective', *IABD 23rd Annual Conference*, New Orleans, Louisiana, USA, 7–9 April.

Rothaermel, F. and Boeker, W. (2008) 'Old technology meets new technology: Complementarities, similarities and alliance formation', *Strategic Management Journal*, 29(1), pp. 47–77.

Salvato, C. (2003) 'The role of micro-strategies in the engineering of firm evolution', *Journal of Management Studies*, 40(1), pp. 83–108.

Sapienza, H.J., Autio, E., George, G. and Zahra, S.A. (2006) 'A capability perspective on the effects of early internationalization on firm survival and growth', *Academy of Management Review*, 31, pp. 914–933.

Schilke, O. (2014) 'On the contingent value of dynamic capabilities for competitive advantage: The nonlinear moderating effect of environmental dynamism', *Strategic Management Journal*, 35, pp. 179–203.

Sciascia, S., Alberti, G.F. and Salvato, C. (2009) 'Firm-level entrepreneurial contents for strategic renewal: A knowledge-based perspective'. In: G.T. Lumpkin and J.A. Katz, eds. *Entrepreneurial Strategic Content* (Advances in Entrepreneurship, Firm

Emergence and Growth, Volume 11), New York: Emerald Group Publishing Limited, pp. 41–75.

Simon, A. (2010) 'Resources, dynamic capabilities and Australian business success', *Journal of Global Business and Technology*, 6(2), pp. 12–31.

Srinivasan, R., Lilien, G.L. and Rangaswamy, A. (2002) 'The role of technological opportunism in radical technology adoption: An application to e-business', *Journal of Marketing*, 66(3), pp. 47–60.

Stam, E. and Wennberg, K. (2009) 'The roles of R&D in new firm growth', *Small Business Economy*, 33, pp. 77–89.

Stam, E., Gibcus, P., Telussa, J. and Garnsey, E. (2007) 'Employment growth of new firms', *Scales Research Reports H200716*, EIM Business and Policy Research.

Stearns, S. (1996) 'Collaborative exams as learning tools', *College Teaching*, 44(3), pp. 111–112.

Teece, D.J. (2007) 'Explicating dynamic capabilities: The nature and microfoundations of (sustainable) enterprise performance', *Strategic Management Journal*, 28(13), pp. 1319–1350.

Teece, D.J., Pisano G. and Shuen, A. (1997) 'Dynamic capabilities and strategic management', *Strategic Management Journal*, 18(7), pp. 509–533.

Telussa, J., Stam, E. and Gibcus, P. (2006) 'Entrepreneurship, dynamic capabilities and new firm growth', *Working Paper H200623*, Netherlands: Scientific Analysis of Entrepreneurship and SMEs.

von Tunzelmann, N. and Acha, V. (2005) 'Innovation in "low-tech" sectors'. In: J. Fagerberg, D.C. Mowery and R.R. Nelson, eds. *The Oxford Handbook of Innovation*, Oxford: Oxford University Press.

Wall, S., Zimmermann, C., Kliengebiel, R. and Lange, D. (2010) *Strategic Reconfigurations: Building Dynamic Capabilities in Rapid Innovation-Based Industries*, Cheltenham, UK: Edward Elgar.

West, III, P.G. and DeCastro, J. (2001) 'The Achilles heel of firm strategy: Resource weaknesses and distinctive inadequacies', *Journal of Management Studies*, 38(3), pp. 417–442.

Winter, S.G. (2003) 'Understanding dynamic capabilities', *Strategic Management Journal*, 24(10), pp. 991–995.

Yli-Renko, H., Autio, E. and Sapienza, H.J. (2001) 'Social capital, knowledge acquisition, and knowledge exploitation in young technology-based firms', *Strategic Management Journal*, 22, pp. 587–613.

Zahra, S.A. and Filatotchev, I. (2004) 'Governance of the entrepreneurial threshold firm: A knowledge-based perspective', *Journal of Management Studies*, 41, pp. 885–897.

Zahra, S.A., Sapienza, H.J. and Davidsson, P. (2006) 'Entrepreneurship and dynamic capabilities: A review, model and research agenda', *Journal of Management Studies*, 43(4), pp. 918–955.

Zollo, M. and Winter, S.G. (2002) 'Deliberate learning and the evolution of dynamic capabilities', *Organization Science*, 13(3), pp. 339–351.

11 How networks and sectoral conditions affect commercialization in a KIE venture in the medical technology industry

A case study of Aerocrine

Jens Laage-Hellman and Maureen McKelvey

1 Introduction

This chapter focuses upon the case study of Aerocrine, a company which is active in the medical technology (or medtech) industry.[1] The case study portrays the commercialization of medical and scientific knowledge, through the starting up and managing phases of a knowledge intensive entrepreneurial (KIE) venture. The case study focuses upon questions about how networks and sectoral conditions influence the process of commercialization, including the development and performance of this KIE venture.[2]

One point of this book – and the conceptual framework in Chapter 2 – is to place the dynamics of developing and managing the KIE venture relative to the wider innovation system context for inputs and outputs. This chapter contributes to this understanding in the following ways. The case study provides an understanding of how one specific firm relies upon the innovation system to access, and further develop, knowledge and resources. More specifically, this chapter focuses upon the role of networks in providing resources as well as the different types of networks that the KIE venture develops over time. The medical technology sector is heavily regulated, and therefore companies must meet particular sectoral conditions related to clinical studies, if they are to be able to identify and exploit the innovative opportunities.

This case study is therefore interesting, as it provides more detailed insights into how a KIE venture develops over time, in relation to the wider innovation system context. Our KIE venture starts as an academic spin-off, but the involvement of the original founders decreased after some years, while financing and ownership shifted from founders to venture capitalist funds. As the company matured, the network relationships also shifted away from the founders and toward other types of partners. This shift also entailed new types of network relationships. The founders had made an initial discovery which was primarily within basic and experimental medicine, but in order to commercialize the idea, the KIE venture had to interact also with other types of medical research, in particular clinical. There was also a need to establish relationships with suppliers and other actors in the field of engineering/technical research and development (R&D) to solve certain issues with the instrumentation. Even though the venture was an academic spin-off, developing the product innovation required the development of much additional scientific and technological knowledge, which is relevant for the medical use, which often relied upon networks. This industry faces particular conditions, and in particular, the need to carry out clinical research, for example, for the purpose of getting the product included in clinical guidelines and reimbursement schemes. In this case study, the KIE venture did not in the early phase of its development carry out a sufficient number of clinical studies, and this helps explain the firm's poor performance in terms of initial sales and its subsequent uneven growth patterns.

The chapter uses the case study in order to enrich our understanding of the following issues facing commercialization in KIE venture, as linked to the innovation system:

Q1: In what ways did the early dynamics of developing and managing the KIE venture depend on links to the innovation system, in terms of accessing and commercializing knowledge and in terms of financing?

Q2: What types of networks were needed and developed, in order to develop from an idea into a KIE venture? Which specific sectoral conditions within the medical technology sector influence the development of the KIE venture?

These questions are used to structure this chapter. Section 2 provides a brief literature overview, which explains the importance of these questions relative to the literature while Section 3 provides the empirical setting of the medical technology industry in Sweden. Section 4 analyses the case study firm Aerocrine, in relation to how the innovation system affected knowledge and financing. Section 5 focuses upon the development of different types of early-phase networks, and their role in developing and managing the company as well as the role of clinical studies and clinical guidelines. Section 6 regards the financing of the KIE venture and Section 7 shows the networking in Aerocrine. Section 8 is about the importance of clinical research to medtech companies. Section 9 concludes and provides some implications for public policy.

2 Literature and research questions

Networks are one way in which the KIE venture interacts with the innovation system, in terms of knowledge and resources. Malerba (2002) defines a broad range of potential actors to analyse within a sectoral system of innovation.

Hence, a detailed study of networks helps us further understand their role in the development and performance of the KIE venture. Networks as a concept and theoretical device represent a huge amount of literature, with conflicting evidence and theories, within social science as a whole. Here, we restrict our literature selection to references that help us identify the role of networks-founder-venture in accessing key knowledge and resources. Thus, we focus particularly upon identifying the different types of actors (partners), with whom the company builds collaborative relationships.

In terms of understanding what types of partners may engage in network relationships with the KIE venture, the literature about business networks is very useful in an industry such as medical technology. According to the so-called Industrial Network Approach (INA), business-to-business markets can be described and analysed in terms of industrial networks. There is a vast amount of literature based upon this theoretical approach.[3] While the bulk of the work is concerned with marketing and purchasing issues there are also a fairly large number of studies focusing more specifically on technological innovation.[4] These studies have shown, *inter alia*, that business relationships are not only important from a commercial point of view but may also have an essential role to play in the development of new products or production processes.

This literature helps us to identify different types of potential partners for the KIE venture, which will be used to discuss the case study. Usually, new companies do not have any customers or suppliers when they are founded. Building up business relationships with *customers* and *suppliers* therefore becomes a natural and important part of the company's development process. As also shown by research on industrial networks, collaboration with the company's direct customers and suppliers may not be enough. For example, in order to gain access to the right resources and influence key actors in the network it may be necessary to involve the *customers' customers* or the *suppliers' suppliers*. The former may be the end-users and those who are most profoundly affected by the features of the new product.

Furthermore, on the marketing side *distributors* represent a type of external actor with whom the firms may need to develop relationships. They are not 'real customers' but trading companies which are performing an intermediary role between the innovating firm and the final customers.

Universities and other types of research organizations constitute another type of R&D partner that companies may wish to establish collaborative relationships with. For obvious reasons, the purpose is different from the industrial collaboration (unless the researchers are customers). Typical benefits sought by the companies are access to research-based knowledge and competencies that can be used in their own R&D process.[5]

There exist a range of other actors in the environment that companies may need to interact with during the innovation process. Here we find, for example, various types of *bridging organizations* which have the task to support commercialization of technology. They may be of particular relevance to science-based start-up companies, since the latter's main focus is on commercialization of academic research results. Typical examples of bridging organizations that interact with start-up companies are the universities' own technology transfer offices ('TTOs'), incubators and science parks. These organizations may provide seed funding of innovation projects as well as other types of support (advice, coaching, project management, contacts, etc.). Bridging organizations are usually public bodies.

Government agencies are a type of actor that some companies may need to interact with. They may provide funding for R&D and commercialization or be important interaction partners if they have a regulatory function (which is common in life science, for example).

Building relationships with *venture capital (VC) firms*, or other types of investors, may also be helpful to start-up companies. Like bridging organizations, VC firms may not only provide money but also support the companies in other ways. This includes, for example, recruitment of skilled management personnel and board members, advisory services and connections to other firms.

Finally, certain types of networks may be conditioned by the specific conditions within an industrial sector. The sectoral system of innovation consists of knowledge, actors, networks and institutions (Malerba, 2002). Thus, there may be specific conditions of a sectoral system of innovation that have major impacts on the development and management of a KIE venture.

Previous research suggests that there are special conditions related to regulation in medical technology and other life science industries, that strongly influence the development and performance of the firm. There is a huge literature on healthcare and pharmaceuticals, so here we restrict to two contributions that study them from a sectoral system of innovation perspective. Lenzi *et al.* (2010) contribute to an understanding of how sectoral systems of innovation are related to knowledge intensive entrepreneurship. A survey was conducted of KIE ventures across European countries, and these firms were active in the sectors of biotechnology, electronics and medical devices. The data included in this KEINS survey of KIE ventures was collected through a long and complex process of sample identification, data collection, questionnaire elaboration and survey administration. The results suggest that the differences across sectors are related to the type of knowledge and competences needed in order to be successful on the market, and that biotechnology and medical devices had specific sectoral conditions of relevance in this context. McKelvey *et al.* (2004) analysed the sectoral system of innovation in the pharmaceutical and biotechnology industry. While not exactly overlapping with the medtech industry, their analysis highlighted the importance of clinical tests and users within the healthcare industry, as well as the regulatory demands in creating markets. Therefore, this chapter will not analyse all aspects of a sectoral system of innovation but instead only focus upon the specific role of clinical research for the KIE venture active in the medtech sector.

3 The medical technology sector in Sweden

The case study company Aerocrine has developed and commercialized a diagnostic method for asthma. It provides a novel diagnostic method, consisting of both equipment and application knowledge, which can be used to improve asthma diagnostics. More specifically, the company is engaged in commercializing a scientific discovery to use nitric oxide (NO) as a marker of airway inflammation (which has important implications for the treatment). This was a university-based discovery and invention, and the founders were researchers at two departments at the Karolinska Institute in Stockholm. Hence, Aerocrine is an academic spin-off.

The Aerocrine case is part of a larger study of Swedish medtech start-ups and their networks. Four in-depth case studies have been completed – covering three university spin-offs and one corporate spin-off (Laage-Hellman, 2012). The data is based upon two primary sources of material, namely archival evidence such as homepages, annual reports, public information, etc., and most importantly semi-structured interviews of approximately 1–3 hours conducted face-to-face with key individuals, including founders in the respective company.

While stimulating KIE entrepreneurship through public policy efforts may be a positive goal, the historical development also shows that few of these KIE ventures in medical technology have, so far, succeeded in the market place and become high-growth companies.[6]

This case study thus helps nuance our understanding of the process of entrepreneurship, from the perspective of the entrepreneur and venture. It illustrates how difficult and time-consuming it is to build a new medtech company from scratch. The inventors and founders who were academic scientists, and later managers of the medtech start-up, experimented with different paths of commercialization of research into products.

An important part of the environment in which Aerocrine was founded and developed is Sweden's long and proud history in medical technology. In fact, Sweden was a pioneer in biomedical engineering research and its application in healthcare. Medical research more broadly has long been an area of strength in Sweden, as linked to historically high investments in public healthcare services. In the decades after the Second World War, several major innovations had their origin in Sweden and contributed to build a growing and highly internationalized medtech industry. Hence, a number of important product innovations have been made in the Swedish medtech industry, among others 'the artificial kidney' (Gambro), the Gamma knife (Elekta), the pacemaker (Siemens-Elema), osseointegration of dental implants (Nobelpharma/Nobel Biocare) and allergy diagnostics (Pharmacia). Many of these innovations came out of close collaboration between academic researchers, the healthcare system and industry. Furthermore, in this period, the collaboration could occur with either new start-ups or large existing firms. Hence, historically (i.e. in the 1950s–1970s) many medtech inventions made at universities or university hospitals were successfully commercialized by Swedish companies.

More recently, that is from about the 1990s, our previous research has shown that the large, established medtech companies have not contributed much to growth and job creation in this industry in Sweden (Laage-Hellman et al., 2009). Some large companies based here have continued to expand their operations, but their investments have been made abroad rather than in Sweden. Instead, the growth of the Swedish medtech industry has come mainly from young research-based businesses in the last decades, usually in the form of new companies but sometimes through corporate venturing and spin-offs in larger firms. The creation of start-up companies has become a key mechanism for commercialization of academic research in this sector and country, and indeed, many KIE ventures in medical technologies have been founded during the past two or three decades. However, for various reasons that will be further commented on below, it is difficult to get the large, established firms to commercialize new product ideas, unless these ideas are closely in line with current strategies of the firm.

The Aerocrine case should be seen and interpreted in this empirical context. Both authors led a recent study on life sciences – including medical technology – and it was carried out on behalf of Vinnova (the Swedish Governmental Agency for Innovation Systems) (ibid.). In that study the long-term effects of public investments in life science research were investigated. Medical technology was one of two sub-sectors chosen for the effect analysis, which focused on two areas where public policy was assumed to make an impact, upon industry and academia respectively. With regard to the effect of public policy on industry, one conclusion was that the formation of new companies is a key mechanism for commercializing results from academic research in the field of medical technology in Sweden (but not in innovative food, another sub-sector covered by the study). It was this conclusion that triggered the AEGIS study that this chapter is based upon.

The Vinnova study also showed that the established firms, despite their reluctance to pick up and commercialize academic product inventions, could benefit from university collaboration (ibid.). For the large firms, the benefit of interacting with universities was primarily to scan technology and develop further knowledge that can be used in the internal product development rather than directly into a product innovation.

Moreover, in the specific context of medical technology in Sweden, this finding was somewhat puzzling. The public investment into universities and public healthcare is very large, and indeed, much of the medtech research carried out at Swedish universities is oriented toward applied research and specific areas of medical application, and often aims to develop new methods and devices for medical diagnosis or treatment.

The previous research on medical technology in Sweden suggests that there are reasons as to why the pathway of moving a specific idea and invention from academic research and directly to large established firms does not work so well. The academic researchers often find it difficult to identify an established firm as a partner, which is interested in taking over the idea and commercializing it. The common reasons (as given in interviews) are that the idea does not fit in well with the company's current strategy; that the technology is perceived to be too unproven; and that the idea or prototype (method) is too far from the market.

These results from the interviews correspond well to the dynamics in the industry, globally. The large medtech companies tend to be niche-oriented and, given the fierce competition in the market, they are also focused on relatively short-term goals and on investing in products and services that lie well within the existing firm strategy and that are proven in the market.

Hence, this case study of commercialization is particularly interesting today, as in many cases, it appears that the only way for the university scientists to commercialize their ideas is to start up a new company. Yet, the case study is also interesting, in that as the developing and managing phase of the KIE venture unfolds, the case suggests that the company moves away from the knowledge and networks of the founders. In other words, the KIE venture becomes less dependent upon the founders and focuses more upon other types of resources and networks needed for commercial success.

4 Aerocrine: underlying discovery and invention

Sections 4-7 address the first question, namely, in what ways did the early dynamics of developing and managing the KIE venture depend upon links to the innovation system, in terms of accessing and commercializing knowledge and in terms of financing?

As we have seen this KIE venture, Aerocrine, is based upon scientific results, made by researchers at a university. Sections 4 and 5 provide a brief overview of how they moved from a scientific discovery to a KIE venture, including some insight into the formation of early networks for venture capital and innovation support, thereby demonstrating the links to the innovation system in the early phase.

This KIE venture is based on a medical discovery, published as scientific results. The first scientific publication showing that nitric oxide (NO) is an important messenger molecule in the human body had appeared in 1987. The invention for asthma diagnostics that is commercialized by Aerocrine many years later is based on mainly pre-clinical research carried out by two groups at the Karolinska Institute. One of the groups, within the Department of Physiology, was headed by Professor Lars Gustafsson. The other group was headed by Professor Jan Lundberg at the Department of Pharmacology.

Both groups had further developed the ideas, and applied them toward use in identifying medical conditions. In 1991, Lars Gustafsson and collaborators were the first in the world to publish the discovery that NO is present at very low levels in exhaled air. Before publication, he also applied for a patent for a lung function test, focusing on a single-breath exhalation measurement. This patent was based upon his realization that exhaled NO mainly originated from the air-carrying parts of the lungs. The discovery of exhaled NO stimulated members of Jan Lundberg's research group to further investigate ideas. They went on to explore this idea, by using an existing research device based on chemiluminescence,[7] the possibility that NO was elevated in patients with inflammatory airway diseases like asthma. In 1993, Kjell Alving, a post-doc researcher, published an article (together with a doctoral student and his supervisor) showing that allergy sufferers had significantly higher levels of NO in their exhaled air.[8] They also applied for a patent, which was partly overlapping with Lars Gustafsson's patent. Almost simultaneously, the Gustafsson group published about NO measurements in a policlinical asthma patient group, and a research group at Imperial College in London also demonstrated that allergen challenge caused elevations in exhaled NO levels. Both articles by the two groups at the Karolinska Institute appeared in the same issue of *The Lancet* in early 1994.

5 Exploring paths for commercializing the scientific research results

There were several possible ways to commercialize the idea, in terms of how to develop it into a product innovation, and the research teams explored several paths, before starting a KIE venture.

Based upon these scientific discoveries, the work in the pharmacology group was shown to have relevance for medical conditions – and hence a possible business application. They had demonstrated that the level of NO in exhaled air could be used as a sensitive marker for inflammation in the airway. This led to the idea of developing a device that could be used to diagnose asthma.[9] Kjell Alving had previously worked for Pharmacia Diagnostics in Uppsala, a world-leader in immuno-assay-based allergy diagnostics. Pharmacia Diagnostics was interested in the invention and helped the researchers to write and finance a patent application – in exchange for the right of first refusal to commercialize the idea.[10]

However, the discussion with Pharmacia Diagnostics advanced very slowly and the university researchers noted that some people in the company were sceptical. This was understandable since the NO measurement method was of a very different kind compared to what Pharmacia Diagnostics was used to (i.e. analysing a blood sample). To 'test' Pharmacia Diagnostics' willingness to invest, the researchers drafted a licence agreement including royalties as well as a significant downpayment. Pharmacia Diagnostics declined this offer, and the option agreement was therefore dissolved in 1996. Following this event, the university researchers took contact with other companies, primarily in the diagnostics industry.

Some showed interest, including an American firm, but nothing came of these discussions.

In parallel, the pharmacology group built an instrument to be used primarily in their own research. This was done in collaboration with a technical consultant and the Swedish distributor of the Swiss analysis instrument which had been used in their previous research projects. The instrument was exhibited at several fairs in order to test the interest of potential customers, and 2–3 potential users showed interest in buying it. This suggested that a potential market existed. This instrument later on became the prototype for Aerocrine's first product.

Lars Gustafsson (on his side) was also interested in commercializing the idea. Some years earlier, he had started a small company, Nitrograf Bioanalys AB. He had also established contact with Sievers Inc., an American manufacturer of chemiluminescence-based analysis instruments. These instruments had up till then mainly been used for environmental applications. With the contact with Gustafsson, the company Sievers saw an opportunity to use their technology in order to develop a new market in healthcare.

From the beginning the two research groups at the Karolinska Institute were 'competitors' in the academic research and had no collaboration. They were also in different fields, where one group consisted of physiologists; the other group worked with pharmacology.

A decisive event for the future KIE venture occurred in 1996 when the CEO of Sievers visited the Karolinska Institute and met with both groups. He made it clear to the researchers that unless they started to collaborate, the commercialization of the invention would be impossible. No firm would be interested in just one of the patents. As a result, representatives of the two groups began to discuss how they could collaborate. This triggered an intensive negotiation process in order to solve the complexities involved in bringing together two competing research groups, each with ongoing patent applications. They finally worked out a deal to value the respective group's contributions, and they agreed to jointly search for a way to take the next step toward commercialization. The final handshake over their agreement took place on 17 June 1996.

The initial idea – and the preferred route of commercialization – was to sell a licence to a big company with an existing market organization. 'This was our picture of the world', as one of the inventors put it. The Pharmacology group wanted to license their idea to Pharmacia Diagnostics, but they did not manage to do so, and so we can say that this pathway of commercialization through selling to a large established company was not realized.

After having failed to find another suitable licensee after Pharmacia Diagnostics, the team changed their mind and decided instead to start their own company. At this stage, there were some contacts with Karolinska Innovation, the technology transfer office of the Karolinska Institute which had recently been established.

However, the researchers chose another alternative to develop an academic spin-off.[11] One of them had a friend working in the venture capital business. As a result of this contact, Sjunnesson & Krook Corporate Finance and Matteus Fondkommission (a stock brokerage company) helped the researchers to found a company and raise start-up capital. This happened in November 1997. The initial owners were ten researchers from the two groups, with varying ownership shares in accordance with the previous deal, and with the university-based Karolinska Innovation making a small investment. Shortly after the founding a public issue of shares brought in some €3 million, which was intended to finance the company during the first two years. After this issue, the founding researchers had some 70 per cent of the shares together.

As a condition for helping the researchers to raise capital, the financial advisors demanded that someone else should manage the company. During the search for a CEO, two of the younger researchers from the pharmacology group asked for a six-month leave during the first half of 1998 in order to manage the company. One of them, Eddie Weitzberg, became acting CEO. Their main task was to start up the business activity in the KIE venture, while waiting for the recruitment of a permanent CEO.

Thanks to contacts arranged by the financial advisors, Acrocrine managed to recruit a competent board of directors. This company board consisted of two of the researchers, Lars Gustafsson and Eddie Weitzberg, as well as four persons with long experience from senior management positions in Swedish pharmaceutical and medtech firms such as Astra and Pharmacia. It was up to the board to recruit a permanent CEO, who should have industrial experience. They chose Thomas Almesjö, a manager with long experience from the Pharmacia Group and at the time, the CEO of the Swedish branch of an American pharmaceutical firm.

In addition, thanks to the researchers' own contact networks in the academic community, Aerocrine was able to put together a very competent scientific advisory board consisting of three world-leading scientists. One of them shared the Nobel Prize in 1998 for his work on NO as a signalling molecule. Another member was a leading American asthma scientist and the third had been research director at a major drug company.

From autumn 1998, under the leadership of the new CEO, Aerocrine began to recruit its staff and build up an organization. Although it was such a small company it became remarkably easy to find competent people. This task was facilitated by the fact that some of the large pharmaceutical and medtech companies in Sweden were downsizing at this time. These lay-offs released a number of competent managers who were searching for a new job. Hence, some of the traditional problems with human resources for KIE ventures were overcome, due to the structural shifts in the industry in Sweden at the time the KIE venture was recruiting.

6 Financing of the KIE venture

Another key link to the innovation system during development relates to financing. Following the initial public issue of shares in 1997, which brought in approximately €3 million, Aerocrine did more than 15 new share issues during the following nine years. Although one can always question whether the degree of capitalization is optimal or sufficient in general, in this specific case, it is clear that the long-term commitment from Aerocrine's lead investors as well as the availability of new investors has been crucial for the company's development.

Most of the capital came from different venture capital (VC) firms. HealthCap, as lead investor, made its first investment in 1999, followed by Investor Growth Capital. These two VC firms became the two largest owners controlling together about half of the equity. Several of the capital raising rounds were marred by local or global financial market difficulties, notably the so-called IT crash in the early 2000s, and also a slump in shares for companies in biotechnology and medicine. One of the founders recalls that the company, under considerable financial stress, was to give a presentation to potential investors at one of the three major Swedish banks. Earlier in the same day, a Swedish financial newspaper had a placard of headlines in war-style letters which only had the words 'Blood-bath in Biotech'.

In 2007, Aerocrine made an Initial Public Offering (IPO) and became listed on the NASDAQ OMX Stockholm stock exchange. The rights issue in connection to the IPO brought in €25 million. Taken together, approximately €90 million in total had been invested in Aerocrine since its foundation (1997) up until 2012.

This also had implications for the founders and their ownership of the company. The founders, who initially owned 70 per cent of the company (after the first share issue) had only 0.75 per cent of equity and voting rights in 2012.

Moreover, the founders had had two representatives on the board of directors since the start, but after the IPO in 2007, the decision was taken that the founders should only have one representative.

In a comment regarding the decreasing ownership for the founders, one of them says that from an economic point of view he would probably have been better off if they had sold the invention to an existing firm. Moreover, without having their own capital it is difficult for the founders to keep a substantial ownership.

In 2010, Aerocrine had become well-established and started to grow, and at that time, they got a new major owner. This owner is a fund belonging to Novo Nordisk in Denmark (a world-leader in diabetes care). This Novo Growth Equity Fund has invested €25 million in the company split in two parts: one half in the form of equity and the other half as a convertible loan. The company's management perceived this investment to be very positive for Aerocrine's future development since it was expected to bring stability and long-term ownership. A senior manager says that if the company had got this money earlier it is possible that it would have been able to grow faster.

7 Networking in Aerocrine

This section addresses the second question, namely, what types of networks were needed and developed, in order to develop from an idea into a KIE venture? Which specific sectoral conditions within the medical technology sector influence the development of the KIE venture?

Networks are seen as ways to access and develop key knowledge and resources for the KIE venture (McKelvey and Lassen, 2013a, 2013b). This section answers the research question, relative to the different types of networks, and partners for collaboration, that were identified in Section 2. We will begin by looking at Aerocrine's interaction with universities. This will be followed by discussions on Aerocrine's relationship-building activities directed at, respectively, customer/users, suppliers and additional types of actors.

7.1 Universities

Universities represent important types of networks for academic spin-offs. For a university spin-off like Aerocrine the invention to be commercialized comes from academic research, in this case basic or experimental research. We have seen that the importance of this relationship from the company (to the founders) was very high in the beginning but has then decreased over time.

In the case of Aerocrine, it seems that the incentives to maintain a close collaborative relationship with the founders at the Karolinska Institute were not so strong. One reason is that some of the founders changed their research focus and headed in a direction that made them less interesting as partners to Aerocrine. Furthermore, what the company most of all needed in the shorter term was results from clinical research, that indicated that their diagnostic method was useful in healthcare. In the longer term, though, when the company has obtained market acceptance, and wants to take the next technological step, then basic and applied medical research at the university or public research institute would become more interesting as network partners, when new generations of equipment are being developed.

Universities also carry out *technical* research of potential relevance to medtech companies. It can be at departments specializing in biomedical engineering or at departments with a broader focus but having medicine as one of several chosen application fields. We can note that it is only more recently that Aerocrine has collaborated with this kind of academic partner, because the instrument itself has been based on well-established technologies. Aerocrine could access these technologies by finding suitable suppliers, and so previously, the company did not need to develop such novel technologies.

However, now when the company has started to develop a completely new product generation, it is trying to take a bigger leap in the product development, it has become more interesting to make use of new technologies coming from front-line technical research. For this purpose Aerocrine has established collaboration with a new partner (i.e. a research group at the Royal Institute of Technology in Stockholm). It is too early to determine what will come out of this.

In general, medtech companies may of course have reasons to use universities also in a more traditional way, that is, as a source of new ideas and competencies. The universities could represent medical, scientific and technological opportunities, not only as related to the founder but also in other disciplines. However, despite the need to broaden, or redirect, the networking activities, a medical start-up should generally also have good reason to maintain a relationship with the founding research group, since it may continue to do relevant research and improve the original technology or method. This may provide future opportunities for the company to access new knowledge and use that collaboration in its own further development of new product generations or new applications.

7.2 Customers and users

Generally, in the context of technological development, customers and users are an especially important category of network actor. For companies in the medtech industry developing products for healthcare, clinical research (carried out on humans, rather than e.g. on animals) is the dominant way of involving customers/users in product development (before and after start of sales). For certain products (e.g. medical implants), clinical trials (similar to what is required for drugs) are a prerequisite for obtaining approval to sell. In many other cases, this is not necessary, but positive results from clinical studies are crucial in order to successfully introduce the product into the market. As further discussed in Section 8, the objective of the clinical studies on Aerocrine's method was to get it incorporated in *clinical guidelines* and gain acceptance from the *reimbursement system*. This was required in each country in order to achieve widespread usage in the daily routine of healthcare. The Aerocrine case offers many insights about the difficulties of running clinical trials from a small, resource-poor company which is dependent upon networks.[12]

Following the initial publications by Aerocrine's founders, clinical researchers in different countries started to make studies and publish results. The first external publication came in 1994 – in *The Lancet*. In 1997, when the company was founded, there were around a hundred articles on NO measurement. However, most of these studies dealt with methodological issues and there were few on the clinical use.

When Aerocrine was founded the most urgent need was to start up the development of a product. But soon clinical research became another high priority. During the first 5–6 years the main focus of the company's R&D was to develop and establish the method itself – i.e. how should NO measurement be used for treatment of asthma patients? In order to convince the healthcare providers and the medical profession about the benefits of using the method as a routine there was great need for clinical research as well as health economic studies.

By using the founders' contact networks Aerocrine was able at an early stage to establish collaboration with several leading clinical research groups, primarily in the USA and Europe. Kjell Alving played a key role in this regard. By co-organizing a couple of international scientific meetings he had established contacts with clinical researchers who already worked in the field. These contacts were later on transferred to Aerocrine and became the basis for the company's clinical collaborations. The three initially most important partners were Imperial College in London, Harvard University in Boston and National Jewish Hospital in Denver. Fruitful collaboration was also established with two university hospitals in the Netherlands and Italy.

Aerocrine's involvement in the clinical studies varied – and still does so. Some of them are initiated, paid and managed by the company itself. They are carried out by clinical partners with which the company has a formal agreement. Others are carried out by independent researchers who approach the company and ask for support. A third category of studies are those carried out by independent researchers who do not have contact with the company.

There are advantages and disadvantages as to how much the company is involved. The availability of a commercial product from 2001 boosted the number of clinical studies.[13] Many groups were interested and it was not difficult to get studies started. However, the quality of studies varied since the measurement method was not standardized. Generally, clinical studies are good for the company and contribute to the development and establishment of the method.

However, certain studies carried out by independent researchers may be negative for the company, for example, if they are not well done and especially if the measurements were not carried out properly. This is a risk, when the company does not have control over the study. Therefore, from the company's point of view sponsored studies are always preferable. The drawback is the high costs. Due to scarce resources Aerocrine has had to limit the number of proprietary studies. This was unfortunate especially since Aerocrine was in a situation where it is introducing a totally new diagnostic method with major implications for therapy. The need for well-controlled clinical studies was therefore higher than for more normal medical devices – and the company needed more control over the studies.

From the beginning the company had two clinical research managers. However, already in 2008 both of them were laid off in connection with a major restructuring of the company. The poor financial performance of the company, caused by lower than expected sales, and the global financial crisis had made it necessary to cut costs.

This also explains why there was for a long time no medical affairs department in the company. The management had recognized the need for such a function, but the board had not been willing to invest. However, around 2003/2004 Aerocrine began to recruit clinical research managers, and in 2007 one of the inventors and co-founders, Kjell Alving, was hired as Director of Scientific & Medical Affairs. Several interviewees maintain that the creation of a medical affairs department should have come at an earlier stage. It is believed that more and better controlled clinical studies would have spurred knowledge development around the method and helped the company to speed up the market introduction and grow faster.

Kjell Alving argues that Aerocrine has had too high expectations on the independent clinical researchers. There has been a need to do more proprietary studies. But these are not only costly but also resource-demanding. Active participation from the medical affairs department is necessary in order to secure an appropriate study design and a correct interpretation of data. Financing can change this situation, and more recently, thanks to the investment from the Novo Growth Equity Fund, Aerocrine has for the first time in 2009 a full-fledged function for medical affairs.

These network relationships also affect the knowledge known and developed in the company. The clinical studies have not affected the design of the instrument itself but have been extremely important for the development of application knowledge (and to some extent for software development).

Not least there is a need, as already mentioned, to standardize the measurement procedure. In fact, consensus on how to use the method must be in place before it becomes meaningful to carry out large-scale clinical studies. Furthermore, once the method has been accepted in the market the company needs to provide this type of knowledge to its customers in order to enable them to use the method in a correct way.

One of the interviewees who was an inventor commented upon the long time it has taken for Aerocrine to get acceptance for the method. He points out that NO diagnostics means a paradigm shift in asthma care. The physicians are used to relying on symptoms and lung function tests. For many of them it has been hard to adopt the idea of using an inflammation marker, since this means a totally new way of thinking. Generally, younger doctors are easier to convince and Aerocrine is therefore trying to reach out to and influence them through their education at medical schools.

The Aerocrine case illustrates a general challenge for innovating medtech companies, namely, to create fruitful collaboration with clinical partners. Large, established firms often have such relationships in place, but start-ups do not. They have to start more or less from scratch. Due to resource scarcity this is not always easy, as our case shows. The results of the clinical research constitute a critical asset in the company's market introduction process. This will be further elaborated below in our discussion of sector-specific conditions.

7.3 Suppliers

Suppliers are another important type of network actor for KIE ventures. Like many other medtech start-ups, Aerocrine decided at an early stage to not manufacture its product in-house (i.e. outsource to one or several suppliers).

After having contacted many potential manufacturers Aerocrine, thanks to the inventors/founders' personal contacts, identified and initiated collaboration with an American company, Monitor Labs. This company could supply the core components needed to build the first generation of instrument. To make the technical design, collaboration was established with a technical consultancy in Sweden. The early recruitment of an experienced technical manager turned out to be very important in establishing these supplier relationships and taking the collaborations to fulfilment.

The responsibility for assembling the final product was given to Amersham Biosciences in Sweden, which acted as a contract manufacturer of biotech and medtech products. Having decided that the second product generation would be based on an electrochemical technology, Aerocrine started to search for a supplier of the sensor, which was a core component to be sold to the customers as a consumable. Aerocrine ended up with a small German company, IT Dr Gambert GmbH, which was specializing in selling sensors to different types of industries. The technical director of Aerocrine knew this company from his previous job at Siemens. From the beginning it was uncertain whether it would be possible to measure NO at the required low concentration levels with a high resolution. To solve the problem the two companies initiated a close technical collaboration and after three years managed to come up with a working solution.

The instrument was designed by Aerocrine in-house. The manufacturing is outsourced to Sanmina SCI in Sweden (an American owned contract manufacturer). Sanmina, once it had been selected as supplier, became involved in making the final design of the product. This collaboration lasted for two years and took place in parallel with the development of the sensor.

The development of the third product generation is now under way, as of 2013. This is a major next step, which means that Aerocrine could enter the potentially huge market for home care. To do so, Aerocrine has established a strategic alliance with Panasonic in Japan – a major large-scale manufacturer of medical devices, including products for the self-care market. Based upon specifications from Aerocrine, which will keep the marketing rights, Panasonic will carry out much of the R&D and take responsibility for all production.

The present case illustrates that suppliers, especially of non-standardized parts or sub-systems, may need to be involved in the start-up's own product development activities. Technical collaboration is required to have these parts effectively designed and manufactured. Like in the customer and user network described above, this kind of collaboration should preferably be established at an early stage of the innovation process.

In the case of Aerocrine, it seems that the establishment of collaborative relationships with suppliers did not encounter big difficulties (thanks, *inter alia*, to the fortunate recruitment of competent and experienced managers). However, we know from other case studies that this is not always an easy task for small start-ups (Laage-Hellman, 2012). For example, given the buyer's small size, lack of resources, lack of track record and uncertain future, it is not uncommon for contacted suppliers to be reluctant to invest own resources in the relationship. An intensive (and costly) interaction may therefore be needed in order to convince the suppliers to mobilize the resources necessary to develop the product.

7.4 Additional actors

The literature also highlights a number of additional actors, but these have not been so influential for the development of this company.

Indeed, we could go so far as to say that in addition to those network relationships mentioned above, there are no other types of collaborative relationships that have been particularly important for Aerocrine's development. For example, Aerocrine has not made use of the services offered by public bridging organizations.[14] When Aerocrine was founded the innovation support system of the Karolinska Institute was not as well developed as it is today. Thanks to the founders' existing contacts initial funding and related support could be received from private actors in the financial market. And since Aerocrine had managed to recruit competent and experienced managers there was no need to get coaching from outside.

Aerocrine presently has a research grant from Vinnova together with the Royal Institute of Technology. This is small money for Aerocrine, but still appreciated. In earlier contacts with Vinnova, Aerocrine failed to get support for its product development, since the company had already begun to sell its product in the market. Aerocrine perceives that in Sweden, unlike in many other countries (e.g. in the US and in Asia), there is a lack of support from the government for large-scale innovation projects. This might be one reason why Aerocrine has been searching for supplier partners abroad for its third product generation. There are consequences, however, in that next product (for home care which is a potentially very large market) will not be produced in Sweden.

8 The importance of clinical research to medtech companies

This section develops the insight from the case study that it is crucial for firms that develop new methods, for diagnostics or therapy, to secure the execution of high-quality clinical studies that prove the benefits of the method. This is a prerequisite in order to convince the medical profession and the payers of healthcare services to buy and use the product.

Aerocrine has its roots in medical research with a mainly basic or experimental character. The case study illustrates how Aerocrine, like other medtech start-ups originating in basic, pre-clinical or technical research, has had a strong need to link up with users (mainly physicians) via clinical research.[15]

In order to successfully commercialize a new medical device, three things need to be in place: product approval, inclusion in clinical guidelines, and reimbursement.

When entering a new market, the first step is to get the product approved for sale. The company must be able to prove that the product is safe for the patients. Aerocrine got such approval in Europe in 2004 and in the US four years later.

However, in order to achieve large-scale usage of the method, this type of approval is not sufficient. In each individual country, there must also be clinical guidelines recommending the method. In Aerocrine's case, NO measurement should be recommended as an effective tool to keep asthma patients' inflammation under control so that they remain symptom free at the lowest medicine dose possible.

Clinical guidelines are usually issued by national healthcare authorities based upon the results of clinical studies and recommendations from specialist physicians' professional associations. For the companies it is usually difficult to approach directly the authorities or associations, but instead they try to influence them indirectly by working with individual physicians and researchers. In particular they try to get the method accepted by key opinion leaders – local as well as international ones.

Clinical studies are thus crucial to get the use of a new product included in clinical guidelines. The principle of evidence-based medicine, applied by regulatory authorities, puts high value on results from large randomized clinical studies, that is, the type of clinical trials carried out by pharmaceutical firms when seeking approval for new drugs. These studies are very costly and cannot be financed by small medtech companies like Aerocrine. Instead, such companies have to rely on the gradually increasing insights that come out of smaller studies. Moreover, the concept of evidence-based medicine was developed for therapeutic intervention and is not well suited to diagnostic products and this is a problem for firms like Aerocrine. The benefits of such diagnostic products are difficult to prove. This is also why it may take such a long time for a diagnostic company to get changes in clinical guidelines.

A third condition for large-scale clinical use is acceptance from the reimbursement system, that is, those who pay for the tests. It can be public authorities and/or private insurance companies. Typically, this follows on the inclusion of the method in clinical guidelines. In other cases, it can be the other way around, that is, the reimbursement comes first and clinical guidelines afterwards.

Like public authorities the insurance companies are used to large randomized clinical trials. The only choice for medtech companies is to work bottom up by trying to influence the physicians and create a demand for the method.

Starting in 2003, Aerocrine has got its method included in clinical guidelines in more than ten European countries. One major exception is Germany. Here, the 700 private asthma clinics have been successfully penetrated, But in order to reach out to the primary healthcare physicians in the public sector, the method must first be included in the national clinical guidelines, which the firm is still waiting for.

The US market is of crucial importance to Aerocrine's growth, because it is the world's largest market for medical devices. Here many people are insured by private insurance companies, and these tend to have their own assessment criteria. The lack of information on health economic effects for a long time hampered Aerocrine's sales efforts in the US. Moreover, many insurance companies considered the measurement of exhaled NO an 'experimental' or 'investigational' procedure and therefore denied payment. However, in 2009 a group of American opinion leaders convened and produced a document recommending clinical use of NO diagnostics in the management of asthma. This resulted in updated clinical guidelines published by the American Thoracic Society in September 2011. This has helped to spur sales in the US market. Another important event was that one of the larger insurance companies in the US adopted a new policy favouring the use of NO diagnostics in the treatment of asthma patients. This is perceived as an important step for the method to gain wider acceptance in the market.

Not only in the United States but also in other countries it is important as a means to influence clinical guidelines and reimbursement to demonstrate that the new method leads to cost-savings for healthcare providers and payers. In order to provide data proving that Aerocrine's method is cost-efficient a first health economic study was started in Germany in 2007 and reported in 2008. The study showed that savings were possible because the pharmaceutical treatment could be optimized by using the results of NO tests.

However, in order to provide better evidence of the cost-efficiency of their devices, the medtech companies would need to carry out large-scale studies. These studies would be based upon prospective health economic data, which is collected and analysed. This is a more recent learning for this company. Aerocrine is now trying to develop ideas for how such studies should be carried out. Under all circumstances, collaboration with healthcare providers is required in order to gain access to data. As a first step, Aerocrine has established collaboration with an American HMO (Health Management Organization). One study has already been completed and a publication is under way. A second larger follow-up study is now being planned.

It can thus be concluded that for firms like Aerocrine, which develops highly innovative medical devices, having access to good and convincing clinical data is a key to successful market introduction and sales growth. That is also why it is so important for such firms to link up with clinical users at an early stage.

A final point to make here also relates to users/customers. What is relatively unique for the medical industry, compared to most other industries, is that there is an overlap between users/customers and academia. The simple reason is that clinical studies are very often carried out at university hospitals. The researchers who carry out the studies do so in their clinics where they have patients and perform healthcare services. These clinics are thus potential regular customers once the product has been approved for sale. In other words, clinical research collaboration is a special form of university-industry interaction.

9 Implications

This chapter has used the detailed case study of one medtech company to illustrate KIE entrepreneurship, relative to research questions about how KIE ventures develop, through networks. Different types of networks are analysed, including ones related to financing, medical and scientific knowledge and users.

One particularly interesting aspect of this case study is the special role of clinical research, and its effects on clinical guidelines and reimbursement. In addition, KIE ventures normally develop under conditions of restrained resources. In our specific case, the KIE venture did not devote enough resources to clinical studies, and this negatively affected the growth and development of the company.

The case also demonstrates how and why the type and value of networks tends to shift over time, due to differing types of networks and the differing needs of the companies as the innovation process proceeds. The case illustrates that the initial relationship to the research environment – or in this case, environments as two groups at the Karolinska Institute developed the ideas – exist from the beginning and are relatively unproblematic. By contrast, the relationships to other types of stakeholders and particularly to users and customers and suppliers are missing de facto and must be developed in the early phase. These types of relationships help reduce the uncertainty inherent in these types of innovations, given that stakeholders and users provide information about specifications of demand that help the KIE venture shape its product to meet market demand.

The case illustrates that network relationships develop over time. The findings can be summarized as follows:

- *Initial relationships* that the new companies have, for example, with founders/inventors or their parent organizations are important in the very early (start-up) phase, but their importance tends to diminish over time.
- There is a great need to develop collaborative relationships with *a broad range of other actors* (than those that the company is linked with at the start).
- In particular early collaboration with *users/customers* is crucial, and in this case this includes teaming up with medical scientists engaged in clinical research. What kind of difficulties, challenges or opportunities the company meets depends partly on its origin (e.g. from what type of academic research the company has spun off).
- Being young, the *lack of resources and track record* often affects the medtech start-up companies' possibilities to find the right partners.
- After the start-up phase collaboration with commercial/market-related partners are more important than academic partners.

This case focused on the KIE venture per se and did not explicitly address the role of public policy. In this particular case, however, it seems that innovation-supporting policy efforts did not affect the company very much. The KIE venture itself was engaged in this challenging task to build up collaborative relationships with users/customers and suppliers.

The deeper understanding of the case study firm helps understand the conditions of the KIE venture, although we do not address the role of public policy per se. In this case, the company hired experienced managers, which is a different path from some public policy initiatives, which try to provide new KIE ventures with external advisors and coaches. This company hired experienced managers, and thereby brought this competence directly into the firm. The industrial experience of the persons hired was very important for explaining the development of the firm. One implication is that the experts and coaches working at incubators need skills and knowledge to help focus the company upon building useful networks – and probably need sector specific knowledge (experience). For example, failure to initiate close contacts with users could lead the company to choose a direction of development for its product which is impractical or unrealistic, relative to market conditions and needs. Developing specialized life science incubators and consultants may be one way to draw upon a wider base of competencies.

Another important implication is that in order to facilitate for start-up companies (and other medtech firms) to gain access to clinical partners the healthcare system should be open to industrial collaboration. Especially the smaller firms tend to be dependent on local partners but, at least in

Sweden, they often experience difficulties in making hospitals interested in testing their new products. One reason is the limitations of low cost demands from public procurement. Public innovation procurement has in recent years attracted great interest and is, for example, promoted by the Swedish government. So far, however, it seems that this policy has not yet been transformed into more concrete action at the regional level. There is obviously a big potential to develop the procurement practices in a way that will improve the future supply of innovative medtech products and also spur industrial growth.

Finally, it is possible that policy initiatives to support cluster development can have indirect positive effects on individual companies, especially small start-ups. It is more difficult for them compared to large firms to find collaboration partners abroad. Thus, a regional agglomeration of companies, research units and healthcare providers may make it easier for individual companies to access the knowledge, competencies and resources they need for their development. The cluster could, for example, provide information linkages about the key variables impacting KIE ventures in their industry or provide contacts to facilitate finding new network partners.

Finally, we should reflect about whether all academic scientists really should be turned into entrepreneurs. On one hand, for this company, it appears to be the only available pathway for commercialization. On the other hand, after a few years, the founders had little ownership left in the company, and several had moved on to other types of research. This is quite normal, it can be argued, in the empirical context of the medical technology industry. Public policy could stimulate other pathways for commercialization, than trying to turn academic scientists into entrepreneurs.

Notes

1 *Medical technology* can be broadly defined as 'Products/solutions/systems used in hospitals, other care centers or for out patient/home care' (ActionMedTech 2007: 65). This includes high-technology devices (equipment and supplies) as well as 'lower'-technology products used to assist healthcare professionals in their care of patients. *Medical devices* and *biomedical engineering* are two other terms commonly used as synonymous with medical technology.
2 The case study was developed during the European Union research project AEGIS (Advancing Knowledge-Intensive Entrepreneurship and Innovation for Economic Growth and Well-being in Europe), project number 225134. IMIT has administered the project, and our work has been funded by IMIT and by the University of Gothenburg. We appreciate all the comments during the AEGIS project on this work.
3 Some key references are Håkansson (1982), Håkansson and Snehota (1995), Håkansson *et al.* (2009) and Ford *et al.* (2011).
4 See, e.g. Håkansson (1987 and 1989), Laage-Hellman (1989 and 1997), Håkansson and Waluszewski (2007) and Ford *et al.* (2011: Ch. 7).
5 In their frequently cited overview article Salter and Martin (2001) identify six major mechanisms for diffusion of university research to industry: Increasing the stock of useful knowledge; Educating skilled graduates; Developing new

scientific instrumentation/methodologies; Shaping networks and stimulating social interaction; Enhancing the capacity for scientific and technological problem-solving; and Creating new firms.

6 This study is part of a longer stream of research about the life science industry in Sweden, and research-based companies in particular, conducted by the authors. See, e.g. Laage-Hellman (1990, 1993, 1998 and 2012) and Laage-Hellman *et al.* (2007 and 2009).

7 Chemiluminescence is the emission of light as the result of a chemical reaction. This phenomenon can be used for different applications, including for example gas analysis for detecting small amounts of impurities in air. NO is one example where the method allows determinations down to one part per billion.

8 Already in early 1993 the researchers had submitted a paper to *The Lancet*, a prestigious medical journal. It was not accepted, which later on turned out to be fortunate since publishing of the findings would have made patenting impossible.

9 Asthma is a chronic airway disease with high and increasing prevalence globally. It is estimated that more than 300 million people are affected. Control of the disease requires long-term and costly treatment adjusted to the degree of asthma. Early diagnosis in combination with appropriate therapy is assumed to substantially reduce the societal costs and improve the quality of life of the patients.

10 The term 'right of first refusal' is a contractual term that means that one party of an agreement has the option to acquire a certain asset from the other party. Only if the holder of this right turns down an offer to enter a business transaction may the owner sell the asset to someone else. This type of contractual right is common, for example, in agreements between researchers and sponsoring companies.

11 One of the founders says that not choosing Karolinska Innovation probably was a good decision. The university's innovation support system was still under development and he does not believe that at the time Karolinska Innovation would have contributed much.

12 For more details, see Laage-Hellman (2012).

13 Today there are more than 2000 studies that have been carried out.

14 As seen in Laage-Hellman (2012), other KIE ventures in medical technologies have benefited greatly from incubators and other publicly funded support organizations.

15 Companies started by clinical researchers often have from the beginning established relationships with clinical environments where the product can be tested.

References

ActionMedTech – Key Measures for Growing the Medical Device Industry in Sweden (2007) A report jointly published by the Royal Institute of Technology, Karolinska Institutet and Karolinska University Hospital.

Ford, D., Gadde, L.-E., Håkansson, H. and Snehota, I. (2011) *Managing Business Relationships*, Chichester: Wiley.

Håkansson, H. (ed.) (1982) *International Marketing and Purchasing: An Interaction Approach*, Chichester: Wiley.

Håkansson, H. (ed.) (1987) *Industrial Technological Development: A Network Approach*, London: Croom Helm.

Håkansson, H. (1989) *Corporate Technological Behaviour: Cooperation and Networks*, London: Routledge.

Håkansson, H. and Snehota, I. (eds) (1995) *Developing Relationships in Business Networks*, London: Routledge.

Håkansson, H. and Waluszewski, A. (eds) (2007) *Knowledge and Innovation in Business and Industry – The Importance of Using Others*, London: Routledge.

Håkansson, H., Ford, D., Gadde, L.-E., Snehota, I. and Waluszewski, A. (2009) *Business in Networks*, Chichester: Wiley.

Laage-Hellman, J. (1989) 'Technological development in industrial networks', Acta Universitatis Upsaliensis, *Comprehensive Summaries of Uppsala Dissertations from the Faculty of Social Sciences 16*, Stockholm: Almqvist & Wiksell International (diss.).

Laage-Hellman, J. (1990) 'Utveckling av ny biomedicinsk teknik – en nätverksstudie, *STU-information 768–1990*, Stockholm: Swedish National Board for Technical Development.

Laage-Hellman, J. (1993) 'Forskningsbaserat medicintekniskt företagande', *B 1993:12*, Stockholm: NUTEK.

Laage-Hellman, J. (1997) *Business Networks in Japan: Supplier-Customer Interaction in Product Development*, London: Routledge.

Laage-Hellman, J. (1998) 'Den biomedicinska industrin i Sverige', *B 1998:8*, Stockholm: NUTEK.

Laage-Hellman, J. (2012) 'Exploring and exploiting networks for knowledge-intensive entrepreneurship', *Deliverable D1.7.7*, AEGIS.

Laage-Hellman, J., Rickne, A. and Stenborg, E. (2007) 'Biomedical firms in Western Sweden: A study of a regional innovation system from a biomedical firm's perspective', *RIDE/IMIT Working Paper No. 84426–024*, Gothenburg.

Laage-Hellman, J., McKelvey, M. and Johansson, M. (2009) 'Analysis of chain-linked effects of public policy: Effects on research and industry in Swedish life sciences within innovative food and medical technology', *VINNOVA Analysis VA 2009:20*, Stockholm: VINNOVA.

Lenzi, C., Bishop, K., Breschi, S., Buenstorf, G., Pllerena, P., Malerba, F., Mancusi, M.L. and McKelvey, M. (2010) 'New innovators and knowledge intensive entrepreneurship in European sector analyses', in Malerba, F. (ed.) *Knowledge Intensive Entrepreneurship and Innovation Systems: Evidence from Europe*, London: Routledge.

Malerba, F. (2002) 'Sectoral systems of innovation', *Research Policy*, 31: 247–264.

McKelvey, M. and Lassen, A.H. (2013a) *Managing Knowledge Intensive Entrepreneurship*, Cheltenham, UK: Edward Elgar Publishers.

McKelvey, M. and Lassen, A.H. (2013b) *How Entrepreneurs Do What They Do: Case Studies of Knowledge Intensive Entrepreneurship*, Cheltenham, UK: Edward Elgar Publishers.

McKelvey, M., Orsenigo, L. and Pammolli, F. (2004) 'Pharmaceuticals analyzed through the lens of sectoral innovation systems', in Malerba, F. (ed.) *Sectoral Systems of Innovation: Concepts, Issues and Analyses of Six Major Sectors in Europe*, Cambridge: Cambridge University Press: 73–120.

Salter, A.J. and Martin, B.R. (2001) 'The economic benefits of publicly funded basic research: A critical review', *Research Policy*, 30: 509–532.

12 Competing for product innovation in knowledge intensive industries

The case of the Digital Audio Players

Roberto Camerani, Nicoletta Corrocher and Roberto Fontana

1 Introduction

One of the most relevant aspects in the literature on knowledge intensive entrepreneurship concerns whether and the extent to what new firms engage in product innovation. The recent literature on this topic has highlighted that firms, in highly dynamic contexts characterized by rapid technical change, choose to compete in product innovation to achieve a competitive advantage and that firms differ in their product innovation strategies in terms of timing and frequencies of new product introduction (Greenstein and Wade, 1998), extent of differentiation (Stavins, 1995), previous experience in the same industry or in a different one (Bayus and Agarwal, 2007). This literature has highlighted how differences across firms in terms of product strategies are likely to lead to important differences in terms of performance and survival (Stavins, 1995; Fontana and Nesta, 2009).

This chapter looks at product innovation strategy in order to highlight differences across categories of firms. By focusing on the case of Digital Audio Players (DAPs), it aims at identifying the main characteristic of the DAPs available in the market, and at investigating whether technical change has led to convergence in product design or to the persistence of heterogeneous products over time, and whether differences exist across firms concerning the product innovation strategies. The analysis carried out in this chapter is two-fold, and focuses on two dimensions: product innovation and differentiation over time, and the strategies of two categories of firms in the market. Regarding the first dimension, our empirical analysis builds upon Koski and Kretschmer (2007) who have analysed the product innovation strategies of firms in the mobile phone industry in terms of changes in the handset design. Their approach looks at product differentiation over time, by focusing specifically on firms' product innovation strategy along two sets of product dimensions: vertical and horizontal.

In particular, vertical innovation occurs when producers improve one of the product's technical characteristics, while horizontal innovation takes place when new additional features are introduced. Regarding the second dimension, the focus is on two categories of firms in the industry: de-novo and diversifiers. De-novo are firms who did not produce portable music players before entering the DAPs industry (such as Apple), while diversifiers are firms who were formerly active in the portable music player industry, before entering the DAPs industry (such as Sony).

Using this approach, we will provide an answer to the following questions. What are the strategies of innovation and product differentiation in the DAPs market? Did firms follow the same innovation strategies or can we identify differences across firm categories (i.e. de-novo vs diversifiers)? The structure of the chapter is as follows. Section 2 provides the relevant background information on the evolution of the DAP industry, in terms of technology evolution and types of firms competing in the market. Section 3 introduces the data set that will be used for the empirical analysis and reports the results of the empirical analysis. Section 4 concludes and draws some economic and policy implication for firms in knowledge intensive industries.

2 The context: the evolution of the DAP sector

Mobile listening of recorded music became a very common practice from the end of the 1970s when the Sony Walkman was developed and launched (Shaw, 2008: 140). Technical change accompanied mobile music listening by gradually improving existing music players and also by developing some radical new products such as CD players and MiniDisc players. However, since the end of the 1990s a series of factors such as the invention of MP3 music codec, the development of higher capacity storage media and the diffusion of the Internet triggered a pervasive process of change that dramatically modified the way that music was listened, exchanged and consumed – changes that revolutionized the whole music industry. One of the main consequences stemming from the advent of digital music has been the proliferation of the so-called Digital Audio Players (DAPs), portable devices able to load and play digital audio files. The extraordinary success encountered by these products is both a consequence and one of the triggers of the digital music revolution.

DAPs are not radically new products, but, similarly to other types of innovations (Levinthal, 1998), they rather represent a significant incremental improvement along an existing 'technological trajectory' (Dosi, 1982) going from analogue, to digital, and eventually to compressed digital music, with different kinds of storage media and music players following one another. In addition, the evolution of music from analogue to digital had a significant impact on the whole music industry and on the way music was consumed and distributed.

2.1 The advent of DAPs

2.1.1 The rise of digital audio compression: the MP3 encoding format

The advent of DAPs started with the introduction of technologies of digital audio compression (audio codecs). The diffusion of these technologies depended on a combination of factors. First of all, although CDs became a very popular audio storage medium, the number of songs that a single CD could store was too limited. In addition, computers equipped with CD-ROM drives allowed users to extract the content of audio CDs and copy it on their hard drives. However, this operation generated music files that were too large to be quickly transferred online, and required hard drives with considerable capacity. In addition, audio compression was required in order to encode digital audio into other formats, such as, for instance, Digital TV, and DVD. For these reasons, during the 1990s a number of audio compression codecs were introduced. Digital audio allowed treating audio tracks as simple data files; audio compression contributed to make them more manageable, more easily storable and transmittable through the Internet. This allowed the creation of portable devices (DAPs) able to store and reproduce these kinds of audio files. In addition, these files could be potentially stored in any kind of memory, be it a digital tape, a hard drive, a solid state memory, a CD-ROM, etc. For the first time there was a separation between music and the physical storage medium containing it.

During the 1990s several codecs were invented. However, one of them (MP3) soon became a standard for audio compression, giving the name to the whole category of devices able to read compressed audio files. MP3 stands for MPEG-1 Audio Layer 3 that is a patented digital audio codec developed by the Moving Picture Experts Group (MPEG) that was approved by ISO/IEC in 1991 and then published in 1993, becoming an international standard.[1] MP3 is one of the audio codecs included in MPEG-1 (MPEG-1 part 3-audio-layer 3), and also used in the more recent MPEG-2 standard. MP3 allowed compressing digital audio, considerably reducing the amount of data required by each audio file. However, MP3 is a lossy codec, meaning that the compression is achieved at the expense of audio quality. In any case, MP3 allowed a very significant reduction, with a compress ratio of $10:1$ or even $12:1$ without a noticeable quality reduction by human hearing.

The main consequence of the introduction of the MP3 was that it became rapidly a de facto standard for home audio encoding (Holmes, 2006: 203). Moreover, in that period, new computers were equipped with more powerful CPUs, which allowed music to be convert from a CD into MP3 in seconds, instead of minutes. Bigger hard drives allowed to store a large amount of MP3s, allowing users to rip their entire collection of CDs and to create large libraries of MP3 files. Software able to reproduce MP3 files (such as Winamp), or able to organize music libraries (such as Music-match Jukebox) became popular. At the same time Internet broadband connections were diffusing rapidly. New Internet applications allowed users not just to download music, but also to share their personal music library with all the other members of the community. This was the case of Napster and of a multitude of other peer-to-peer (P2P) applications.

2.1.2 The early stages

Saying that the invention of compression codecs, and in particular MP3, made possible the introduction of DAPs is certainly right. However, the invention of compression codecs has most probably influenced the timing of introduction of DAPs, but not determined their existence. The introduction of compression codecs that took place during the 1990s was very timely, especially considering that the current hard drive sizes and Internet connection speed were limiting the use and the transfer of digital music. In fact, the increase in hard drives size (and the drop of their price) and the diffusion of much faster Internet connections that have been experienced in the following years, would eventually have allowed users to copy their music into their computers and portable players and transfer it online without the need of any compression codec.

The first kinds of digital portable music players using MP3 format have been CD players able to read and reproduce MP3 files (MP3-CD). The media used by this kind of players were CD-ROMs in which MP3 files were saved as data files. In this way, a single CD could include much more music.[2] These CD players compatible with MP3 and Sony's MiniDisc players can be de facto considered portable players of digital audio. However, a DAP (or MP3 player) is a portable device able to store and play compressed digital audio files, in which there is also a separation between audio file and the physical storage medium containing it. In fact, the term Digital Audio Player is most commonly used to describe portable players that use non-removable erasable digital media, such as CDs and MDs (Holmes, 2006: 75). According to this definition of DAP, MP3-CD and MD players are only considered precursors of DAPs.

DAPs can be classified into several categories: flash players, hard drive (HD) players and Microdrive players, depending on the storage medium they use. Usually, flash players are small and lightweight devices, but with a limited storage space, while HD players are generally bigger and heavier, but with a much higher storage capacity. The last group of DAPs uses a Microdrive, which is still a hard drive. However, since it is very compactly sized, it has been used to produce DAPs more similar in size to flash based players. Microdrive players only achieved a limited use, since flash memories quickly overcame Microdrive's capacity, making them economically obsolete for DAPs.

In general, although some miniaturized MP3 players do not have any display, DAPs are often equipped with a screen (at the beginning mono-chromatic, then with colours). The DAPs display allows browsing the music library stored in the internal memory, and selecting the songs to play. Usually, MP3 players are able to read the metadata contained in the MP3 files tags, showing artist name, song title and other information during playback.

In addition to the main function of music listening, some models of DAPs have been equipped with additional features such as FM radio player or a voice recorder. After this, many more functions have been added, such as photo display, video playback, games, alarm/calendar, etc. DAPs are generally low consumption devices, since they do not necessitate mechanical parts to be operated, in contrast, for instance, with a CD player, which has to spin a CD in order to play it. This means that DAPs generally have a longer battery life. The main difference among DAPs regarding the battery is whether the player is equipped with a rechargeable battery or not.[3] Over time, the number of players with non-rechargeable battery gradually decreased, eventually having all the DAPs launched equipped with rechargeable battery. Figure 12.1 plots a timeline of the major events characterizing the evolution of the DAP industry.

The history of DAPs begins at the end of the 1990s when some firms started to patent inventions regarding MP3 players or to announce the launch of new products. In any case, the first MP3 players available were the MPMan created by the South Korean company SaeHanin 1998, and the Rio PMP300 launched by Diamond Multimedia a few months later

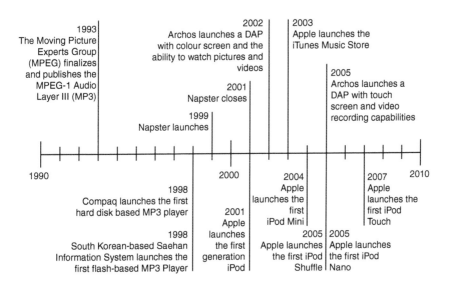

Figure 12.1 Major events in the evolution of the DAP industry.

(Knopper, 2009: 166).[4] Both players were equipped with a 32 MB flash memory and therefore providing a very limited space for storing MP3 files (not more than 10/12 songs). A potential solution to this lack of storage space was to use a hard drive as memory for DAPs. In 1998, Compaq used a 2.5" laptop hard disk to create the first hard drive based DAP, the Personal Jukebox (PJB-100) manufactured under licence by HanGo Electronics. This player had a 4.8 GB hard drive, making it possible to store more than 1,000 songs. In 2000, Creative launched the Nomad Jukebox, equipped with a 6 GB hard drive. These hard drive based DAPs coped with the issue of limited storage space of the first flash players; however, they had the disadvantage of being heavy and quite slow in loading the MP3 files (Knopper, 2009: 167).

In fact, the first DAPs suffered from at least three issues (Kahney, 2005; Knopper, 2009). First of all, they had problems related to the storage media. Flash memories still had a too limited storage space, while 2.5" hard drives (the same drives usually installed in laptops) could store much more music, but they were bulky and heavy, limiting the portability of the DAPs. Second, the first MP3 players had a problem of loading speed. Besides the very first models equipped with parallel links, most of the players had a USB 1.1 connection cable.[5] This type of connection was fast enough for flash players containing only a few songs, but too slow to fill up a 5 or 6 GB hard drive. Third, these first players were not very user friendly. In particular, both the user interface was not very easy to use, and also the software organizing music and allowing loading it onto the player was still at a very early stage.

2.1.3 Apple's iPod

In October 2001, Apple entered the MP3 players market, by launching its first iPod. The iPod, still rather far from being a perfect product, was only the first one of a long series of MP3 players that Apple launched, and that eventually led the firm to take over the industry. With this product, Apple attempted to provide a response to the above-mentioned issues that early DAPs were suffering from. One of the major advantages of the first Apple iPod was the storage medium. Apple used a Toshiba 1.8" hard drive with 5 GB storage space. This drive was significantly smaller than the hard drives used in the other DAPs (usually a laptop 2.5"), making the iPod much smaller than competitors' HD players. In addition, Apple signed an exclusive deal with Toshiba, preventing competitors from using the same technology (Knopper, 2009: 168). This hard drive could be used to store both audio and data, potentially making the iPod also a backup device. Regarding the transfer speed, Apple opted for a FireWire connection, which was much faster than parallel and USB 1.1.[6] All the MACs sold in that period were equipped with a FireWire port. In addition, the FireWire cable was also used to recharge the iPod battery. The iPod was also equipped with a quite large screen for the time being, and with a very intuitive user interface based on a mechanical scroll wheel. The software that connected Apple's iPod to MAC computers was iTunes. Thanks to iTunes, users were able to easily organize and manage their music libraries, and to load this music into their iPod.

Apple's iPod was certainly a highly innovative and groundbreaking product (Kahney, 2005: 39). It was small, compact, with an appealing design, and easy to use. However, at the beginning, Apple's market was still limited, since the product was quite highly priced (US$399), and not compatible with Windows based PCs (Knopper, 2009: 171), but only with MACs. Moreover, in that period, the FireWire connection was mostly used to transfer video streams recorded with portable camcorders, and it was not equipped in many Windows based PCs.

After the first iPod, Apple released several improved versions. Since the very beginning, the user interface evolved into a touch sensitive scroll wheel. Then, the iPod became compatible with the Windows operating system, first in 2002 through the software Musicmatch, and then in 2003 thanks to the launch of iTunes 4.1 for Windows. In addition, the release of the USB 2.0 standard made FireWire unnecessary.[7] For this reason, Apple started selling iPods equipped with both cables, with USB 2.0 eventually substituting FireWire connection. Apple dedicated a relatively small budget to the promotion of the iPod, spending only $25 million to promote the launch of the first iPod (Kahney, 2005: 44). However, since 2001, iPod sales increased steadily, as reported in Figure 12.2.[8]

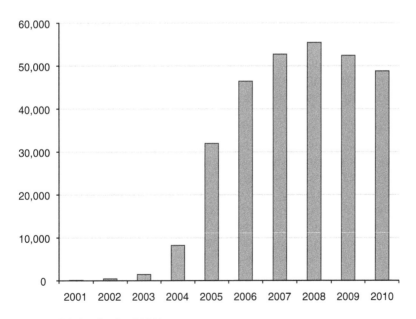

Figure 12.2 iPod sales ('000).

Note
* Only October–December.

More or less the sales tripled every year: 125,000 units in 2001, 470,000 in 2002, and 1,451,000 in 2003. One of the main forces driving this success was word-of-mouth, facilitated by the easy recognisability of the white iPod's ear buds, and also the constant attention that media dedicated to the iPod. A major increase in sales occurred in 2004, when Apple launched its first iPod with colour screen and photo display capability, with up to 60 GB memory, and also started differentiating the production. In fact, in that year, Apple launched the first iPod Mini, based on a Hitachi's 4 GB Microdrive. This kind of memory is a miniature hard drive, which combines a sufficient high storage capacity with a very small size. It allowed to produce an iPod even more portable than the classic iPod, but with more storage capacity than flash based players sold by competitors. The combined sales of iPod Classic and iPod mini overcame eight million units in 2004, making the iPod the undisputed market leader in the DAP sector.

Apple innovative activity did not rest. In 2005, a new iPod with video capabilities and memory up to 160 GB was launched, together with two new different iPods based on flash memory. The first model was the iPod Shuffle, a highly miniaturized player without screen and with the shape of a USB memory stick. This player was the most simple and portable device sold by Apple. The other product was the iPod Nano, replacing the Mini with a very slim size, colour screen and up to 4 GB storage space. Both iPod Shuffle and iPod Nano experienced great success, allowing Apple to sell almost 32 million iPods in 2005. After 2005, Apple periodically launched new versions of iPod Nano, Classic and Shuffle, with new colours, redesigned aesthetics, new features and more storage space. Finally, in 2007 Apple launched another line of DAPs, the iPod Touch, a player with a multi-touch screen that served also as user interface, with also another set of features, such as Wi-Fi connection, Internet browsing and games.

Certainly, one of the factors that contributed to iPod's success was its seamless integration with iTunes software. Also iTunes evolved with the iPod, making it possible to load videos, share music within local networks, rip and burn CDs, etc. Moreover, in April 2003 iTunes became a digital media online store, selling legal music in digital format, and later also video content, such as movies and TV series episodes.

A slight decline in sales occurred in 2009 and 2010. This may depend on two causes. First of all, in 2007 Apple launched its smartphone, the iPhone, whose sales are not reported in the figure. This phone is also a DAP and probably attracted some previous or potential iPod customers. Second, even considering product replacements and upgrades, the diffusion process of iPods was already reaching its final phase, since most of its potential adopters had already purchased it.

2.2 The technical evolution of DAPs

From the technical point of view, DAPs significantly improved during the last ten years, in two ways. On one side, DAPs improved in some technical characteristics, such as memory, size, etc. The main technical improvement of DAP regarded the storage space. In fact, HD players gradually increased their capacity reaching 320 GB in 2008 (64 times bigger than the first 5 GB hard drive player). Flash memories lagged behind for some years, but caught up rapidly. For many years, some early models of flash players had such a limited storage space that they could almost only be used as voice recorders. Until 2004 the storage space of flash players was not more than 1 GB. However, flash memory capacity increased dramatically during the end of the 2000s, reaching 64 GB in 2009 (more than 2000 times bigger than the first 32 MB flash player). In addition, DAPs became smaller and smaller. This trend mostly regarded flash players, which, considering the very small size of a flash memory, were more predisposed for miniaturization. Also the use of more powerful and slimmer batteries contributed to the development of more miniaturized models. In addition, the vast majority of DAPs producers gradually discontinued non-rechargeable batteries, in favour of rechargeable lithium batteries.

On the other side, DAPs have been progressively equipped with an increasing number of additional features. Some features installed since the very first years have been voice recording, FM radio player and FM radio recorder. This was the case, for example, of several early models of flash based players. Another stream of visual features was added later starting from the proliferation of colour displays. In fact, at the beginning, most of the DAPs had very small monochromatic screens, sometimes with only 2–3 lines of text. Then some early models with colour displays started appearing already in 2002; however they widely diffused only in the period 2004/2005. Together with colour displays, DAPs started to be equipped with several additional functions such as photo display and video playback (especially in the case of HD players that had a sufficiently large memory to store video files). In addition, some models have even been equipped with a video camera, making it possible to take pictures and record videos.

Another feature that encountered a certain success has been audio and video podcast.[9] Finally, some more recent technical developments regarded the user interface, with the launch of some models controlled through sophisticated touch screens. In general, these kinds of product also had several other capabilities, such as Internet browsing and emailing through wireless connection, games playing, etc.

2.3 Competition in the DAP sector

Besides Apple, many companies entered into the DAP market. CNET, a website specialized in reviewing consumer electronics with a specific section about DAPs, since 1999 has reviewed a large number of MP3 players, listing about 80 different producers (even though most of them only produced one single model). However, only a small number of companies have seriously attempted to erode Apple's supremacy. These firms can be divided in two groups: diversifiers and de-novo firms.

Diversifiers are firms which were formerly active in the portable music player industry (producing, for instance, portable CD players), before entering in the DAPs industry. The most important firms in this category include Sony and Philips who shaped the portable CD player industry for decades, but failed to successfully maintain their leadership in the new emerging DAPs industry. These companies reacted to iPod success, launching new products, which were not distant from Apple in terms of price, characteristics and features. However, they never met Apple's sales. At the end of the 1990s, when the MP3 codec was invented and the DAPs began to emerge, the innovative activity of these companies was mostly directed to the development of new storage media, such as MiniDisc (MD), Digital Compact Cassette (DCC) and Digital Audio Tape (DAT). However, one of the major innovations brought by audio compression was to free music from any specific storage medium. In other words, songs could be stored in every kind of memory, such as a hard drive, a Microdrive or a flash memory.

These developments notwithstanding, these firms were still concentrating on an old conception of music players, in which music almost coincided with the storage medium (Knopper, 2009). Audio compression allowed by MP3 and other audio codecs broke this idiosyncrasy and apparently incumbents have not been able to react to this change. Moreover, Sony had for many years a sort of disregard for MP3, aiming at diffusing its proprietary codec (ATRAC1, ATRAC3 and ATRAC3plus). For this reason, some of the first Sony DAPs were not MP3 compatible. This meant that the whole users' collections of MP3 files had to be converted to ATRAC3 before they could be loaded onto the player. It is true that other competitors had a preferred audio coding, starting from Apple that sold songs in AAC (Advanced Audio Coding). However, the majority of DAPs were still backward compatible with the MP3 format. Finally, Sony, being both a DAP producer and a music label (Sony Music Entertainment), always had an internal conflict regarding digital music. In fact, Sony was selling MP3 players, which could also contain audio files exchanged through the Internet, but at the same time was part of RIAA (Recording Industry Association of America), strongly opposing file sharing (Knopper, 2009: 174).

Other diversifiers include Creative, iRiver and Samsung. Creative Technology is a company based in Singapore established in 1981 and it is one of the world's market leaders in the production of sound cards for computers, sound systems and speakers. It also entered into the sector quite early, offering one of the first HD based players (Nomad), followed by the

Muvo and Zen series. However, Creative never managed to transfer the knowledge acquired with the production of sound and audio components to the market of portable devices, becoming a follower of Apple.

De-novo are firms which, like Apple, had never produced portable music players before entering the DAPs industry. This is the case, for instance, of Archos and Microsoft. Archos is a French company established in 1988, initially producing different kinds of computer peripherals during the 1990s. Archos was also an early entrant into the DAP market, soon emerging as one of the most innovative and venturesome companies in the sector. In fact, Archos has been a pioneer for many incremental innovations of DAPs. For instance, Archos Multimedia Jukebox, launched in September 2002, had a colour display and the capability of showing pictures and video two years before the launch of iPod Photo and three years before the iPod Video. Moreover, Archos PMA400, launched in January 2005, was equipped with a touch screen, Wi-Fi connection and the possibility to record video, more than two years before the launch of the iPod Touch.

Microsoft entered into the market more recently, trying to challenge Apple's leadership by offering a system-type of product very similar to iPod/iTunes. Microsoft Zune was launched in 2006, and was followed by a series of improved models with higher storage capacity and more functions. Zune worked with Zune software, an application similar to iTunes, which also started selling audio and video contents through the Zune Marketplace. One of Microsoft's advantages was its very large customer base already using Microsoft operating systems. Moreover, even if Microsoft did not have any direct experience in portable audio players, it had some kind of expertise with digital audio, having developed a proprietary audio codec, WMA (Windows Media Audio), that was mostly used for online streaming applications. Moreover, most of its customers already used Microsoft's software to manage and listen to music (Windows Media Player). In any case, despite these potential advantages and besides a considerable economic and advertising effort, Microsoft Zune never threatened Apple leadership. Other firms in this category include Cowon and Sandisk.

It has to be noted that Apple was neither the first player entering the market, nor the first one introducing some of the major innovations (hard drive, colour screen, touch screen interface, etc.). Moreover, Apple could not count on specific knowledge on audio players, since it did not have direct experience in the sector. In addition, Apple's iPods were not necessarily superior to competitors' products, at least from a purely technical point of view. However, none of the above mentioned players managed to weaken Apple leadership in the sector. Some of the major strengths of Apple were its attention to usability, to product design (both architectural design and aesthetical) and to the demand side. In particular, Apple has been able to recognize and in some cases to anticipate users' needs, and continuously innovate in order to fulfil them (Kahney, 2005). Another aspect that deserves particular attention is iPod's seamless integration with iTunes. In fact, Apple did not just sell a DAP, but a bundle of product and services, materializing in a piece of hardware, but usable only thanks to a software (iTunes), which expanded iPod capabilities, by offering an additional series of services to users.

3 Measuring innovation in the DAP sector

The DAPs industry has experienced a very rapid rate of technical change during the last decade. In order to capture the technical evolution of the sector, an original set of data on 586 DAPs launched from 2001 to 2009 has been built. The data set includes the launch date and launch price, as well as several technical characteristics of the DAPs (size, storage space, functions, etc.). These technical characteristics are listed in Table 12.1 below.

The main source of data has been the website CNET.com, a website offering buyers' guides and reviews of these products. Other additional sources have been PCMagazine.com, Wikipedia and the producers' websites. The products have been selected by including the ten DAP brands with the highest numbers of products, according to CNET's classification. Considering that the DAP sector is a very concentrated market with the market leader accounting for a very high market share, including the ten top brands will ensure that the data set includes most of the products actually available on the market. In addition, even though CNET lists a higher number of producers, the vast majority of them only launched one DAP.

Table 12.1 List of product characteristics

Characteristic name	Variable type
Memory type	Categorical (hard disk, flash, Minidisc)
Display	Categorical (no screen, monochromatic, colour)
Storage space (in GB)	Continuous
Screen size (no. of pixels, e.g. 128 × 64)	Continuous
Size (width, depth, high in inches)	Continuous
Weight (in ounces)	Continuous
Estimated battery life (in hours)	Continuous
Rechargeable battery	Dummy
Radio FM	Dummy
Voice recorder	Dummy
Video recorder	Dummy
Radio FM recorder	Dummy
Photo display	Dummy
Video playback	Dummy
Built-in speakers	Dummy
Touch screen	Dummy

These ten DAP producers have been classified as de-novo or diversifiers according to their previous experience in the portable music players industry. In particular, the data set includes five de-novo firms (Apple, Archos, Cowon, Microsoft and Sandisk) launching 211 DAPs in total, and five diversifiers (Creative, iRiver, Philips, Samsung and Sony) that launched 375 DAPs.

The data set contains only verifiable variables. For this reason, although the sources of data provided also some users' opinions on product aesthetics or usability, this type of information has not been taken into consideration. The only variable with some missing cases is launch price (14.8 per cent of missing cases). All the other variables are complete.

DAP players can be divided into three product families – flash, hard disk (HD) and Microdrive players – depending on the type of memory used to store music files. In some cases, these types of players will be analysed separately, in order to test whether these groups of products evolved in a different way. Most of the DAPs in the data set are flash players (437); HD players are 126, while Microdrive players are only 23. The number of Microdrive players is too small to be analysed separately. A Microdrive is a small hard drive used in some DAPs models in order to achieve a storage space comparable to the one of HD players but with the size of a flash player. They have been used only for a short period of time since they were discontinued when flash memories overcame Microdrive's storage space making their use pointless. For these reasons Microdrive players will be analysed together with flash players.

Figure 12.3 plots the number of DAPs launched in each year by type of player, and the cumulative number of players.

The number of players launched rises over time, reaching a peak in the period 2004–2005 and then declines over time. This makes the cumulative trend follow a sort of s-shaped curve, similar to a diffusion curve. The graphs show also that flash players always outnumber HD players, and that the decline in the launch of HD players in the last periods is much sharper than in the case of flash players.

Figure 12.4 shows the number of DAPs launched by the two categories of firms (de-novo and diversifiers) in each period.

For simplicity, only the cumulative curves are displayed. First of all, we notice that diversifiers have been much more prolific than de-novo firm in terms of number of products. Each diversifier launched on average 75 players, compared to only 42 launched by de-novo firms. In addition, looking at the curves, we can see that the two kinds of firms followed quite different strategies. De-novo firms kept a balance between flash and HD players over time, and they also significantly reduced the overall number of products launched over time, with both lines becoming flatter over time. On the contrary, the products launched by diversifiers are very unbalanced towards flash players, as they nearly stopped producing HD players after 2005. In addition, their production of new flash players significantly expanded after 2005, and increased at a much higher rate.

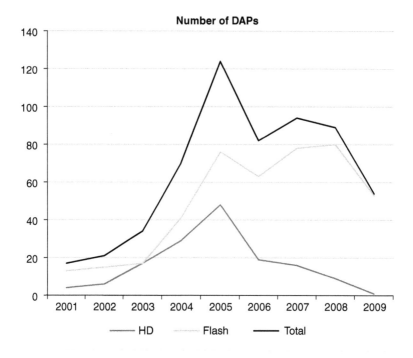

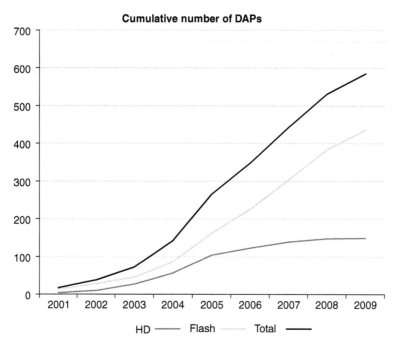

Figure 12.3 Frequency and cumulative distribution of DAPs launched in each year.

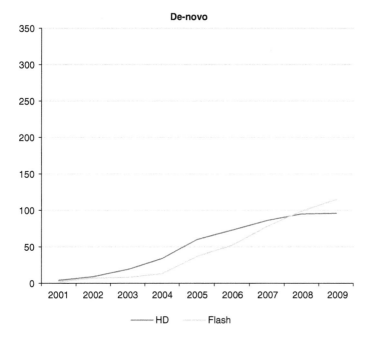

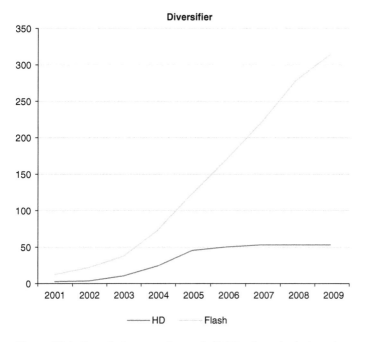

Figure 12.4 Cumulative number of DAPs launched by de-novo firms and diversifiers.

While analysing these graphs one should bear in mind that launch of a new product only reflects the innovation and diversification strategies of a firm, but it is not an indicator of success. For instance, we know that Apple (which is part of the de-novo group), has been quite parsimonious in the number of products launched compared with other companies, but, at the same time, it became the market leader in the sector.

Regarding product characteristics, DAPs have improved in several ways during recent years. In general, they have become smaller, with larger storage memories, and equipped with new functions. Since the main objective of this section is to study the technical innovation in the sector, the first step will be to present the definition of innovation that will be used in the analysis. Product innovation can occur in two ways. First of all, DAP producers can improve any of the product's technical characteristics (e.g. storage space, size, etc.). This kind of innovation will be defined (for the purposes of this chapter) as vertical innovation. On the other side, innovation can occur by offering new products with new additional features (e.g. picture display, video playback, touch screen, etc.). This kind of innovation will be defined as horizontal innovation. Table 12.2 reports the reclassification of the characteristics according to these dimensions.

The evolution of the products along this set of characteristics will be used to map technical change in the industry. Moreover, another dimension that will be taken into consideration is the degree of similarity among products. By measuring the average differences among products in each period, it will be possible to test whether firms are converging towards similar products or they continue to offer differentiated products. Convergence or similarity will be assessed by coefficients of variation calculated for each characteristic in each period of time. In particular, the coefficient of variation is calculated by dividing the standard deviation of a certain

Table 12.2 Classification of product characteristics

Vertical	Horizontal
Storage space (in GB)	Graphic features
Screen size (in pixel units)	Colour screen
Size (in cubic inches)	Pictures display
Weight (in ounces)	Video playback
Battery life (in hours)	Audio and multimedia features
	Radio FM
	Voice recording
	Radio FM recording
	Video recording
	Extra features
	Rechargeable battery
	Built-in speakers
	Touch screen

characteristic by its mean each year. Therefore, a coefficient approaching zero indicates that firms' product strategies are converging towards a similar design, regarding that particular characteristic.

Figure 12.5 reports technical change in the DAP industry concerning one of the most important characteristics: storage space. The values observed in the graph on the left hand side represent the mean of the storage space (in GB) offered by the models launched in that year. The observations on the graph on the right hand side display the maximum storage space offered by at least one of the models launched in that year.

The figure indicates that storage space increased significantly over time both for HD players and flash players. HD players started from a 5 GB hard drive reaching a maximum of 320 GB in 2008. Flash players have a much smaller storage space than HD players, however, they showed a much greater increase, passing from 32 MB to a maximum of 64 GB.

Figure 12.6 plots the evolution in the number of pixels.

This variable measures the screen resolution, but it can be used as a proxy for screen size.[10] Also the average number of pixels increased over time. The period of highest growth in screen size is around 2005–2006. This is also the period in which an increasing number of players started to be equipped with colour screen, giving also the possibility to show pictures and videos. These new functions also required a bigger screen in order to provide a better user experience. The drop during the last period may be due to the declining number of players introduced annually combined with the fact that the data collection has been carried out in the period October–November 2009 and hence the products launched after that period have not been considered, resulting in a right truncation of the last year. On average hard disk players have much bigger screens than flash players. However, in 2007 flash players reached their maximum number of pixels, which is equivalent to the maximum for HD players reached one year before. In any case, the screen size cannot grow unlimitedly, given the size of the device. Some touch screen DAPs have a display already covering the entire surface of the device. In addition, another limit to the growth of screen resolution is that a further increase in pixel density in a handheld device might not even be discernible by the human eye.

The next product feature taken into consideration is the size of the player (see Figure 12.7).

In particular, two measures are considered: the volume in cubic inches and the weight in ounces. As expected, flash players are considerably smaller and lighter than HD players. Moreover, the average and minimum sizes of players declined considerably over time. However, this trend is not monotonic for HD players, since this type of player experienced an increase in both the average size and weight in the period 2006–2007. This seems to be linked with the emergence of colour screens. In fact in that period a number of HD players with new functions, bigger batteries and

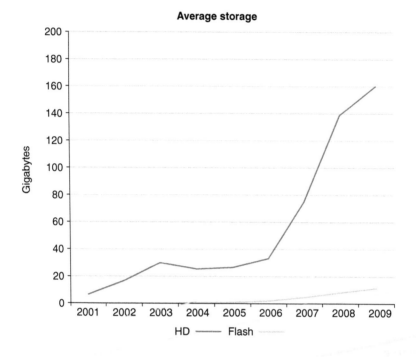

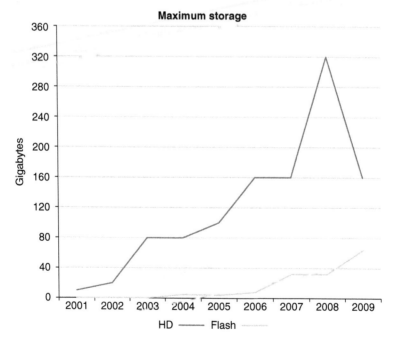

Figure 12.5 DAPs' average and maximum storage space by year.

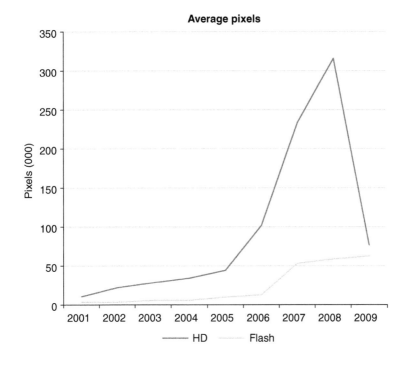

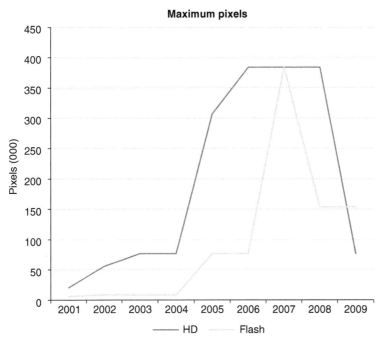

Figure 12.6 DAPs' average and maximum number of pixels by year.

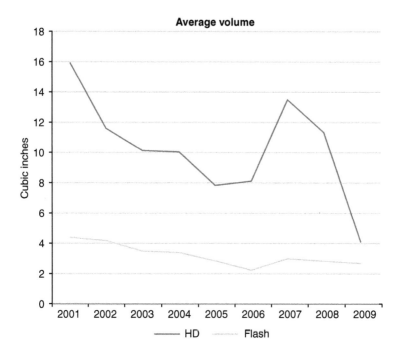

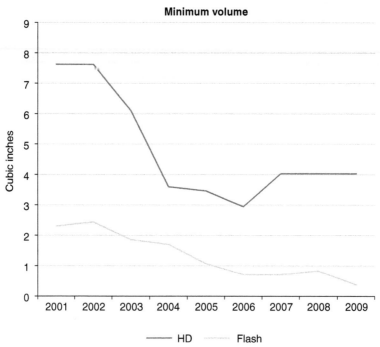

Figure 12.7 DAPs' average and minimum size (volume and weight) by year.

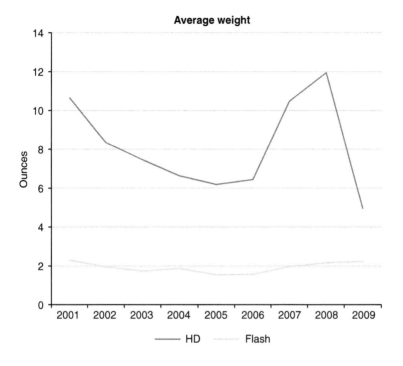

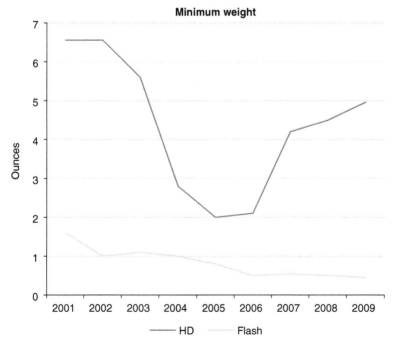

Figure 12.7 Continued.

screens were launched, but these improvements came at the expense of the size of the devices, which were necessarily bigger than their predecessors.

The last vertical innovation characteristic considered is battery life (Figure 12.8).

In this case there is a trade-off between HD and flash players. On one side, HD players are bigger, and consequently they can be equipped with a bigger and more powerful battery. On the other side, although flash players cannot accommodate large batteries, they do not have any mechanical part to operate (such as a hard drive) and thus they have the advantage of having a lower power consumption, and hence a longer battery life. This trade-off among HD and flash players makes them quite similar regarding their battery life, with HD players lasting longer than flash players in every period except for the last one. In particular, the average battery life of the players started around ten hours of audio playing reaching a maximum of 60 hours for HD players and 40 hours for flash players.

The next set of figures regards horizontal innovation. This type of innovation is carried out by equipping the product with new functions. These functions have been divided in three groups: graphic features (colour screen, picture display and video playback), audio and multimedia features (radio FM, voice recording, radio FM recording and video recording) and extra features (rechargeable battery, built-in speakers and touch screen).

The first figure plots the evolution of graphic features (Figure 12.9).

Since the variables considered by this kind of graphs are all dichotomous, the vertical axis represents the percentage of players in a specific period of time that were equipped with that particular characteristic. First of all, colour displays were launched for the first time in 2003 for HD players and in 2004 for flash players. This feature has been adopted by an increasing number of players, and it was followed by the implementation of both picture and video display. Video playback was possible also before colour screen, however, only a limited number of monochromatic players were equipped with this feature.

Figure 12.10 shows the trend for audio and multimedia characteristics.

First of all, radio FM and voice recording are the most common features. Moreover, both radio FM and voice recorders have been installed more frequently in flash players than HD players. This issue needs some further considerations. In fact, already in the first periods almost 50 per cent of the flash players were also radio players and voice recorders. Since in the same period most of these players also had a very limited storage space (e.g. 32 MB), it is possible to say that a certain group of flash players, at least in the first years, were mainly radio players and voice recorders.

The players belonging to this particular market niche were still Digital Audio Players; however, their main task was to record voice. On the other side, also FM recording is a feature much more used by flash players, which however, has been progressively dismissed after 2004.[11] Finally, video recording is still a feature used by only a limited number of products.

The last group of features are summarized in Figure 12.11.

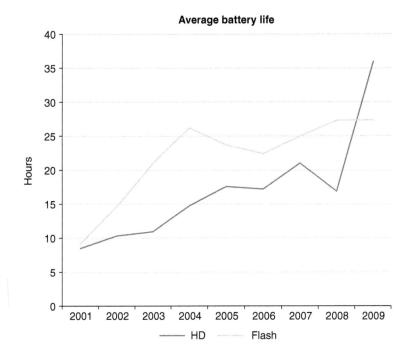

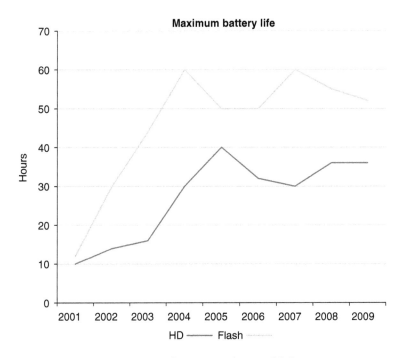

Figure 12.8 DAPs' average and maximum battery life by year.

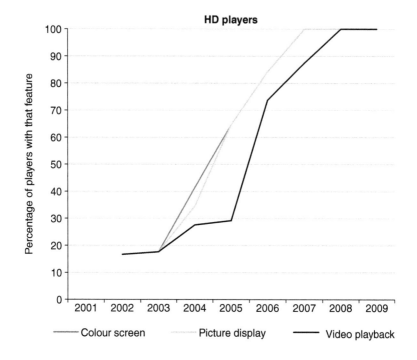

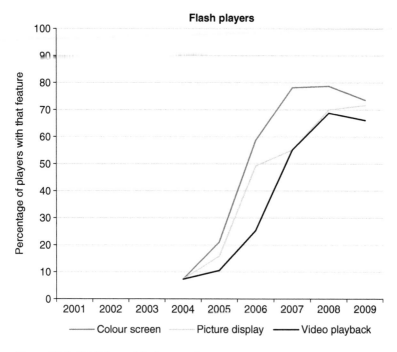

Figure 12.9 DAPs' graphic features by year.

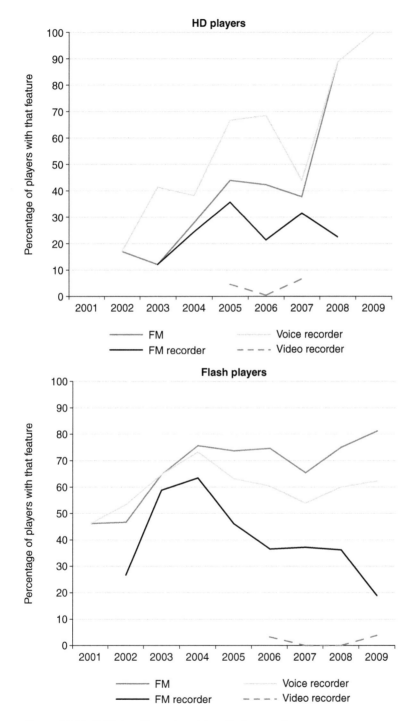

Figure 12.10 DAPs' audio and multimedia features by year.

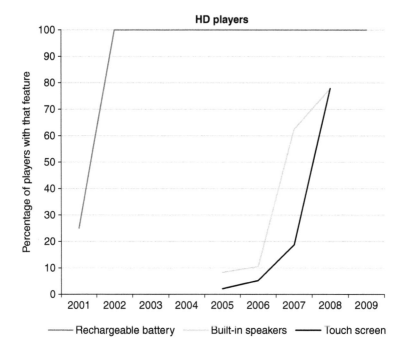

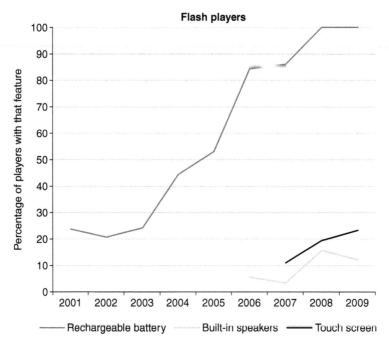

Figure 12.11 DAPs' extra features by year.

One of these features is quite relevant: rechargeable battery. Since users do not have to purchase and provide the player with new batteries each time, the usability and the value of a player with rechargeable battery is higher than the value of a product without them. This feature has been provided to all HD players since 2002, perhaps because the costs of replacing batteries for these devices would be much higher, since HD players need more energy as they have to power a hard drive. However, flash players show a much slower trend in the adoption of rechargeable batteries. Regarding the other features, built-in speakers are increasingly installed in HD players, after 2004. On the other side touch screens were launched for the first time in 2005 for HD players and 2006 for flash players, and encountered increasing application, especially in the case of HD players.

The trends of vertical and horizontal characteristics over time are useful to give an idea of which kind of technical innovation occurred in the DAP sector. However, it does not ensure that all the products followed the same pattern or, more importantly for our purpose, that product innovation strategies are converging across categories of firms. The next step in the analysis tries to shed some light on this issue.

3.1 Product innovation and firms' differentiation strategy

In this section we employ coefficients of variations to assess whether differences or similarities in the product innovation strategies across the two firm categories exist. The coefficients of variation have been calculated for the product characteristics analysed in the previous section. The analysis of the coefficients of variation will be visual and by firm category. In particular, within a specific firm category, a decreasing coefficient, approaching to zero, highlights a convergence around a specific design. On the contrary, a stable or increasing coefficient would signal that DAPs producers are still competing through product differentiation.

Figure 12.12 shows the coefficients of variation for our set of vertical innovation features.

First, we note that the level of the coefficients tend to be slightly higher for diversifiers than for de-novo producers, thus suggesting less convergence within the former and more convergence within the latter group. Second, though within each group and for most of the product features, we witness a general pattern of convergence, this convergence is achieved in rather different ways. In fact, while in the case of diversifiers the coefficient for most characteristics has always been flat, for de-novo firms differentiation in some characteristics has actually increased starting from 2003. This is the case for instance of weight and volume. Third, there is one characteristic, storage space, for which we observe opposite strategies: convergence among diversifiers but divergence among de-novo firms.

All in all, this evidence suggests that different types of firms choose to compete on specific characteristics and to pursue different strategies of

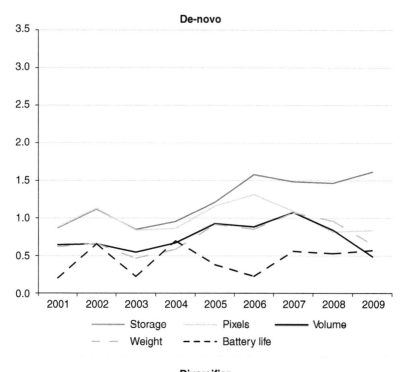

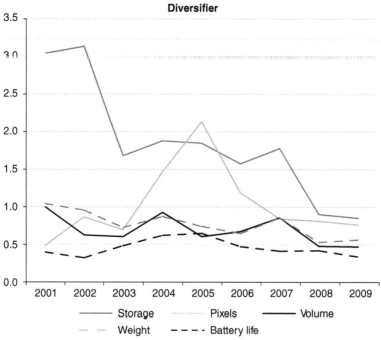

Figure 12.12 Coefficients of variation on vertical characteristics.

differentiation or convergence depending on the stage of the industry life cycle. The conclusion is that DAPs are still quite differentiated products, along vertical dimensions, and different designs of DAPs still coexist in the market as a result of specific strategies chosen by different types of firms.

Regarding the horizontal features the picture changes depending on the characteristics. Figure 12.13 shows the coefficients of variation for three horizontal graphical characteristics such as colour screen, picture display and video playback.

Both in the case of de-novo and in the case of diversifiers, the lines show a sharp and decreasing trend, suggesting that DAPs are actually converging towards a design in which the average player is equipped with colour screen and it is able to show pictures and play videos. Some differences seem to exist between the two groups of firms in terms of the time it took for convergence to occur with a process that seemed to have been faster for diversifiers than for de-novo firms. Also we can notice that diversifiers introduced graphical features later than de-novo firms.

In Figure 12.14 we report the coefficients of variation for another group of horizontal characteristics related to audio and multimedia.

In this case the pattern appears to have been rather different across type of firms. In the case of de-novo, we witness divergence until 2004 (particularly concerning FM and voice recording) and then convergence in the second half of the period, suggesting that attempts to diversify their products occurred along these dimensions. In the case of diversifiers instead, the coefficient of variation is low at the beginning of the period and then increases in the second half of the period particularly for FM recording, suggesting an increasing differentiation along this dimension.

Finally, in Figure 12.15 we consider a third group of horizontal characteristics: rechargeable battery, built in speakers, presence of touch screen.

In this case the following observations are in order. First, the coefficient of variation is much higher for de-novo than for diversifiers, suggesting that there is much more heterogeneity of product design strategies within the former than within the latter group. Second, different characteristics display rather different pattern of evolution over time and across firm categories. While the pattern is almost flat and stable for 'rechargeable battery' suggesting convergence in this characteristic, much more variety exists for speakers and touch screen with a rapid and substantial convergence in the case of de-novo firms and a much slower process in the case of diversifiers. Similarly to the case of graphic characteristics, diversifiers took longer to introduce touch screen features compared with de-novo.

4 Summary, conclusions and policy implications

In this chapter we have analysed product innovation in a very dynamic knowledge intensive industry characterized by rapid technical change, i.e. the Digital Audio Player sector. Our empirical analysis has highlighted that

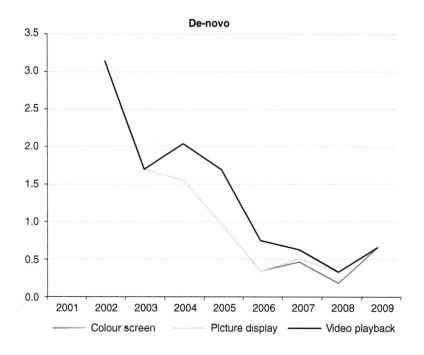

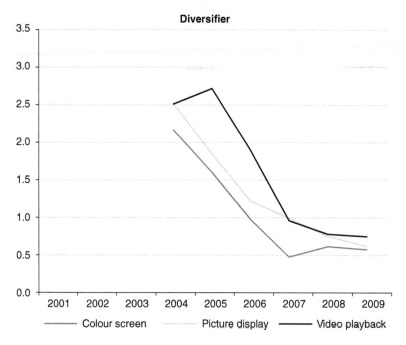

Figure 12.13 Coefficients of variation on horizontal characteristics (1).

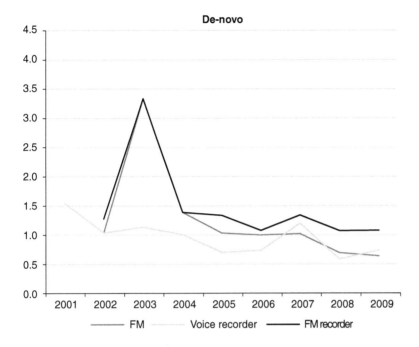

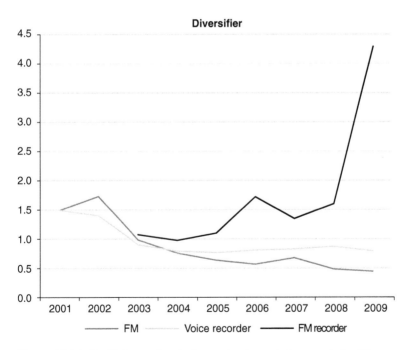

Figure 12.14 Coefficients of variation on horizontal characteristics (2).

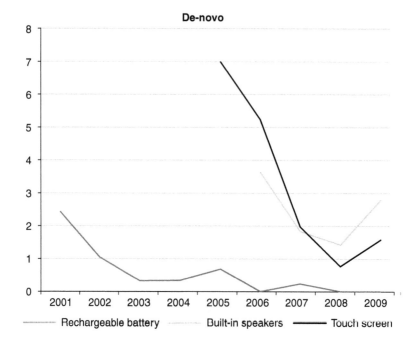

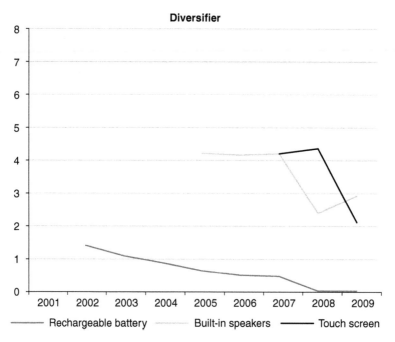

Figure 12.15 Coefficients of variation on horizontal characteristics (3).

product innovation occurred rapidly and focused upon two broad sets of product characteristics (horizontal and vertical).

Despite the fact that both de-novo firms and diversifiers engage in product innovation along these two dimensions, they seem to have followed quite different strategies.

First of all, de-novo firms engaged in innovation particularly in the first half of the period under consideration. As a result of that, convergence to a similar product design was achieved in the most recent period for most of the characteristics though some important differences still exist particularly for vertical dimensions. Diversifiers innovated more continuously and did not concentrate in a specific period of time. Also in this case products converged to a similar design; however our findings suggest that their level of design heterogeneity is generally higher than in the case of de-novo.

Second, the two kinds of firms decided to introduce some key features in different periods of time. This is the case of graphical characteristics (such as photo display and video playback) and touch screen; even though both groups of firms eventually equipped their products with these features, diversifiers took more time to do so.

Finally, we found significant differences in terms of number and kinds of product launched over time. De-novo firms continued to produce both lines of product in parallel. However, they reduced the rate of new product launch. Conversely, diversifiers mostly concentrated on flash players, and they dramatically expanded the launch of new products over time.

As a result of these different product innovation strategies pursued by the firms in the industry, a substantial variety of supply in the industry exists as convergence toward a similar design occurred but was rather low.

Three types of policy implications can be drawn from our findings. A straightforward policy implication is the need for any policy addressed to knowledge intensive entrepreneurship to nurture and sustain variety in order to promote innovation and competition. Despite the presence of an undisputable leader (Apple) in the industry, our evidence suggests that the DAP sector is largely innovative in terms of speed of new product introduction and variety of designs. From a policy perspective, ensuring that product variety is maintained is important to cater to different types of users. The second implication is that variety is the consequence of competition among firms that are heterogeneous in terms of product innovation strategy. This finding suggests that any policy intervention in support of innovation in knowledge intensive industries should take into account the heterogeneity of firms and strategies. The final implication that can be drawn from our finding concerns the timing of policy intervention. Our analysis has highlighted that firms engaged in innovation unevenly over time and that product design variety generally decreased over time. Thus the most effective policies aimed at sustaining variety should be implemented in the early-mid stages of industry life cycle when competition in knowledge intensive industries is still high.

Notes

1 ISO is the International Organization for Standardization, while IEC is the International Electrotechnical Commission. The MPEG is a working group of experts established by ISO and IEC in 1988 with the specific purpose to develop standards for audio and video encoding. The expert group was formed by members from industry, universities and research institutions and worked on some international standards that become very widespread, such as MPEG-1 (the encoding used for Video CDs) and MPEG-2 (used for Digital TV and DVD Video). A MPEG standard contains several encoding algorithms for both audio and video.

2 In fact, while an ordinary music CD can contain not more than 15/18 tracks, a CD-ROM can store even 200 MP3 files (depending on the songs' length and encoding bitrate).

3 Some players used one or two AA or AAA non-rechargeable batteries, which had to be substituted each time. Other players used built-in rechargeable batteries (usually lithium polymers or lithium ions batteries). Some other players allowed disposable batteries or rechargeable batteries (in general AA or AAA rechargeable batteries) to be used in the same device.

4 The MPMan was distributed in North America by Eiger Labs under the name MPMan F10. The company SaeHan Information System has then been acquired by iRiver in 2004.

5 Universal Serial Bus (USB) 1.1 was released in 1998 with a data transfer rate of 12 Mbit/s.

6 FireWire is Apple's brand name for IEEE 1394 serial bus interface standard. The first FireWire standard was released by the EEE P1394 Working Group in 1995 with a data transfer rate of up to 400 Mbit/s.

7 USB 2.0 was made available at the end of 2001 and has a data transfer rate of 480 Mbit/s.

8 Source: Apple Inc. Press Releases (http://en.wikipedia.org/wiki/File:Ipod_sales_ per_quarter.svg; last accessed 27/01/2011).

9 The name podcast derives from the combination the words *pod* (from Apple's iPod) and broadcast. However, this naming could be misleading, since the use of podcasts is not limited to iPods. In fact, all computers and several portable devices can download podcasts.

10 The pixels of the screen measure the resolution, and not necessarily the size of the screen. However, considering the small size of the DAP screen (not more than 4"), the screen resolution can be also used as a measure of the screen size.

11 This seems to coincide with the popularity gained by podcasting in the same period. An increasing number of radio stations started offering the possibility to regularly download some of their radio programmes (or part of them) through podcasting, making the FM recording function less useful.

References

Bayus, B.L. and Agarwal, R. (2007) 'The role of pre-entry experience, entry timing, and product technology strategies in explaining firm survival', *Management Science*, 53(12), 1887–1902.

Dosi, G. (1982) 'Technological paradigms and technological trajectories: a suggested interpretation of the determinants and directions of technical change', *Research Policy*, 11(3), 147–162.

Fontana, R. and Nesta, L. (2009) 'Product innovation and survival in a high-tech industry', *Review of Industrial Organization*, 34(4), 287–306.

Greenstein, S.M. and Wade, J.B. (1998) 'The product life cycle in the commercial mainframe computer market, 1968–1982', *The RAND Journal of Economics*, 772–789.

Holmes, T. (2006) *The Routledge Guide to Music Technology*. New York, NY: Routledge.

Kahney, L. (2005) *The Cult of iPod*. San Francisco, CA: No Starch Press.

Knopper, S. (2009) *Appetite for Self-destruction: The Spectacular Crash of the Record Industry in the Digital Age*. London: Simon & Schuster UK.

Koski, H. and Kretschmer, T. (2007) 'Innovation and dominant design in mobile telephony', *Industry and Innovation*, 14(3), 305–324.

Levinthal, D.A. (1998) 'The slow pace of rapid technological change: gradualism and punctuation in technological change', *Industrial and Corporate Change*, 7(2), 217–247.

Shaw, D. (2008) *Technoculture: The Key Concepts*. Oxford: Berg.

Stavins, J. (1995) 'Model entry and exit in a differentiated-product industry: the personal computer market', *The Review of Economics and Statistics*, 77, 571–584.

Part III
Countries

13 Entrepreneurial orientation of knowledge-based enterprises in Central and East Europe[1]

Slavo Radosevic and Esin Yoruk

1 Introduction

There is a widespread recognition that entrepreneurship is not simply an individual matter but also refers to characteristics of entire organizations. In that context, the key features of organizations are their entrepreneurial orientation. Since the pioneering paper by Miller (1983), a sizable literature has grown up that investigates the entrepreneurial activity of the firm and employs measures of the degree to which a firm can be classified as entrepreneurial (Covin and Slevin, 1989; Lumpkin and Dess, 1996; Zahra, 1996; Shane and Venkataraman, 2000; Shane, 2003; Wiklund and Shepherd, 2003; Salaran and Maritz, 2009). Entrepreneurial orientation (EO) is seen as consisting of a number of different dimensions. Miller and Friesen (1982, 1983), Miller (1983) and Covin and Slevin (1989) have defined entrepreneurially oriented organizations as those that are innovative, proactive (pioneering) and risk taking. More precisely, according to Miller (1983: 771) 'an entrepreneurial firm is one that engages in product-market innovation, undertakes somewhat risky ventures, and is first to come up with "proactive" innovations'. For Covin and Slevin (1989: 77) 'entrepreneurial firms are those in which the top managers have entrepreneurial top management styles, as evidenced by the firms' strategic decisions and operating management philosophy'.

This chapter explores the factors influencing entrepreneurial orientations of firms but it adds an important new dimension – the role of networks in EO. This may seem quite logical in the context of a volume that adopts a systemic perspective on entrepreneurship. Indeed, external networks may influence entrepreneurial orientation. They may differ across different sectors depending on their networking, learning and competitive strategies (March, 1991; Shane and Venkataraman, 2000; Lumpkin and Dess, 2001; Shane, 2003), especially as these relate to technological, market and institutional opportunities (Radosevic, 2007; Radosevic and Yoruk, 2013). Equally, EO is shaped by external factors like knowledge infrastructure, FDI linkages and business environment.

The research is based on an in-depth survey of 60 knowledge-intensive entrepreneurial (KIE) firms in four Central and East European countries[2]

(CEEC). The issue of EO to the best of our knowledge has not been explored in the context of this region. CEE is largely a middle-income region, which has undergone tremendous institutional transformation as well as integration into the world and EU economy with widely differing outcomes (World Bank, 2005; Pisani-Ferry *et al.*, 2010; EBRD, 2013; IMF, 2013). The issue of entrepreneurship and within it primarily the role of individuals has been relatively widely explored (for example, see Smallbone and Welter, 2001; Estrin *et al.*, 2005; Estrin and Mickiewicz, 2010). However, the KIE in CEE has not been to the best of our knowledge explored (for an exception see Radosevic *et al.*, 2010).

The last 25 years in this region represent a historically unique period for exploring if there is anything unique or specific about EO of CEE firms. In view of the large-scale systemic change, which is usually labelled as 'transition' (EBRD, 2013), it is quite interesting to explore whether external networks have facilitated or hindered EO of firms. KIE is embedded in systems composed of heterogeneous actors and networks of various types, and is shaped by institutions (regulatory systems). In that respect, our inquiry takes a broader perspective and goes beyond a focus on the innovativeness, proactiveness, risk taking, autonomy and aggressiveness which characterize current approaches. We also take into account the role of networks as an important new element of EO. We explore this issue in the context of the region where external networks of firms have undergone deep transformation and thus the role of networks is quite a pertinent issue. More specifically, we explore EO of KIEs, which are usually perceived as the key promoters of technology upgrading and structural change (Coad and Reid, 2012). In the context of the CEE, networking strategy has been described as one of firms' major strategies (Peng, 2000) both as a reflection of opportunities or as a survival strategy, i.e. a response to fundamental uncertainties of the institutional context (Stark, 1996). In Radosevic *et al.* (2010) we showed that EO is inherently different in different sub-populations of firms depending on their sources of knowledge.

In the next section we present the extended theoretical background on entrepreneurial orientation (EO). Section 3 describes the sample of firms studied as well as the data and methodology, while Section 4 presents the results. Section 5 concludes.

2 The concepts

2.1 Firm level entrepreneurial strategies based on dimensions of entrepreneurial orientation

In this chapter we follow Miller (1983) who was the first to perceive entrepreneurial activity in the firm as the activity that arises from the effective complementary and simultaneous entrepreneurial innovativeness, proactiveness and risk taking. Following Miller (1983), Covin and Slevin (1989) and Lumpkin and Dess (1996, 2001) developed the notion of *entrepreneurial orientation* defining it as strategy-making processes and styles of firms that engage in entrepreneurial activities. The concept was well-received in the entrepreneurship literature. Further studies comprise Zahra (1993) and Zahra and Covin (1995: 44) who used the concept of corporate entrepreneurship and suggested that 'it provides a potential means for revitalizing established companies through risk taking, innovation, and proactive competitive behaviours'. Ireland *et al.* (2009: 21) define corporate entrepreneurship strategy as 'a vision-directed, organization-wide reliance on entrepreneurial behaviour that purposefully and continuously rejuvenates the organization and shapes the scope of its operations through the recognition and exploitation of entrepreneurial opportunity'. Morris *et al.* (2008) contend that a firm is employing an *entrepreneurial strategy* when the actions taken in a large firm to form competitive advantages and to exploit them through a strategy are grounded in entrepreneurial actions. Therefore, dimensions of EO, to the extent that they are undertaken in a firm, determine its *entrepreneurial strategy*. Further, when establishing direction and priorities for the product, service and process innovation efforts of the firm, the company is formulating its entrepreneurial strategy. In this chapter, we primarily refer to EO though we recognize that developed dimensions of EO may implicitly or explicitly lead to entrepreneurial strategy.

Lumpkin and Dess (2001) added two other dimensions to the original dimensions of EO – innovativeness, proactiveness and risk taking proposed by Miller (1983): autonomy and competitive aggressiveness. For Covin and Slevin (1989) and Lumpkin and Dess (2001: 431), these five dimensions are as listed:

- *innovativeness* refers to willingness to support creativity and experimentation in introducing new products/services, and novelty, technological leadership and R&D in developing new products and processes;
- *proactiveness* is an opportunity-seeking, forward-looking perspective involving introducing new products or services ahead of the competition and acting in anticipation of future demand to create change and shape the environment and it captures the tendency of a firm to lead rather than follow, to be the first to introduce new products, processes and/or services;[3]
- *risk taking* embraces a firm's predilection for risk, its perception of risk as necessary for success in the competitive environment in which it finds itself, and its tendency to act boldly and aggressively under conditions of uncertainty, as well as tendency to take actions such as venturing into unknown new markets, committing a large portion of resources to ventures with uncertain outcomes, and/or borrowing heavily;[4]

- *autonomy* is defined as independent action by an individual or team aimed at bringing forth a business concept or vision and carrying it through to completion; contrary to autonomy, dependence of the entrepreneur would prevent him from exercising any of the other features of EO; and
- *competitive aggressiveness* reflects the intensity of the firm's efforts to outperform industry rivals, characterized by a combative posture and a forceful response to competitors' actions. It differs from proactiveness in the sense that proactiveness is about creating opportunities (i.e. getting to a place where the competition hasn't been yet), but competitive aggressiveness is about defending them (i.e. keeping the competition out of place, or eliminating them if they arrive).

In continuation we use this conceptual framework but we extend it by exploring the role of networks in EO. Overall, we aim to explore whether firms in emerging markets like CEE have all the attributes of developed EO and how the specific external constraints or opportunities affect their EO.

2.2 Network orientation

The importance of networks for entrepreneurship emerges from the interactive nature of knowledge generation and utilization. For KIEs to innovate the firm needs to access external knowledge through its networks and process that knowledge combining it with internal knowledge. When favourable, networks operate as external scale economies which impact a firm's EO through benefits of close proximity, through backward or forward linkages or joint infrastructure, they improve a firm's rate of growth, reduce risks and improve innovativeness. If developmental or opportunity driven networks surround KIEs they could facilitate their growth through knowledge exchange with other firms. On the other hand, rent-seeking networks can block entry and growth of entrepreneurially oriented firms. It is not obvious in which direction networking affects proactiveness and autonomy as these seem to have ambiguous effects – i.e. they may both increase and decrease these two dimensions of EO.

Malerba (2010) argues that successful entrepreneurs are 'consummate networkers' who thrive in communities. Referring to views of the firm as a 'processor of information', Cohendet and Llerena (2010) see the governance of the firm as consisting primarily in 'the coordination of distributed pieces of knowledge and distributed learning processes'. Lazonick (2002a, 2002b) in his theory of innovative enterprise explains how transformation of external technological and market conditions is the essence of the innovative firm. For such a process to take place, an enterprise has to pursue organizational integration or a set of incentives to employers and managers to cooperate in contributing their skills and efforts toward the achievement of common goals. Business enterprise is a social structure that is embedded in a broader (typically national) institutional environment. The industrial, organizational and institutional conditions of which networking is very important do promote or constrain the EO of an enterprise. Network oriented entrepreneurial strategies are especially important in the context of emerging markets where firms are deprived of various local knowledge sources.

Access to external knowledge may come from a number of sources, including cooperation with supply chain partners, but also from cooperation with other kinds of organizations specifically devoted to research, or from various published sources, such as journals and patent disclosures (Shaw, 1994). It has become commonplace to note that the importance of networking for innovation has grown in recent decades due to the distributed nature of the innovation process and the complexity of knowledge. A number of studies have demonstrated a positive link between a firm's R&D intensity and the number and intensity of its strategic relationships (Powell and Grodal, 2005). Eisenhardt and Schoonhoven (1996) point to a link between networking and various dimensions of EO, with evidence from the US semiconductor industry, the more a company's strategy is oriented toward risk taking, the more alliances it forms. This confirms the view that networking may be a risk reducing strategy in conditions of highly uncertain technological opportunities. How various aspects of networking (both internal and external to the organization) relate to EO has been studied by Walter *et al.* (2006) and Salaran and Maritz (2009). Stam and Elfring (2008) investigate whether the intensity of networking can lead to higher levels of EO.

The relationship between networking characteristics of the firm and its EO is important for catching up economies where coupling of different knowledge sources is one of the key entrepreneurial challenges. Based on Table 13.1 below, we explore the extent of autonomy, innovativeness, risk taking, proactiveness, competitive aggressiveness and networking orientation. We refer to network orientation as a firm's perception about the importance of taking part in collaborative agreements and awareness regarding advantages of collaborating en route to innovation. Elements of networking are also embedded in autonomy, innovativeness and competitive aggressiveness dimensions (see Table 13.1 additions in italics). Network orientation, on the other hand, captures the 'perception' of the firm with regard to importance of networks.

Given the absence of this type of research in the context of the CEE we are not able to formulate prior hypotheses and thus this chapter is largely of an exploratory nature. Very tentatively we assume that all elements where external factors play a very important role like networking (knowledge infrastructure, value chains) and risk taking (financial system, venture capital) may be constrained, i.e. EO may be deficient in these dimensions.

Table 13.1 Dimensions of entrepreneurial orientation (based on Covin and Slevin, 1989, 1991; Lumpkin and Dess, 1996, 2001) including network orientation

Autonomy	Innovativeness	Risk taking	Proactiveness	Competitive aggressiveness	Network orientation
1. Firm origin 2. Factors influencing company formation: a. Market and financial opportunities b. Technical knowledge c. *Network experience*	1. Basic indicators: a. Number of new products/ processes/services introduced into the market during the last three years b. Share of new products/ processes/services in total sales during the last three years c. Innovation productivity d. Share of income/ payment from/ for licensing/ royalties during the last three years 2. Sources of knowledge for developing new products: a. *Value chain and market networks* b. *External R&D* c. In-house R&D	1. Source of funding to start the company 2. Factors creating obstacles in the entrepreneurial activity of the company: a. Technology, market-and labour-related factors b. Know-how related factors c. Financial constraints 3. Institutional barriers in setting up and operating company: a. Corruption and informal obstacles b. Regulatory impediments	1. Main strategy of the firm 2. Implementation of strategic activities: a. Technology upgrading b. Management and personnel training 3. Sources of knowledge for exploring new ideas: a. *External R&D* b. *Market networks* c. *Value chain and in-house R&D*	1. Primary competitive advantage of the company 2. Factors creating and sustaining competitive advantage 3. Export performance	1. *Participation in collaborative agreements:* a. *Production capability acquisition* b. *Technology acquisition/ knowledge generation* 2. *Contribution of networking to the activities of the company:* a. *in market-related areas* b. *in technology-related areas*

Note
Italics denote elements that we have added to dimensions of EO developed by cited authors.

3 Data and research methods

3.1 Selection of sectors and firms

We study two sectors, computer and related activities (NACE Rev 1.1, K72) and manufacturing of machine tools (NACE Rev 1.1, DK29.4). CEECs have inherited good competencies in mechanical technologies from the socialist period, which explains why we have chosen machine tools. Also, CEEC are integrated into global value chains in IT which is quite a new sector for these economies and where EO issues may be quite different when compared to old sectors such as machine tools. Finally, two sectors are capital goods (machine tools) and 'knowledge capital goods' sectors (IT) and, despite their limited sizes as specialized supplier sectors, they play a very important role in knowledge systems of these economies.

We have selected a sample of firms in both sectors that can be considered KIEs. These are defined as firms that are innovative, have significant knowledge intensity in their activity, and which explore and exploit innovative opportunities. KIEs have internal management, business models and organizations that enable them to transform knowledge into innovation. KIE operates based on new products and processes (innovations), which are knowledge intensive, and, hence both use and generation of knowledge are essential parts of KIE.

The major operational criterion for selection of firms from machine tools and IT is that they are innovative. They should have introduced new products, processes or services onto the market during the last three years. However, in addition to this criterion, a selected firm should meet at least one of the auxiliary criteria below:

1   It is employing highly skilled personnel (MSc, PhDs) in engineering sciences;
2   It is continuously (not intermittently) investing in R&D; or
3   It has registered patents.

The use of these criteria would have made quite difficult use of a random sample. Hence, we have selected the overall portfolio of firms so that they are diverse in several dimensions (success, strategy, etc.). Unlike AEGIS definition of KIEs firms in our sample are both new and old firms, but they are all innovating and knowledge intensive as proxied by our auxiliary criteria. Also, KIEs could be of domestic, foreign or mixed origin. A restriction of sample on new and young firms only would go against the systemic view of entrepreneurship. Last but not least, our strict criteria regarding knowledge intensity of firms would significantly limit the portfolio of potential firms to be selected, especially in small CEE economies.

3.2 Data collection and the sample

Data that form the basis for this chapter have been gathered based on face-to-face structured interviews with managers in 60 firms in Czech Republic, Hungary, Poland and Croatia during April–May 2011. The sample involves 18 Czech, 15 Croatian, six Hungarian and 21 Polish firms. Table 13.2 details the firms by sector. The managers were asked questions related to the formation stage of their companies, market conditions, their networks, research activities and institutional structure.

The sample consists of 30 software (SW) and 30 machine tools (MT) firms. For both sectors in the sample, more than 60 per cent of the firms are SMEs older than eight years. Moreover, more than 80 per cent of all firms in the sample are independently located indicating that they are not members of a physical cluster. Only a minority of software firms are located in S&T parks and city clusters, which are formed spontaneously.

3.3 Indicators of entrepreneurial orientation

We use a number of individual indicators as proxies to measure the dimension of EO (cf. Table 13.1). These comprise a combination of observable measures (both numeric and string) and scale indicators formed by presenting the respondents with statements using a five-level Likert scale approach ranging from 'not important' to 'very important'. We employ factor analysis to collapse a number of indicators into representable concepts explaining the dimensions of EO. Table 13.3 below presents a summary of indicators in operationalizing the concepts. Respondents were either directly asked about the answers to particular questions or were presented statements to assess the importance of certain indicators at a five-level Likert scale approach from 'not important' to 'very important'. For autonomy, selected indicators aim to explain the extent of (in)dependence in an established firm along with the exploration of factors that the owners have identified or possessed when setting up the firm. For innovativeness, indicators explain whether the firm showed substantial effort in innovating or not. Risk-taking indicators assess first the financial aspect when starting up the company; second the technological, market and financial factors

Table 13.2 Number of firms by country and sector

	Software	Machine tools
Czech Republic	4	14
Poland	12	9
Hungary	2	4
Croatia	12	3
Total	30	30

influencing the entrepreneurial activities in the company, and third the institutional barriers which have significant relevance, particularly in the case of CEECs. The indicators of proactiveness show commitment to innovation, including the use of external sources of knowledge. Competitive aggressiveness indicators show determinants of the competitive advantage of the company and actions to sustain their competitive advantage including exporting. Finally, we have added the dimension of network orientation to EO by using indicators that show the importance of participation in different kinds of networks and the contribution of these networks to the company growth.

4 Results

This research is of an exploratory nature and where appropriate we employ factor analysis to group individual indicators used within the framework in Table 13.1.

4.1 Autonomy

The conventional view of entrepreneurship is that it is a 'sheer individual act' be it either individual person or organization. Hence, the issue of organizational independence of firm and the type of opportunity that lies behind its formation are relevant in understanding autonomy issues.

In our sample of firms 90 per cent of SW firms are independent start-ups, while 60 per cent of MT firms are corporate spin-outs, indicating that starting a business in the latter necessitates an initial nurturing phase under a larger, established firm. This may be expected as MT firms are older with competencies inherited from the socialist period while SW firms are new ventures which most often have not been part of larger enterprises.

4.1.1 Importance of factors for company formation

A factor analysis applied to the indicators assessing the importance of factors for company formation identified three conceptually meaningful components (i.e. underlying constructs) (Table 13.4). The entrepreneurial activity as an independent action demands capabilities and opportunities with regard to the market related, networks related and technical functional areas. Component 1 highlighted the market and finance related opportunities and capabilities. Component 2 highlighted the technical capability including design and software knowledge. Component 3 highlighted the network related experiences especially those that are outcomes of the previous work experience and networks built during the previous career. These three factors highlight the importance of coupling as well as relative independence of markets, technology and networks in the formation of new firms.

Table 13.3 Indicators for assessing entrepreneurial orientation of enterprises and networking orientation

	A. Categories that emerged from exploratory factor analysis of all statements in B.	B. Respondents were asked to give answers about Aluere presented statements to assess the importance of A (five level from not important to very important).

Autonomy	1. Firm origin
	2. Factors influencing company formation:
	  a. Market and financial opportunities
	  b. Technical knowledge
	  c. Network experience
		1. Independent company, corporate spin-out, partner firm.
		2a. Knowledge of the market, Availability of finance and Opportunities in a public procurement initiative.
		2b. Technical/engineering knowledge in the field, Design knowledge, Software knowledge.
		2c. Work experience in the current activity field, Networks built during previous career.

Innovativeness	1. Innovation: types and commercial relevance
	
	2. Sources of knowledge for developing new products:
	  a. Value chain and market networks
	  b. External R&D
	  c. In-house R&D
		1. Number of new products/processes/services introduced into the market during the last three years, Share of new products/processes/services in total sales during the last three years, Innovation productivity, Share of income/payment from/for licensing/royalties during the last three years.
		2a. Clients: Suppliers, Competitors, Trade fairs, conferences and exhibitions.
		2b. Government or public research institutes, Universities or other higher education institutes, External commercial labs/R&D firms, Scientific journals and other trade or technical publications including patent disclosures.
		2c. In-house (know-how, R&D unit in your firm).

Risk taking	1. Source of funding to start the company
	2. Factors creating obstacles in the entrepreneurial activity of the company:
	  a. Technology, market and labour related factors
	  b. Know-how related factors
	  c. Financial constraints
		1. Own resources, family member, business angel, etc.
		2a. Technology risk, Demand or market constraints, Marketing problems (i.e. lack of marketing and management know-how), Difficulty in finding employees with technical skills, Difficulty in keeping employees with technical skills.
		2b. Lack of technological know-how, Difficulty in finding partners for technological collaboration.
		2c. Large sunk investment (Capital stock in which we have invested has limited flexibility), Funding constraints.

3. Institutional barriers in setting up and operating company:
   a. Corruption and informal obstacles
   b. Regulatory impediments

3a. Poorly enforced copyright and patent protection, High level of corruption, Government officials favour well connected individuals.

3b. Too complex taxation regulations, High tax rates, Time consuming regulatory requirements for issuing permits and licences, Insufficient competition law to curb monopolistic practices, Bankruptcy legislation making the cost of failure too great, Unsupportive labour market legislation.

Proactiveness

1. Main strategy of the firm

1. To produce distinctive products, to target new markets or to produce standardized products.

2. Implementation of strategic activities:
   a. Technology upgrading
   b. Management and personnel training

2a. Renewal of advanced machinery or other equipment, Large-scale update of computer hardware and software, Purchase or licensing of patents from other companies or organizations.

2b. Preparation of formal business plan, Internal or external training of personnel.

3. Sources of knowledge for exploring new ideas:
   a. External R&D
   b. Market networks
   c. Value chain and in-house R&D

3a. Government or public research institutes, Universities or other higher education institutes, External commercial labs/R&D firms.

3b. Clients or customers, Competitors, Trade fairs, conferences and exhibitions.

3c. Suppliers, In-house (know-how, R&D unit in your firm), Scientific journals and other trade or technical publications including patent disclosures.

Competitive aggressiveness

1. Primary competitive advantage of the company

1. Product/service novelty, Product/service quality, Product customization, Cost competitiveness.

2. Factors creating and sustaining competitive advantage

2. R&D activities, Alliances/partnerships, Marketing and promotion to sustain their competitive advantage.

3. Export performance

3. Share of exports in total sales of the company during 2009.

4. Employment strategies:
   a. Employee trend from start to 2010
   b. Skilled employee trend

4a. Ratio of number of employees at the start of the company to number of employees in 2010

4b. Share of skilled labour (at different levels, i.e. BSc, MSc and PhD holders) in total employees.

Table 13.3 Continued

	A. Categories that emerged from exploratory factor analysis of all statements in B.	B. Respondents were asked to give answers about Alwere presented statements to assess the importance of A (five level from not important to very important).
Networking orientation	1. Participation in collaborative agreements: a. Production capability acquisition■ b. Technology acquisition/knowledge generation	1a. Outsourcing, Subcontracting, Technical cooperation agreement, Supply agreement, Value added reseller. 1b. R&D agreement, Licensing agreement.
	2. Contribution of networking to the activities of the company: a. in market-related areas b. in technology-related areas	2a. Finding clients, Finding suppliers, Gathering information about competitors, Accessing distribution channels, Assistance in obtaining business loans/attracting funds, Advertising and promotion, Managing production and operations, Assistance in arranging taxation or other legal issues, Exploring export opportunities. 2b. Developing new products, Recruiting skilled labour.

Table 13.4 Factor analysis for 'Importance of factors for the formation of company'

	Market and financial opportunities	Technical knowledge	Network experience
Knowledge of the market	**0.791**	−0.146	−0.100
Availability of finance	**0.688**	0.026	0.323
Opportunities from a public procurement initiative	**0.718**	0.328	−0.004
Technical/engineering knowledge in the field	−0.112	**0.465**	0.528
Design knowledge	0.019	**0.734**	0.164
Software knowledge	0.111	**0.839**	−0.121
Work experience in the field	−0.040	−0.022	**0.865**
Networks built during the previous career	0.354	0.028	**0.609**

Note
KMO measure of sampling adequacy = 0.61; Bartlett's test of sphericity significant at 0.002 level; Cumulative % of variance explained is 61.38%.

Table 13.5 Important factors for formation of company (% of firms expressing the factors as 'important' and 'very important') ($N_{SW} = 30$, $N_{MT} = 30$)

	SW	MT	All firms
1. Market and financial opportunities			
Knowledge of the market	53.3[3]	60[1]	56.7[4]
Availability of finance	16.7[3]	30[1]	23.3[4]
Opportunities from a public procurement initiative	6.7[2]	3.3[1]	5[3]
2. Technical knowledge			
Technical/engineering knowledge in the field	86.7[1]	93.3	90[1]
Design knowledge	63.3	53.3[2]	58.3[2]
Software knowledge	90[1]	36.7[2]	63.3[3]
3. Network experience			
Work experience in the field	80	100	90
Networks built during the previous career	43.3[3]	50[1]	46.7[4]

Notes
1 1 missing value.
2 2 missing values.
3 3 missing values.
4 4 missing values.

Descriptive results show that these are KIEs where technological skills play a role but also that these capabilities have to be coupled with knowledge of the market (Table 13.5). The firms in the sample are mainly self-funded even in the MT sector where a firm necessitates more capital-intensive investment than in the SW sector. As expected, technical/engineering knowledge in the field of activity is rated as highly important by more than 90 per cent of the companies which confirms that firms in the sample are indeed KIEs. Work experience in the activity field is rated as highly important for company formation by almost 90 per cent of the firms. More than 85 per cent of the firms' value networks built in employees' previous careers as very important and moderately important. Table 13.6 summarizes the major features of autonomy dimension of entrepreneurial orientation in the two industries.

4.2 Innovativeness

4.2.1 Innovation: types and commercial relevance

We investigated the number of new products/processes/services introduced by the firms onto the market during the 2007–2009 period, their share in total sales and innovation productivity calculated as the number of new products/processes/services per employee in the firm. Innovation productivity of the firms in the sample ranges between 0 and 7.2, with an outlier firm with the score of 24.4 innovations per firm. The majority of the firms,

Table 13.6 Major features of autonomy dimension of entrepreneurial orientation in machine tool and software sectors in CEE

EO dimension	Dimension category		Results	Synthesis
Autonomy: Independent action by an individual or team aimed at bringing forth a business concept or vision and carrying it through to completion.	Firm origin		90% of SW firms are independent start-ups, 60% of MT firms are corporate spin-outs	Autonomous or corporate driven entrepreneurship exploiting existing knowledge based on previous experience and recognizing market opportunities.
	Factors influencing company formation	Market and financial opportunities	Knowledge of the market is very important for 57% of firms, availability of finance for financial 23%	
		Tech knowledge	Technical knowledge is very important for 90% of firms, software knowledge 63%, design knowledge 58%.	
		Network experience	Work experience in the activity field is highly important for almost 90% of the firms. 47% of the firms value networks built in the previous career as very important.	

in both sectors, characterize themselves as producing distinctive products and identify customers as the most important source of knowledge for developing new products. These indicate that the sample is formed of specialized suppliers. Thus, when they were asked about innovations, we made sure that innovation is defined as a radically new or significantly improved product compared to other bespoke products produced by the firms. Hence, similar bespoke products are not counted as separate innovations.

Table 13.7 shows that by absolute numbers, 50 per cent of the firms have introduced more than ten innovations onto the market during the last three years. There are no differences between the two sectors with regard to absolute number of innovations. In addition, half of the firms have more than 50 per cent of sales based on new products during the last three years. The sales as proxy are quite unreliable as innovations may not have an immediate success or may have an immediate success but this may not last. Therefore, innovation productivity (number of innovations per employee) may be a better proxy, particularly because it is also an input indicator.

Table 13.7 Innovations, share of innovations in total sales and innovation productivity (%)

	SW	MT	All firms
1. New products/processes/services introduced onto the market during the last 3 years	N = 30	N = 30	N = 60
More than 10	50	16.7	18.3
Between 5 and 10	16.7	23.3	20
Less than 5	33.3	30	31.7
Total	100	100	100
2. Share of new products/processes/services in total sales during the last 3 years (%)	N = 28	N = 30	N = 58
Equal to or more than 50%	53.3	43.3	48.3
Between 10% and 50%	26.7	46.7	36.7
Equal to or less than 10%	13.3	10	11.7
Total	93.3	100	96.7
3. Innovation productivity (innovations per employee)	N = 29	N = 30	N = 59
Equal to or more than 2	16.7	6.7	11.7
Between 0.5 and 2	23.3	3.3	13.3
Between 0.1 and 0.5 or equal to 0.5	33.3	30	31.7
Equal to or less than 0.1	23.3	60	41.7
	96.7	100	98.3

Notes
1 1 missing value.
2 2 missing values.
3 3 missing values.
4 4 missing values.

Table 13.8 Licensing income and payment as percentage of total revenues (%)

	SW	MT	All firms
1. Share of payment for licensing	N = 28	N = 15	N = 43
Between 1 and 49%	50	3.3	26.7
0	43.3	46.7	45
Total	93.3	50	71.7
2. Share of income from licensing	N = 29	N = 27	N = 56
100%	16.7	3.3	8.3
Between 50% and 99%	20	–	10
Between 1 and 49%	33.3	–	18.3
0	26.7	86.7	56.7
Total	96.7	90	93.3

Almost 40 per cent of the firms in the sample pay for licences while 20 per cent receive payments for their licences. However, there are major differences between the two sectors. The vast majority of MT firms neither pay for formalized knowledge nor sell it indicating that untraded know-how is more important in the sector. In contrast, half of the SW firms pay 1–49 per cent of their revenues for other organizations' licences as a way to acquire knowledge and innovate (Table 13.8). Moreover, 70 per cent of SW firms have an income from the sale of their own licences, which indicates they are able to innovate independently.

4.2.2 Importance of sources of knowledge for developing new products and processes

The results of factor analysis (Table 13.9) suggest that there are three major sources of knowledge in developing new products/processes: value chain and market networks or external R&D networks or in-house R&D. In that respect, component 1 highlighted the networks with clients, suppliers, competitors and fairs and exhibitions. Component 2 highlighted the external R&D organizations as the major source of knowledge. Component 3 highlighted the in-house know-how which in some cases is formalized R&D.

Of the firms, 90 per cent rate their clients as very and moderately important sources of knowledge for developing new products (Table 13.10). Only half of them consider suppliers as significant sources for product development. At most 10 per cent of firms in both sectors assess knowledge sources such as universities, government research institutes and private R&D labs as significant for developing new products. This result is similar to results from innovation surveys and it confirms that these sources are not important direct sources of new knowledge in the CEE. Internal know-how is the most important source of knowledge for developing new products/processes in both sectors (Table 13.10). Table 13.11

Table 13.9 Factor analysis for importance of sources of knowledge for developing new products/processes

	Innovativeness via value chain & market networks	Innovativeness via R&D	Innovativeness via external R&D	Innovativeness via in-house R&D
Clients	**0.758**	0.089		0.052
Suppliers	0.476	-0.237		-0.557
Competitors	**0.782**	0.052		-0.037
Trade, fairs, conferences and exhibitions	**0.789**	0.203		0.014
Government or public research institutes	0.044	**0.860**		-0.017
Universities or other higher education institutes	0.003	**0.773**		-0.071
External commercial labs/R&D firms	0.278	0.338		-0.281
Scientific journals/trade/technical publications including patent disclosures	0.210	**0.768**		0.100
In-house know-how (R&D unit in your firm)	0.198	-0.096		**0.828**

Note
KMO measure of sampling adequacy = 0.62; Bartlett's test of sphericity significant at 0.000 level; Cumulative % of variance explained is 60.55%, all firms (N=60).

Table 13.10 Importance of sources of knowledge for developing new products/processes (% of firms expressing the sources of knowledge as 'important' and 'very important')

	SW	MT	All firms
1. Innovativeness via value chain and networks			
Clients	73.3	50	61.7
Suppliers	20	30[1]	25[1]
Competitors	23.3	20[1]	21.7[1]
Trade, fairs, conferences and exhibitions	26.7	20[1]	23.3[1]
2. Innovativeness via external R&D			
Government or public research institutes	6.7[1]	6.7[2]	6.7[3]
Universities or other higher education institutes	10	6.7[2]	8.3[2]
External commercial labs/R&D firms	13.3	6.7[2]	10[2]
Scientific journals/trade/technical publications including patent disclosures	23.3	10[1]	16.7[1]
3. Innovativeness via in-house R&D			
In-house know-how (R&D unit in your firm)	83.3[1]	63.3[2]	73.3[3]

Notes
1 1 missing value.
2 2 missing values.
3 3 missing values.

summarizes the major features of innovativeness dimension of entrepreneurial orientation in the two industries.

4.3 Risk-taking orientation

In the context of CEE countries, the market, technological and institutional conditions affects risk taking including the institutional barriers to setting up a company.

4.3.1 Source of funding to start a company

The main source of funding for company establishment in 90 per cent of cases is the founder(s)' own finances. There are no significant differences with regard to the two sectors in that respect. Venture capital is almost non-existent even in the SW sector.

4.3.2 Factors creating obstacles for entrepreneurial activity of the company

The results of factor analysis suggest that entrepreneurial activity is constrained by technology, market and labour factors; by know-how and by financial constraints (Table 13.12). Component 1 highlights the technology

Table 13.11 Major features of innovativeness dimension of entrepreneurial orientation in machine tool and software sectors in CEE

EO dimension	Dimension category	Results	Synthesis
Innovativeness: Willingness to support creativity and experimentation in introducing new products/services, and novelty, technological leadership and R&D in developing new products and processes.	Innovation: Types and commercial relevance	Number of new products/processes/services introduced into the market during the last three years	50% of the firms have introduced more than ten new products/processes/services onto the market during the last three years. No differences between the two sectors. 50% of the firms have more than 50% share of 'innovative sales' during the last three years.	Oriented towards developing new/distinctive products; Customers as the most important source of knowledge > specialized suppliers. Innovation active firms; specialized suppliers dependent on own R&D, and value chains, only 10% on external R&D. SW firms are involved in licence trade; no patentors.
		Share of new products/processes/services in total sales during the last three years	50% of the firms have more than 50% share of 'innovative sales' during the last three years.	
		Innovation productivity (IP)	IP ranges between 0 and 7.2 and differs considerably between sectors. SW has higher IP.	
		Share of income/payment from/for licensing/royalties during the last three years	Almost 40% of the firms pay and almost 20% receive payments for their licences. MT firms are not buying licences. In contrast, 50% of the SW firms pay 1–49% of their revenues for licences. Moreover, 70% of SW firms have an income from the sale of their own licences. Only one firm (SW) has a registered patent.	

Sources of knowledge for developing new products	Value chain and market networks	90% rate clients as very and moderately important source (60% rate as very important). Trade fairs and exhibitions are important for only 20% of firms in product development.
	External R&D	Only 10% of firms rely on external R&D (universities, government research institutes and private R&D labs) for product development.
	In-house R&D	For almost 80% of firms in-house knowledge is a very important source of knowledge. This is more so in SW and somewhat less in MT where suppliers and buyers take more part in innovation.

Table 13.12 Factor analysis for 'Factors creating obstacles for the entrepreneurial activity of the company'

	Technology, market and labour constraints	Know-how constraints	Financial constraints
Technology risk	0.715	0.158	-0.198
Demand or market constraints	0.601	0.239	-0.015
Marketing problems (lack of marketing and management know-how	-0.495	0.480	-0.186
Difficulty in keeping employees with technical skills	0.843	-0.038	0.051
Difficulty in finding employees with technical skills	0.372	0.386	-0.051
Lack of technological know-how	0.169	0.785	-0.030
Difficulty in finding partners for collaboration	0.069	0.757	0.154
Large sunk investment	-0.217	-0.109	0.768
Funding constraints	0.117	0.147	0.743

Note
KMO measure of sampling adequacy = 0.59; Bartlett's test of sphericity significant at 0.002 level; Cumulative % of variance explained is 55.47%, all firms (N = 60).

risk related to the innovation, limited demand or market constraints, and the difficulty in finding and keeping employees with good technical skills. This indicates a scarcity of skilled employees which is the emerging problem in CEE. Component 2 highlights the lack of intra-firm technical know-how as well as external know-how (difficulty to find partners for technological collaboration). Finance does not seem to be a problem for the formation of firms but much more for firm growth which requires high fixed investments (sunk costs).

The majority of the firms (60–70 per cent) consider technology risk, demand and market constraints, and difficulties in finding and keeping employees with technical skills as highly or moderately important factors to their entrepreneurial activities (Table 13.13). For almost 80 per cent of firms, lack of technological know-how and difficulty in finding partners is not a major constraint. Lack of problems in technical collaboration may well be explained by weak demand by firms for this type of cooperation which includes universities, research institutes and commercial labs. For some firms, financial constraints represent one of the major barriers to product innovation. However, large sunk costs or fixed investments do not seem to be an important obstacle. This may be expected given the relatively low development ambition of firms. However, funding constraints in

Table 13.13 Factors creating obstacles for the entrepreneurial activity of the company (% of firms expressing the factors as 'important' and 'very important')

	SW	*MT*	*All firms*
1. Technology, market and labour constraints			
Technology risk	26.7[1]	50[2]	38.3[3]
Demand or market constraints	40[2]	60[1]	50[3]
Marketing problems (lack of marketing and management know-how)	20[1]	3.3[2]	11.7[3]
Difficulty in keeping employees with technical skills	23.3[1]	46.7[1]	35[2]
Difficulty in finding employees with technical skills	20[1]	50[1]	35[2]
2. Know-how constraints			
Lack of technological know-how	13.3[1]	13.3[2]	13.3[3]
Difficulty in finding partners for collaboration	10[1]	3.3[2]	6.7[3]
3. Financial constraints			
Large sunk investment	26.7[2]	16.7[2]	21.7[4]
Funding constraints	43.3	30[1]	36.7[1]

Notes
1 1 missing value.
2 2 missing values.
3 3 missing values.
4 4 missing values.

firm growth are seen as very and moderately important by almost 75 per cent of the firms.

4.3.3 Institutional barriers to setting up a company

A factor analysis applied to nine statements to assess barriers to setting up their companies reveals that these can be grouped in two (Table 13.14), indicating differences between formal and informal barriers. Corruption and informal obstacles include poorly enforced patent protection, a high level of corruption and favouring of well-connected individuals by government officials. Regulatory impediments relate to issues with regard to taxation, licences, competition law, bankruptcy and labour market legislations.

Almost 65 per cent of the firms regard poorly enforced patent protection as an insignificant barrier to setting up a company. This is probably due to the fact that firms in the sample do not have any patenting activities during the last three years. Still, 35 per cent of firms consider this issue as moderately or very important. Firms are divided in their opinions about the level of corruption and favouring of individuals in acting as a barrier for starting a company. Some consider these as an important barrier, while for others they are not important. The regulatory barriers to setting up a company – i.e. complex and high taxes, time consuming regulatory requirements for licences, insufficient competition law, costly bankruptcy legislation and unsupportive labour market legislation, are assessed as not important by more than 60 per cent of the companies. These findings show

Table 13.14 Factor analysis for 'institutional barriers for setting up a company'

	Corruption and informal obstacles	Regulatory impediments
Poorly enforced copyright and patent protection	0.726	0.160
High level of corruption	0.929	0.055
Government officials favour well-connected individuals	0.943	−0.097
Too complex taxation regulations	−0.244	0.897
Too high tax rates	−0.061	0.897
Time consuming regulatory requirements for issuing permits and licences	0.187	0.403
Insufficient competition law to curb monopolistic practices	0.405	0.555
Bankruptcy legislation makes the cost of failure too great	0.507	0.520
Unsupportive labour market legislation	0.482	0.516

Note
KMO measure of sampling adequacy = 0.70; Bartlett's test of sphericity significant at 0.000 level; Cumulative % of variance explained is 63.18%.

that legal institutional reforms have been in place in the CEECs, whereas issues with regard to informal barriers need to be tackled. Differences between the two sectors in terms of regulatory impediments are insignificant. Table 13.15 summarizes the major features of risk taking dimension of entrepreneurial orientation in the two industries.

4.4 Proactiveness

4.4.1 Core strategy of the company

Almost 90 per cent of the firms state that their core strategy involves production of distinctive products and targeting new markets. This requires proactiveness and vision in order to grasp market opportunity for a new product or entering a new market by the firm's existing products where these products were not traded before.

4.4.2 Implementation of strategic activities in the firm

A factor analysis applied to five statements about the extent of strategic activities resulted in two components pertaining to technology upgrading and management and personnel training (Table 13.16). These are both knowledge-intensive activities as would be expected from KIEs.

Table 13.17 shows the frequency with which firms upgrade their existing technologies as a way to stay ahead of competition. These comprise activities such as renewal of advanced machinery, update of computer and software and purchasing patents from other organizations. Frequent implementation of these activities means that firms are proactive and keep up with changes in technology in order to introduce innovations ahead of the competition and acting in anticipation of future demand to create change and shape the environment. On the whole, a majority of firms invest in machinery and computer update; but purchase of licensing is limited to at most 30 per cent. Firms also need to continuously improve their management plans and make sure their personnel holds up-to-date knowledge in the field. About 60 per cent of the firms in both sectors implement these activities often (Table 13.17).

4.4.3 Importance of sources of knowledge for exploring new ideas

The use of external sources of knowledge for exploring new ideas, not necessarily developing new products in any form, indicates the extent of proactiveness. The respondents were presented with five statements as shown in Table 13.18. A factor analysis applied on the indicators resulted in three components pertaining to external R&D, value chain relationships and market networks.

Table 13.15 Major features of risk-taking dimension of entrepreneurial orientation in machine tool and software sectors in CEE

EO dimension	Dimension category		Results	Synthesis
Risk taking is a firm's tendency for risk, its perception of risk as necessary for success in the competitive environment in which it finds itself, and its tendency to act boldly and aggressively under conditions of uncertainty, as well as tendency to take actions such as venturing into unknown new markets, committing a large portion of resources to ventures with uncertain outcomes, and/or borrowing heavily.	Source of funding to start the company		The main source of funding is the founders' own finances (90%). No differences between SW and MT.	Risk taking is constrained by weak demand and markets, technology risks, and skills shortages as well as by regulatory impediments.
	Factors creating obstacles in the entrepreneurial activity of the company	Technology, market and labour related factors	Majority of the firms (60–70%) consider demand and market constraints, technology risk and skills shortages as highly or moderately important factors to their entrepreneurial activities. Lack of marketing and management know-how is not considered to be a major problem.	Corruption is present but unevenly.
		Know-how related factors	Lack of technological know-how and difficulty in finding partners is an issue only for 20% of firms.	Financial constraints are not the major obstacles.
		Financial constraints	Financial constraints are one of the major barriers for more than 20–40% of firms.	

| Institutional barriers in setting up and operating the company | Corruption and informal obstacles | For almost 65% of the firms poorly enforced patent protection is not an important barrier > firms in the sample do not have patenting activities. Still, 35% of firms consider this issue as moderately or very important. Firms are divided about the level of corruption and favouring of individuals as a barrier. |
| | Regulatory impediments | The formal barriers for setting up a company – i.e. complex and high taxes, time consuming regulatory requirements for licences, insufficient competition law, costly bankruptcy legislation and unsupportive labour market legislation, are assessed as not important by more than 60% of the companies. |

Table 13.16 Factor analysis for 'Implementation of strategic activities in the firm'

	Technology upgrading	Management and personnel
Renewal of advanced machinery and other equipment	0.474	−0.247
Large-scale update of computer hardware and software	0.701	0.277
Purchasing and licensing of patents from other organizations	0.820	−0.033
Preparation of formal business plan	−0.345	0.796
Internal and external training of personnel	0.309	0.808

Note
KMO measure of sampling adequacy = 0.48; Bartlett's test of sphericity significant at 0.000 level; Cumulative % of variance explained is 60.58%.

Table 13.17 Implementation of strategic activities (% of firms expressing the strategic activities as 'important' and 'very important')

	SW	MT	All firms
1. Technology upgrading			
Renewal of advanced machinery and other equipment	30[3]	40	35[3]
Large-scale update of computer hardware and software	53.3	26.7	40
Purchasing and licensing of patents from other organizations	30	6.7[2]	18.3[2]
2. Management and personnel training			
Preparation of formal business plan	53.3	56.7[2]	55[2]
Internal and external training of personnel	60	56.7[2]	58.3[2]

Notes
2 2 missing values.
3 3 missing values.

Table 13.19 shows that public research institutes, universities and private R&D labs are not major sources for exploring new ideas. This suggests that the R&D system is not involved in firms' upstream activities. This can be due to differences in knowledge profiles of these organizations in the CEECs or due to the absence of 'interface' institutions. Still, for approximately 30 per cent of firms universities are either very or moderately important as sources of new ideas. These results are broadly similar to results from innovation surveys in other countries.

Market networks like links with clients, competitors and trade fairs and exhibitions are rated as important by almost 70 per cent of the firms (Table 13.19). More than 60 per cent of the firms assess particularly their clients

Table 13.18 Importance of sources of knowledge for exploring new ideas

	External R&D	Market networks	Value chain
Government or public research institutes	**0.862**	-0.149	-0.073
Universities or other higher education institutes	**0.760**	-0.039	0.220
External commercial labs/R&D firms	**0.648**	0.201	-0.270
Suppliers	0.050	0.086	**0.783**
Scientific journals/trade/technical publications including patent disclosure	**0.503**	0.081	**0.609**
In-house know-how (R&D unit in your firm)	0.175	0.064	**-0.500**
Clients	-0.120	**0.641**	-0.171
Competitors	-0.016	**0.880**	0.022
Trade, fairs, conferences and exhibitions	0.195	**0.769**	0.293

Note
KMO measure of sampling adequacy = 0.42; Bartlett's test of sphericity significant at 0.000 level; Cumulative % of variance explained is 60.17%.

Table 13.19 Importance of sources of knowledge for exploring new ideas (% of firms expressing the sources of knowledge as 'important' and 'very important')

	SW	MT	All firms
1. External R&D			
Government or public research institutes	3.3	3.3[2]	3.3[2]
Universities or other higher education institutes	13.3	6.7	10
External commercial labs/R&D firms	6.7	6.7	6.7
2. Market networks			
Suppliers	26.7	26.7[2]	26.7[2]
Scientific journals/trade/technical publications including patent disclosures	30	23.3[1]	26.7[1]
In-house know-how (R&D unit in your firm)	90	66.7[2]	78.3[2]
3. Value chain			
Clients	63.3	63.3[1]	63.3[1]
Competitors	40	33.3	36.7
Trade, fairs, conferences and exhibitions	33.3	36.7	35

Notes
1 1 missing value.
2 2 missing values.
3 3 missing values.

as very important sources of knowledge for exploring new ideas. Around 80 per cent of the firms confidently state that they rely on their own in-house knowledge for exploring new ideas in order to be proactive. More than 60 per cent of the firms value suppliers and trade journals as important sources of such knowledge. Interviews revealed that specific trade journals are good sources of information for catching up with the recent developments in the field. Suppliers, on the other hand, have contacts with most of the firms in the field; thus they transfer knowledge from one firm to another. In that sense, the information they provide is valuable. Table 13.20 summarizes the major features of proactiveness dimension of entrepreneurial orientation in the two industries.

4.5 Competitive aggressiveness

To measure the extent of competitive aggressiveness in firms we asked them to identify their major competitive advantage and what actions do they undertake to create and sustain it. Export performance is also an important measure to assess a firm's intensity of effort to outperform its rivals and thus we used it as a proxy. This is a very important proxy in CEE where good local firms are often struggling to become established exporters.

Table 13.20 Major features of proactiveness dimension of entrepreneurial orientation in machine tool and software sectors in CEE

EO dimension	Dimension category		Results	Synthesis
Proactiveness is an opportunity-seeking, forward-looking perspective involving introducing new products or services ahead of the competition and acting in anticipation of future demand to create change and shape the environment and it captures the tendency of a firm to lead rather than follow, to be the first to introduce new products, processes and/or services.	Core strategy of the firm		Core strategy of almost 90% of firms involves production of distinctive products and targeting new markets. In MT this is more important strategy than in SW. This can possibly be explained by more distinctive nature of MT products vs stronger service component of SW.	Proactiveness is realized through distinctive products and new markets and based on technology upgrading and training.
	Implementation of strategic activities	Technology upgrading	Majority of firms invest often or sometimes in machinery and computer updates; but purchase of licensing is limited to at most 30% of firms. MT is more inclined to renewal of machines, whereas SW is more into upgrading of computer systems.	Main sources of new ideas are own know-how, market networks and value chain partners.
		Management and personnel training	About 60% of the firms in both sectors implement these activities often.	
	Sources of knowledge for exploring new ideas	External R&D	Public research institutes, universities and private R&D labs are marginally involved as sources for exploring new ideas. Still, for around 30% of firms universities are either very important or moderately important source for new ideas.	
		Market networks	Market networks like links with clients, competitors and trade fairs and exhibitions are rated as important by almost 70% of the firms. More than 60% of the firms assess particularly their clients as very important sources of knowledge for exploring new ideas.	
		Value chain and in-house R&D	80% of firms rely on their own in-house knowledge. More than 60% of the firms value the suppliers and trade journals as important sources of knowledge for exploring new ideas.	

4.5.1 Primary competitive advantage of the company

A large majority of firms (75–95 per cent) rate all factors of primary competitive advantage (product/service novelty, quality and customization) as very important while costs are somewhat less important indicating again that they are specialized suppliers.

4.5.2 Creating and sustaining competitive advantage

Entrepreneurial firms need to be able to sustain the competitive advantage they have. This involves continuous effort into R&D activities, alliances/partnerships and marketing. R&D activities within the firm are very important factors to sustain competitive advantage for 60 per cent of firms (Table 13.21). This is true for 80 per cent of SW firms and 50 per cent of MT firms. Alliances and partnerships are more important for SW to maintain the competitive advantage, whereas they are less significant for MT with almost 60 per cent of these firms declaring it as not important. This reflects differences in sector characteristics since SW firms are customizers of generic solutions supplied by international software firms via alliances and partnerships, on the other hand MT firms are more independent when focusing on customer-oriented projects. Finally, marketing and promotion are important for 60 per cent of SW firms, but less significant for MT. Again, SW firms depend more on successful promotion and advertising as they often produce end-user products, while the specialized MT firms do not need to incur such costs as they are in closer links with their clients.

4.5.3 Export performance

Lastly, we asked firms about the share of exports in their total sales. If this ratio is equal to or more than 95 per cent, we consider the firm as 'sole exporter'; if equal to or below 5 per cent 'not exporter'; and as 'exporter' for values between 5 and 95. This provides us with a tangible indicator to assess the competitiveness strategy based on an aggressive approach to conduct of export. Within the whole sample 40 per cent of the firms are

Table 13.21 Factors creating and sustaining competitive advantage (% of firms expressing the factors as 'important' and 'very important')

	SW	MT	All firms
R&D activities	76.7	46.7[1]	61.7[1]
Alliances and partnerships	53.3[1]	36.7	45[1]
Marketing and promotion	50	13.3[1]	31.7[1]

Note
1 1 missing value.

'sole exporters'. Broken down by industry, this corresponds to 60 per cent of SW firms and 20 per cent of MT. Only a minority of the firms aim solely at national markets. Overall, a high share of sole exporters suggests that our sample has picked up 'better' or more aggressive firms in both sectors. Table 13.22 summarizes the major features of competitive aggressiveness dimension of entrepreneurial orientation in the two industries.

4.6 Network strategies

In addition to Lumpkin and Dess' (2001) dimensions for entrepreneurial strategies, we also wanted to investigate the networking strategies of the firms. From a systemic perspective, entrepreneurship is a collective and not only individual level activity and it may influence a firm's performance, especially growth. Yet the network component of entrepreneurial strategies is barely touched upon in the entrepreneurship literature.

4.6.1 Importance of participation in collaborative agreements

We investigated the firms' assessment of participation in collaborative agreements such as outsourcing, subcontracting, R&D/technical cooperation/licensing agreements, supply agreement and as value added reseller. In a sense, we aim to find out why firms engage in collaborative activities, if indeed they do? Respondents were presented with seven different types of collaborative agreements and were asked to assess it from 'not important' to 'very important' using a five-level Likert scale approach. A factor analysis resulted in two components that differentiated between production capability acquisition and technology acquisition/generation agreements (Table 13.23).

Descriptive results indicate that, on the whole, involvement in collaborative agreements to acquire production capabilities is important for at most 40 per cent of the firms. These findings confirm the previous findings that firms are mostly engaged in close relationships with their clients. Similar to the production capability acquisition component of collaborative agreement participation, the importance of R&D agreement and licensing agreement within the technology acquisition component is also rated as significant by only 40 per cent of firms at most. These findings confirm the previous findings, i.e. importance of sources of knowledge for developing new products were mainly pointing to clients and in-house sources of knowledge.

4.6.2 Contribution of networks with other firms/institutions/ suppliers to the activities of the company

In what contexts do firms' interactions with other organizations facilitate their activities? These may change from finding clients to exploring export

Table 13.22 Major features of competitive aggressiveness dimension of entrepreneurial orientation in machine tool and software sectors in CEE

EO dimension	Dimension category	Results	Synthesis
Competitive aggressiveness: reflects the intensity of firm's efforts to outperform industry rivals, characterized by a combative posture and a forceful response to competitor's actions. It differs from proactiveness in the sense that proactiveness is about creating opportunities, but competitive aggressiveness is about defending them.	Primary competitive advantage of the company	The major factors of competitive advantage of companies are the product/service novelty, product/ service quality, product customization and cost competitiveness.	Firms are competing on all competitive factors (novelty, quality, customization and costs) by largely serving both domestic and export markets. SW firms rely more on R&D and alliances in sustaining these advantages.
	Factors creating and sustaining competitive advantage	R&D, alliances and promotion activities are important factors in sustaining firms' competitive advantages. These factors are significantly more important in SW than in MT.	Employment growth is based on generic expansion.
	Export performance	40% of firms are sole exporters (export 95% or more of sales) of which SW firms 60% and MT 20%. Only a minority of the firms aim solely at national markets.	

Table 13.23 Network strategies: importance of participation in collaborative agreements

	Production capability acquisition	*Technology acquisition for knowledge generation*
Outsourcing	**0.669**	−0.445
Subcontracting	**0.711**	−0.380
Technical cooperation agreement	**0.695**	0.146
Supply agreement	**0.702**	0.097
Value added reseller	**0.632**	0.340
R&D agreement	−0.111	**0.744**
Licensing agreement	0.327	**0.720**

Note
KMO measure of sampling adequacy = 0.65; Bartlett's test of sphericity significant at 0.000 level; Cumulative % of variance explained is 57.26%.

opportunities: firm activities can therefore be grouped into market related and technology related areas.

Of the firms, 75 per cent stated that such networks play an important role for finding clients and gathering information about competitors (Table 13.24). On the contrary, about 50 per cent of the firms stated that these networks are not important for activities such as finding suppliers, accessing distribution channels, exploring export opportunities and advertising.

We also investigated how important these networks are for technology related issues, i.e. for recruiting skilled labour as an input to innovation, and developing new products as an output of the innovation process. Of the firms, 55–70 per cent stated that such networks play an important role

Table 13.24 Contribution of networks with other firms/institutions/suppliers in market and technology related areas (% of firms expressing the factors as 'important' and 'very important')

	SW	*MT*	*All firms*
1. Market related areas			
Finding clients	66.7	40	53.3
Finding suppliers	10	23.3	16.7
Gathering information about competitors	36.7	33.3[1]	35[1]
Accessing distribution channels	26.7	20[1]	23.3[1]
Advertising and promotion	26.7	10[1]	18.3[1]
Exploring export opportunities	23.3	16.7[1]	20[1]
2. Technology related areas			
Developing new products	40	30[1]	35[1]
Recruiting skilled labour	26.7	13.3[1]	20[1]

Note
1 1 missing value.

for developing new products and recruiting skilled labour (Table 13.24). However, one must recall clients were stated as the most important source of knowledge for developing new products.

The data presented here show that networks are very important in the entrepreneurial strategies of firms and that there are no significant differences between SW and MT sectors in this respect. Moreover, informal networks seem to be much more important than formal, collaborative agreement based networks. Table 13.25 summarizes the major features of network orientation dimension of entrepreneurial orientation in the two industries.

5 Conclusions

Our main research question is whether firms in emerging markets like CEE have all the attributes of developed EO or whether the specific external constraints and opportunities affect their EO. The picture that emerges from our analysis is sharply different from the dominant 'individual – opportunity nexus' as depicted in GEM-style research on entrepreneurship. Within this perspective, and in a very simplified interpretation, the individual entrepreneur is conceptualized as a person that has grasped market opportunity and is constrained in its realization by a variety of institutional obstacles. In contrast, our data show **a combination of individual start-ups as well as corporate spin-outs whose establishment and growth are closely interdependent with a variety of networks or network related factors.** Similar to Klepper and Sleeper (2005) and Klepper (2009) CEE firms are spin-offs which have inherited specific knowledge from parent firms. They are either organizational spin-offs (MT) or new start-ups (SW) but whose founders brought accumulated work experience and network capital built during their previous career. This autonomous or corporate driven entrepreneurship is geared towards exploiting existing knowledge based on previous experience and recognizing new market opportunities. New KIEs are repositioning themselves in terms of markets or products, but not in terms of technology. In that respect, CEE entrepreneurship is of a cumulative and evolutionary rather than disruptive nature.

In the dominant I-O nexus perspective, the focus is on factors inhibiting firm formation and these are usually sought in a variety of institutional factors. Indeed, the departing rationale for our research was the assumption that there are numerous transition factors that inhibit knowledge-intensive entrepreneurship, especially risk taking. On the contrary, **institutional barriers in setting up and operating a company are present but far less than would be expected.** The range of regulatory barriers for setting up and operating a company are assessed as not important by more than 60 per cent of the companies while corruption and discriminatory treatment of companies as barriers are quite divided between companies.

Table 13.25 Major features of network orientation dimension of entrepreneurial orientation in machine tool and software sectors in CEE

EO dimension	Dimension category	Results	Synthesis
Network orientation. Reflects ability to form networks and accessibility to external knowledge through its networks and process that knowledge, combining it with internal knowledge in order to innovate.	Participation in collaborative agreements	The involvement in collaborative agreements to acquire production capabilities is very or moderately important at most for 40% of the firms. The involvement in collaborative agreements to acquire technology capabilities is very or moderately important at most for 40% of the firms.	Networks are very important in entrepreneurial strategies of firms and there are not significant differences between SW and MT in this respect. Informal networks seem to be much more important than formal collaborative agreements based networks.
	Production capability acquisition (outsourcing, subcontracting, supply agreement, technical cooperation and value added reseller) Technology acquisition/ knowledge generation (R&D/licensing agreements)		
	Contribution of networking to the activities of the company	Networks are important in finding clients (for 75% of the firms) and gathering information about competitors (for 70%). For 50% of the firms these networks are not important for finding suppliers, accessing distribution channels, exploring export opportunities and advertising. Networks play important role for developing new products (for 70% of the firms) and recruiting skilled labour (for 55% of the firms).	
	In market-related areas (finding clients, suppliers, gathering information about competitors, accessing distribution channels, exploring export opportunities and advertising) In technology-related areas (for recruiting skilled labour as an input to innovation and developing new products as an output of the innovation process)		

So, institutional barriers still exist but they are weaker than expected and seem to be more firm – rather than sector or country – specific. **The major barriers are related to demand and market constraints, technology risks and skills shortages, i.e. barriers are more developmental than institutional.** Equally, finance is usually portrayed as the major constraint to new firm formation and growth. Our data suggest that this is much less a problem in firm formation but is more present in firm growth. The finance factor is one of the major barriers for growth of 20–40 per cent of firms which again suggests that demand and market constraints, technology risks and skills shortages are much more important factors inhibiting risk taking.

Innovation is commercially quite relevant for CEE KIEs. Around 50 per cent of the firms have more than 50 per cent share of 'innovative sales' during the last three years which is significantly above the EU average of 9.9 per cent of turnover from new or significantly improved products new to the market in 2008 (calculated based on Eurostat). SW and MT firms are specialized suppliers firms, which largely innovate based on their in-house knowledge (own R&D) and value chains. For only 10 per cent of firms, external R&D is a very important source of innovation for product development. For 90 per cent of firms, clients are a very or moderately important source for product development. All this points to innovativeness which is embodied in a firm's 'know-how' and shared with value chain partners, especially in the MT sector. Disembodied knowledge trade is important in the SW sector while protection is not embodied in patents but largely in organizational capabilities. This mode of innovativeness of CEE KIEs becomes clearer if we take into account how firms operate pro-actively.

Their proactiveness is realized through distinctive products and new markets which are initially developed or thought through based on their own know-how, market networks and value chain partners. **A collective nature of their innovativeness reflects their interdependence with partners in the physical or knowledge value chain.** As specialized suppliers, they are naturally oriented towards clients and suppliers. They maintain their proactiveness through hardware renewal (technology upgrading) and management and personnel training.

CEE KIEs are not new technology based firms that grow based on commercialization of proprietary technology. Instead, these firms are competing on all competitive factors (novelty, quality, customization and costs) by serving both domestic and export markets. Hence, their innovativeness is much more embodied in their overall entrepreneurship orientation and cannot be reduced to new 'gadgets', i.e. artefacts or disembodied knowledge (patents). **The basis of their entrepreneurship is in accumulation of firm-specific know-how and in understanding of clients' needs.** In order to sustain these wide competitive advantages, KIEs (especially SW firms) rely on in-house knowledge and alliances.

Networks are very important in entrepreneurial strategies of firms and there are no significant differences between the two sectors in this respect.

Formal collaboration agreements are important in terms of both production and technological capabilities for 40 per cent of firms. However, much more important are informal networks especially with clients, competitors, in developing new products and in recruiting skilled labour. Our research suggests that indeed networks are quite positively important in establishing company (networks inherited from previous employment), in new product development or innovativeness (value chain partners and market networks), in exploring new ideas or proactiveness (value chain partners and market networks), and partly in sustaining competitive advantages (alliances in SW). Networks are neither hindering nor positive factors in risk taking. This may suggest that already strong network linkages are confined to incremental and low risk projects. This all suggests that, **because of specific features of SW and MT as specialized supplier sectors, networks are their important feature. But these networks are not improving risk-taking ambition and do not generate potential economies of scale and scope through labour pool or joint specialized services.** This may be partly due to the small size of the CEE markets and the lack of inter-country support networks.

Overall, different factors that shape EO in CEE point to the increasing importance of limited demand, small markets, technology risk and skills as inhibiting factors to increased risk taking by entrepreneurs. **The institutional factors that fall within the realm of a structural reforms agenda or transition continue to play a role but much less when compared to 'developmental' factors.** The major limiting factors call also for policies which focus on public procurement, stimulation of demand, technology risk funds and for sector specific skills enhancement programmes. Policies to increase entrepreneurial orientation in knowledge-intensive sectors should be embedded in their specific market context and thus be very much sector or technology specific. This requires in-depth understanding of the major drivers of competition in specific sectors and firm-oriented policies appropriate to open market context.

Finally, our analysis has justified the addition of networking as an additional component of EO. Without it, the very important networking dimension of entrepreneurship would be undermined or overlooked. Of course, our results are limited to two sectors explored and future research should further test key stylized facts of our research.

Acknowledgements

A research that forms the basis for this chapter was funded by the EU FP7 Project AEGIS – Advancing Knowledge Intensive Entrepreneurship and Innovation for Economic Growth and Well-Being in Europe (project number: 225134) coordinated by Franco Malerba. The authors would like to thank Martina Hatlak, Attila Havas, Anna Kaderabkova, Mira Lenardic, Wojciech Pander, Slavica Singer, Elżbieta Wojnicka and Richard Woodward for data collection.

Notes

1 We are deeply grateful to Maureen McKelvey for insightful and very useful comments on the previous version of this chapter.
2 Croatia, Czech Republic, Hungary and Poland.
3 This suggests that timing of innovation is important and thus companies that are pioneers are considered as more entrepreneurial than followers.
4 There are different proxies regarding this aspect. These could be differentiated as risk based on (a) diversification (i.e. entry into new area), (b) specific sectoral risks (i.e. high technology activities being more risky than low technology activities) although this is only for technology risk, and c) size of investments or size of loans.

References

Coad, Alex and Reid, Alasdair (2012) *The Role of Technology and Technology-based Firms in Economic Development: Rethinking Innovation and Enterprise Policy in Scotland*, Technopolis group, Brussels, August.

Cohendet, P. and Llerena, P. (2010) The knowledge-based entrepreneur: The need for a relevant theory of the firm, in F. Malerba (ed.), *Knowledge-Intensive Entrepreneurship and Innovation Systems: Evidence from Europe*, Routledge, London.

Covin, J.G. and Slevin, D.P. (1989) Strategic management of small firms in hostile and benign environments, *Strategic Management Journal*, 10(1), 75–87.

EBRD (2013) *Transition Report 2013: Stuck in Transition*, European Bank for Reconstruction and Development, London.

Eisenhardt, K.M. and Schoonhoven, C.B. (1996) Resource-based view of strategic alliance formation: Strategic and social effects in entrepreneurial firms, *Organization Science*, 7(2), 136–150.

Estrin, Saul and Mickiewicz, Tomasz (2010) Entrepreneurship in transition economies: The role of institutions and generational change, IZA Discussion Papers, No. 4805.

Estrin, Saul, Meyer, Klaus E. and Bytchkova, Maria (2005) Entrepreneurship in transition economies, in M.C. Casson *et al.* (eds) *The Oxford Handbook of Entrepreneurship*, Oxford University Press, Oxford.

IMF (2013) *German-Central European Supply Chain*; Cluster report, International Monetary Fund, Washington DC.

Ireland, R.D., Covin, J.G. and Kuratko, D.F. (2009) Conceptualizing corporate entrepreneurship strategy, *Entrepreneurship. Theory and Practice*, January, 33(1), 19–46.

Klepper, S. (2009) Spinoffs: A review and synthesis, *European Management Review*, 6(3), 159–171.

Klepper, S. and Sleeper, S. (2005) Entry by spinoffs, *Management Science*, 51(8), 1291–1306.

Lazonick, W. (2002a) Innovative enterprise and historical transformation, *Enterprise & Society*, (March), 3, 3–37.

Lazonick, W. (2002b) The theory of innovative enterprise, in Malcolm Warner (ed.), *International Encyclopaedia of Business and Management*, Thomson Learning, London, 3055–3076.

Lumpkin, G.T. and Dess, G.G. (1996) Clarifying the entrepreneurial orientation construct and linking it to performance, *Academy of Management Review*, 21(1), 135–172.

Lumpkin, G.T. and Dess, G.G. (2001) Linking two dimensions of entrepreneurial orientation to firm performance: The moderating role of environment and industry life cycle, *Journal of Business Venturing*, 16, 429–451.

Malerba, F. (2010) Knowledge-intensive entrepreneurship and innovation systems in Europe, in F. Malerba (ed.), *Knowledge-Intensive Entrepreneurship and Innovation Systems: Evidence from Europe*, Routledge, London.

March, J.G. (1991) Exploration and exploitation in organizational learning, *Organization Science*, 2(1), 71–87.

Miller, D. (1983) The correlates of entrepreneurship in three types of firms, *Management Science*, 29, 770–791.

Miller, D. and Friesen, P.H. (1982) Innovation in conservative and entrepreneurial firms: Two models of strategic momentum, *Strategic Management Journal*, 3(1), 1–25.

Miller, D, and Friesen, P. (1983) Strategy-making and environment: The third link, *Strategic Management Journal*, 4, 221–235.

Morris, M., Kuratko, D. and Covin, J. (2008) *Corporate Entrepreneurship and Innovation*, Thomson/South-Western Publishers, Mason, OH.

Peng, W.M. (2000) *Business Strategies in Transition Economies*, Sage IBS Series, London.

Pisani-Ferry, Jean, Rosati, Dariusz, Sapir, André and Weder Di Mauro, Beatrice (2010) *Whither Growth in Central and Eastern Europe? Policy Lessons for an Integrated Europe*, Bruegel, Brussels.

Powell, W. and Grodal, S. (2005) Networks of innovators, in J. Fagerberg, D. Mowery and R. Nelson (eds), *The Oxford Handbook of Innovation*, Oxford University Press, Oxford, 56–58.

Radosevic, S. (2007) National system of innovation and entrepreneurship: In search of a missing link, Economics working paper No. 73, UCL, SSEES, Centre for Economic and Social Change in Europe.

Radosevic, S. and Yoruk, E. (2012) Synthesis: New member states. Deliverable 4.2.3 for Project AEGIS – Advancing Knowledge-Intensive Entrepreneurship and Innovation for Economic Growth and Social Well-being in Europe, EU FP 7, September.

Radosevic, S. and Yoruk, E. (2013) Entrepreneurial propensity of innovation systems: Theory, methodology and evidence, *Research Policy*, 42, 1015–1038.

Radosevic, Slavo, Savic, Maja and Woodward, Richard (2010) Knowledge intensive entrepreneurship in Central and Eastern Europe: Results of a firm level survey, in F. Malerba (ed.), *Knowledge-Intensive Entrepreneurship and Innovation Systems Evidence from Europe*, Routledge, London, 198–219.

Salaran, M.M. and Maritz, A. (2009) Entrepreneurial environment and research performance in knowledge-based institutions, *Journal of International Entrepreneurship*, 7, 261–280.

Shane, S. (2003) *A General Theory of Entrepreneurship: The Individual–Opportunity Nexus*, Edward Elgar, Cheltenham.

Shane, S.A. and Venkataraman, S. (2000) The promise of entrepreneurship as a field of research, *Academy of Management Review*, 25, 217–226.

Shaw, B. (1994) User/supplier links and innovation, in M. Dodgson and R. Rothwell (eds), *The Handbook of Industrial Innovation*, Aldershot, Edward Elgar.

Smallbone, David and Friederike Welter (2001) The distinctiveness of entrepreneurship in transition economies, *Small Business Economics*, 16(4), 249–262.

Stam, W. and Elfring, T. (2008) Entrepreneurial orientation and new venture performance: The moderating role of intra- and extraindustry social capital, *Academy of Management Journal*, 51(1), 97–111.

Stark, David (1996) Recombinant property in East European capitalism, *American Journal of Sociology*, 101, 993–1027.

Walter, A., Auer, M. and Ritter, T. (2006) The impact of network capabilities and entrepreneurial orientation on university spin-off performance, *Journal of Business Venturing*, 21, 541–567.

Wiklund, J. and Shepherd, D. (2003) Knowledge-based resources, entrepreneurial orientation, and the performance of small and medium-sized businesses, *Strategic Management Journal*, 24(13), 1307–1314.

World Bank (2005) *Economic Growth in the 1990s: Learning from a Decade of Reform (Lessons from Experience)*, World Bank, Washington DC.

Zahra, S.A. (1993) Environment, corporate entrepreneurship, and financial performance: A taxonomic approach, *Journal of Business Venturing*, 8(4), 319–340.

Zahra, S.A. (1996) Technology strategy and financial performance: Examining the moderating role of the firm's competitive environment, *Journal of Business Venturing*, 11, 189–219.

Zahra, S.A. and Covin, J.G. (1995) Contextual influences on the corporate entrepreneurship–performance relationship: A longitudinal analysis, *Journal of Business Venturing*, 10(1), 43–58.

14 The determinants of innovation

A patent- and trademark-based analysis for the EU regions

Víctor Ferreira and Manuel Mira Godinho

1 Introduction

This chapter addresses the relationship between innovation and knowledge-based entrepreneurship (KBE). Innovation has played a high profile role on both research and policy agendas in recent decades. A large consensus on its importance to economic growth and development emerged and there is now widespread acceptance that countries and regions must foster innovation in order to generate growth and improve their overall wellbeing. In parallel agreement also exists on the economies' reliance on entrepreneurship as a driver of the structural change that is needed to remain competitive in the long term. Nevertheless, the research on entrepreneurship points out that the contribution of new firms for such long-term dynamics varies in accordance to their knowledge intensity. Thus the focus of the analysis on the impact of KBE in innovation.

Although the idea of innovation may seem rather simple, the fact remains that its underlying concepts are rather more complex. When we think of physical investment, or human capital (or labour), we broadly understand what to do to improve these factors of production. However, when referring to boosting innovation, we imply we should improve the factors leading to a higher rate of new or improved products or processes launched onto the market. Hence, to begin with, we are faced with two difficulties to operationalize the concepts. First, what is innovation and how do we measure it and, second, just what are the inputs able to drive more innovation.

The Organisation for Economic Co-operation and Development's (OECD) Oslo Manual defines innovation as the implementation of products or production and delivery processes with new or significantly improved characteristics. The third edition of the Oslo Manual extends the definition to include new organizational methods in business practices, workplace organization or external relations (OECD, 2005).

It seems clear that the innovation process involves two key areas each respectively related to inputs and outputs (Nasierowski and Arcelus, 1999). Therefore, relying solely on the study of input measurements, such as the level of research and development (R&D) seems to be an oversimplification of the phenomenon.[1]

In this chapter, we try to steer away from simpler traditional measurements and encompass a measurement of innovation closer to practical application and to exploitation, more in line with the definition of innovation quoted above. As Rose *et al.* (2009, 4) put it, 'commercialization – the mechanism through which the consumer obtains the benefits of innovation and the innovator obtains the return – is therefore critical to the innovative process'. Hence, we have decided to include trademarks together with patents in a composite measure of innovation. In doing so we are aware of the limitations of trademarks as a measure of commercial innovation, but we assume that it is better using them as an approximation to that type of innovation rather than simply overlooking this dimension.

On the other hand, to understand innovation we should realize that it involves the application of knowledge in creative activities through the combination of specific process inputs. Therefore, we need to research the resources, the technologies and the market dynamics that lead to innovation. Firms understand this and as a consequence invest heavily in knowledge production to acquire capabilities that will in the future lead to more competiveness and to new and improved products or processes (Rose *et al.*, 2009).

Further, to account for the innovation phenomena at a larger scale, at the sectorial, regional or national level, a broader approach is required. Indeed, understanding which inputs are important to the innovation process is a crucial factor for policy makers trying to improve their regions' performances. Given our work being geographical in nature, we will thus maintain a focus closer to the macroeconomic approaches that have attempted to account for innovation. There are several studies and conceptual frameworks indicating just what clues to search for when studying the inputs to innovation at such a broader scale. Our main ideas, adopting a perspective similar to Muller and Nauwelaers (2005), Muller *et al.* (2006) and Buesa *et al.* (2010), follow the innovation systems approach, recognizing the importance and the role of different actors in the generation of innovation. More specifically we use the Regional Innovation Systems (RIS) concept emphasizing the role of a localized and tacit dimension to the innovation phenomenon. The tacitness and complexity of new knowledge seems to make it 'sticky'. Thus, spatial proximity is important to facilitating interactive learning and knowledge flows. Hence, how economic actors are distributed over the geographic space does influence the creation of innovation, therefore making the RIS approach adequate for analysing innovation activities (Fritsch, 2002).

The concept of RIS gained importance and usage by political authorities and researchers (Cooke *et al.*, 2004) in the sequence of an earlier recognition of the importance of systemic innovation at the national level (Freeman, 1988; Lundvall, 1992). The development of this RIS approach has been associated with the rebirth of the regional level analysis and decision-making structures (primarily by recognizing the existence of industrial clusters and the need for local action).

Hence using the RIS concept and attempting to grasp some of the relevant factors leading to innovation, we will build an innovation production function to analyse the regional innovation dynamics in Europe building upon previous research which has tried to account for innovation (Griliches, 1979; Jones, 1995; Romer, 1990, Furman *et al.*, 2002; Furman and Hayes, 2004).

This methodology allows us to discern which factors are contributing most to innovation in different regions, by testing some of the traditional theoretical hypotheses while at the same time attempting to validate some new ones. Further we assess our composite measure of innovation vis-à-vis the conventional innovation indicators used by similar studies.

Other works, such as Rodríguez-Pose and Crescenzi (2006), deploy similar analysis to that undertaken here but with different combinations of factors as suggested by different approaches to the study of regional innovation. Much of this research has pointed out that further to the R&D effort also the local socio-economic conditions and the geographical proximity (of local and neighbouring knowledge) are important variables in the generation of innovation.

Buesa *et al.* (2010) adopt a similar approach to the studies mentioned above but with a factorial analysis of a set of variables measuring the national environment, the regional environment, innovating firms, universities and R&D before incorporating the obtained factors into a Knowledge Production Function (KPF) to account for innovation. Krammer (2009) uses a very similar methodology to study Eastern European countries.

This study is organized as follows. In the next section, we assess our new variable to measure innovation. Section 3 discusses the proposed model and the estimation procedures, and then presents the results. Finally, Section 4 concludes, discussing findings, policy implications, possible caveats and lines of further research.

2 Assessing a new variable to measure innovation

2.1 Trademarks and innovation

While the use of patents as a proxy for innovation has been quite widespread over the most recent decades, the use of trademarks for this end is much more recent.

The use of patent data in innovation assessment was first proposed by Jacob Schmookler (Schmookler, 1966). According to Marzal and Tortajada-Esparza (2007), the use of patent-based indicators offers many advantages: to be granted a patent requires the development of an inventive technology, patent databases give easy access to information and enable comparison between countries, with patents also allowing for the understanding of knowledge flows (through citations).[2]

The use of trademarks for measuring innovation has been the subject of some attention in recent years. The Oslo Manual (OECD, 2005) was written under the main assumption that patents do not reflect the different sources and ways in which innovation occurs, particularly in the services sector, where organizational change and co-creating new solutions with customers often happens beyond the scope of R&D laboratories. This is clearly reflected in the OECD's own definition of what is innovation.

The joint utilization of data from patents and trademarks has the additional advantage of providing a more reliable perspective on the potential for innovation. As previously stated, patents are used in advanced economies in several ways, which go far beyond their traditional role as a means of protecting innovation. In this context, many studies have affirmed the need for further indicators, which, in conjunction with patents, might provide a more realistic and comprehensive portrayal of the capacity for innovation.

Within this context, there has been increasing interest in the usage of trademarks as an innovation indicator (Mendonça *et al.*, 2004). Statistical studies on trademarks were carried out so as to obtain information on issues such as international differences in trade participation (Baroncelli *et al.*, 2004a), trade specialization (Fink *et al.*, 2003) and the usage of trademarks as protectionist devices (Baroncelli *et al.*, 2004b).

Applications for new trademarks are related to broader marketing strategies within which companies seek to enhance a brand to differentiate their products. In most cases, this differentiation involves incremental changes in relation to other goods or services within existing product lines but in some cases the use of new brands can also be related to more radical changes in products. Normally, new brands involve a variety of measures, such as changes in packaging and labelling and communicating with the potential market through public relations, advertising and promotion (Elliott and Percy, 2006), which in total may involve major changes in company behaviour. What can also be argued is that trademarks are more closely related to the launch of new products, rather than the inventive process, as is the case with patents.

Several studies have highlighted that trademarks related to new services have grown steadily in recent years (Greenhalgh *et al.*, 2001; Schmoch, 2003) while others have shown that brands are more intensively used in the consumer goods sectors (Greenhalgh *et al.*, 2001; Mainwaring *et al.*, 2004). Still other studies point out, through the use of empirical data, that there is a correlation between usage of brands and innovative activities. These studies have found a significant positive relationship between applications in different sectors of brands and different indicators of innovation such as patents, R&D and new product launches (Millot, 2009). This correlation seems to be stronger in service sectors (Schmoch, 2003; Mendonça *et al.*,

2004) and in high technology sectors (Mendonça *et al.*, 2004), particularly in sectors such as pharmaceuticals (Malmberg, 2005; Millot, 2009).

2.2 Creating a new dependent variable to measure innovation

Taking into account the previous discussion we set out to create a new variable that may allow us to measure innovation in a more accurate way (looking into the 'market' dimension). Therefore, considering the afore-mentioned vantages of trademark application counts, we decided to analyse the variations of trademark demand in Europe and proceeded to evaluate them as part of our measure of innovation, combining them with patent application counts.

As we are using EPO patents, we decided to consider requests for com-munity European trademarks (also, European trademarks are more costly and require an extra effort for companies thus signalling a service or product that may be new or significantly improved, thus signalling an innovation). The data were collected from the Office of Harmonization for the Internal Market (OHIM), covering all European localities between 1996 and 2007. This database contained the entries for all resident and non-resident European trademark applicants, and representing a total of about 70,000 entries per year. The database then had to be broken down, gathering only data for EU residents. However, the database referenced only the address/location of the applicant's headquarters while we needed to locate each application in a specific European NUTS 2 region. By cross-referencing the Eurostat LAU 2[3] (European Union municipalities) database with the OHIM database, with the help of an adapted advanced match formula,[4] we were able to relate about 99 per cent of the applica-tions to specific NUTS 2 regions. We thus obtained the first ever existing database of Community Trademark applications for the EU's NUTS 2 level.

Our second step was creating the composite variable that would account for patent and trademark intensity, allowing us to better evaluate regional innovation.

To generate this composite of patents and trademarks, the simplest approach was to add the two variables (or add them with different weight-ings, thus increasing the importance of each variable). However, this approach resulted in the production of one variable with a distribution that was somewhat different from the original ones.

We decided then to run factor analysis thereby checking the feasibility of reducing the two variables to one. Thus, a reduction strategy was fol-lowed, starting with two variables and iteratively reducing them. The elim-ination method with principal component analysis generated a new variable component. However, the KMO statistic indicated that factor analysis was not fully appropriate for these variables and the Bartlett test of sphericity confirmed the conclusion (Pereira, 2004).

Therefore, we introduced a third alternative, combining the two variables into a composite indicator. Combining different variables into one dimension provides a single composite image that enables the evaluation of the innovative capacity of any given region. This results in a multidimensional variable, reflecting the characteristics of complex and nonlinear situations. In its statistical glossary, the OECD (2004) states that a composite indicator represents an aggregation under the same mathematical index of individual indicators that do not alone necessarily attain the necessary significance, and is based on an underlying model of the multidimensional concept that is to be measured.

The first step in the aggregation of the two variables was therefore a normalization process (Z-score method).[5] This avoids introducing bias into the aggregation of indicators, basically leveraging the scale and unit of measurement and retaining the amplitude of variation (Gravetter and Wallnau, 2004).

Next, we constructed the composite indicator we were aiming at, which was found by a simple average of the values of the two synthetic dimensions, after normalization to a common scale by the min-max method.[6]

These procedures (factor analysis, simple aggregation or Z-scores based aggregation) allowed us to create three potential dependent variables to measure innovation output.

However, as we will see in the next section, the estimation procedure led us to change our data set from 14 years to two time periods (1990s average and 2000s average). This led us to discard the initial three variables, establishing three new dependent variables.

In the new data specification for the two periods mentioned above, we cross-correlated (and conducted linear regressions) for the new factor variable, the sum variable and the normalized variable (all produced from the new panel) with our variables that accounted for patent and trademark applications in Europe. The factor variable and the sum variable (simple sum of patents and trademarks) retained more explanatory power. In the two periods specification, the KMO statistic indicated the factor analysis to be fairly reasonably appropriate for summarizing the two initial variables and the Bartlett test of sphericity confirmed the conclusion, with the new variable explaining 77 per cent of the variance from the two originals.[7]

Finally, using data from the regional innovation scoreboard (Hollanders et al., 2009),[8] we created an index of the most innovative regions (weighing an average of all indicators in this scoreboard) and compared it with our own measures of innovation.

To make this comparison possible, we adopted cluster analysis in order to identify 'natural' groupings of regions based on the new variables. When comparing the different regional clusters that resulted from the use of different variables (patents, trademarks, factor variable, sum variable and average of regional innovation scoreboard indicators), the new variables that minimized the difference between the original regional clusters measured by trademarks per capita, or patents per capita, or average regional innovation scoreboards indicators, were the sum of patents and trademarks variable and the factor variable, thus confirming our previous result. In addition, the regional clusters seem to vary slightly across variables even though in the majority of cases this did not cause regions to drop or climb more than one position across the different clustering results that were generated by the different variables.[9]

3 Formulating the model

At the core of our analysis is an innovation production function inspired by idea-driven growth models (Jones, 1995; Romer, 1990, Furman *et al.*, 2002 and Furman and Hayes, 2004) augmented with a set of extra variables.

Rodríguez-Pose and Crescenzi (2006) followed a similar innovation production function perspective and found, through the application of factor analysis to a set of variables that not only the traditional linear models of R&D innovative efforts are important but also that the local socioeconomic conditions and proximity are relevant in accounting for innovation. Buesa *et al.* (2010) also undertook a factor analysis on a set of variables measuring the national environment, the regional environment, innovating firms, universities and R&D and used the resulting factors as the independent variables of an innovation production function. Similar approaches were followed by Baumert (2006 and 2007) and Buesa *et al.* (2005) but as in our study now they focused on the regional level.

Following Krammer (2009) our theoretical function is:

$$\dot{A}_t = \delta h_t^\beta \, L_t \, A_t^\gamma \, E_t^\omega \, \theta_t$$

where $\dot{A}_t$ stands for the innovation/new ideas flux, h stands for the average skill of labour and the δ subscript is productivity adjusted for one unit of labour. L_t is the labour input devoted to the 'production of innovation sector' (originally 'ideas sector') and θ_t stands for the factors linked to several streams of literature. We augmented the original expression with E that stands for 'entrepreneurship capital', which has been proposed as the missing link between knowledge and the market (Audretsch and Keilbach, 2004).

L_t refers to the employment in R&D activities, as the labour devoted to this type of activities has been shown to be critical in accounting for innovation (Krammer, 2009). In accordance to previous studies we distinguish between Private Business R&D and Public R&D (Bassanini and Ekkerhard, 2002; Hu and Mathews, 2005, Krammer, 2009). We complemented this information with the intensity of high-tech employment within each region.

For the regional ideas stock (A), we use real Gross Domestic Product per capita (2000 prices) as a proxy for technological sophistication (Furman et al., 2002). Other studies use patent stock variables proxying the accumulated ideas/innovation (Krammer, 2009), but the task of building a patent and trademark stock through the use of a perpetual inventory method for all regions in the study, with large quantities of missing data, was not feasible.

Regarding the proxy for entrepreneurship (E) we used the variation of new businesses in a region divided by its population. This rate may reflect the ability of inhabitants of a given region to create a new company (Audretsch and Keilbach, 2004). A current strand in the literature highlights the role entrepreneurship may play as a factor linking knowledge produced and the creation of innovations, a vehicle which encourages the usage of knowledge spillovers. Acs et al. (2004) and Audretsch and Keilbach (2005) argue that the exploitation of knowledge depends on several factors and institutional regulations, which in their opinion constitute a 'knowledge filter'. This filter represents the gap between new knowledge and knowledge that is marketed. Thus, entrepreneurs take on a crucial role in transforming knowledge into new products and services, i.e. knowledge spillovers are often enhanced by the activities of entrepreneurs. Audretsch et al. (2006) went so far as to propose a new factor of production called 'entrepreneurship capital', linked to the extensive literature on 'social capital'. As the number of new firms set up is subject to a large degree of stochastic disturbance over a short period of time, following Audretsch and Keilbach (2004) we applied a three-year moving average. Also in accordance with Audretsch and Keilbach (2004) we divided entrepreneurship into 'total entrepreneurship' and 'KIBS entrepreneurship' in order to see whether this differentiation has an impact on the different estimation results.

As for θ we considered several determinants included in the literature.

In line with many other works (for example, Amable and Petit, 2001; Acs et al., 2004; Audretsch and Keilbach, 2004; Godinho et al., 2005; OECD, 2005), we included a variable that proxied human capital. As Griffith et al. (2004) encapsulated it, human capital adds to R&D efforts (Krammer, 2009) while higher levels of schooling are also expected to positively impact on growth and innovation (Barro and Sala-i-Martin, 1995; OECD, 1995; Amable and Petit, 2001).

We also included the role of universities since not only do they provide resources but simultaneously serve as key actors generating spillovers feeding back into industry (Jaffe et al., 1993; Mansfield, 1995; Adams et al., 2001; Laursen and Salter, 2004; Mowery and Sampat, 2005; Krammer, 2009; Buesa et al., 2010; among others).

Reflecting the investment in innovation we further included gross expenditure on R&D (2000 prices) divided into public and private business spending (Bassanini and Ekkerhard, 2002; Hu and Mathews, 2005, Krammer, 2009).

In accounting for geographical or agglomeration factors, we considered the degree of urbanization and the potential market of each region. Specifically, we used the values computed for potential regional accessibility by the European

Spatial Planning Observation Networking (ESPON) with the measure of potential accessibility based on two elements: population in the NUTS 2 regions and the effort (time, distance) to reach them. The accessibility model used by ESPON measures the minimum travel time between all NUTS 2 regions. In this case, multimodal accessibility integrates the accessibility by road, rail and air into one indicator expressing the combined effect of these modes for each NUTS 2 region. In summary, potential accessibility describes how easily people in one region can reach people located in other regions (see www.ESPON.eu/main/).

Diffusion is a key variable in innovation systems that particularly depends on the existence and strength of network-based relations as well as on the activity of Knowledge-Intensive Business Services (KIBS) (Muller and Zenker, 2001). Within an innovation system, KIBS are responsible for disseminating knowledge and are able to support knowledge users in implementing new knowledge (Thomi and Böhn, 2003). Therefore we included the percentage of employment in the KIBS sector and, as previously stated, entrepreneurship in this sector.

Referring to the role of institutions, Cooke *et al.* (1997) make the case that regional policies should be directed towards establishing better relations between the different interested parties to the innovation process and minimize uncertainties. Correspondingly, the financial system should increase the flows of information between parties while simultaneously implementing specialized financing formulas that boost innovation. Other authors (such as Christensen, 1992; Perez, 2002; Lamoreaux and Sokoloff, 2004; O'Sullivan, 2005; Buesa *et al.*, 2010) highlight the role of finance in innovation. We decided to include this dimension, weighted by the employment in the financial sector in a NUTS 2 region.

Since institutions seem to take a relevant role in RIS efficiency (Cooke *et al.*, 1997), we also sought to factor this dimension into our model. Nevertheless, due to restraints on available data at the regional level, we constructed a variable that took into account the mortality rate attributed to tuberculosis and physical assault, thus reflecting the crime and poverty rate in a region (several studies link tuberculosis with poverty).[10] Nevertheless, we should acknowledge that this specification actually assesses the social conditions within a region and not the quality of the institutional setting, so we have a measure related to the social conditions within a specific region.

Finally, we took into account some control variables, such as the absolute investment in a region (2000 prices), the population of a region and the number of firms within each region. Summing up, we ended up with the following specification:

$$\dot{A}_t = \delta h_t^\beta L_t A_t^\gamma E_t^\omega \theta_t$$

where $\theta = \{RD, G, Uni, N, S, F\}$.

Thus, in terms of proxies employed, we have the variables which are listed in Table 14.1.

For the majority of the estimations we used log variables and specified the flow of innovation as a production function:

$$\log \dot{A} = \beta \log h + \delta \log L + \log \delta A + \omega \log E + \delta \log \theta$$

3.1 Data set and variables

The scope of our study is all of the European Union NUTS 2 regions. NUTS 2 regions were selected since there is a set of policies and local efforts that contribute to innovation at this level.[11] In addition, there is statistical data supplied by Eurostat available at this level thus facilitating analysis. All data were first taken for the time period between 1994 and

Table 14.1 Variables

A	pib	GDP per capita, 2000 prices
$\dot{A}$	pat	Number of patents
$\dot{A}$	trademark	Number of trademarks
$\dot{A}$	Counttp	Number of patents + number of trademarks
$\dot{A}$	Fac	Factor variable (aggregate of patents and trademarks)
E	vkibs	Rate of KIBS variation, three year moving average
E	vemp	Rate of total firm variation, three year moving average
F	emplcred	% of employment in the financial sector
G	urb	Degree of urbanization
G	espon2	Market space (potential accessibility)
RD	htempl	% of employment in high-tech industries
h	edu	% of active workforce with tertiary education
RD	pubicrdp	Public expenditure in R&D – 2000 prices
RD	businessrdp	Business expenditure in R&D – 2000 prices
N	emplkibs	% of employment in KIBS
L	pexrd	Public personnel in R&D, FTE
L	bexrd	Business personnel in R&D, FTE
S	sociac	% of deaths related to tuberculosis and physical assault
Uni	uni	Number of students in secondary stage of higher education
Control		
	Invest	Gross investment, 2000 prices
	Market	Number of companies
	Pop	Population

Source: own elaboration.

Note
Whenever in the text the variables are preceded by "l", that means we took into account the natural logarithm of that variable.

In the first stage estimation, with the full set of years, we did not distinguish between private and public R&D expenditures and personnel.

2008. The statistical information was collected from the Eurostat Regional Database and the data on trademarks applications were, as stated before, collected from the OHIM database.

We initiated our study with 252 NUTS 2 regions (Eurostat, 2006), and withdrew all Bulgarian regions given the lack of data for the period 1994–2008. The data set included therefore 26 European Union member states and their regions.

In a second stage of our study, we reduced our data set to two periods. We averaged all available observations regarding our variables to two periods – 1994–1999 and 2000–2008. All observations were averaged to the available years and when no data were available for the first time period we took into account the first year available on the second period as the proxy for the first period average. Using this procedure and considering only NUTS 1 regions for Denmark, Ireland, Belgium and Slovenia and dropping all French overseas regions, we were able to maximize the number of cases making up our data set without using abusive imputation techniques. Such decisions were necessary as some of the variables in our initial panel registered in excess of 50 per cent of observations missing for that period.

3.2 Estimation

Our first estimations started with data pooled over all regions and years within the 1994–2008 period. As we previously stated, we performed different estimations with different dependent variables: number of trademark applications (trademark), number of patent applications (pat), sum of trademarks and patents (Counttp), normalized composite variable (nbnp) and a factor component (Fac1) that resulted from the counts of patents and trademarks.

When using sum of trademarks and patents and the isolated trademark and patent counts we decided to employ count models, since they better fitted the structure of our data (discrete, non-negative), while when using the component and the normalized composite variables that had positive and negative values we utilized more linear models.

When estimating the models with both the component variable and the normalized component variable, we went through a set of different estimators. We used Panel OLS and OLS with PCSE for all our panel data, but a simple exogeneity test showed us that some of the regressors were endogenous and we therefore decided to deploy GMM system estimations, instrumenting the endogenous variables with various lags. We also accounted for regional fixed effects, since non-observed differences between regions may arise mainly due to the following types of factors: differences in regional industrial structures, differences in local labour market conditions and real estate prices and different regional cultural attitudes. Nevertheless, we believe our variables are capable of grasping the majority of individual effects. Also, all our estimations took into account year dummies to capture as much as possible unobserved heterogeneity (Wooldridge, 2002) (only for our initial specification and not for the two periods specification).

One important factor that should be noted is that some of our variables were highly collinear. We performed VIF tests (variance inflation factors for the independent variables) using all the variables in the set as dependent variables and we decided to exclude several, based on these tests and based on the pair-wise correlations, since our models often found multicollinearity.

In performing the count model estimations, we were not able to deploy the Poisson distribution in the present study due to the high variability in the number of patents/trademarks across NUTS 2 regions. In cases where there is overdispersion, i.e. where the sample variance is higher than the sample mean, the Poisson variance assumption does not hold (Cameron and Trivedi, 2005). A Pearson residuals test was performed and confirmed the inadequacy of the Poisson distribution for our sample. Thus, we deployed a Negative Binomial (NB) distribution. Within the context of NB estimation, we applied a fixed effect model (FE) and an averaged population model where the interpretation of results is harder but better able to deal with both heteroskedasticity and autocorrelation.

Unfortunately, in the first stage our results seemed hardly consistent with an estimation providing conclusions for all of Europe since missing data meant very few groups of regions were accounted for in each estimate.

The second stage of our work led us, as already stated, to decrease the number of time periods within the panel to two. For all variables, we considered the average of the available years in each decade (1990 and 2000). Nevertheless, we still found some missing cases in the first period, which led us to take the first year available in the second period as the average value for the previous. Furthermore, we dropped all French overseas regions and considered only NUTS 1 regions for Denmark, Ireland, Belgium and Slovenia, thus ending up with a total of 222 regions and two time periods.

In what follows we will not refer to the results from the initial panel as our estimations in that panel accounted for only 279 observations and 76 regions, due to missing data in several years leading to the exclusion of most of the NUTS 2 regions in the sample.

3.3 Results

As stated, we transformed our panel reducing it to two periods (average 1990s and average 2000s), thus avoiding most problems with the missing data.

Since it proved to be one of the most reliable options that both explained the propensity to patent and to trademark in a region (while also close to the average of the regional innovation scoreboard average index) we used the logarithm of the sum of patents and trademarks (lpt) as a dependent variable when estimating the panel OLS, a FE model, a OLS with PCSE (a linear estimation corrected for panel specific heteroskedasticity) and an Instrumental Variable GMM. We also run the NB estimation, using the Sum of patents and trademarks as the dependent variable. The results of our estimations are presented in Table 14.2.

Going through each variable, education (edu) was statistically significant in the PCSE, IV GMM and NB models. All models attributed a positive coefficient to the variable, and the values were close. This result is consistent with the theory since one should expect regions with larger percentages of their active labour force with higher education degrees to perform better in terms of innovation.

The business expenditures on R&D (lbexrd) variable was statistically significant in all models (except FE), and the coefficient was similar across models. Public expenditure on R&D (lpexrd), although positive and statistically significant in PCSE and IV estimations, was not in the NB estimation, thus this may confirm that to some extent public R&D expenditure may be less inductive of innovation in the short term (Buesa *et al.*, 2010).

The geographic dimension, computed through the espon2 variable, was statistically significant and positive in the PCSE and in the NB models, which could mean, as might be expected, that regions where more people are quickly and easily accessible are more prone to innovation.

The coefficient of the variable that represented 'social conditions' (lsocialc) was positive in the NB estimation. This counterintuitive finding was not confirmed across the other estimations as the estimated regressor was negative and statistically significant (this was the expected result, as the inference was that regions with more poverty and crime may be less able to innovate).

The evidence for the importance of universities (uni) was mixed but overall seemed less important than other variables. As one would expect, the technological level (or wealth) measured by the GDPpc (lpib) in a region was positive and statistically significant in most models.

Finally, we should refer to the entrepreneurship variables. The variation of KIBS (lvkibs) was statistically significant with a positive coefficient, while general entrepreneurship (lvemp) was slightly negative overall. Thus, this may imply that general entrepreneurship seems less innovation inducing than KIBS entrepreneurship. Such a result may not be surprising as most of the new firms tend to be born out of 'necessity entrepreneurship' rather than 'opportunity entrepreneurship'.

When using the factor variable extracted from the PCA as a dependent variable, we obtained very similar results, especially with the PCSE estimation.

Finally we estimated functions accounting for trademark and patent counts. When performing NB FE estimations, we detected that for trademark counts, while several variables were statistically significant, education

Table 14.2 Count models – estimating functions (NB – FE accounting for 'sum of trademarks and patents' (counttp), 'trademarking' and 'patenting'

counttp			trademarking			patenting		
Variables	Coef.	Std. Err.	Variables	Coef.	Std. Err.	Variables	Coef.	Std. Err.
_cons***	-1.3347	0.4280	_cons	-0.1334	0.6827	_cons	0.1178	0.5157
bexrd***	0.0004	0.0001	bexrd*	0.0002	0.0001	bexrd	0.0004	0.0002
edu***	3.3005	0.5997	edu***	4.4758	0.9710	edu***	3.3418	0.8370
emplkibs	0.0036	0.0140	emplkibs	0.0156	0.0263	emplkibs ***	-0.0560	0.0186
espon2***	0.0182	0.0038	espon2	0.0016	0.0048	espon2	0.0075	0.0051
htempl	0.0042	0.0481	htempl	0.0083	0.0707	htempl	0.0002	0.0614
pexrd	-0.0001	0.0001	pexrd **	-0.0005	0.0002	pexrd	-0.0003	0.0002
pibpc**	0.0000	0.0000	pibpc **	0.0000	0.0000	pibpc***	0.0001	0.0000
socialc ***	0.4206	0.0668	socialc***	-0.3738	0.0928	socialc ***	0.3590	0.0883
uni	0.0000	0.0000	uni***	-0.0001	0.0000	uni	0.0000	0.0000
vkibs ***	0.0045	0.0009	vkibs ***	0.0052	0.0011	vkibs ***	0.0035	0.0011
vemp	-0.0032	0.0089	vemp *	-0.0274	0.0120	vemp	0.0058	0.0141

counttp:
Conditional FE negative binomial regression
Number of obs=298
Group variable: regio Number of groups=149
Obs per group: min=2
avg=2.0
max=2
Wald chi2(11)=936.90
Log likelihood=-604.70505
Prob>χ2=0.0000

trademarking:
Conditional FE negative binomial regression
Number of obs=298
Group variable: regio Number of groups=149
Obs per group: min=2
avg=2.0
max=2
Wald chi2(11)=369.49
Log likelihood=-533.47991
Prob>χ2=0.0000

patenting:
Conditional FE negative binomial regression
Number of obs=298
Group variable: regio Number of groups=149
Obs per group: min=2
avg=2.0
max=2
Wald chi2(11)=416.66
Log likelihood=-495.88996
Prob>χ2=0.0000

Source: own calculations.

Note
* Significance level: *0.1, **0.05, ***0.01.

was the single most important factor inducing the probability of trademarking, while the second most important factor was entrepreneurship in KIBS, and the regressors for social conditions and general entrepreneurship came again as negative. In terms of patenting, the NB FE model still maintained education as the most important variable while social conditions were positive and significant. This last result is somehow unexpected, but still since our social conditions index measures crime and health problems, perhaps dense urban areas which are more prone to have these problems are also the ones with more patenting.[12]

Summing up, our results seem fairly consistent with much of the literature that employs innovation (knowledge) production functions. Buesa *et al.* (2010), as referred to earlier, state their own research indicates the importance of the 'innovation environments' on which we can include some of the variables that are consistent across models (espon2, or a geographic dimension, GDPpc, R&D expenditure and human resources with higher education). Also consistent with Buesa *et al.* (2010), the weight of innovatory firms (reflected in our business expenditure on R&D variable) seems relevant across estimations (with similar results to be found in Jaffe, 1989; Feldman, 1994; Anselin *et al.*, 1997; Acs *et al.*, 2002; Buesa *et al.*, 2010). When accounting for patenting, this is in line with earlier research that stresses that innovation is driven by the behaviour of firms in the productive sector (Nelson and Winter, 1982; Dosi, 1988; among many others).

The finding that 'education' is one of the most important variables seems consistent with other works (Acs *et al.*, 2002; Krammer, 2009), while the finding that the role of universities seems neither very obvious nor significant across estimations when explaining our composite variables is consistent with the notion that even if universities are important drivers of invention (the variable seems relevant in our first stage estimations and highly significant for patents in the complete panel), they are not, at least in European regions, direct sources of innovation.

Audretsch and Keilbach (2004), among others, proposed the idea that entrepreneurship may serve as the missing link in the transformation of knowledge spillovers into real economic opportunities. Our average KIBS variation rate, which is not a true entrepreneurship rate but just a proxy, seemed to play a significant role in the creation and fostering of innovation (measured by patent and trademark sums). In relation to total entrepreneurship, when significant, it had a slightly negative impact and thus potentially indicating the two way effect of entrepreneurship (Hartog *et al.*, 2010). As these authors state, it seems that when entrepreneurship happens in less technologically intensive sectors (or less developed countries) it is less prone to generating competitiveness (since human resources are deviated to less knowledge-intensive and competitive activities), a conclusion that is in line with our findings.

4 Concluding remarks

This chapter addressed the relationship between innovation and knowledge-based entrepreneurship (KBE) bringing into the analysis different dimensions of the innovation systems through an innovation production function approach. Specifically the study contributes to the regional innovation literature and to the study of innovation metrics by investigating the influence of KIBS, space, institutions and entrepreneurship in regional innovation outcomes in regions across the European Union.

Our work departs from many similar studies in its inclusion of trademark applications and the quasi-validation of a composite measure with patents and trademarks thereby maintaining the practical advantages of both and minimizing some of the disadvantages.

We should also emphasize the importance of the creation of a data set of trademarks distributed by NUTS 2 regions. While previous studies have focused mostly on Western Europe, we also studied Eastern European regions.

Following studies such as Krammer (2009), Buesa *et al.* (2010), Furman *et al.* (2002) and Furman and Hayes (2004) that in turn drew upon Porter (1990), Romer (1990) and Nelson (1993), we employed an innovation function to account for the main determinants of innovation in the EU's NUTS 2 regions.

Our results seem broadly robust and imply that the majority of factors considered contribute to the regional innovative performance as proxied by a variable that combines patenting and trademarking. In addition, our approach allowed us to compare different measures and to link trademarking, patenting and innovation, through the comparison of our aggregate variables, our count variables and outputs taken from the regional innovation scoreboard (Hollanders *et al.*, 2009). In doing so we recognize the limitations of both patents and trademarks to approximate respectively technological and commercial innovation, though we also assume that in the absence of better alternatives patent and trademark applications (or grants) are useful indicators to study innovation dynamics.

The results allowed us to draw some relevant points. While education, business R&D, market space and wealth[13] (or 'technological sophistication', as measured by GDP per capita) seemed important across our different estimations with the full set of years or only one of two periods, we detected persistently and across all estimations that KIBS entrepreneurship (as a variable that approximates the dynamics of KBE in the regions) had a positive relationship with our dependent variables. This result contrasts with the fact that general entrepreneurship was not found to have a significant impact on innovation. Furthermore, while urban concentration (whether actually measured or implied in the second panel by the social conditions) seemed to play a vital role in patent counts, education and the market dimension seem more important in accounting for trademarking activities.

It is relevant to point out that the percentage of population with higher education has an important role, whether regions are producing more technological knowledge (patents) or more marketable knowledge (trademarks). Thus, as repetitive as this may seem, it was confirmed that the 'human endowment' of a region is essential for its innovation performance.

It was also confirmed that regions should promote business R&D and that new KIBS firms seem important for fostering patenting and trademarking. On this regard, it shall be recalled that the indicator used to measure KIBS entrepreneurship is a three-year moving average, therefore even if some younger KIBS firms may be directly innovating (i.e. applying for trademarks or patents), many of them may be acting as providers of specialized services that induce greater innovative capability in a region through networking.

In sum, we were able to establish an innovation production function based on concepts linked to entrepreneurship, KIBS, geographic dimension of market, and other traditional factors (public and business R&D, education, etc.) and apply it to the NUTS 2 regions across the EU. In doing so, we proposed and validated a new measure for innovation that comprises two different types of intellectual property: patents and trademarks. Further, the data set that was created may in the future be important to developing different regional studies, whether in the innovation field or in other economics or business management areas of study.

Notes

1 An OECD report entitled *Measuring Innovation: A New Perspective* (OECD, 2010) has summarized some of the problems of the more commonly used measures that, as will be highlighted by this chapter, have been pointed out by several other studies.
2 See Griliches (1990) for a summary of the literature on the use of patents as economic indicators. Previous studies include among others Griliches (1979, 1984 and 1990), Jaffe (1986), Acs and Audretsch (1989), Blundell *et al.* (1995), Cohen (1995), Cohen and Klepper (1996), Jacobsson *et al.* (1996), Cincera (1997), Crepon and Duguet (1997), Cantwell and Janne (1999), Pavitt and Patel (1999), Malerba and Orsenigo (2000).
3 http://epp.eurostat.ec.europa.eu/portal/page/portal/nuts_nomenclature/local_administrative_units.
4 We adapted the formula found on www.mrexcel.com/forum/showthread.php?t=195635.
5 This consists of dividing the difference between the value of each indicator (number of patents and trademarks) in a given region and the average of this indicator, by the standard deviation of this same distribution, thus ensuring standardized values with zero mean and standardized units.
6 The min-max method is, in terms of formulation: $MMXi = [Xi - \min (X)]/[\max (X) - \min (X)]$ where MMXi represents the normalized value given by region i in the X dimension, Xi represents the value assumed by region i in the X dimension,

min (X) represents the minimum distribution of aggregates in the X dimension in all regions, and max (X) represents the maximum distribution of aggregates in the X dimension in all regions.

7 We tried a different method to extract a factor variable, with covariance matrixes, where the new variable explained 84 per cent of the original two. Nevertheless the correlation with one of the original variables (Trademarks) was very poor and hence we discarded it.

8 The regional innovation scoreboard adopts the European Innovation Scoreboard approach at the regional level (NUTS 2 and 1). The European Innovation Scoreboard (EIS) (now 'Innovation Union Scoreboard') is developed to provide a comparative assessment of the innovation performance of EU Member States (Hollanders *et al.*, 2009).

9 These results are available on request.

10 www.nowpublic.com/health/tuberculosis-tb-and-poverty-partners-default.

11 Note the cases that the European funds and programmes are often distributed according to the levels of economic development of each region and the goals set for these.

12 The results of the alternative estimates that were carried out can be obtained on request.

13 And universities, in the case of the panel with the complete set of years.

References

Acs, Z. and Audretsch, D. (1989) Innovation, market structure, and firm size, *The Review of Economics and Statistics* 69(4), 567–574.

Acs, Z., Anselin, L. and Varga, A. (2002) Patents and innovation counts as measures of regional production of new knowledge, *Research Policy* 31, 1069–1085.

Acs, Z., Audretsch, D., Braunerhjelm, P. and Carlsson, B. (2004) *The missing link: The knowledge filter, entrepreneurship and endogenous growth*, Working Paper. Centre for Economic Policy Research, London.

Adams, J.D., Chiang, E.P. and Starkey, K. (2001) Industry-university cooperative research centers, *The Journal of Technology Transfer*, 26, 73–86.

Amable, B. and Petit, P. (2001) *The diversity of social systems of innovation and production during the 1990s*, Paper presented at the DRUID Conference, Aalborg, June.

Anselin, L., Varga, A. and Acs, Z. (1997) Local geographic spillovers between university research and high-technology innovation, *Journal of Urban Economics* 42, 422–448.

Audretsch, D. and Keilbach, M. (2004) Entrepreneurship and regional growth: An evolutionary interpretation, *Journal of Evolutionary Economics* 14(5), 605–616.

Audretsch, D. and Keilbach, M. (2005) Entrepreneurship capital and regional growth, *Annals of Regional Science* 39(3), 457–469.

Audretsch, D., Keilbach, M. and Lehmann, E. (2006) *Entrepreneurship and Economic Growth*, Cambridge University Press, New York.

Baroncelli, E., Fink, C. and Smarzynska Javorcik, B. (2004a) *The global distribution of trademarks: Some stylized facts*, World Bank Policy Research Working Paper, 3270.

Baroncelli, E., Krivonos, E. and Olarreaga, M. (2004b) *Trademark protection or protectionism?*, World Bank Policy Research Paper, 3214.

Barro, R.J. and Sala-i-Martin, X. (1995) *Economic Growth*, McGraw Hill, New York.

Bassanini, A. and Ekkerhard, E. (2002) Labour market regulation, industrial relations and technological regimes: A tale of comparative advantage, *Industrial and Corporate Change* 11(3), 391–426.

Baumert, T. (2006) *Los determinantes de la innovación. Un Estudio aplicado sobre las regiones de la Unión Europea*, Ph.D. Thesis, Universidad Complutense de Madrid. www.ucm.es/bucm/cee/iaif.

Baumert, T. (2007) *Los determinantes de la innovación regional en España y la Unión Europea*. In Buesa, M., Heijs, J., *et al.* (eds), *Sistemas regionales de innovación: Nuevas formas de análisis y medición*, Fundación de las Cajas de Ahorros, Madrid.

Blundell, R., Griffith, J. and Reenen, V. (1995) Dynamic count data models of technological innovation, *The Economic Journal* 105(429), 333–344.

Buesa, M., Heijs, J., Martínez Pellitero, M. and Baumert, T. (2005) Regional systems of innovation and the knowledge production function: The Spanish case, *Technovation* 26, 436–472.

Buesa, M., Heijs, S. and Baumert, T. (2010) The determinants of regional innovation in Europe: A combined factorial and regression knowledge production function approach, *Research Policy* 39(6), 722–735.

Cameron, A.C. and Trivedi, P. (2005) *Microeconometrics: Methods & Applications*, Cambridge University Press, Cambridge.

Cantwell, J. and Janne, O. (1999) Technological globalisation and innovative centres: The role of corporate technological leadership and location hierarchy, *Research Policy* 28(2–3), 119–144.

Christensen, J.L. (1992) The role of finance in national innovations systems. In: Lundvall, B.-A. (ed.), *National Systems of Innovation: Towards a Theory of Innovation and Interactive Learning*, Pinter, London.

Cincera, M. (1997) Patents, R&D and technological spillovers at the firm level: Some evidence from econometric count models for panel data, *Journal of Applied Econometrics* 12(3), 265–280.

Cohen, W. (1995) Empirical studies in innovative activity. In Stoneman, P. (ed.), *Handbook of the Economics of Innovation and Technological Change*, Blackwell, Oxford, 182–264.

Cohen, W. and Klepper, S. (1996) A reprise of size and R&D, *The Economic Journal* 106, 925–951.

Cooke, P., Uranga, M.G. and Etxebarria, G. (1997) Regional systems of innovation: An evolutionary perspective, *Environment and Planning A* 30, 1563–1584.

Cooke, P., Heidenreich, M. and Braczyk, H.J. (eds) (2004) *Regional Systems of Innovation*, Routledge, London.

Crepon, B. and Duguet, E. (1997) Research and development, competition and innovation pseudo-maximum likelihood and simulated maximum likelihood methods applied to count data models with heterogeneity, *Journal of Econometrics* 79(2), 355–378.

Dosi, G. (1988) Sources, procedures and microeconomic effects of innovation, *Journal of Economic Literature* 26, 1120–1171.

Elliott, R. and Percy, L. (2006) *Strategic Brand Management*, Oxford University Press, Oxford.

Eurostat (2006) *NUTS – Nomenclature of Territorial Units for Statistics: Overview*. http://ec.europa.eu/eurostat/web/nuts/overview.

Feldman, M. (1994) *The Geography of Innovation*, Kluwer Academic Publishers, Dordrecht, Boston, London.

Fink, C., Smarzynska Javorcik, B. and Spatareanu, M. (2003) *Income-related biases in international trade*, World Bank Policy Research Paper, 3150.

Freeman, C. (1988) Japan, a new national system of innovation. In Dosi, G., Freeman, C., Nelson, R., Silverberg, G. and Soete, L. (eds), *Technical Change and Economic Theory*, Pinter, London.

Fritsch, M. (2002) Measuring the quality of regional innovation systems: A knowledge function approach, *International Regional Science Review* 25(1), 86–101.

Furman, J. and Hayes, R. (2004) Catching up or standing still? National innovation productivity among follower nations, 1978–1999, *Research Policy* 33, 1329–1354.

Furman, J., Porter, M. and Stern, S. (2002) The determinants of national innovation capacity, *Research Policy* 31, 899–933.

Godinho, M.M., Mendonça, S. and Pereira, T.S. (2005) *Towards a taxonomy of innovation systems*, Working Papers 2005/13, Department of Economics at the School of Economics and Management (ISEG), Technical University of Lisbon.

Gravetter, J. and Wallnau, L. (2004) *Statistics for the Behavioural Sciences*, 6th edn, Wadsworth/Thomson Learning, Belmont, CA.

Greenhalgh, C., Longland, M. and Bosworth, D. (2001) *Protecting intellectual property: British, European and American patents and trademarks of selected UK companies 1986–95*, OIPRC Working Paper 01/01.

Griffith, R., Redding, S. and Van Reenen, J. (2004) Mapping the two faces of R&D: Productivity and growth in a panel of OECD industries, *The Review of Economics and Statistics* 86(4), 883–895.

Griliches, Z. (1979) Issues in assessing the contribution of research and development to productivity growth, *Bell Journal of Economics* 10, 92–116.

Griliches, Z. (1984) Interindustry technology flows and productivity growth: A reexamination, *Review of Economics and Statistics* 66, 324–329.

Griliches, Z. (1990) Patent statistics as economic indicators: A survey, *Journal of Economic Literature* 28(4), 1661–1707.

Hartog, C., Parker, S., van Stel, A. and Thurik, R. (2010) *The two-way relationship between entrepreneurship and economic performance*, EIM Research Reports, reference number H200822.

Hollanders, H., Tarantola, S. and Loschky, A. (2009) *Regional Innovation Scoreboard 2009*, Pro Inno Europe, Inno Metrics.

Hu, M. and Mathews, J. (2005) National innovative capacity in East Asia, *Research Policy* 34, 1322–1349.

Jacobsson. S., Oskarsson, C. and Philipson, J. (1996) Indicators of technological activities – comparing educational, patent and R&D statistics in the case of Sweden, *Research Policy* 25(4), 573–585.

Jaffe, A. (1986) Technological opportunity and spillovers of R&D: Evidence from firms' patents, profits, and market value, *American Economic Review* 76(5), 984–1001.

Jaffe, A. (1989) The real effects of academic research, *American Economic Review* 79(5), 987–970.

Jaffe, A., Trajtenberg, M. and Henderson, R. (1993) Geographic localization of knowledge spillovers as evidenced by patent citations, *The Quarterly Journal of Economics*, MIT Press, 108(3), 577–598.

Jones, C. (1995) R&D based models of economic growth, *Journal of Political Economy* 103(4), 759–784.

Krammer, S. (2009) Drivers of national innovation in transition: Evidence from a panel of Eastern European countries, *Research Policy* 38(5), 845–860.

Lamoreaux, N. and Sokoloff, K. (eds) (2004) *The Financing Innovation in Historical Perspective*, MIT Press, Cambridge, MA.

Laursen, K. and Salter, A. (2004) Searching high and low: What types of firms use universities as a source of innovation? *Research Policy* 33, 1201–1215.

Lundvall, B. (1992) User-producer relationships, national systems of innovation and internationalisation. In Lundvall, B.-A. (ed.), *National Systems of Innovation, Towards a Theory of Innovation and Interactive Learning*, Pinter, London, 45–67.

Mainwaring, L., Moore, N. and Murphy, P. (2004) *Trademark holdings of production firms in Britain and Ireland*, Working Paper, Department of Economics, University of Wales.

Malerba, F. and Orsenigo, L. (2000) Knowledge, innovative activities and industrial evolution, *Industrial and Corporate Change* 9(2), 289–314.

Malmberg, C. (2005) *Trademarks Statistics as Innovation Indicator? – A Micro Study, Center for Innovation*, Research and Competence in the Learning, Lund.

Mansfield, E. (1995) Academic research underlying industrial innovations: sources, characteristics, and financing, *Review of Economics and Statistics* 77, 55–65.

Marzal, J. and Tortajada-Esparza, E. (2007) Innovation assessment in traditional industries: A proposal of aesthetic innovation indicators, *Scientometrics* 72(1), 33–57.

Mendonça, S., Pereira, T.S. and Godinho, M. (2004) Trademarks as an indicator of innovation and industrial change, *Research Policy* 33(9), 1385–1404.

Millot, V. (2009) *Trademarks as an indicator of product and marketing innovations*, STI Working Paper, OECD.

Mowery, D. and Sampat, B. (2005) Universities in national innovation systems. In Fagerberg, J., Mowery, D.C. and Nelson, R. (eds), *The Oxford Handbook of Innovation*, Oxford University Press, Oxford, 209–239.

Muller, E. and Nauwelaers, C. (2005) *Enlarging the ERA, identifying priorities for regional policy focusing on research and technological development in the New Members States and Candidate Countries*, Final report COP6, CT.2004. 00001.

Muller, E. and Zenker, A. (2001) Business services as actors of knowledge transformation: The role of KIBS in regional and national innovation systems, *Research Policy* 30, 1501–1516.

Muller, E., Jappe, A., Héraud, J. and Zenker, A. (2006) *A regional typology of innovation capacities in New Member States and Candidate Countries*, BETA, Document de travail n° 2006–18.

Nasierowski, W. and Arcelus, F. (1999) Interrelationships among the elements of national innovation systems: A statistical evaluation, *European Journal of Operational Research* 119(2), 235–253.

Nelson, R. (ed.) (1993) *National Innovation Systems: A Comparative Analysis*, Oxford University Press, Oxford.

Nelson, R. and Winter, S. (1982) *An Evolutionary Theory of Economic Change*, The Belknap Press of Harvard University Press, Cambridge and London.

O'Sullivan, M. (2005) Finance and Innovation. In Fagerberg, J., Mowery, D.C. and Nelson, R. (eds), *The Oxford Handbook of Innovation*, Oxford University Press, Oxford.

OECD (1995) *The Measurement of Scientific and Technological Activities*, Manual on the Measurement on Human Resources Devoted to S&T (Canberra Manual), OECD, Paris.

OECD (2004) *The OECD-JRC Handbook on Practices for Developing Composite Indicators*, OECD, Paris.

OECD (2005) *The Measurement of Scientific and Technical Activities, Proposed Guidelines for Collecting and Interpreting Technological Innovation Data*. Oslo Manual, DSTI, 3rd edn, OECD, Paris.

OECD (2010) *Measuring Innovation: A New Perspective*, OECD, Paris.

Pavitt, K. and Patel, P. (1999) Global corporations and national systems of innovation: Who dominates whom?, In Archibugi, D., Howells, J. and Michie, J. (eds), *Innovation Policy in a Global Economy*, Cambridge University Press, Cambridge, 94–119.

Pereira, A. (2004) *SPSS Guia Prático de Utilização*, Análise de Dados para Ciências Sociais e Psicologia. 5th edn, ed. Sílabo, Lisboa.

Porter, M. (1990) *The Competitive Advantage of Nations*, Free Press, New York.

Rodríguez-Pose, A. and Crescenzi, R. (2006) *R&D, spillovers, innovation systems and the genesis of regional growth in Europe*, College of Europe – Bruges European Economic Research Papers No. 5.

Romer, P. (1990) Endogenous technical change, *Journal of Political Economy* 98(5), 71–102.

Rose, S., Shipp, S., Lal, B. and Stone, A. (2009) *Frameworks for measuring innovation, initial approaches*, Science and Technology Policy Institute, Working Paper Series 6, Athena Alliance.

Schmoch, U. (2003) Services marks as novel innovation indicator, *Research Evaluation* 12(2), 149–156.

Schmookler, J. (1966) *Invention and Economic Growth*, Harvard University Press, Cambridge, MA.

Thomi, W. and Böhn, T. (2003) *Knowledge intensive business services in regional systems of innovation: Initial results from the case of Southeast-Finland*, 43rd European Congress of the Regional Science Association, Jyväskylä, Finland, 27–30 August 2003, 22 pp.

Wooldridge, J.F. (2002) *Econometric Analysis of Cross-section and Panel-data*, MIT Press, Cambridge, MA.

15 Knowledge based entrepreneurship and emerging economies

Franco Malerba, Sunil Mani, Valero Sterzi, Xiaobo Wu and Andrei Yudanov

1 Introduction

In the last decade China, India and Russia have developed significantly and have been involved in a process of catching up in many sectors. In this process, knowledge-intensive entrepreneurship (KIE) has played a key role by introducing innovations and fostering growth. KIE involves the creation of innovation networks of different actors such as firms, universities and other public organizations, which allow entrepreneurs to share information and to create new knowledge.

Its success clearly depends on structural factors and on innovation-related policy reforms aiming at removing barriers for entrepreneurs to bring ideas to markets, such as the access to finance and the effectiveness of the intellectual property rights. In this context innovative firms, start-ups and spin-offs, especially in new technology-based high-tech industries, become the key factors in the catching-up process characterizing these three big players.

This chapter is organized in the following way. In Section 2, we start by exploring the characteristics of innovation activities and of the 'new innovators', defined here as those private and public organizations that start to patent and innovate, in China, India and Russia. We provide a picture of new innovators and the patterns of technological entry; the post-entry innovative behaviour of new firms and the technological value generated by the new firms, distinguishing the number of citations received by new entrants and incumbents. In Sections 3, 4 and 5 we examine the cases of China, India and Russia. Finally, in Section 6 we draw some conclusions by highlighting similarities and differences behind the growth of knowledge-intensive entrepreneurship in China, India and Russia.

2 A quantitative overview of innovators and new innovators in China, India and Russia

Large emergent economies have grown dramatically in technological terms in recent years. Figure 15.1 (a, b, c) shows the patenting activity of selected

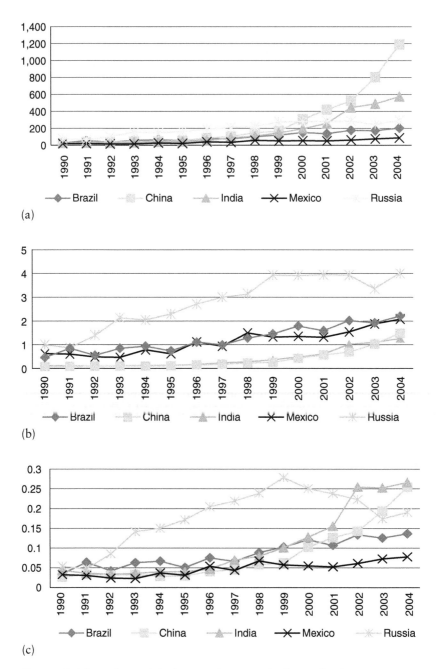

Figure 15.1 Patenting activity in emerging countries by application years.

large emergent economies according to the application date of the patent. There are two ways of assigning a patent to a country: it is possible to look at the country of the applicants or at the country of the inventors. If in the first case we observe the patenting activity of companies with legal address in one of the selected emerging countries, in the second case we observe the inventive activity of individuals according to their residence. We have chosen the one based on the inventor's address because, especially for developing and emerging countries where the presence of foreign multinationals is important, this should reflect more directly the inventive activity of laboratories in a given country (Dernis *et al.*, 2001; Montobbio and Sterzi, 2011, 2013).

In particular, Figure 15.1a shows the simple count of patent applications from the European Patent Office (EPO) from 1990 to 2004. If the absolute numbers are particularly low for all countries throughout the first half of the 1990s,[1] it is also true that in the period 1996–2004 China and India, but also Brazil and Russia, experienced a high growth in international patent applications. Figure 15.1b however points out that in terms of number of workers the Russian Federation shows the highest productivity: the number of patent applications per number of workers is about twice that of all the other economies. However, also China and India have experienced an increasing level of productivity since the last years of the 1990s. Finally, Figure 15.1c shows the ratio of patent to GDP which corrects for the effects of country size and improves comparability across the countries. Since the 2000s India and China have experienced a strong growth in patenting activity, which enabled them to perform better than the Russian Federation in the number of patent applications in terms of GDP.

For what concerns technological differences, Figure 15.2 (a, b, c) shows the number of patenting firms in five main sectors (*Telecommunications, Technology for Control/Measures/Analysis, Pharmaceuticals/Cosmetics, Information Technology* and *Biotechnology*) for three periods (1990–1994, 1995–1999, 2000–2004).

Strong differences that appear especially in India (Figure 15.2b) are not surprising since the role and effectiveness of patents vary considerably across technologies and industries (Orsenigo and Sterzi, 2010). In particular, *Pharmaceuticals/Cosmetics* and *Biotechnology* fields in India have been experienced as strong since the 1990s and now the Pharmaceutical industry in India is the world's third largest in terms of volume. China shows an impressive growth in all the selected sectors, while the Russian Federation shows it in *Telecommunications* and *Information Technology*.

There are various factors behind the substantial growth of patenting activity (in particular in China and India) beyond their impressive economic growth. These factors are related to high R&D growth, increases in the level of human capital, considerable inflows of FDIs, reforms conducive to the entry and creation of new innovative companies, the structural

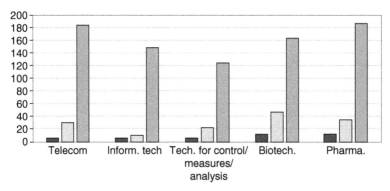

(a)

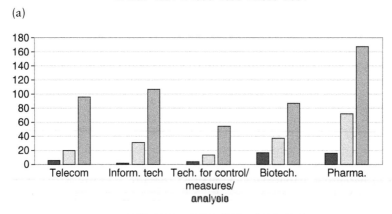

(b)

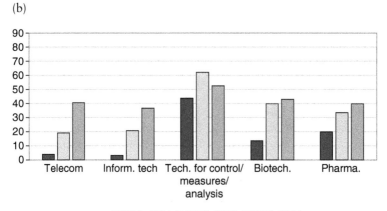

(c)

Figure 15.2 Patenting activity in emerging countries by technological fields and application years.

transformation of these economies towards the production of goods and services with higher technological intensity and reforms in intellectual property legislation.

2.1 Patterns of technological entry

In this section we analyse new innovators, defined as firms and other organizations which innovate for the first time,[2] in China, India and Russia, using the methodology used by Malerba and Orsenigo (1999). In more detail, we consider technological entrants (new innovators) those firms and other types of organizations that patent for the first time in a specific technological field. The data used in this work are based on patent applications to the European Patent Office (EPO). In the 2000s, new innovators are in general foreign companies (around the 80 per cent of total innovators in China and the 70 per cent in the Russian Federation) with still a persistent role played by the national public sector (around 10 per cent both in China and in the Russian Federation).

For the technologies examined, we have adopted the INPI-OST-FhG-ISI classification, developed by Institut National de la Propriété Industrielle (INPI, Paris), Observatoire des Sciences and des Techniques (OST, Paris) and Fraunhofer Gesellschaft-ISI (Karlsruhe). The 13 technologies selected[3] have been chosen from the 30 technological fields classified by the INPI-OST-FhG-ISI nomenclature. It is important to point out that the classification used is technology-based and not market-based. As a result, the names of sectors represent specific technologies in which the patent has been classified by the Patent Office, and not the sector in which the firm operates. Some firms may patent in some technologies and then use those patents in completely different markets.

In this section we use the term 'firm' for both companies and other institutions (such as universities and PROs). A technological entrant – i.e. an organization applying for a patent for the first time – can be a *de novo* entrant, when the patent is the first patent ever, or a technological diversifier, when the patent is the first in a certain technology. It is important to remark that technological entry does not necessarily imply economic entry or the establishment of a new company. Although case studies and analyses in progress confirm that the date of the first patent of a firm is highly correlated with its foundation, in general a firm can patent shortly after its foundation or after many years. In our analysis, we consider the *application date* of the patent, since that date is the closest to the date of production and sale of the related new product.[4] The period of analysis is 1990–2003.

Besides the simple count of the number of total technological entrants, both *de novo* and diversifiers, other indicators are used. The first is the rate of technological entry, calculated in terms of firms or in terms of patents. The *entry rate* in terms of firms is the ratio between the number of entrants in a certain sector divided by the total number of firms patenting in the same sector in a given period. The same ratio can be expressed in terms of patents: the *entrants share* is the ratio between the patents held by new entrants and those held by all the companies patenting in the same sector in a given period. Results show that technological entry is a very common process. Tables 15.1 and 15.2 report some general figures about technological entry for the countries included in the analysis.

First of all, the total entry average rate in terms of firms for 2002–2003 ranges from 63.5 per cent to 77.7 per cent, a level substantially higher than the 42.5 per cent for the USA in the same period but similar to other large emergent economies such as Mexico and Brazil (for further figures about technological entry in developed countries, see Camerani and Malerba, 2010). Second, there are some differences among the three emerging countries: Table 15.1 shows that India on average presents a lower level of technological entry in terms of firms compared to China and Russia. This result is also confirmed looking at *de novo* firms where the percentage of patenting firms in the period 2002–2003 that have not patented before is 47.7 per cent in India, while it is substantially higher in China and the Russian Federation (respectively with 76 per cent and 77.7 per cent). Third, the ratio of new innovators to the total innovators (both measured as *total technological entry* and the *de novo technological entry*) has decreased over time in the Russian Federation and in China, but not in

Table 15.1 Technological entry in terms of firms (%)

Years	China		Russia		India	
	Total	De novo	Total	De novo	Total	De novo
1990–1991	100.0	95.7	82.9	73.2	62.5	45.8
1992–1993	92.3	92.3	95.3	89.4	55.0	45.0
1994–1995	85.3	85.3	82.6	77.7	80.0	60.0
1996–1997	94.6	89.3	86.2	73.8	64.0	48.0
1998–1999	88.2	81.4	72.1	63.9	70.7	59.8
2000–2001	83.0	71.0	78.6	67.7	67.8	55.5
2002–2003	76.0	63.7	77.7	68.0	63.5	47.7
	Mexico		Brazil		USA	
	Total	De novo	Total	De novo	Total	De novo
2002–2003	77.1	72.9	79.3	62.2	42.5	27.3

Notes
Total *(technology entry)* is the ratio of new patenting organizations (both *de novo* entrants, organizations that start to patent for the first time, and *technological diversifiers*, organizations that start to patent in a given technology) to the total number of patenting firms active in the period. De novo *(technology entry)* is the ratio of *de novo* entrants to the total number of patenting organizations active in the period. Own elaborations.

Table 15.2 Technological entry in terms of patents (%)

	China		Russia		India	
	Total	De novo	Total	De novo	Total	De novo
1990–1991	90.9	86.4	73.2	65.9	50.0	36.7
1992–1993	91.3	91.3	82.7	76.5	50.0	40.9
1994–1995	84.4	84.4	73.8	69.0	60.5	44.7
1996–1997	85.5	83.6	66.7	58.0	48.8	36.9
1998–1999	75.9	71.4	59.6	53.2	46.9	39.8
2000–2001	57.8	49.3	61.9	53.2	36.8	30.0
2002–2003	42.9	35.8	62.7	54.7	28.1	21.2
	Mexico		Brazil		USA	
	Total	De novo	Total	De novo	Total	De novo
2002–2003	68	64	68.4	54.7	14.5	9.4

Notes
Total (technology entry) is the ratio of the number of patents of new patenting organizations (both *de novo* entrants, organizations that start to patent for the first time, and *technological diversifiers*, organizations that start to patent in a given technology) to the total number of patents of firms active in the period. *De novo (technology entry)* is the ratio of number of patents of *de novo* entrants to the total number of patents of organizations active in the period. Own elaborations.

India, meaning that the differences among the three emerging countries have been reduced in the last years. Fourth, Table 15.2 reports statistics about the number of patents held by the entrants divided by the total patents in the period. As expected, new innovators are on average smaller in terms of patenting activity than incumbents. This is true especially for China and India, where in 2002–2003 the *de novo innovators* are the 63.7 per cent and the 47.7 per cent of the total number of patenting firms but held respectively only 35.8 per cent and 21.2 per cent of total patents.

2.2 A characterization of the new innovators

Among the new innovators, at least 74 per cent in China and 60 per cent in the Russian Federation are foreign companies, that is foreign multinationals that patent for the first time with inventors residing in China and in the Russian Federation.[5] This is particularly evident for China in Pharmaceuticals and Biotechnology, where the *de novo* innovators represent 75 per cent of total patenting firms. Public domestic firms are still 10 per cent in 2004 even though as time goes by we observe an increasing role of private business.

For what concerns the post-entry behaviour of technological entrants we consider the persistency in the patenting activity of technological

398 F. Malerba et al.

entrants. This statistic takes into consideration only *de novo* entrants, since entrants by diversification can be considered by definition in some way persistent, as they already patented before entering into the technology. In more detail, *de novo* entrants are divided in three groups: *occasional*, if they have only one patent; *sporadic*, if they have more than one patent but less than the average; *persistent*, if they have more than one patent and they patent more than the average. Table 15.3 calculates the persistence in patenting activity of *de novo* entrants by period. China shows the lowest level of persistency in the last years (14.2 per cent), while India and Russia have respectively values of 21.7 per cent and 23.1 per cent. Moreover, in terms of persistency, these countries seem to be in the middle between the advanced countries (for example USA, with 12.9 per cent of persistency) and other large emergent economies (such as Mexico and Brazil with 31.4 per cent and 24.6 per cent). A possible reason is that in China new innovators are often individual and small and medium enterprises (SMEs) that are among the major force (accounting for 40 per cent) behind the growth of national GDP (Chang and Li, 2007), but also have fewer chances to survive given the worldwide intense competition.

Finally, in order to measure the quality and the technological impact of the patenting activity we consider the number of forward citations received[6] by the patent within the first five years after the priority date. Interestingly, in terms of quality of patenting activity we do not observe any significant difference either between innovators and new innovators or between China, India and the Russian Federation. Moreover, we find similar figures also for the United States and for some other emerging countries such as Brazil and Mexico.[7]

3 The growth of knowledge-intensive entrepreneurship in China

Thus, overall China, India and Russia present a high level of technological entry rate with respect to the advanced countries, due to the presence of foreign multinationals and, in recent years, to the innovative activity of private domestic firms.

We now move from the introductory quantitative analysis of new innovators in China, India and Russia to a discussion of knowledge-intensive entrepreneurship in China, India and Russia. We will examine one country at a time. We examine the case of China first.

In the last 30 years, China has been transforming to be a much more market-oriented economy. Along with this process, entrepreneurial activities have become quite high and have contributed a lot to economic prosperity (Anderson *et al.*, 2003; Dana, 1999). Strategies and organizational behaviours of firms have also changed greatly, acknowledging knowledge as one of the most important factors in building up and maintaining competitive advantages.

Table 15.3 Post-entry behaviour (%)

	China			Russia			India		
	Persistent	Occasional	Sporadic	Persistent	Occasional	Sporadic	Persistent	Occasional	Sporadic
1990–91	36.4	59.1	4.5	10.0	90.0	0.0	54.5	45.5	0.0
1992–93	25.0	70.8	4.2	22.4	65.8	11.8	44.4	55.6	0.0
1994–95	37.9	55.2	6.9	22.3	69.1	8.5	55.6	38.9	5.6
1996–97	28.0	64.0	8.0	23.4	59.8	16.8	30.6	47.2	22.2
1998–99	21.7	57.8	20.5	17.9	70.9	11.1	23.6	54.5	21.8
2000–01	15.3	66.3	18.4	15.5	69.7	14.8	24.7	59.3	16.0
2002–2003	14.2	65.1	20.7	23.1	70.9	6.0	21.7	51.9	26.4
	Mexico			Brazil			USA		
2002–2003	31.4	60.0	8.6	24.6	55.1	20.3	12.9	52.8	34.2

It takes a long time for Chinese firms to realize the importance of knowledge and associated entrepreneurial activities. The People's Republic China was a laggard in literally every sector compared to developed countries at the beginning of its foundation in 1949. The reform and openness since 1978 have led to a remarkable economic growth and social changes. Entrepreneurial activities were completely prohibited before 1978, and also restricted in terms of scale (no more than seven employees) in the early 1980s. Chinese government officially recognized the status of private economy in 1988 (7th National People's Congress). Even with certain restrictions, private businesses in the form of private enterprises (*siying qiye*), township and village enterprises (*xiangzhen qiye*) and individual businesses (*getihu*) developed very fast (Liao and Sohmen, 2001). They plunged actively into providing consumer goods and services that rigid state owned enterprises could not provide at the time. During this transition period, central and local government also reformed laws and regulations to promote free market.

On the other hand, in order to acquire foreign technology, the Chinese government aggressively encouraged foreign direct investment. However, the direct application of those technologies was not always efficient or effective, partly because the demand conditions of China were different from those of the source countries. China's domestic market is huge but highly segmented in terms of consumer demands. Based on the understanding of local markets, Chinese firms learned to combine foreign technology with demand, and came up with innovative products that could satisfy market needs. This process does not fit with the U-A model (Utterback and Abernathy, 1975), in which technological innovation emerges first and is then followed by process innovation. Wu (1995) and Wu *et al.* (2009) propose a 'Secondary Innovation' model to explain the unique phenomenon in China: Chinese firms tend to conduct process innovation based on foreign technologies and their understanding of local needs. During this process, technological capabilities are built and become the basis of further technological innovations, the performance of which, in some cases, would surpass the original foreign technologies. 'Secondary Innovation' is still a common practice for Chinese firms today.

'Secondary Innovation' proves to be a suitable strategy for Chinese firms to compete with foreign firms whilst building up their technological capabilities. However, the dependence on imported technology is not enough for Chinese firms to compete with foreign firms on a global scale. Thus, novel and original innovations are becoming the key to the future competitiveness of Chinese firms. Many Chinese firms are now the top technological innovators in their industrial sectors. For example, Huawei and ZTE are ranked 11th and 26th in EPO patent applications in 2013. Innovation and entrepreneurship however have been uneven across regions, with the highest intensity in the eastern regions and the lowest intensity in the south-west regions, as Chang and Li (2007) and the GEM report (Gao *et al.*, 2006) show (see Figure 15.3).

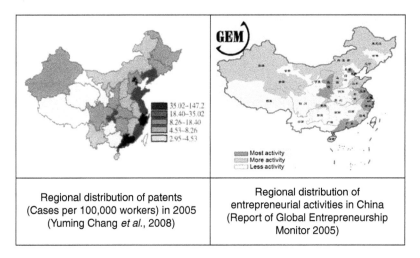

| Regional distribution of patents (Cases per 100,000 workers) in 2005 (Yuming Chang *et al.*, 2008) | Regional distribution of entrepreneurial activities in China (Report of Global Entrepreneurship Monitor 2005) |

Figure 15.3 Entrepreneurial and patent activities by region.

Following the framework introduced in Chapter 2, in order to discuss driving factors of KIE in China, we follow on the following variables (Figure 15.4).

3.1 Driving factors of KIE in China: demand and market segmentation

China's market is highly segmented, owing to uneven regional development and income inequality (Cui and Liu, 2000; Mu and Lee, 2005). The requirements of a high-end customer from the Eastern Coastal region might be very different from a low-end customer from the Western region. This highly diversified customer requirement calls for entrepreneurs who

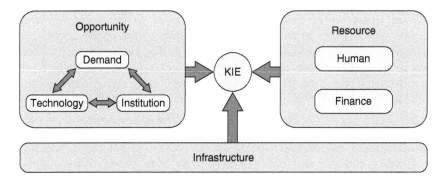

Figure 15.4 Driving factors of KIE in China.

can flexibly leverage market knowledge, technological knowledge and social knowledge to succeed in this highly segmented market (Liao and Sohmen, 2001). Entrepreneur Jack Ma and his online C2C platform Taobao.com can serve as a good example: Taobao is created free for both sellers and buyers (social knowledge), inclusive of diversified needs (market knowledge), and it provides a reliable trading platform (technological knowledge). Jack Ma is now one of the most successful entrepreneurs in China.

3.2 Technology

The main sources of technological innovation for Chinese firms are the technologies acquired from foreign countries. However, with the accumulation of available capital, both industry and government are investing heavily in scientific and technological (S&T) activities. The intensive investments in S&T lead to significant output and contribute to the catching-up of domestic firms in both traditional and high-tech industries (Hu and Mathews, 2008). This pattern is verified by substantial increases in R&D expenses and patent application in the last decade (Figure 15.5). In this dynamic technological environment, domestic entrepreneurs play an important role in the catching-up process, and their ability to acquire and apply new knowledge is key to the success of their organization.

3.3 Institutional support

Other than policies that promote private economy, laws and regulations directly related to entrepreneurship were enacted. In 2000, the 'Sole Proprietorship Enterprise Law of the People's Republic of China (PRC)' was put into effect, aiming at broadening investing areas, improving policy environment, opening financing channels and services. Tax incentives were provided to promote the growth of these businesses. In 2008, 'PRC Employment Promotion Law' was carried out, bringing up a series of guidelines to promote entrepreneurship. Regional governments also took various measures to encourage entrepreneurship and employment. For example, Shanghai Industry and Commerce Bureau announced 'Some Opinions on Encouraging Business for Promoting Employment', which put forward eight measures to promote university students' entrepreneurial activities.

There are also several science and technology parks and incubators which provide favourable entrepreneurial environment and encouraging high-tech entrepreneurship, such as Zhongguancun in Beijing, Zhangjiang in Shanghai and International S&T Park in Suzhou. There are also numerous entrepreneurial parks established to attract overseas returnees in order to utilize their knowledge learned in other countries or regions. By 2010,

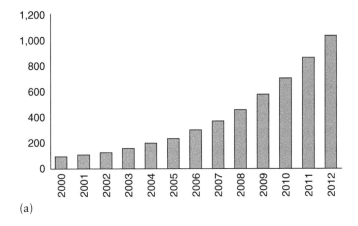

(a)

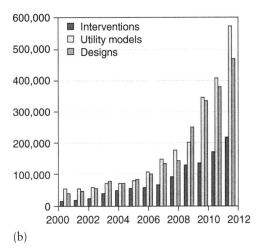

(b)

Figure 15.5 R&D expenses (billion RMB) and patent application (source: *China Statistics Yearbook on High Technology Industry*, 2013).

there were more than 150 returnees' parks, with more than 8,000 enterprises.

3.4 Human capital

Since the resumption[8] of the college entrance examination in 1978, the average educational level of the Chinese labour force has improved a lot. Market economy stimulates people's incentive to pursue wealth by conducting business. Entrepreneurial intention of individuals drives them to continuously look for opportunities in every possible area. Higher education helps them to perceive and seize these opportunities. They can use their knowledge to correctly understand technological potential, access resource holders and combine these into a feasible business model.

Except for general education, entrepreneurial education has been implemented from the early 2000s in China. In April 2002, the 'Forum on experiment of entrepreneurial education in selected places' was held by the Ministry of Higher Education, appointing nine universities as the first experimental units to cultivate undergraduates to be individuals with innovative spirits and entrepreneurial abilities. There were circa 600 universities offering curriculums in entrepreneurship, and 85 per cent of higher education institutes confirmed a function of promoting entrepreneurial spirits and skills (Entrepreneurship Education Report China, 2011).

3.5 Financial capital

As one of the key resources of running business, financial capital is especially vital for high-technology entrepreneurship. In recent years, the number and scale of venture capital (VC) companies has increased rapidly in China (Figure 15.6). The combination of capital, science and technology is part of the successful story of the USA, as seen in Silicon Valley. In China, domestic VC companies are less experienced compared to their international counterparts. On the other hand, their advantage is to have a better understanding of local customers.

Difficulty in receiving financial support represents the major challenge for new ventures in China. The state dominated financial system and capital market does not provide sufficient support for entrepreneurs in order for their businesses to take off (Boyreau-Debray and Wei, 2005). This is especially true for small enterprises in traditional industrial sectors and rural areas. Entrepreneurs have to rely on other sources of funding (e.g. personal loans). The government has realized the importance of the issue but reforms still have to take place.

3.6 Infrastructure

The advance of ICT technology has played a significant role in supporting entrepreneurial activities in China: entrepreneurs in China rely heavily in *guanxi* (personal relationship) to achieve information (Guthrie, 2002). The emergence of ICT technology has made business-related information easier to achieve thus reducing information asymmetry (Avgerou and Li, 2013). Internet platforms realized by ICT technology also significantly cut the cost of capturing and maintaining customers (Ansari and Mela, 2003), who are geographically dispersed in a big country like China. This feature of ICT technology allows entrepreneurs in China to start their business on internet platforms such as Taobao.

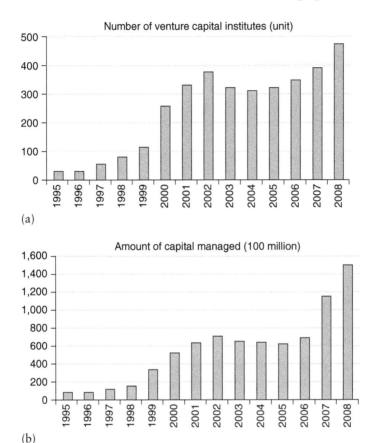

Figure 15.6 Venture capital and institutes in China.

3.7 Policy implications

Although entrepreneurial activities had been banned for decades before the economic reformation in 1978 (Liao and Sohmen, 2001), they are now the key driver behind the country's economic growth. Therefore, successful entrepreneurs are recognized by the public as role-models. In the meantime, China's government has been persistently promoting innovative activities (the 10th, 11th and 12th 5-Year Plans). Thus, a significant increase in both quality and quantity in EPO patents filed by Chinese companies and research organizations has been observed. With government support, the increased supply of human resource and the improvement of financial and business infrastructure, we have reason to believe that Chinese entrepreneurs and entrepreneurial activities will continue to contribute significantly to the country's competitiveness, innovation and productivity (Yue, 2008).

4 The growth of knowledge-intensive entrepreneurship in India

One of the distinguishing aspects of India's growth performance especially since 2000 is that its knowledge intensity has increased: in 2005–2006 about 14 per cent of overall NDP of the country derived from knowledge-intensive production.[9] Mirroring the general trend, much of the knowledge-intensive production comes from the services sector. Further, the growth performance of the knowledge-intensive production sector is larger than that of the overall economy (Mani, 2010). In the following pages the term knowledge-intensive entrepreneurship means entrepreneurship in the context of medium- and high-technology industries, both in the manufacturing and service sectors as well. The medium- and high-technology industries that we consider are the following: Chemical and chemical products, Metal products and machinery, Electrical machinery, Transport equipment, Communication services, Computer relating services and R&D services. Our discussion of the growth of knowledge-intensive entrepreneurship is in terms of first a set of two macro indicators and second a micro indicator. We begin with the former.

4.1 Macro indicators

The two macro indicators are based on the new company formation and on the size of India's corporate sector in relation to her GDP. According to the former, the number of new companies formed has increased quite tremendously, from about 250,000 in 1992 to about 730,000 in 2006. On average about 34,000 new companies have been established every year since 1992, although the rate of growth of new company formation has actually decelerated during the post liberalization period. Deceleration in the rate of growth may be purely statistical. It may be that the rate of growth of companies in the pre-liberalization period was high because it started from a low base. Although there has been an increase in the absolute number of new companies during the post-liberalization period, its rate of growth has decelerated. Unfortunately, we do not have further data on whether these companies are started by new entrepreneurs or by existing entrepreneurs. However, there is indirect evidence to show that most of the companies that have entered new technology-based industries, such as IT, BT and even the auto parts industries, are new companies set up by hitherto not-so well-known entrepreneurs.[10] As result of the phenomenal growth of new companies, the size of the corporate sector in India measured by the share of its paid-up capital[11] to the country's GDP has increased by 12 percentage points to about one-fifth of GDP by 2006 – the latest year for which such data are available. Another interesting aspect is that the gross domestic saving and investment rates of the private sector have increased. For instance the gross domestic savings rate of the sector has increased from 3.4 per cent in

2001–2002 to 7.8 per cent in 2007–2008 and the gross domestic investment rate has increased from 5.4 to 14.5 per cent during the same period (Reserve Bank of India, 2008: 70–71). All this points to an improvement in entrepreneurial activity in the country.

4.2 Growth in knowledge-intensive ventures

For measuring this aspect, we employ a director indicator, which is the number of new company registrations in India according to the level of technological activity (National Knowledge Commission, 2008). According to the National Knowledge Commission, there are four levels of entrepreneurship in terms of the level of technology involved with low-technology activities such as agriculture and allied activities at the bottom of the pyramid (Level 1) and knowledge-intensive sectors at the top of the pyramid (Levelone 4):

- Level 1: Agriculture and other activities: crop production, plantation; forestry, livestock, fishing, mining, and quarrying,
- Level 2: Trading services: wholesale and retail trade; hotels and restaurants,
- Level 3: Old economy or traditional sectors: manufacturing, electricity, gas and water supply,
- Level 4: Emerging sectors (including knowledge-intensive sectors): IT, finance, insurance and business services, construction, community, social and personal services, supply chain, transport, storage, communications, etc.

The data on new company formations that we discussed earlier could be cross-classified according to these four levels. They show that new companies belonging to knowledge-intensive sectors account for the largest share (for over 50 per cent) and the number of new companies formed has significantly increased since 2003 or so.

This dominance of technology-intensive sectors in total company formation is further corroborated by our proxy – namely the technology content of all industrial proposals[12] actually implemented since 1991. Once again, with the exception of a few industries such as textiles, the majority of the new proposals are in technology-oriented industries such as chemicals, fuel, electrical equipment, etc. This once again suggests that technology-oriented ventures have been on the rise in India since the initiation of economic reforms in 1991. However, we do not have any data on the survival rates of these new ventures, as it is quite possible that some of these[13] would have exited from business due to a variety of reasons.

A still another indicator of growing knowledge-intensive entrepreneurship is the growing Indian investments abroad. An increasing number of Indian companies are now investing abroad in order to access high-growth markets, technology and knowledge, boost their positioning in the value chain, attain economies of size and scale of operations, tap global natural resource banks and leverage international brand names for their own brand building. Over time, outward FDI from India has reached, on an average, 42 per cent of inward FDI. Further, counter to one's intuition much of this investment has gone towards the manufacturing sector. Within manufacturing a number of technology-oriented industries such as pharmaceuticals, automobiles, basic metals, telecommunications and electrical equipment have been important. This increase in FDI from India has been facilitated by a number of favourable policy changes at the home front, which encouraged such investments beginning with the Foreign Exchange Management Act (FEMA) of 1999. The amended Foreign Exchange Management Act of 1999 has permitted Indian companies to invest abroad up to 400 per cent of their net worth in India.

4.3 Micro indicators

An analysis of a unique data set on entrepreneurship based on the nominees at the Tata-NEN hottest start-ups competition run by a not-for-profit organization, National Entrepreneurship Network (NEN), has thrown up some additional insights into the emergence and growth of technology-based entrepreneurship in the country in recent times.

Approximately 40 per cent of the start-ups are technology-based (IT and telecoms), mostly based in the large cities with a quarter of them in Bangalore and most of them established in the last three years. The earliest one in the sample was set up in 2003. This latter finding is quite consistent with our earlier finding in that the real fillip to entrepreneurial activity took place only in the current millennium and specifically since 2004: the period 2004 through 2008 is generally referred to as the boom period in India's economy. The GDP grew at an average rate of 9 per cent during this period. The background of these new entrepreneurs also presents us with some interesting results. The majority of them are in their twenties, are first-generation entrepreneurs having their first business and have studied abroad or in Tier I institutions in India where they were exposed to the nitty gritty of starting a new business venture. Women formed only 8 per cent of the total number. In terms of head count, the total employee strength ranged from five to 15 employees.

In sum, the macro and micro indicators that we have presented reinforce the point that the process of economic liberalization and international integration of India's economy has served to unleash a spate of entrepreneurship that was hitherto not seen or experienced in India's recent economic history.

How does one explain this sudden emergence of knowledge-intensive entrepreneurship? In order to understand this we identify a set of facilitating factors.

4.4 Facilitating factors

The basic proposition that we have advanced so far, with the help of a variety of macro and micro indicators, is that there has been an increase in knowledge-intensive entrepreneurship in India since the onset of economic reforms in 1991. In this section, we will attempt to identify those facilitating factors and those which are still constraining a faster emergence of this activity. According to the GEM,[14] there are ten facilitating factors or framework conditions for this activity to flourish and sustain. These are: financial support, government policies, government programmes, education and training, R&D transfer, commercial, professional infrastructure, internal market openness, access to physical infrastructure, cultural and social norms and Intellectual Property Rights protection. While all these factors are important, in the case of India, we could identify five facilitating factors.[15] These are:

I   the new market opportunities presented by a liberalizing economy;
II the availability of financial support schemes from both official and private sources;
III the existence of a large number of governmental programmes and public-private partnership programmes;
IV the emergence of a number of private sector initiatives for supporting knowledge-intensive entrepreneurship by complementing government programmes and by reducing information asymmetries; and
V   the increased availability of technically trained manpower due to a phenomenal increase in the enrolment rate for engineering and technology education at especially the tertiary level in the country.

We elaborate on only the first two as these are the most important determinants.

4.4.1 Growth in market opportunities

An important aspect of liberalization that has been set into motion since 1991 pared down the discretionary role of the government with respect to economic matters and increased the scope of market forces. One of the important components of this increased space was the dispensing of industrial licensing and other regulatory measures thereby reducing the height of barriers to entry to new entrepreneurs. This ease of entry, we argue, is one of the reasons for the rise of entrepreneurship in general. Against this background, an aspect that has engineered knowledge-intensive entrepreneurship is the emergence and growth of new technology-based industries such as IT, which really opened up new opportunities. A run through the list of the top 20 enterprises (in terms of domestic and export sales) in each of the two technology-based industries such as IT and Biotechnology (BT) industries show that almost all the enterprises in these two industries were established during the 1990s or in the more recent period. Most of these are small and medium type enterprises initially set up by technology-oriented entrepreneurs. We further argue that a common factor in spurring opportunities in these two areas is the growth of knowledge process outsourcing. KPOs (proxied by receipts of R&D services, architectural, engineering and other technical services) has been on the rise indicating further market opportunities in addition to the organic growth that is taking place in both the IT, BT and other high-technology industries such as mobile telecommunications.

4.4.2 Availability of finance and especially risk capital

One does not have to emphasize the relevance of the availability of financial resources, equity and debt, for new and growing firms including grants and subsidies. The availability of external risk capital has often been a constraining factor for financing company formation in India. Firms in India have increasingly relied on internal sources of capital and on debt capital rather than on equity for financing their long-term investment goals. It is interesting to note that with the onset of the reforms and the liberalization of the capital markets, the external sources of funds have actually come down since 2004–2005 and in the last two years external financing has, once again, become important but with debt capital becoming more important. It should of course be mentioned that the data for the last two years 2005–2006 and 2006–2007 need to be taken with some caution as the number of companies covered by the Central Bank of India (RBI) survey on the basis of which these numbers have been arrived at shows a dramatic halving compared to those covered in the previous years. So, it may well be possible that the increased share of external finances may actually be a statistical artefact. Companies seem to be depending, increasingly, on self-generation. Within the external source of finance, bank borrowings are more important (due to the current global financial crisis and with the likely existence of a liquidly crunch within the banking system bank borrowings, despite the steps taken by RBI, can become very tight). More recent data from RBI (contained in RBI 2008) too confirm this trend.[16] While this pattern of financing with the internal generation accounts for the larger share and therefore is important for existing companies, new companies may have to depend on external sources. For this the emergence and growth of the private equity market and the venture capital funding has been somewhat helpful.

Finally it may be said that, given the dynamic entrepreneurial ecosystem (consisting of market opportunities, government and private support systems of various kinds, VC, etc.) is beginning to have a positive impact on the students graduating from Tier I institutes taking up entrepreneurship as a career compared to the lure of the labour market (Bansal, 2008; Basant and Chandra, 2006).

5 The predominance of non-R&D-oriented knowledge intensive entrepreneurship in Russia

The main specific feature of contemporary knowledge-intensive entrepreneurship (KIE) in Russia stems from the paradoxical combination of extremely low levels of current R&D expenditures and remaining high potential in research (strong education system; a multitude of specialists representing high academic culture, etc.), which has been the precondition for gazelle-type development of Russian KIE. When the former, centrally planned NIS in the Soviet Union ceased to exist, the entire R&D activities in the country collapsed. Under almost complete stop of the state orders many centers of science and research turned out to be unviable (while in the Soviet epoch they held leading positions in the world).

The reduction in the state innovative activity could be in principle compensated by the private sector. However, it didn't happen either at the moment of state leaving the sphere of innovations, or even many years later. The Russian economy was being transformed from a planned one into a market one under extremely liberal conditions of international openness. There were practically no signs of protectionism. Consequently, the qualitative superiority of imported products due the Soviet industry's lagging behind the developed countries, and the inexperience of the former socialist enterprises to operate under the market conditions have caused the mass replacement of domestic high-tech production with imports and with foreign knowledge.

The process of borrowing foreign knowledge had distinct competitive advantages over domestic R&D. Instead of its own R&D activities, the Russian firms got and/or copied (legally or illegally) foreign technologies. In other cases the Soviet vertically integrated system of knowledge creation (from fundamental scientific research to the production of finished goods) was replaced with directly imported products, embodying foreign knowledge.

As an evaluation of the R&D activity in the largest Russian corporations, made by the author of the '400 Largest Russian Enterprises' ranking list (better known as 'Expert-400') claims (Grishankov, 2008):

> We are labouring under a dangerous misapprehension regarding innovations. The point is, there has not been any. More precisely, there are some innovative processes, but their scale is appallingly small. According to our rating data, many large Russian companies spend more on corporate parties than on research and development. So at the very least it would be naive to speak of innovative development.

The quote above sounds even more tragic in view of the fact that it is about largest Russian firms, obviously much better provided with financial resources to sustain R&D expenditures than other companies in the country. Nevertheless, there is no exaggeration: the R&D expenditures of the large business in Russia are very small. In 2009 they did not exceed 0.2 per cent of the total revenue of 'Expert-400'. For the comparison, we would like to remind that by the OECD classification the companies with the above indicator lower than 0.9 per cent are attributed to the 'low-tech' category. It is no wonder that, as has already been shown in this chapter, the patent activity of Russian companies is not growing as much as for China and India in the last years (see Figure 15.1a and 15.1c).

At the same time, the high educational and scientific potential of the nation has proved to be more stable against shocks, than other elements of the Russian NIS. Despite the possibility of a brain drain, millions of highly qualified specialists stayed in the country, while universities kept on training more and more of them. Under changed conditions these people found jobs in business, often far away from the academic specialization. In Russia the cases when a successful shoe firm is headed by a Ph.D. or certified nuclear physicist, or a confectionery firm is governed by a group of former military engineers became the rule rather than the exception. No wonder that the combination of a solid educational background among the leaders of the Russian business (in particular for the heads of successful middle-size enterprises) and low commercial return from own R&D expenditures stimulated and promoted informal innovative activities The trained eyes of these people promoted high 'entrepreneurial alertness', as it is called in the terminology of the Austrian school. In such a case, innovations are to a lesser degree connected with persistent inventive activity, than with the ability to notice what is lying underexploited and has not been used by other firms (Kirzner, 1997).

As a result, the knowledge-intensive entrepreneurships in Russia started to develop not as R&D-oriented enterprises, but as a type of KIE that is similar to the one observed in the developed countries among so-called high-growth or gazelle-firms (Birch and Medoff, 1994), that the innovative activity of gazelles is usually described the following way: 'with regard to gazelles, in particular, innovation is understood in a broad sense i.e. managerial, organizational and technological'. Moreover, 'innovation in gazelles is more remarkable in the new applications of resources and in new organizational structures than in the generation of new technologies'. It is also noted that 'contrary to popular perception, only around one-third of gazelles are 'high-tech' companies. Fast-growing firms whose success comes from innovative approaches to marketing, organization or distribution can be found across a wide range of activities' (Inno Grips, 2007: 18).

In our empirical study of Russian gazelles we took as a basic principle the original David Birch algorithm according to which any company that has grown at 20 per cent per year or more for at least five years is considered a gazelle. Birch's algorithm places emphasis not only on high rates of firm growth, but also on the sustainability of this growth over some period of time. This cuts off firms whose significant revenue growth is only accidental ('one-day success') and gives some a-priori relevance of the knowledge-based nature of gazelles growth: evidently, the ability of gazelles to show rapid growth over long periods of time proves that these companies possess long-term competitive advantages that are unlikely to appear without the intensive use of knowledge. The results of our study are showing that KIE is developing in Russia mainly as gazelle-type KIE, instead of a R&D-intensive-type KIE. According to direct estimates, in the pre-2008 period gazelles made up 7–8 per cent of the total number of Russian firms (Yudanov, 2011), i.e. they are about twice as numerous as gazelles in the West.[17] The peculiarities of the Russian accounting system (for details see Yudanov, 2010) make us believe that even these high figures dramatically underestimate the number of gazelles, and the correct assessment should be about 12–13 per cent of all companies. Impressive are also growth rates of Russian gazelles. In times of prosperity (2003–2007) they increased their annual revenues by 78 per cent (in constant prices), while the average growth rate of all firms did not exceed 18 per cent. In times of crises (2006–2010) gazelles demonstrated only slightly slower yearly growth of revenue (69 per cent in constant prices) in sharp contrast with only 5 per cent growth shown by the rest of the national business population. Despite the well-known institutional instability Russia should be called the 'country of gazelles', offering the possibility of rapid and sustainable growth for a strikingly large percentage of firms.

In our opinion, the extremely high density of population of gazelles in Russia stems from the excellent possibilities of a rapid growth in a young, emerging market economy combined with the potential of highly educated entrepreneurs to create and/or absorb knowledge. Russia's large and potentially rich economy offers a multitude of promising unoccupied niches making possible long-term dynamic development. The transformation of a firm into a gazelle in almost every case was underpinned by the aspiring gazelle's deliberate search for a vital but unsatisfied market need, and by extraordinary efforts to correct the situation. In other words, the success of gazelles is knowledge-based.

This is most evident from the analysis of individual firms. Russian gazelles display innovativeness of the most wide-ranging nature. It can be purely technological, as in case of *Energomera* that grows the world's largest sapphire crystals required in manufacturing cell phones. Marketing innovations are very numerous: the Soviet era led to a total loss of marketing skills, so that a firm acquiring such skills leaves its competitors far behind (Kolodnyaa, 2007). In other cases, success is achieved by breaking marketing stereotypes. For example, the *Splat* firm gained ground against its much more powerful Western rivals by breaking the global marketing taboo on black toothpaste (this is the colour it gets from natural herbal extracts often required for medicinal purposes).

No wonder that the new knowledge introduced by gazelles into economy works as a strong factor of structural change. In areas where gazelles began to operate, the innovations introduced by them in just a few years changed the profile of the corresponding lines of business. And the fact that these innovations in technological terms turned out to be relatively simple, and were often only adaptations of the world experience to the Russian conditions, does not belittle their value. On the contrary, it represents their strongest side: the most powerful result was achieved with minimal efforts. In some cases networking processes (Dumnaya, 2009) were observed when, for example, the innovative consumer goods produced by some gazelles were promoted through the innovative marketing networks organized by other gazelles, and were financed by the innovative credit products brought to the market by a third category of gazelles.

The development of Russian gazelles has had a spontaneous character, being based on the private initiative, without any interference and/or support from the government. In fact, it was the process of creation of what in NIS theory is often called 'innovation ecosystem',[18] meaning innovations as 'the result of the interaction among an ecology of actors'.

Lately, the government has been seen returning to the innovation sphere. For the first time in the history of post-socialist Russia the goals of modernization of the economy are formulated and measures to support R&D-intensive firms are developed; national projects on the major lines of scientific and technical development are affirmed. As a result, knowledge-intensive entrepreneurship exists in modern Russia on two different and loosely interconnected levels.

The first of them is gazelles' innovation ecosystems. Its member-firms are, as a rule, far from conducting formal R&D activity. Moreover, very often gazelles' innovations represent a recombination, adaptation and integration of knowledge to Russian conditions, rather than innovation in the narrow meaning of the word. Even more often, the innovative activity of gazelles is not connected with technological change at all, and lies in marketing or management sphere. Apparently, only such a type of system can develop and survive spontaneously without any state support under conditions of a strong foreign competition in an ultra-liberal transition economy.

At the same time, gazelles' innovation ecosystem is an extremely viable community of firms, actively and positively influencing the structure of the Russian economy. Modest in size (at least, at the initial stages of the development) gazelles proved to be capable to create in a few years new industries and/or to change considerably the features of old branches. Exponential nature of the growth (Yudanov, 2011), typical for gazelles, leads to innovations spreading through the economy at a high speed after getting market support. Powerful networking effects have been revealed – we can observe how a gazelle forces other firms to innovate, involves them in innovations or supports innovations of the others.

The second level of Russian KIE is represented by high-tech companies re-established with an active support of the government. These days Russia can boast all the institutions and public policies of support for KIE used in the developed countries (Russian Venture Company, Russian Corporation of Nanotechnologies, Skolkovo Technological Park, special economic zones, etc.). The main emphasis is placed on stimulating the creation and early-stage growth of high-tech companies. This is undoubtedly an important task, because the entrepreneurs building an innovative firm in Russia without any help and support face huge difficulties trying to overcome various obstacles.

People involved in practical high-tech business in Russia know, however, that in real life the problem is not solved once the company has successfully made its first steps in business, far from it. The main hurdle is that an innovative enterprise in Russia, having reached a certain size, ceases to grow and never matures to a world-class player. We are not talking here about the specialized suppliers of the Western type, which serve a narrow market niche. These companies' products simply lack sufficient demand. In the simplified Russian economy, which during the period of reforms shifted its focus towards primary products, sophisticated high-tech products often remain unpopular even in cases where they have excellent characteristics. 'Russian innovative companies attempt to skip several institutional barriers in their evolution. They need access to capital at the early stage and later some help in conquering markets' (Medovnikov and Imamutdinov, 2009: 24). Direct stimulation of innovators by the state at this later stage is almost powerless, if the market offers no demand for their products. In the case of Russia, we are talking about demand-side problems: dealing with very weak domestic demand for innovative domestic products and having no experience of working abroad (with the exception of some successful software companies), the majority of Russian high-tech enterprises are unable to bring even very promising products to the market.

This is the point of why Russian gazelles may come to the fore. In terms of the structure of the industries, they are not typically high-tech firms. On the contrary, most of them concentrate in traditional industries (trade, construction, food industry) or industries of moderate technological level (machine building, chemistry). It has been fully understood, however, that a strong high-tech component grows not where it feeds itself (i.e. satisfies the demand within high-tech branches), but where its products are demanded by the entire economy, including low-tech industries. (Hirsch-Kreinsen and Jacobson, 2008). Gazelles reign supreme in identifying and building demand for their products at the consumer end, and are therefore natural consumers/implementers of new technologies. The fact that gazelles have this ability to stimulate consumer demand in any (including traditional) industry additionally expands the scope of use of innovations. Owing to gazelles, high-tech firms may gain potential access to large sales of their products.

We have collected documented examples of borrowing, adapting and implementing technological advance by a number of gazelles (Yudanov,

2007). This has not yet become a large-scale phenomenon in Russia because manufacturers of high-tech product in this country do not know yet which specific innovations are in demand by gazelles while gazelles have no information on what the Russian high-tech can supply to them. Obviously, the current predominance in Russia of policy of stimulation for the creation of high-tech companies requires also the facilitation of contacts with those agents that generate demand for innovations, such as gazelles.

Two potential barriers have to be overcome for the successful development of a high-tech company. During the first stage of the company's development (i.e. while the market tests the innovative product – we estimate annual revenue of such enterprises up to $10 million), the state support for innovative companies as such plays an important role. In the second stage, when the firm reaches annual turnover of about $100 million, the main success factor lies in the access of their high-tech products to the mass market. The 'transparency ratio' of this second barrier is a function of the presence in the country of a strong layer of companies that are capable of and interested in using innovations in products and that enjoy strong demand by consumers. It is this ability which is the characteristic of many gazelles.

Under these conditions, the most reasonable decision is that the state's participation in the process of entrepreneurship generation and growth should be expanded from an exclusive support of R&D-intensive firms to the support to all types of knowledge-intensive entrepreneurship, including the gazelles' innovation ecosystem which already practically exists in the country: the state policy is particularly important in providing access to investment resources, supporting export activities, solving infrastructure problems and protecting from unlawful hostile takeovers.

6 Conclusions

6.1 What are the factors behind the growth of knowledge-intensive entrepreneurship in China, India and Russia?

In sum, from the above analysis we can advance some conclusions on the factors behind the growth of knowledge-intensive entrepreneurship in China, India and Russia. In analytical terms, they can be linked to those factors related to (a) technology, (b) market and demand, and (c) institutions and public policy, which have been discussed in this book in detail in the conceptual chapter by Malerba and McKelvey (Chapter 2) and in the analysis of the role of market, technological and institutional opportunities in Central and Eastern Europe by Radosevic and Yoruk (Chapter 13). To these chapters one may add also recent work by the editors of this book which has been related to innovation systems and opportunities in developing countries, including China and India, as in Malerba and Nelson

(2011 and 2012) and McKelvey and Bagchi-Sen (2014). However, rather than identifying the specificities of each country (which has been done in the previous sections on China, India and Russia) we will try to identify some common factors.

6.1.1 Economic growth, increase in income and the growth of domestic market opportunities

Economic growth and increase in income per capita have greatly expanded domestic demand, changed demand preferences and augmented the variety of new needs, in turn triggering entrepreneurial activities. Given the fact that it is usually difficult for most individuals to gain capital support in their initial entrepreneurial phrase, personal wealth is the main source of entrepreneurial capital.

6.1.2 Increase in skills and education and growth of supply of engineers, technicians and managers

China, India and Russia have increased their level of skills and the quality of their human capital. A larger supply of engineers and scientists in the last years has characterized China and India, while Russia has always had a good scientific base. In addition, in these countries – particularly in China and India – there have been university courses to cultivate undergraduates to have an innovative spirit and entrepreneurial abilities. Nowadays there are several universities offering entrepreneurial curriculum.

6.1.3 Growth of R&D

In few years China and India have increased their absolute effort in R&D. The share of R&D over GDP has also increased. This has created a very active learning environment for companies and generated spillovers in the whole economy.

6.1.4 Spread of information technology

The spread in the use of ICT in the economy has meant a new organizational method to business processes, which may generate entrepreneurial opportunities. With the development of information technology, many new business models have been emerging because firms need less physical investment and can display products online.

6.1.5 Returnees from advanced countries

The growth of knowledge-intensive entrepreneurship in China and India has been fuelled by the inflow of Chinese and Indian students and entrepreneurs coming from advanced countries. These students and entrepreneurs grew up and developed experience in the United States and Europe and were able to transfer into China and India knowledge, ideas and managerial talent.

6.1.6 Rise of venture capital

In recent years, venture capital organization and venture capital firms have increased rapidly. Also the types of venture capital have become more diversified, which means plentiful sources of capital. Private capital has been the main source of funding given its flexibility and efficiency.

6.1.7 Increase in the extent and variety of policy support

A series of policies have been launched in order to specifically support entrepreneurship, in particular in China and India and in Russia more recently. These policies improved the financing channels, supported services for entrepreneurs and provided tax incentives. Regional governments also took measures to promote entrepreneurship and employment. Finally, a large amount of science and technology parks and incubators providing favourable entrepreneurial environment and encouraging high-tech entrepreneurship have been launched.

Notes

1 USPTO patents confirm these figures.
2 Please note that new innovators may be firms and other organizations that have been in existence for some time before going to patent. Thus, we analyse technological, rather than economic, entry.
3 Five broad technologies according to the OST30 classification are considered: *Electrical Engineering and Electronics* (Audiovisual technology (class 2), Telecommunications (3), Information technology (4), Semiconductors (5)), *Instruments* (Optics (6), Technologies for Control/Measures/Analysis (7), Medical engineering (8)), *Chemicals and Materials* (Materials and Metallurgy (14), Macromolecular chemistry (11)), *Pharmaceuticals and Biotechnology* (Biotechnologies (15), Pharmaceuticals and Cosmetics (16)), and *Mechanical Engineering, Machines and Transports* (Machine tools (23), Space technology and Weapons (28)).
4 Instead of the application date, it is also possible considering the priority date to be the formal date of invention for patent law purposes.
5 Data are available upon request by the authors.
6 Since Trajtenberg (1990), forward patent citations have often been used as an indicator of patent value. They are in fact highly correlated with the technological importance of the invention and with the expected profits from the inventions.
7 Data are available by the authors on request.
8 The selection of college students were not based on the academic achievements but political and family backgrounds during the culture revolution between 1966 and 1976.
9 This is computed by taking the share of value added of certain knowledge-intensive manufacturing and services industries in total GDP of the country.

Knowledge-intensive manufacturing includes Chemical and chemical products, Metal products and machinery, Electrical machinery and Transport equipment. Knowledge-intensive services include communication, computer-related services and R&D services.

10 Not-so well-known entrepreneurs refers to new entrepreneurs not affiliated to any of business-houses.

11 Paid-up capital is the amount of a company's capital that has been funded by shareholders. Paid-up capital can be less than a company's total capital because a company may not issue all of the shares that it has been authorized to sell. Paid-up capital can also reflect how a company depends on equity financing.

12 An examination of all industrial proposals actually implemented during 1992 through 2013 reveals that the majority of the industrial proposals implemented fall into industries that are knowledge-intensive, such as metallurgy, electrical equipment, pharmaceuticals and motor vehicles. The source of these data are sector-wide proposals implemented during 1992 through 2013 and published in the data source, Department of Industrial Policy and Performance (2014), *SIA Statistics – March 2014*, Ministry of Industry and Commerce, New Delhi: Government of India.

13 This means the new ventures that may have failed and perhaps would have ceased operation. This is because the bankruptcy laws in India are such that there are strong legal barriers to exit.

14 See Global Entrepreneurship Monitor (2007).

15 See also National Knowledge Commission (2008).

16 New firms in India have typically relied on internal sources of finance in the form of family and personal savings. This is corroborated by the micro level data from the New Entrepreneurship Network (Section 4.3). In this chapter we do not claim that there has been a deceleration in external source of funding. We only speculate that this will become even more difficult to obtain in view of the global financial crisis. In fact the main argument is that market opportunities and liberalization of governmental rules have opened up possibilities for new firms to emerge, but the availability of risk capital from institutional sources has been a constraining factor. Converting ideas to business propositions has thus been limited by the availability of risk capital as there will be a limit to which entrepreneurs can reply on internal sources of finance.

17 Birch's algorithm is sufficiently rigorous, and in developed countries its requirements are usually met by only 3–5 per cent of firms.

18 In the West where the government has never left the sphere of innovation, similar processes of self-organization in the innovative firms community are applicable to technologically complex sectors (see Chesbrough, 2003), for example software open platforms.

Bibliography

General

Acs, Z. and Audretsch, D. (1990) *Innovation and Small Firms*, Boston: MIT Press.

Agarwal, R. and Gort, M. (1996) 'The evolution of markets and entry, exit and survival of firms', *The Review of Economics and Statistics*, 78(3), pp. 489–498.

Bain, J.S. (1956) *Barriers to New Competition*, Cambridge MA: Harvard University Press.

Breschi, S., Malerba, F. and Orsenigo, L. (2000) 'Technological regimes and Schumpeterian patterns of innovation', *The Economic Journal*, 110(463), pp. 388–410.

Camerani, R. and Malerba, F. (2010) 'Patterns of technological entry in different fields: An analysis of patent data', in F. Malerba (ed.), *Knowledge Intensive Entrepreneurship and Innovation Systems*, London: Routledge.

Cefis, E. (2003) 'Is there persistence in innovative activities?', *International Journal of Industrial Organization*, 21, pp. 489–515.

Cefis, E. and Orsenigo, L. (2001) 'The persistence of innovative activities: A cross-countries and cross-sectors comparative analysis', *Research Policy*, 30, pp. 1139–1158.

Chang, Y.M. and Li, K. (2007) 'Research on the spatial distribution and dependence of Chinese innovation output: Spatial econometrics analysis based on province-level patent data', *China Soft Science Magazine*, 2007(11), pp. 97–103 (in Chinese).

Chesbrough, H.W. (2003) *Open Innovation, The New Imperative for Creating and Profiting from Technology*, Harvard: Harvard Business Press.

Dernis, H., Guellec, D. and van Pottelsberghe, B. (2001) 'Using patent counts for cross-country comparisons of technology output', *STI Review*, 27, Paris: OECD. Available at www.oecd.org/dataoecd/26/11/21682515.pdf – Accessed 14 January 2015.

Dosi, G., Cimoli, M. and Stiglitz, J. (2009) *Industrial Policy and Development: The Political Economy of Capabilities Accumulation*, Oxford: Oxford University Press.

Geroski, P.A. (1989a) 'Entry and the rate of innovation', *Economics of Innovation and New Technology*, 1, pp. 203–214.

Geroski, P.A. (1989b) 'Entry, innovation and productivity growth', *Review of Economics and Statistics*, 71, pp. 572–578.

Geroski, P.A. (1995) 'What do we know about entry', *International Journal of Industrial Organization*, 13(4), pp. 421–440.

Geroski, P.A. and Jacquemin, A. (1988) 'The persistence of profits: A European comparison', *Economic Journal*, 98, pp. 375–389.

Geroski, P.A. and Schwalbach, J. (1991) *Entry and Market Contestability: An International Comparison*, Oxford: Basil Blackwell.

Griliches, Z. (1990) 'Patent statistics as economic indicators: A survey', *Journal of Economic Literature*, 28(4), pp. 1661–1707.

Jaffe, A. and Trajtenberg, M. (2002) *Patents, Citations, and Innovations: A Window on the Knowledge Economy*, Cambridge, MA: MIT Press.

Kingston, W. (2001) 'Innovation needs patent reform', *Research Policy*, 30(3), pp. 403–423.

Klepper, S. (1996) 'Entry, exit, growth and innovation over the product life cycle', *American Economic Review*, 86, pp. 526–583.

Malerba, F. (ed.) (2010) *Knowledge-intensive Entrepreneurship and Innovation Systems*, London: Routledge.

Malerba, F. and Mani, S. (2009) *Sectoral Systems of Innovation and Production in Developing Countries: Actors, Structure and Evolution*, Cheltenham, UK: Edward Elgar.

Malerba, F. and Nelson, R. (2011) 'Catching up in different sectoral systems', *Industrial and Corporate Change*, 6, pp. 1646–1676.

Malerba, F. and Nelson, R. (2012) *Economic Development as a Learning Process: Evidence from Sectoral Systems*, Cheltenham, UK: Edward Elgar.

Malerba, F. and Orsenigo, L. (1995) 'Schumpeterian patterns of innovation', *Cambridge Journal of Economics*, 19(1), pp. 47–65.

Malerba, F. and Orsenigo, L. (1996) 'Schumpeterian patterns of innovation are technology-specific', *Research Policy*, 25, pp. 451–478.

Malerba, F. and Orsenigo, L. (1999) 'Technological entry, exit and survival', *Research Policy*, 28(6), pp. 643–660.

Mani, Sunil (2011) 'Promoting knowledge-intensive entrepreneurship in India', in Eddy Szirmai, Wim Naudé and Micheline Goedhuys (eds), *Entrepreneurship and Innovation in Developing Countries*, Oxford: Oxford University Press, pp. 194–227.

Marsili, O. (2001) *The Anatomy and Evolution of Industries: Technological Change and Industrial Dynamics*, Cheltenham, UK: Edward Elgar.

McKelvey, M. and Bagchi-Sen, S. (2014) *Innovation Spaces in Asia: Entrepreneurs, Multinational Enterprises and Policy*, Cheltenham, UK, Edward Elgar.

Montobbio, F. and Sterzi, V. (2011) 'Inventing together: Exploring the nature of international knowledge spillovers in Latin America', *Journal of Evolutionary Economics*, 21(1), pp. 53–89.

Montobbio, F. and Sterzi, V. (2013) 'The globalization of technology in emerging markets: A gravity model on the determinants of international patent collaborations', *World Development*, 44, pp. 281–299.

Nelson, R.R. and Winter, S.G. (1982) *An Evolutionary Theory of Economic Change*, Cambridge, MA: Harvard University Press.

Orsenigo, L. and Sterzi, V. (2010) 'Comparative studies of the use of patents in different industries', KITeS Working Paper No. 33.

Roycroft, R.W. and Kash, D. (1999) *The Complexity Challenge: Technological Innovation for the 21st Century*, London: Francis Pinter.

The Economist (2010) 'The World turned upside down: A special report on innovation in emerging countries'.

Trajtenberg, Manuel (1990) 'A penny for your quotes: Patent citations and the value of innovations', *The RAND Journal of Economics*, 21(1), pp. 172–187.

Utterback, J. (1994) *Mastering the Dynamics of Innovation*, Cambridge, Boston, MA: Harvard University Press.

WIPO (2005) *International Patent Classification*, 8th edition, core level, volume 5 Guide.

Bibliography for China

Anderson, R., Li, J., Harrison, R. and Robson, P. (2003) 'The increasing role of small business in the Chinese economy', *Journal of Small Business Management*, 41(3), pp. 310–316.

Ansari, A. and Mela, C. (2003) 'E-customization', *Journal of Marketing Research*, 40(2), pp. 131–145.

Avgerou, C. and Li, B. (2013) 'Relational and institutional embeddedness of Web-enabled entrepreneurial networks: Case studies of entrepreneurs in China', *Information System Journal*, 23(4), pp. 329–350.

Boyreau-Debray, G. and Wei, S. (2005) 'Pitfalls of a state-dominated financial system: The case of China', World Bank working paper series.

Chang, Y.M. and Li, K. (2007) 'Research on the spatial distribution and dependence of Chinese innovation output: Spatial econometrics analysis based on province-level patent data', *China Soft Science Magazine*, 2007(11), pp. 97–103 (in Chinese).

Cui, G. and Liu, Q. (2000) 'Regional market segments of China: Opportunities and barriers in a big emerging market', *Journal of Consumer Marketing*, 17(1), pp. 55–72.

Dana, L. (1999) 'Small business as a supplement in the People's Republic of China (PRC)', *Journal of Small Business Management*, 37(3), pp. 76–80.

Entrepreneurship Education Report China (2011) KAB Entrepreneurship Education Research Institute (in Chinese).

Gao, J., Jiang, Y.F., Li, X.B. and Cheng, Y. (2006) *Global Entrepreneurship Monitor China Report: An Analysis Based on 2005 Data*, Tsinghua: Tsinghua University Press.

Guthrie, D. (2002) 'Information asymmetries and the problem of perception: The significance of structural position in assessing the importance of guanxi in China', in Thomas Gold, Doug Guthrie and David Wank (eds), *Social Connections in China: Institutions, Culture, and the Changing Nature of Guanxi*, London: Cambridge University Press.

Hu, M. and Mathews, J. (2008) 'China's national innovation capacity', *Research Policy*, 37(9), pp. 1465–1479.

Li, H. and Atuahene-Gima, K. (2001) 'Product innovation strategy and the performance of new technology ventures in China', *Academy of Management Journal*, pp. 1123–1134.

Liao, P. and Sohmen, P. (2001) 'The development of modern entrepreneurship in China', *Stanford Journal of East Asian Affairs*, 1, pp. 27–33.

Mu, Q. and Lee, K. (2005) 'Knowledge diffusion, market segmentation and technological catch-up: The case of the telecommunication industry in China', *Research Policy*, 34(6), pp. 759–783.

Shane, S.A. (2003) *A General Theory of Entrepreneurship: The Individual-opportunity Nexus*, Cheltenham, UK: Edward Elgar.

Statistics of Ministry of Science and Technology of the People's Republic of China.

The Twelfth Five-Year Plan for National Economic and Social Development of the People's Republic of China (2011–2015), Central Compilation and Translation Press.

White, S., Gao, J. and Zhang, W. (2005) 'Financing new ventures in China: System antecedents and institutionalization', *Research Policy*, 34(6), pp. 894–913.

Wu, X. (1995) 'Secondary innovation circle and organizational learning mode', *Management World*, pp. 168–172 (in Chinese).

Wu, X., Ma, F. and Mao, Q. (2009) 'Organizational learning model evolution based on dynamic secondary innovation dynamic process: Longitudinal case study of Hangyang 1996–2008', *Management World*, 2, pp. 152–164 (in Chinese).

Utterback, J.M. and Abernathy, W.J. (1975) 'A dynamic model of process and product innovation', *Omega*, 3(6), pp. 639–656.

Yue, L. (2008) 'China's entrepreneurs', *CentrePiece*, 13(1), pp. 15–18.

Zhang, Y. and Li, H. (2009) 'Innovation search of new ventures in a technology cluster: The role of ties with service intermediaries', *Strategic Management Journal*, 31(1), pp. 88–109.

Bibliography for India

Bansal, R. (2008). *Stay Hungry, Stay Foolish*, Ahmedabad: Indian Institute of Management.

Basant, R. and Chandra, P. (2008) 'Role of educational and R&D institutions in city clusters: An exploratory study of Bangalore and Pune regions in India', *World Development*, 35(6), pp. 1037–1055.

Basu, K. (2008) 'The enigma of India's arrival: A review of Arvind Virmani's *Propelling India: From Socialist Stagnation to Global Power*', *Journal of Economic Literature*, 46(2), pp. 396–406.

Global Entrepreneurship Monitor (2007) *2007 Executive Report*, www.gemconsortium.org/docs/download/263 – Accessed 23 November 2012.

Mani, Sunil (2010) 'Are innovations on the rise in India since the onset of reforms of 1991? Analysis of its evidence and some disquieting features', *International Journal of Technology and Globalization*, 5(1&2), pp. 5–42.

National Knowledge Commission (2008) *Entrepreneurship in India*, New Delhi: National Knowledge Commission.

Panagariya, A. (2008) *India: The Emerging Giant*, New York: Oxford University Press.

Reserve Bank of India (2008) *Annual Report 2007–08*. Mumbai: Reserve Bank of India.

Bibliography for Russia

Birch, D. and Medoff, J. (1994) 'Gazelles', in L.C. Solomon and A.R. Levenson (eds), *Labor Markets, Employment Policy, and Job Creation*, Boulder, CO: Westview, pp. 159–168.

Dumnaya, N. (2009) 'Network growth of the companies: The contribution to economic well-being of the nation', in Christof Pforr, Bella Butler and Werner Soontiens (eds), *Wealth and Prosperity of Nations in the Period of Global Transformation*, Perth, Western Australia: Curtin University of Technology.

Grishankov, D. (2008) 'Expert-400', http://raexpert.ru/ratings/expert400/2008/ (in Russian) – Accessed 14 January 2015.

Hirsch-Kreinsen, H. and Jacobson, D. (2008) *Innovation in Low-Tech Firms and Industries*, Cheltenham, UK: Edward Elgar.

Inno Grips (2007) Mini Study 01 – 'Are gazelles leaping ahead? Innovation and rapidly growing small firms' (John Rigby, Mercedes Bleda, Kathryn Morrison, Jong-Seok Kim), 13 April 2007.

Kirzner, I.M. (1997) 'Entrepreneurial discovery and the competitive market process: An Austrian approach', *Journal of Economic Literature*, 35(1), pp. 71–90.

Kolodnyaa, G. (2007) *Looking Through the Prism of Practice: The Neo-institutional Theory of the Firm*, Moscow: Finance and Credit (in Russian).

Medovnikov, D. and Imamutdinov, I. (2009) 'To leave puberty behind', *Ekspert*, 2(19), pp. 21–27 (in Russian).

Yudanov, A. (2007) *The Experience of Competition in Russia: Causes for Success and Failure*, Moscow: KnoRus (in Russian).

Yudanov, A. (2010) 'Embodiments of entrepreneurial spirit: "Gazelle-firms" in Russia', *Jurnal Novoi ekonomicheskoi associacii*, 5, pp. 91–109 (in Russian).

Yudanov, A. (2011) 'High-growth firms in Russia: Experimental data and prospects for the econophysical simulation of economic modernization', *Physics-Uspekhi*, 54(7), pp. 733–737.

Part IV
Policy

16 Public policy for knowledge intensive entrepreneurship

Implications from the perspective of innovation systems

Yannis Caloghirou, Patrick Llerena,
Franco Malerba, Maureen McKelvey and
Slavo Radosevic

1 Introduction

This final chapter focuses upon public policy for knowledge intensive entrepreneurship and advances previous analyses on policies regarding knowledge intensive entrepreneurship (Malerba, 2010). We are arguing for a more complex view of the role of public policy which should go well beyond the current focus on stimulating the entry of new small firms. This chapter is based on the analyses in the chapters in this book, as well as on the work done in the EU project AEGIS about public policy.

Public policy is one of the ways in which society can change. The recent economic crisis in Europe turned out to be one of the most severe of the last decades. The costs have been significant in terms of the strong negative impact on real economic activity, as well as increasing unemployment, especially in southern European Union countries and in new EU member states. Furthermore, economic recovery seems to be rather weak, indicating that new challenges have emerged at the policy level, especially in terms of designing new entrepreneurial policies.

Entrepreneurship should not be considered as a silver bullet for growing out of the crisis, and yet it is indeed a key element in any growth agenda. We do know that certain types of entrepreneurial firms appear to impact growth more than others. Heterogeneity implies that different types of newly established firms have different potentials for growth and societal impact. In fact, this heterogeneity is known, in that the positive impact of new firms on the economy is extensively skewed by atypical firms (Storey, 1999; Nightingale and Coad, 2014). Recent research suggests that only some particular kinds of entrepreneurship matter for economic development (Autio and Acs, 2007; Delmar and Wennberg, 2010; Henrekson and Johansson, 2010; Nightingale and Coad, 2014). The peculiarities of high potential entrepreneurship have been given a number of labels, such as 'high potential', 'innovative', 'knowledge-intensive', 'gazelles', 'quality' or in some cases 'extraordinary'. Within the broader entrepreneurial community each category tends to focus upon a specific kind of new venture.

This book started with the assumption – and has shown it empirically – that knowledge intensive entrepreneurship is a multi-dimensional, systemic and context dependent phenomenon. KIE firms can display different degrees of innovativeness and knowledge intensity, and can be cultivated and promoted both in high-tech and low-tech sectors. Therefore, knowledge intensive entrepreneurship can be affected and influenced by the decisions taken by diverse sets of public policies. For us, what public policy needs to do is to take a systemic perspective. By this, we mean that public policy should take into account systemic interdependencies as well as the impact of different ecologies such as sectors, countries, networks and markets in the creation and growth of ventures started in knowledge intensive entrepreneurship (KIE).

Section 2 presents some indications for a system of policies for fostering knowledge intensive entrepreneurship, in order to understand the implications of this research for public policy. Section 3 presents some specific implications for policy makers, organized around the model presented in Chapter 2, and based upon research results from this book. Section 4 stresses the need for better policy measures, in order to assess innovation and entrepreneurship policies. Finally, Section 5 draws conclusions.

2 Promoting a system of policies for KIE in Europe

2.1 *What do we mean by entrepreneurship being a heterogeneous and systemic phenomenon?*

In this book, entrepreneurship has been argued to be a multi-dimensional, systemic and complex economic and social phenomenon. Entrepreneurship, as analysed here, encompasses different aspects, including the act of engaging (undertaking) entrepreneurship, the process of bringing together resources and entrepreneur(s), the starting of a venture, enterprise or business as well as its performance and societal impacts. Entrepreneurship is therefore a heterogeneous phenomenon, both in terms of 'behaviour, structure, and performance' and in terms of its 'impact on the economy'.

This book as well as the AEGIS project aimed to analyse various aspects of knowledge intensive ventures, according to the four characteristics defined in Chapter 2. Figure 16.1 provides the conceptual model of the dynamics of knowledge intensive entrepreneurship used in this book.

Figure 16.1 is relevant for understanding, and structuring our discussion of public policy because it includes the dynamics of the venture itself, its interaction with other actors and institutions through networks and its performance, and also visualizes the various elements of the surrounding system of innovation. Through this representation, we are assuming that knowledge intensive entrepreneurship is very much related to knowledge

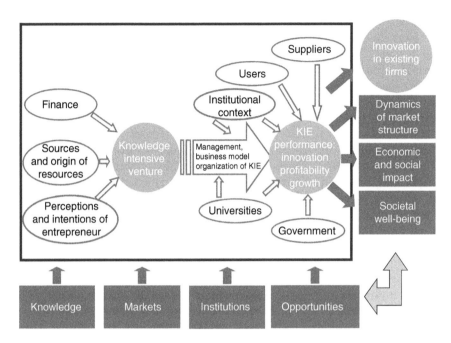

Figure 16.1 The process model of KIE dynamics (source: Malerba and McKelvey, Chapter 2 in this volume).

generation and the innovation process, which are influenced by different contexts such as regional and sectoral systems of innovation. More specifically, knowledge intensive entrepreneurship has been here defined in terms of a transformative mechanism, which helps determine the effectiveness of the conversion of knowledge originated both from R&D and other non-R&D sources into business and economic activity.

Thus, the ways in which public policy can induce knowledge intensive entrepreneurship has proven to be far more complex than considered before. In this respect, modern entrepreneurship policy needs to be much broader, more diverse and more indirect compared to traditional policy approaches like support to formation and growth of SMEs (small and medium enterprises) through state subsidies.

2.2 A framework of policies by linking KIE, innovation and economic growth

Our argument is that advancing KIE should be conceptualized as a set of systemic policies. In our view, a new approach to KIE policy can therefore be developed through the union between traditional policy for entrepreneurship, on the one hand, and a broader set of policy related to stimulating knowledge and innovation, on the other hand (see also Dahlstrand and Stevenson, 2010).

Thus the scope of knowledge intensive entrepreneurship policy should go beyond traditional policies of support for small enterprises. Policy makers should consider a coherent set of policies for promoting KIE, rather than a bunch of isolated and separate measures. The fact that knowledge intensive entrepreneurship can flourish also in non-research intensive industries broadens the range of policy instruments and enriches the necessary targeting also to low- and medium-tech sectors. This also calls for strengthening the interrelationships among policies through policy mixes. Therefore, in order to develop knowledge intensive entrepreneurship and foster innovation and economic growth, an interrelated system of policies is required to activate both knowledge creation and exploitation. As a start, one can consider the sets of policies that enhance (a) market opportunities, (b) technological opportunities and (c) institutional opportunities for knowledge intensive entrepreneurship (Radosevic, 2010).

Another way of conceptualizing this is that public policy instruments will affect overall KIE by promoting new ventures through the inclusion of both supply side and demand side aspects. By supply side, we mean policies such as science and technology, education and training, information provision, knowledge infrastructure, industry structure, networking, clustering, finance, risk management, and the like. By demand side aspects, we mean policies which affect things like overall aggregate demand, demand induced through sector specific standards and regulations, as well as innovative public procurement.

While it is important that policies address specific dimensions of KIE, there is also a need to have a process view and a system dimension of KIE. This implies that policies should use often more than one instrument at a time and that a system of policies rather than single, isolated and uncoordinated ones should be used. This requires that policies for KIE should be coordinated and integrated and that they should take into account both the short run as well as the long run effects.

Policies and measures for stimulating knowledge intensive entrepreneurship can be grouped according to the time-horizon of their impact, where according to Hart (2003) policies can be classified according to a taxonomy of influences on short term, intermediate and background conditions. This insight is useful when designing policy instruments.

Let us take the example of public procurement, which is an emerging issue in Europe. AEGIS project empirical findings suggest that the role of public demand in promoting and supporting innovative activity is extremely limited/weak for KIE in Europe, in the sense that few KIE ventures respond to public demand. Potentially, therefore, a mix of policy measures related to public procurement could be used to induce KIE. A first issue to consider is the stage of the innovation lifecycle. In the early stage, new technological opportunities can be created and technology and market risks reduced. At a later stage, market opportunities can be created for the products/services that successfully passed the pre-commercial stages and that are likely to be procured by a public organization. For the latter phases, policies could be more focused on the diffusion of innovations and on the development of market and institutional opportunities for KIE. A second issue is the potential size of the market. Here, the EU could play a role in combining and developing a larger market. As long as public procurement is confined to individual countries, the potential markets may be quite limited. Hence, there may be a huge untapped potential for innovative procurement though coordinated unbundling of demand among European states and regions.

This points to another relevant feature of public policy related to the high heterogeneity and diversity of KIE ventures. Evidence provided in this book (see for example Chapter 3) suggests that different sources of knowledge, different innovation strategies and, thus, different pathways of development of KIE ventures can be identified. All too often entrepreneurship and innovation policy that overlooks the diversity of paths towards successful innovation and growth slips into myopic strategies related to oversimplified quantitative targets such as R&D spending and the like.

Along the same line of argument, findings based upon the insights and perspectives of entrepreneurs in KIE ventures (Chapter 6) indicate that public policy initiatives and relevant instruments should take into account specific goals and targets of different forms of start-ups. This, for instance, suggests the need to obtain distinct tools and analysis for university spin-offs, or for corporate spin-offs.

Finally, we would like to point out that a more systemic view of public policy also requires that public policy makers need to have increased capabilities to analyse the heterogeneity of KIE in various settings and the ability to react to changes in the system. One major implication of a system and process oriented policy set is the need for a knowledge intensive policy decision process, and for policy makers with explicit and integrated 'dynamic capabilities'.

2.3 Alleviation of systemic risk

On average 50 per cent of new firms fail to survive within the first three to five years of their life. This high failure rate is partly due to internal management weaknesses but also due to external constraints. New businesses often lack an appropriate or favourable ecosystem that will help them grow. Therefore, greater resources should be devoted to European entrepreneurs in order to help them get through this highly demanding period.

Given this perspective, this means that policy intervention should primarily concentrate in reducing systemic risks, i.e. risks that the companies cannot hedge or diversify. Again, Figure 16.1 provides an overview of the key aspects of KIE venture development in relation to the environment: the types of risks discussed below can be seen in this context.

The concept of technology risk appears to be the easiest for individual companies to deal with. They treat it as unsystematic, manage it actively and decrease it by networking. So, it seems that there is little room for direct government intervention in alleviating technology risk for young KIEs. However, there is a very important indirect role for the public sector in supporting the scientific and technological context within which firms pursue their specific goals.

A much bigger risk for KIEs seems to be recruitment risk, reportedly one of the most important obstacles for our firms' growth. Availability of skilled personnel is a key issue. The role of governments in this respect is essential in ensuring well functioning educational systems at all levels, including vocational and other professional training.

Market risk and competition risk, while also perceived by companies as systematic, do not lend themselves easily to government intervention. This is because the public sector is often incapable of assessing the market potential of new products (beyond those that it itself utilizes such as for defence). It is also difficult to see how the government can alleviate competition risk for a company without falling back into practices of picking the winners.

However, there is a legitimate role for public policy in maintaining well functioning markets and healthy competition. Competition policy should aim to nurture and sustain variety in a market or industry to promote innovation and competition. Variety is the consequence of competition among firms that are heterogeneous in terms of product innovation strategies. Thus any policy intervention in support of KIE should take into account the heterogeneity of firms and strategies. In this respect, the most effective policies aimed at sustaining variety should be implemented in the early-mid stages of industry life cycle when competition is still high.

3 Policy implications

3.1 Policy implications of the pre-formation stage and of the firm development stage

Based upon the model of the dynamics of knowledge intensive entrepreneurship found in Figure 16.1, this section moves onto implications grouped according to pre-formation and to firm development. The implications are based upon the research in AEGIS. One important source is Lassen and McKelvey (2011), which engaged in a large scale literature review and also developed a set of policy implications. This was further developed into an entrepreneur and firm perspective analysis in McKelvey and Lassen (2013a, 2013b).

Table 16.1 Policy implications of the pre-formation phase

Topic	Policy implications
Financing	
	KIE ventures are highly dependent upon their own financial resources. From a policy perspective, there is a need to differentiate different types and sources of financing – such as venture capital, corporate investments and personal and family savings.
	Other types of financing are public, where complementary policy instruments like incubators, can affect the performance of firms.
	Also, new alternative forms of financing for start-ups (e.g. platforms for crowd sourcing) should be facilitated. European structural funds resources could be used to set up microfinance support schemes under the respective EU investment priorities. This indicates the need to address the interactions amongst different domains of policy.
	Financing is not a one-off need of the company, but continuing.
	This points to the need to stimulate intermediary policy goals, such as reviewing regulatory conditions for buy-outs or bankruptcy as well as considering fiananacing over time.
	For example, rules regarding personal credit and bankruptcy laws, and public financing schemes should consider the importance of not focusing only on *de novo* entrepreneurs but also capitalize on those that already have certain experience.
	For corporate spin-offs, financing related to developing products close to their industrial partner may be positive. This can lead to uneven development, whereby regions with R&D intensive large corporations may be able to stimulate spin-offs but regions lacking this type of enterprise structure cannot do so. Public policy may need to ameliorate the unevenness.
Sources and origins of resources	
	Policy should consider providing simpler policy instruments, where individuals can easily partake of the initiative, without heavy demands on applications and reporting.
	Public policy instruments must clearly identify specific goals and targets of different forms of start-ups, to be effective. This suggests the need to obtain more distinct tools and analysis of especially university spin-offs but also of corporate spin-offs, and for the development of intermediary policy.
	Policy may need to more focus upon the process of venture creation, rather than on the upstream creation of opportunities, since existing research to a large extent has focused upon issues that are outside the direct control of public policy. One such issue might be to examine the role of the competencies of university and policy administrators, rather than their existence and relationships to other organizations.
Perceptions and intentions of the entrepreneurship	
	Specific demographic groups are underrepresented within the entrepreneurial population in Europe are founders of young companies, women and migrants (European Commission, 2013). These facts are also confirmed by the AEGIS survey data. Therefore, specific policy actions based on the needs of each group should be taken.
	Women usually face more difficulties than men mainly in access to finance, training, networking, and in reconciling business and family.
	National and European policies should consider the potential of qualified migrants in creating entrepreneurial ventures and should develop and launch support measures and policy initiatives to attract talented would be entrepreneurs.
	Young people such as students are the most exposed to scientific and technological knowledge, and thus in favourable position to embark on technological entrepreneurship projects. Therefore, European higher educational systems should be more geared to develop the appropriate competences, stimulating the entrepreneurial spirit of students and providing initial assistance in their entrepreneurial activities (incubating activities, coaching and mentoring activities, etc.).
	Further consider instruments and goals that indicate how to bring together (entrepreneurial) opportunities and resources. One goal would be to stimulate (or increase the likelihood) of serial entrepreneurship, i.e. the launching of multiple ventures by the same entrepreneur, which would enable knowledge spillovers across a portfolio of start-ups.

Source: AEGIS research and Lassen and McKelvey (2011: Table 6).

By pre-formation, we mean persons, resources and capabilities that had an impact upon the starting-up of a KIE venture. In Figure 16.1, this is exemplified by financing, by sources and origins of resources, and by perceptions and intentions of the entrepreneurship. For pre-formation, the implications for public policy are summarized in Table 16.1.

By firm development, we mean the management and development of the KIE venture which includes internal managerial issues such as resources and opportunity recognition as well as networks and performance, as also visualized in Figure 16.1. For firm development, the implications for public policy are summarized in Table 16.2.

Table 16.2 Policy implications from the development and management phase

Topic	Policy implications
Internal management issues, such as resources and opportunity recognition	
	A key policy issue is especially how to balance between a focus on knowledge intensive development and a focus on bringing the knowledge efficiently to market in terms of product, processes or services, and thereby creating wealth.
	Policy might intervene in order to promote a more market oriented, and less technology oriented perspective for the firm, by e.g. introducing subsidies for demonstration projects or soft loans for products to be introduced into markets.
	These types of policy instruments try to provide incentives and resources for firms which are more oriented towards the market, and market opportunities
	Internationalization is particularly important for the KIE service firms, which appear to be more immediately focused upon internationalization, suggesting that their market is global rather than local.
	On the flip side, public policy which primarily focuses upon regional networks and relationships may be counterproductive for these types of firms.
	A clear issue is the need to develop learning not only about technological knowledge but also, or even especially, about market knowledge, such as the demands of customers. This is likely through networks (see below).
Networks	
	AEGIS research findings suggest that the most important knowledge sources for young firms are customers, suppliers and competitors. The main place for policy may be in supporting diverse intermediary actors (industry associations, chambers of commerce, etc.) that can facilitate access to customers, suppliers and competitors.
	Formal or informal collaboration with scientific actors is also limited for some KIE ventures.
	Programmes facilitating networking with universities and research institutes as well as EU policy measures promoting the young firms' participation in EU funded research networks may help young companies complement and expand their limited technological resource and knowledge bases.
	However, the empirical findings in the context of the AEGIS project show that it is not network participation per se that matters, but the 'right' type of links, especially at the beginning of network activity.
	There is a need of policy instruments to differentiate the types of alliances that different types of KIE need. For instance, for small ventures in science based industries, university collaborations are critical for enhancing credibility and reputation while inter-firm collaborations are critical for product development and commercialization.
Performance	
	Firm formation is a key indicator, often used to assess and evaluate the impact of public policy. As such, the proxy is often taken as given, e.g. as a useful and relevant measure of the impact of policy upon entrepreneurship. The research outlined above suggests that the process of new firm formation is somewhat more complex than previously imagined. Policy may thus need different measures of what constitutes a high level of firm formation, in different regions or different types of technologies.
	Especially the indirect effect of knowledge intensive entrepreneurship on the development of clusters and new industries seems to be a potentially interesting area.

Source: AEGIS research and Lassen and McKelvey (2011: Table 6).

3.2 Taking systems of innovation into account in KIE policy: high-tech and low-tech sectors

This book suggests that KIE differs in different national and sectoral systems of innovation. Public policy can influence and shape all the various factors determining the demand side and the supply side of entrepreneurship as well as the availability of relevant resources (knowledge, information, finance, etc.), the cultural aspects and the risk-reward profile of entrepreneurship. Contextual conditions, including social and cultural, as well as the major characteristics of the prevailing innovation systems in different European areas, should be taken into consideration. Therefore, we can also presume that the relative effects of demand and supply side instruments of entrepreneurship policy mentioned above will also differ across different socio-techno-economic environments. Different countries will have different aspects of supply and demand for KIE developed and articulated to very different degrees.

In other words, there is more than one profile of sectoral systems in which KIE firms operate (see the discussion in Chapter 8). As visualized in Figure 16.1, this suggests that the environment in which entrepreneurs are active can be very diverse.

Specific policies supporting knowledge intensive entrepreneurship must also be aware of the sectoral influence on the survival and performance of young firms. This does not necessarily imply that policies need to be sector specific. It means however that even general entrepreneurship policies should take into account that the actual impact of horizontal policies may drastically differ across sectors, because the channels and ways through which policies affect KIE vary accordingly (from sector to sector).

Moreover, a sectoral system view of KIE recognizes not just one, but several systems of policies that affect entrepreneurship in sectors. This point highlights on the one hand the importance of interdependencies, links and feedbacks among policies, and on the other that these interdependencies may greatly differ across sectoral systems. Thus the most effective policies may vary according to the type of knowledge, actors, networks and institutions that entrepreneurs face in their activities in the different sectors.

One category of KIE to promote is present in high-tech sectors. KIE ventures in high-tech sectors differ with respect to the origin of their business idea on which the firm is founded, i.e. whether they stem from a corporation or a university. The AEGIS findings suggest however that there are marked differences between corporate spin-offs and university spin-offs within high-tech sectors. These differences are such that policy needs to distinguish between different kinds of knowledge intensive firms when developing measures to support entrepreneurship. For example, university spin-offs, at least compared to corporate spin-offs, seem much more likely to contribute to change and renewal in various regional innovation systems. However, they are also characterized by considerable uncertainties, which make them more prone to failure, especially in the early stage of their development.

Policies in high-tech sectors imply that often they have to be made in continuously changing technologies and markets. New technologies may often emerge, together with high expectations which are not always realized. A public policy perspective may imply to establish a system of monitoring and assessment which can generate early warning signals so that funding can be withdrawn before major failures in new technologies take place. Once again, this statement implies a KIE policy making process and policy frame equipped with some sort of 'dynamic capability'.

Another category of KIE ventures to promote are those found in low-tech sectors. One finding is that KIE in low- and medium low-tech (LMT) industries usually occurs without any major and targeted support of innovation policy at the national and European level (see the discussion in Chapter 9). Most of the state funded innovation projects are often targeted towards high-tech innovation activities, or have a bias towards high-tech bias. Thus, there is room for improvements to foster KIE activities in LMT sectors. KIE can be a major mechanism for translating knowledge into innovation (and consequently growth) even in low-tech industries. However, a better understanding of the role of knowledge creation and capability development in LMT sectors is required for introducing measures that could foster their competitiveness and strengthen their role in highly competitive international markets. Such measures may be different. One is the access to trans-sectoral knowledge for LMT firms which often have limited resources to engage in search for knowledge which is outside their narrow speciality area. In this respect, promoting the creation of external knowledge and competence networks could be crucial in order to facilitate collaboration with actors from other sectors, and also to increase the opportunities for closer interaction with customers. A second one regards the fostering of the transfer of the globally available knowledge to the local LMT firms and entrepreneurs. This may require the establishment of bridging institutions between low-tech industries and science, which would consult LMT firms about potential new technological and market developments. Another one may focus on enhancing the capabilities of firms to absorb, integrate and utilize new knowledge. This can be done by upgrading and promoting R&D related activities at LMT firms, and/or enhancing the skills of staff, so as to improve the overall management competences of the firms, especially the capability to cooperate and network internationally. Even though most of the aforementioned relevant tasks can be realized through support programmes at EU and national levels, measures aimed at upgrading knowledge and skills may be better developed by local authorities close to LMT firms, as they understand local firms' specific needs better than supranational policy makers.

4 The need for better measures for policy

Despite that entrepreneurship is often taken as a self-evidentially positive feature of market economies, it has long been acknowledged that it brings costs as well as benefits. Thus, there is a need for taking into consideration additional indicators when assessing innovation and entrepreneurship policies.

While an increasing number of entrepreneurs are generally accepted as a useful objective for public policies in Europe, a closer look at the data shows that a significant part of this increase is mostly self-employment and has only a minor impact on employment and growth. Moreover, it may be very difficult to separate these types of start-ups from the much smaller number of knowledge intensive start-ups, some of which eventually become major contributors to growth and employment. A consequence is that promotional policies regarding entrepreneurship may often be a 'blunt instrument', directing resources to the aspirations of individuals for self-employment. Efforts to sharpen instruments by establishing 'knowledge' qualifications or 'knowledge related' business plans may be helpful, but difficult to implement and need useful indicators that may support policies.

However, there is also a need for public policy to reconsider what venture creation and firm growth means. Venture creation as a proxy is often taken as a useful and relevant measure of the impact of policy upon entrepreneurship. However, research suggests (see for example Chapter 6) that the process of new firm formation is somewhat more complex than previously imagined. Policy may thus need different measures of what constitutes a high level of firm formation, in different regions or different types of technologies. Public policy needs to keep in mind both the expected effects of growth and performance, as well as the expected timeline. This matters in terms of policy assessment, because many effects may take a long time to create observable outcomes, and also because the performance may vary widely in different time periods. In addition, one could also further develop intermediary policy measures that stimulate knowledge development and diffusion. For example, the assessment of public policy could focus more upon mechanisms that increase knowledge intensity in existing companies through technology transfer such as consultancy rather than focusing upon the formation of ventures per se.

Finally, indicators of entrepreneurship should also include welfare measures of well-being and measures of societal progress that go beyond traditional measures of income.

5 Conclusions

In conclusion, this book is based on the statement – proven empirically with the survey and the case studies – that knowledge intensive entrepreneurship is a multi-dimensional, systemic and context dependent phenomenon.

Therefore in this concluding chapter we call for a system of public policies that takes into account the systemic and evolutionary nature of knowledge intensive entrepreneurship. In this respect, public policy should take into account systemic interdependencies and the different contexts within which knowledge intensive entrepreneurship develops.

On that basis, we claim that a new approach to KIE policy can therefore be developed by joining the traditional policies for entrepreneurship with policies that aim at stimulating innovation and knowledge creation and diffusion. In this respect knowledge intensive entrepreneurship policy should go beyond traditional policies of support for small enterprises and (a) encompass a coherent set of policies for promoting this type of entrepreneurship, (b) be coordinated and integrated and (c) take into account both the short run as well as the long run effects.

In particular, the book emphasized two dimensions that public policy should consider in its intervention. The first dimension regards the distinction between supporting the pre-formation stage or firms' later development. The second concerns the contexts in which knowledge intensive entrepreneurship takes place, because contexts may greatly differ in terms of sectoral, national or regional system of innovation. In this respect public policy can influence the various factors determining the demand side and the supply side of entrepreneurship, the characteristics and effectiveness of networks and the role of institutions.

On this basis, the chapter concludes with a plea for new indicators that are able to capture the key dimensions of the system, interdependencies and evolution of knowledge intensive entrepreneurship.

References

Autio, E. and Acs, Z.J. (2007) 'Individual and country level determinants of growth aspirations in new ventures', Paper presented at the Third Global Entrepreneurship Research Conference, October 2007, Washington.

Dahlstrand, A.L. and Stevenson, Lois (2010) 'Innovative entrepreneurship policy: linking innovation and entrepreneurship in a European context', *Annals of Innovation & Entrepreneurship*, 1: 5602-DOI: 103402/aei:v1/1.5602.

Delmar, F. and Wennberg, K. (2010) 'The knowledge intensive sector: theoretical concerns, research design and data'. In: F. Delmar and K. Wennberg (eds), *Knowledge Intensive Entrepreneurship: The Birth, Growth and Demise of Entrepreneurial Firms*, Cheltenham, UK: Edward Elgar.

European Commission (2013) 'Entrepreneurship 2020 Action Plan: Reigniting the entrepreneurial spirit in Europe'. Communication from the Commission to the European Parliament, the Council, the European Economic and Social Committee and the Committee of the Regions, Brussels, 9.1.2013 COM(2012) 795 final.

Hart, D.M. (2003) *The Emergence of Entrepreneurship Policy: Governance, Start-ups and Growth in the US Knowledge Economy*, Cambridge: Cambridge University Press.

Henrekson, M. and Johansson, D. (2010) 'Gazelles as job creators: a survey and interpretation of the evidence', *Small Business Economics*, 35(2), pp. 227–244.

Lassen, A.H. and McKelvey, M. (2011) 'Conceptualizing knowledge-intensive entrepreneurship: a literature review for analyzing case studies and defining policy implications'. AEGIS Deliverable 7.2.1. Delivered to EU Commission and at AEGIS webpage.

Malerba, F. (2010) *Knowledge-Intensive Entrepreneurship and Innovation Systems: Evidence from Europe*, London and New York: Routledge.

McKelvey, M. and Lassen, A.H. (2013a) *Managing Knowledge Intensive Entrepreneurship*, Cheltenham, UK: Edward Elgar.

McKelvey, M. and Lassen, A.H. (2013b) *How Entrepreneurs Do What They Do: Case Studies of Knowledge Intensive Entrepreneurship*, Cheltenham, UK: Edward Elgar.

Nightingale, P. and Coad, A. (2014) 'Muppets and gazelles: political and methodological biases in entrepreneurship research', *Industrial and Corporate Change*, 23(1), pp. 113–143.

Radosevic, S. (2010) 'What makes entrepreneurship systemic?' In: F. Malerba (ed.), *Knowledge-Intensive Entrepreneurship and Innovation Systems: Evidence from Europe*, London and New York: Routledge, pp. 52–76.

Storey, D.J. (1999) 'Six steps to heaven: evaluating the impact of public policies to support small business in developed economies'. In: D.L. Sexton and H. Landström (eds), *Handbook of Entrepreneurship*, Oxford: Blackwell, pp. 176–194.

Index

Page numbers in *italics* denote tables, those in **bold** denote figures.

For Product Safety Concerns and Information please contact our EU
representative GPSR@taylorandfrancis.com
Taylor & Francis Verlag GmbH, Kaufingerstraße 24, 80331 München, Germany

www.ingramcontent.com/pod-product-compliance
Ingram Content Group UK Ltd.
Pitfield, Milton Keynes, MK11 3LW, UK
UKHW021024180425
457613UK00020B/1045